3 0400 00595 236 7

D0600497

11/14

How to Build Your Own
Greenhouse

How to Build Your Own
Greenhouse

Designs and Plans
to Meet Your Growing Needs

ROGER MARSHALL

Storey Publishing

*The mission of Storey Publishing is to serve our customers by
publishing practical information that encourages
personal independence in harmony with the environment.*

Edited by Elaine M. Cissi
Art direction by Cynthia McFarland
Cover design by Kent Lew and Cynthia McFarland
Text design by Erin Dawson
Text production by Jennifer Jepson Smith
Cover photographs © Bryan Mullenix / Photographer's Choice RF / Getty Images: left;
© George Doyle / Stockbyte / Getty Images: middle; © Doug Menuez / Photodisc /
Getty Images: right
Cover illustrations © Elayne Sears: front and back cover top
Finished building illustrations © Elayne Sears; CAD drawings by Sean Batho,
TSB Consulting; other plans and technical drawings by Brigita Fuhrmann
Indexed by Daniel Brannen

Text © 2006 by Roger Marshall

All rights reserved. No part of this book may be reproduced without written permission from the publisher, except by a reviewer who may quote brief passages or reproduce illustrations in a review with appropriate credits; nor may any part of this book be reproduced, stored in a retrieval system, or transmitted in any form or by any means — electronic, mechanical, photocopying, recording, or other — without written permission from the publisher.

The information in this book is true and complete to the best of our knowledge. All recommendations are made without guarantee on the part of the author or Storey Publishing. The author and publisher disclaim any liability in connection with the use of this information. For additional information please contact Storey Publishing, 210 MASS MoCA Way, North Adams, MA 01247.

Storey books are available for special premium and promotional uses and for customized editions. For further information, please call 1-800-793-9396.

Printed in the United States by Versa Press
10 9 8 7 6 5

Library of Congress Cataloging-in-Publication Data

Marshall, Roger.
    How to build your own greenhouse : designs and plans to meet your growing needs /
Roger Marshall.
        p. cm.
    Includes bibliographical references and index.
    ISBN 978-1-58017-647-7 (pbk. : alk. paper)
    ISBN 978-1-58017-587-6 (hardcover : alk. paper)
    1. Greenhouses — Design and construction. 2. Greenhouse gardening. 3. Greenhouses — History.
    I. Title.
SB416.M37 2007
690'.8924—dc22
                                                                            2006035837

CONTENTS

Acknowledgments

This book draws on my more than forty years of gardening experience and greenhouse ownership to tell you everything you need to know about building a greenhouse, but I didn't rely solely on my experiences to write it. I talked to other greenhouse owners, researched manufacturers and their Web sites, and found many technical articles that taught me even more about greenhouses. Many manufacturers allowed me access to information and to pictures of their greenhouses, for which I thank them. Their input has greatly enriched the content of this book.

I'd especially like to thank Tamara Pugh of Charley's Greenhouse and Garden for supplying many images virtually overnight, Sharon Gamba for her insights into greenhouse gardening, Linda Broden for sharing her greenhouse and orchid knowledge, Leeann Foss West for her comments on growing in warmer climates, and Steve and Paul at Jamestown Hardware for answering my questions on materials and structures. I also owe a debt of gratitude to serendipity: I was working on the chapter on glazing while on a plane to London when I discovered that sitting next to me was Don Mather, a former glazier from Middletown, New Hampshire. He patiently answered myriad glazing questions as we hurtled toward England.

Of course, these are just a few of the people who helped with this book. There are many others who, over the years, have given me advice on gardening and greenhouse growing. To all of them, thanks.

Roger Marshall
Jamestown, Rhode Island

INTRODUCTION

IMAGINE A WORLD where a family, using a greenhouse, can produce free, organic food year-round. A citrus tree sits in one corner, a fig tree in another. Carrots and lettuce sprout in growing beds a few feet away. Assorted herbs grow in pots that are scattered here and there. The greenhouse also has space for flowers: Paperwhites, orchids, and other blossoms perfume the air. In another section, the water in a pool housing koi and carp adds gentle resonance to the warm and humid air. If you want, you can add to this picture a few butterflies or ladybugs, or perhaps a friendly gecko or anole patrols the environment, helping to eliminate unwanted insects without the use of pesticides. Now imagine turning this picture into reality by building your own greenhouse. That is what this book will help you do.

For a home gardener, having a greenhouse has a great many advantages. A greenhouse puts you in control of what you sow and what you eat. It enables you to grow vegetables and fruits out of season and allows you to keep away from your produce insects and rodents that might damage it. If you are not inclined to grow vegetables and fruits, your greenhouse might be full of orchids or geraniums or African violets. Imagine the aroma of bulbs in bloom at any time of the year. This is what owning a greenhouse can bring to your gardening lifestyle.

Greenhouses need not be expensive. I built both of my 300-square-foot greenhouses for under $500 each, using recycled materials. The amount of money you put into a greenhouse is directly related to how much you want to spend. You can go to a garden center and spend less than $1,000 for a perfectly adequate greenhouse, or you can go to an architect and spend $50,000 or more having one built to his or her design speci-fications. Both greenhouses could grow exactly the same plants. A greenhouse structure itself does not necessarily affect what you can grow in it, although it can affect both some of the intangible enjoyment that you get out of your home and its resale value.

A greenhouse definitely helps you get more out of your gardening without requiring a huge time commitment. After all, flowers and vegetables grow slowly, but I know from experience that with a greenhouse, you can bring fresh vegetables, fruits, or flowers to your table almost all year long in most parts of the country. A greenhouse can be attached to your home or it can be freestanding, and it can be constructed in myriad ways. The options are many. Start with a small greenhouse and expand as you gain more experience. It is the pleasure that you get out of your year-round greenhouse environment that makes it worthwhile. Given its potential benefits, why not start building one for yourself today?

1 Questions to Ask before You Begin

IT'S WINTER and a snowstorm has deposited a foot or so of the white stuff everywhere. With the departing of the storm, the sun is shining on a beautiful cold, white landscape. As you scrape the snow off your greenhouse roof, you feel like heading south to warm weather . . . so you change out of your winter clothes and walk into the greenhouse abutting your home.

Inside, the temperature is almost 80°F, the humidity is high, and a waterfall is babbling into a pond. Green plants and flowers send their aromas your way. Everything is right with the world. No need to fly south. You have a choice of climates without traveling beyond your own home.

Sound too good to be true? It's not. As I write this in the middle of December in Rhode Island, the door from my studio into the attached greenhouse is wide open. Outside, the sun is shining brightly. Warm, moist air floods my studio from the greenhouse, where the thermometer reads 78°F. Impatiens, geraniums, and fuchsias are in bloom. In a week or so, paperwhites will also be in flower, adding their powerful fragrance to the other scents in the air. Outdoors, I have to trudge through the snow, but in here it's warm and tropical. A greenhouse exists to create a microclimate in which plants can grow, people can stay warm, fish can be raised, and the sun's heat can be harnessed and distributed. In other words, with a greenhouse you can keep a little bit of summer within easy reach year-round.

In this chapter we'll look at the first questions to ask and the primary considerations as you explore constructing your own greenhouse. In many cases, these go hand in hand with determining how you plan to use your greenhouse (see chapter 3).

How Much Time Does a Greenhouse Require?

You can spend as much time as you want or can afford to spend in a greenhouse, but if you are like many of us, you have many things that need doing and your time is limited. From my experience working in them, I've found that greenhouses do need tending fairly often. Beyond necessary time, you may be lucky enough to free up many more hours to spend among the plants in your greenhouse.

I find that my greenhouse chores require a few hours per week, depending on the season. In spring, for example, the greenhouses are packed with flower and vegetable seedlings. In the middle of January, I generally spend three or four nights setting up seedling trays and starting plants in the germination chamber (see page 172 for information on how to build your own). After the plants have germinated, I spend about half an hour each day watering, fertilizing, and adjusting the lights. By the end of February, I move these fast-growing seedlings into the heated greenhouse under grow lights (which provide enough light to prevent the plants from getting leggy). I check and water them there every day, which takes about an hour. In late fall or early winter (December or early January) I also spend a few hours each week in the greenhouse potting up hanging baskets and tending the plants I propagated in the early fall. During the winter, I spend 1 or 2 hours a week in the heated greenhouse.

Schedules can be individual, however. I have a friend who owns a heated greenhouse and she can spend almost an entire weekend just puttering around in it. She tells me that her husband complains that she spends too much time there. For many people, the amount of time spent in a greenhouse varies dramatically depending on the time available.

For about two months during the summer, my heated greenhouse usually stands empty, although I might keep in it any expensive plants that could be gnawed by squirrels or deer and plants that need a little more heat than that provided by normal summer weather. This is the time when I paint and do routine maintenance with the structure's windows and vents open. During this time, I plan what will take place in the fall.

Around late August or early September, I move back into the greenhouse all plants I placed around the deck and property for the summer. This can take one or two weekends. I thoroughly check each plant and spray each one with pesticide. (I prefer to use an organic pesticide such as Safer's insecticidal soap. I spray each plant twice about ten days apart to eliminate any newly hatched insects.) I repot some plants and lightly fertilize all of them. Once the plants are under cover, despite the spraying, insect explosions may occur (some eggs may be missed and sometimes insects can hitch a ride in the potting soil) and these will need to be treated, so I spend 30 minutes to an hour each day checking plants and treating problems.

By early November insect infestations, late growth spurts (from plants just been moved into a warm greenhouse from the cooler outdoors), and other modulations have settled down. Now shortening days, limited light, and cool temperatures slow plant growth, so fertilizing and watering slow too. By late December, I might go into the greenhouse only twice a week for an hour or two to water and check plants, looking for insect problems, removing yellowing leaves, cleaning up any leaves that have dropped, and simply making sure that everything is as it should be.

My unheated greenhouse works on a different cycle from the heated one. During January and February, our coldest months, it holds little except for Chinese greens, spinach, herbs, and other hardy plants that we use in the kitchen. I use this time to dig over the beds, adding compost and manure to them, and to repaint the inside of the greenhouse or make any needed repairs to the interior structure. Come March, the beds contain greens and peas started in the basement germination chamber. These can take the freezing nighttime temperatures. As soon as I harvest the greens, in middle to late May, I refresh the soil and transplant tomatoes, peppers, melons, and eggplant seedlings into the growing beds. By this time, I've moved the greens and peas outdoors and the brassicas are about to be transplanted from the cool greenhouse as well. During summer, when everything is growing, I spend a couple of hours each week in the cool greenhouse, weeding, tending plants, and watering.

The heated greenhouse, which is usually empty during summer, may need painting and maintenance work during that season. Because I work at home on the property, I can manually open and close the windows and vents as required, which takes a few minutes each day, but this is a chore that can easily be automated. Whenever possible, I perform maintenance on the exterior of the unheated greenhouse because it's in use in all but the coldest months.

On average, I'd say that half a day each week year-round is a fair estimate of the time required to run and maintain a single greenhouse. Once you have a greenhouse, you will adopt a routine and adjust your schedule to suit its requirements. In general, assume that you will spend at least an hour a day there from spring to midsummer, although you might combine these on the weekend instead of spacing them out over each day. In winter, you probably won't spend more than an hour a week in the greenhouse. Of course, you may enjoy the heat and humidity of a warm greenhouse on a sunny day, and on those days, who knows how much time you'll spend in there? For more on greenhouse maintenance schedules, see chapter 12.

What Is Your Budget?

In your final greenhouse decision, budget is often *the* controlling factor, determining size, materials used, whether or not you can heat your structure, and, thus, how you'll use it. If you want large, you can scale back considerably when it comes to materials and heating systems. Because I wanted large greenhouses, I made mine out of low-cost recycled materials. In my original cold frames, for instance (where heat wasn't an issue), I used old storm windows. Later, in sizable structures, I recycled old windows by using panes of double-glazed glass with broken seals. The broken seals meant that each side of the double glazing could be used as a single pane. I became such an avid collector of old glass that one time a local store called me and, for the price of removing them, offered me double-glazed windows that were going out of stock. Using these panes, I built a 30-foot by 10-foot lean-to greenhouse. The lesson here is that the cost of a large greenhouse need not be very high if you're willing to get creative with the materials you use — which may also mean rethinking how you want to use the structure.

In determining your budget, take into account such factors as the cost of the foundation, glazing, plumbing, wiring, and landscaping. Part of your budget equation should also include the cost of operating a greenhouse, such as lighting needs, heating it in the colder months (if you plan to use it during this time), and cooling it in hot weather. If you build a greenhouse that is bigger than you can afford, you may end up not using it because it costs too much to heat, cool, and light the structure. By planning your budget before you build and knowing what you can afford, you'll get more enjoyment out of your greenhouse and have money left over for plants. The checklist on page 100 will help you in the process of determining your budget. In addition, the table on page 7 rates various elements of greenhouse construction by cost.

How Large Should Your Greenhouse Be?

As explained above, one way of determining the size of your greenhouse is to base dimensions on what you can afford to build and heat. Before building, you should find out how much it will cost to heat the structure you are considering. I know of one greenhouse owner who built a large greenhouse without predetermining the heating cost and found that she spent almost $700 per month to heat it in the middle of winter!

One way of determining the size of your greenhouse is to base dimensions on what you can afford to build and heat.

This heating caveat aside, though, if you are an experienced gardener, make your greenhouse just as big as you can. You *will* fill it with plants. I built a 280-square-foot greenhouse, then decided that it needed to be heated. Now it is full of tropical plants and even has a fishpond. It is so full that during the winter months I find it is difficult to move around inside. I've since built a second 280-square-foot greenhouse for growing vegetables. It has served well, but I have a strong urge to set up a heated growing bed or two and add heat to this structure. I also use an unheated, plastic-covered hoop house to extend the growing season and to protect winter greens from deer and rodents. That's how it is with greenhouses — once you start, who knows where you will end up?

If, however, a large greenhouse seems daunting, you might want to build or buy a hobby greenhouse that is 8 feet by 10 feet or 8 feet by 12 feet. If you don't want to heat it, you can use it simply to extend your season in the spring and fall. Another way to begin greenhouse gardening without investing in a sizable structure is to try using cold frames and other small season extenders (see Small Season Extenders on page 31 and the cold-frame project in chapter 13). These can be only about 4 feet by 4 feet — a manageable size. Through these smaller structures, you may find that you enjoy pushing the limits of your growing season and that you'd like to put some cash and effort into buying or building a larger greenhouse.

> Another way to begin greenhouse gardening without investing in a sizable structure is to try using cold frames and other small season extenders.

In determining the size of a structure that's right for you, remember that the larger the greenhouse, the easier it is to maintain a constant temperature inside it. The mass of air inside a large structure takes longer to heat and cool than that in a smaller structure, thus a large greenhouse helps moderate the swings between soaring temperatures on hot, sunny days and abruptly cooling temperatures at night. Conversely, the smaller your greenhouse or cold frame, the more quickly it will both heat up and cool down. In fact, without venting of some kind, smaller structures can overheat very quickly.

See chapter 4 for more on the factors that will help you decide on a size that's right for you.

What about Structure and Systems?

In tandem with determining your budget, you'll need to consider structural elements (such as building materials, glazing, and heating). See later chapters in this book for more detailed information on each of these components.

Structural Materials

Also important to consider are the structural materials used to build the frame of the greenhouse. They should be strong yet light. Aluminum framing meets both requirements, but it also transfers heat out of the greenhouse via the metal. Wood framing takes up more space than aluminum framing and cuts down on the amount of light that enters the greenhouse — but it does allow less heat loss than aluminum. You'll need to balance these structural factors when you choose your greenhouse frame.

For more on structural building materials, see chapter 6.

Light and Glazing Options

Generally, plants in a greenhouse require plenty of light. In most cases, the easiest way to get enough light in the greenhouse is to make sure the structure is located where nothing is obstructing sunlight. In addition, the orientation of your greenhouse and the placement of its glazing can affect light exposure: If you plan on growing in midwinter, for instance, you'll need to make sure that your structure's glazing is at or near a right angle to the sun's path. This allows more light to pass through the glazing and less to be reflected away from it.

The type of glazing you use also affects the amount of light that gets to your plants. Single-pane glass, if kept clean, allows the most—about 96 percent of the total light available. But single-pane glass is both heavy and expensive, and if you drop a pane, it makes a real mess. In addition, there are certain building requirements that must be met for glass in different areas of the country. Some jurisdictions require the glass to be hurricane-proof or tempered and others require all installed glass to be safety glass. You'll have to check your local building codes before you plan your structure.

If your plants don't require maximum light, you have other options for glazing: acrylic or polycarbonate panels, polyethylene sheeting, fiberglass sheeting, and corrugated fiberglass sheeting. They all differ in the amount of light they allow into the greenhouse and each provides certain benefits and drawbacks in cost,

Comparative Costs for Building and Running a Greenhouse			
COMPONENT	LOW COST	MEDIUM COST	HIGH COST
Frame materials	Recycled/scavenged	Building lumber	Quality cedar
Foundation	None	Lumber/slab	Concrete knee walls, stone or brick knee walls
Glazing	Plastic, polyethylene, recycled glass	Polycarbonate, single-pane glass	Double-pane glass
North wall*	Noninsulated wall	Insulated, partly glazed wall	Foam-insulated full-height wall
Insulation	None	Polystyrene	Fiberglass foam with reflective covering
Automation	None	Window openers, thermostat	Thermostat-controlled fans and vents
Heating system	Solar wall	Propane under-bench heater	Oil-fired water heater/electric heat

Usually the north side of a greenhouse is a glazed wall, but to reduce heating costs, consider making it an insulated wall.

installation, and other areas. (See chapter 7 for more on glazing options.)

Heating Options

Freestanding greenhouses can be heated or unheated, but an unheated greenhouse glazed with single-pane glass may not be usable for the coldest part of the year north of the Mason-Dixon Line. Depending on its size, location, and time of the year, an unheated greenhouse has a nighttime temperature of about 8 to 10 degrees F above the surrounding area. This means that in your greenhouse you can grow plants that would survive in one USDA plant hardiness zone warmer than your area. In other words, if you live in Zone 6, in your greenhouse you can support plants that would survive outdoors in USDA Hardiness Zone 7; you can use the frost dates for Zone 7 to determine dates for growing plants in your greenhouse. By contrast, sunny daytime temperatures in a greenhouse can climb to 50 to 60 degrees warmer than the surrounding area. For example, on a sunny day, the temperature in my single-pane unheated freestanding greenhouse is 75°F to 85°F when the temperature hovers around freezing outside and there is snow on the ground. (Refer to the USDA Hardiness Zone map, page 249.)

Though you may have a use for your greenhouse in mind as you begin to plan, consider whether you can afford to (or want to) heat the structure. Heating costs can vary widely, depending on the size of the structure and the kind of system you use. (For more on heating a greenhouse, see chapter 5.)

What Are the Pros and Cons of Kit Greenhouses?

A major consideration at the start of your planning is whether to buy a kit greenhouse or build your own structure from scratch. With the introduction of aluminum framing, polyethylene film, and galvanized steel, kit greenhouses have become affordable for everyone. Hobby or kit greenhouses can be made of wood, steel, extruded aluminum, or PVC, with glass, acrylic, polycarbonate, or even polyethylene sheeting as glazing.

Common kit green-houses can fill the bill for many hobby growers.

A hobby greenhouse is the most basic kind available and can be purchased from a home or garden center or through any of the company Web sites listed in Resources (pages 246–247). If you order a simple, smaller model (which may require a foundation), you can assemble a kit greenhouse yourself, while larger models (which will require a foundation) are usually assembled by a contractor. There are hundreds of retailers of kit and hobby greenhouses, which range from the simplest PVC pipe–frame greenhouses to elaborate wood- or metal-frame buildings. In general, less expensive styles are usually freestanding and single-glazed with a door at one end and one roof vent. As the price goes up, so do the options and the construction quality.

In general, kit greenhouses are small (often as small as 4 feet by 6 feet or 8 feet by 12 feet) and unheated and raise the nighttime temperature by only 3 to 5 degrees F. Consequently, they should add half a hardiness zone to the zone of your area as determined by the USDA Hardiness Zone map (page 249). Of course, this can be altered with additional insulation (often in the form of bubble wrap or polyethylene sheeting), space heaters, or fans. Be aware, however, that adding space heaters may make your greenhouse very expensive to heat if your daytime temperatures hover at 0°F or plunge lower.

When trying to determine which kit greenhouse to purchase, look at the quality of each kit. You can begin by exploring greenhouses on the Internet using the addresses found in Resources. When comparing features, consider price, construction, glazing, accessories available and their additional cost, delivery charges, and the cost of adding a foundation, heat, electricity, and plumbing if these are required. Look, too, at frame color options. I prefer either natural wood or, if the frame is metal, a green painted or anodized frame to blend in with the surroundings, but you can often order a white frame (to maximize interior light) or a bronze-finished frame. After comparing features and analyzing costs in the comfort of your home, you can look at greenhouses offered by local suppliers. Of course, buying locally and picking up the greenhouse yourself may eliminate delivery charges, but you should compare any delivery charges from Internet companies with the cost of local taxes on your purchase.

When looking at greenhouses at local suppliers, inspect the thickness of the supporting frame and each greenhouse's potential structural resistance to twisting or warping in high winds. Greenhouses do move in the wind, but if a structure moves too much, the glazing could break or detach.

If you have the opportunity to look at a model greenhouse, try to determine how easy it will be to clean the glazing inside and out. Check to see if the greenhouse can be expanded; how difficult it will be to install benches, lighting, and heating; and whether you can fit a wheelbarrow through the door and inside the structure. Also look at how the greenhouse is ventilated and how air will flow through it and around your plants. Many kit greenhouses do not have adequate ventilation (see chapter 5 for more on greenhouse ventilation). Most have a single large vent at the top and rely on opening the door to allow air to pass through the structure. Open doors are often an invitation for rodents and pets to enter a greenhouse. If you must leave the door open, use a screen door.

Kit greenhouses range in price from around $1,000 to $20,000. In general, you get what you pay for. More expensive greenhouses usually are sturdier and have better glazing — in most cases double- or even triple-pane glass or double- or triple-wall polycarbonate. Some come with decorative ridgeline cresting and finials. Although these Victorian-style details may not complement the style of your house, they keep birds from perching on top of the greenhouse and leaving droppings on the glass in hard-to-clean areas. Be aware that shipping, building a foundation, and assembly (if you hire a contractor to do this) can add $15,000 to $20,000 to the cost of a top-quality kit greenhouse.

You can also hire a company to design a "custom" factory-built structure and install it on your property. All you need to do is write the checks. You'll find many such companies on the Internet and some are listed in Resources on page 247. Many are located overseas and export their products worldwide, though importing a greenhouse from another country can be very expensive.

Build It Yourself or Hire a Contractor?

In 1986, when I looked into having an attached greenhouse built, I received a quote of $18,600 from a professional greenhouse contractor for a 28-foot-long, 10-foot-wide, 12-foot-high greenhouse. This price did not include the foundation, wiring, or plumbing. My wife commented: "You can buy an awful lot of vegetables for that amount of money." The contractor insisted that we needed the structure he could provide because "almost any kind of home-built greenhouse will leak." I planned to use the structure to grow vegetables and flowers and felt that I could put up with a leak or two if I saved most of the money the installer wanted.

I built both of my greenhouses on the same foundation that the contractor was going to use and spent less than $500 on each, using lumber recycled from other jobs and glass recycled from patio doors. Yes, I do have a leak or two, but the leaks are over plant beds, so I'm not too concerned.

Certainly, if you don't have the skills or inclination required to build a greenhouse, you can hire a contractor to build it for you. Contractors calculate the cost of building in terms of hours and materials and then add in their profit. For some, the profit margin may be as high as 50 percent of the total cost to allow for cost overruns and a longer construction time than they might have estimated.

If you don't have the skills or inclination to build a greenhouse, you can hire a contractor to build it for you.

In most states, contractors must be licensed and insured, and in some states they must be bonded to ensure that their work is of a high standard. Many large contracting companies may consider a greenhouse job too small to take on, so you may have to find a one- or two-person company. To find a competent contractor, ask friends and neighbors for a recommendation. If you can't find a good contractor through word of mouth, you can try the Yellow Pages. The Better Business Bureau, your local chamber of commerce, or your state's building regulatory agency may also have a list of licensed contractors.

Your contractor should specify who will get the permits; the grade of the materials used; who will build the foundation; who will provide the plumbing and electricity lines; whether the contractor will provide and install the heating, sprinkler, and ventilation or cooling system; and whether the contractor will remove the waste and landscape the area after the project is finished. If you are installing a premade or kit greenhouse, your agreement with the contractor should list the manufacturer's name and model name or type of greenhouse, any additional materials required, and, if landscaping is included, the number and type of landscaping materials and shrubs that are to be planted on the site when the building is finished. The agreement should also spell out how the contractor will be paid and whether a warranty on the work is provided and for how long.

Generally, the last payment of 10 to 15 percent of the total cost is made when all the work

Communicate your expectations and ideas to the contractor at the start and remain involved in the building process.

is finished and the area has been blessed by the local building inspector (if the job requires a certificate of occupancy). If payment is made before the project is finished, some less reputable contractors have no incentive to finish the job and, as has happened to me, a few may simply walk away with the final payment before the job is complete.

Once you find a reputable contractor and all these details are ironed out, however, don't just tell him where you want the greenhouse and then walk away. That's a sure way to get the job the contractor thinks you want rather than the one you actually have in mind. Communicate your expectations and ideas at the start and remain involved in and aware of the building process.

Rather than hiring a soup-to-nuts contractor, you may decide that you have the skills and tools

required to do part of the work — perhaps you can handle the carpentry but not the foundation work, for instance. If you don't know how to do part of the job, don't be afraid to ask a local contractor if you can hire him or her to guide you or to take on a portion. For an hourly rate, you often can get expert help. You can also check with a local college or technical school for students who might want to take on a spare-time project. A greenhouse is an ideal short-term project for many tech-school students and, possibly, their instructor. Another source for information is the local garden club. Many clubs have greenhouse growers who can give you practical guidance on building and using your greenhouse. See Resources (page 246) for organizations that can provide information on building a greenhouse.

What Aesthetics Are Important to You?

Because it is a structure that you'll be living with for a long time, a greenhouse's aesthetics are an important consideration before you build. A greenhouse can be an eyesore — especially if it is a do-it-yourself project — or it can add value to your home. According to real estate agents, beyond providing a wonderful winter environment for plants, fish, and people, a well-designed conservatory adds several percentage points to a home's value. A greenhouse adds less, but still increases home value. Of course, if you are selling your home to a nongardener who isn't interested in owning a greenhouse, you can always take apart a freestanding greenhouse and move it to your new home.

Obviously, you want a greenhouse to add value to your property, and this requires both some thought about design and some basic building skills if you plan to complete the project yourself. Regarding design, the architectural style of the greenhouse should complement that of your home. If you have a cedar-shingled home with green trim, a greenhouse will look more integrated if it too has cedar shingles and green trim.

A complementary style is especially important if you are constructing a lean-to greenhouse or other type of attached structure. If you are building a new home, perhaps you'd like to have a greenhouse designed into the plans. If you are adding a greenhouse to an existing home, you might want to use the design services of a professional architect or greenhouse manufacturer to ensure that it matches the style of your home. If you plan to build the greenhouse yourself, adequately research house styles and architecture ahead of time to make a successful job of it.

It's also important to consider landscaping around your greenhouse. Try not to plant trees or shrubs that will eventually grow tall enough to shade the greenhouse, unless you intend to take advantage of their shade benefits. To avoid finding a tree root growing through the greenhouse floor, don't plant landscaping shrubs too close to the greenhouse. If you can, repeat plant species already growing in your yard; this helps to integrate the greenhouse structure into your property.

A greenhouse can help increase the long-term value of your property by allowing you to contribute to all the landscaping on your lot through the propagation of trees, shrubs, and less common plants grown from seed. Good landscaping can add 10 to 15 percent to the value of your home, and it has been estimated that a single mature tree can have an appraised value of $10,000 or more. Propagating your own plantings for landscaping — even starting and growing plants for hanging baskets for your porch — will save money too. Purchasing young trees, shrubs, and plants at a nursery or garden center can get very expensive.

2 The First Glasshouses

BEFORE YOU GET TOO DEEPLY INVOLVED in building your own greenhouse, let's take a brief historical tour of those "glasshouses" that we've turned to again and again for both pleasure and purpose.

The Start of Growing under Glass

Of course, greenhouse development could not begin until glass had been discovered. Most experts say that glass was first made about 4000 years ago in or near ancient Persia or Mesopotamia in the Middle East, when people used cooking fires to heat the local sand, melting the silica in it to form glass globules. These globules were then melted into molds and used for arrowheads and knives. Eventually, methods for producing glass improved and it was used to create objects for both practical and decorative purposes.

By 600 B.C.E., glass "recipes" were being recorded, but another 2,000 years passed before glass could be made cheaply enough for use in greenhouses and windows. This, however, did not stop the Roman emperor Tiberius from trying to grow out-of-season cucumbers under cover. Tiberius craved cucumbers all year long and demanded that his gardeners find a way to produce them. The workmen reputedly split off pieces of semitransparent mica and used them against a south-facing wall or in a small bed to cover tender crops in heated cold frames called *speculariums*. We don't know for sure whether this method worked, but the concept of growing plants under cover had been born.

It did not catch on quickly, however. The art of gardening under cover was lost for many years until the sixteenth century, when people attempted growing plants under semiopaque oiled paper and canvas and when, in the middle of the century, glass was "reinvented" in Europe. Yet it wasn't until glass became easier to make and less expensive that it was used for glasshouses, as greenhouses were first called.

Most sources give credit to Jules Charles, a French botanist, for designing the first glasshouse in 1600 or earlier. It was built in Leiden, Holland (perhaps giving an early start to the Dutch greenhouse industry). From that time onward, until the 1690s, affluent people experimented with glasshouses, and many large and very expensive structures were built throughout Britain, France, and Holland.

The First Conservatories

One of the first recorded conservatories, another name for greenhouses, was the one owned and written of by the Englishman John Evelyn, F.R.S. (Fellow of the Royal Society). Evelyn lived around the same time as the famous diarist Samuel Pepys, and like Pepys and other rich landowners of the day, he kept a diary. While Pepys's diary dealt with more topical events, Evelyn wrote about the gardens and plants of his time. He also wrote several books, the best known of which is *Elysium Britannicum,* a huge work that was not finished or published until after he died. He also published a gardener's almanac and *Acetaria: A Discourse of Sallets.* Evelyn's conservatory, heated by an enormous woodstove, was used for preserving delicate plants, many of which he had collected on his travels around the European continent during the English Civil War, which started in 1648.

During Evelyn's time, the use of glass in general slowly became more popular, but most glass could be made only in small panes of varying thicknesses and densities. To make these small panes into something large and more useful, a technique was employed that had been used for the stained-glass windows in many churches constructed in the medieval era: They were held together with lead casing.

Orangeries and Pineries

Around 1700, a few very rich merchants tried growing warm-weather plants under glass in England's moderate winter climate. The most successful of these designs was the orangery. In most cases, an orangery was built against a brick wall, with a sloping roof and the other three sides constructed of glass. As you might guess, its intended use was to grow citrus fruits. To keep the ground warm in the orangery, the gardeners of the time either built deep garden beds that were partly filled with horse manure and straw and covered with a foot or two of loam in which the trees were grown or placed pots containing the orange trees directly into beds of manure and compost. The decomposition of the manure kept the bed temperature at around 110°F to 140°F, which allowed citrus trees to grow. Moving large orange trees and spreading new compost around the tree roots or pots each fall must have been quite a laborious chore.

The term *greenhouse* came into use late in the eighteenth century, when growers noted the green appearance of the fruits and vegetables growing in these orangeries in the middle of an English winter.

In the United States, one of the first greenhouses on record was built in 1737 in Boston for Andrew Faneuil. Like his English counterparts, Faneuil wanted to grow fresh fruit in winter — and he was not alone. George Washington is reputed to have grown pineapples at Mt. Vernon so that he could serve them to his dinner guests. His glasshouse used the same manure-heating techniques used in the English orangery, but he called his structure a pinery.

Orangeries and pineries became much more popular after 1850 or so, when glass was first produced in large sheets and became a relatively inexpensive product. At that time, wrought iron, instead of wood, which tended to rot fairly quickly, became the glass (or glazing) support of choice. Eventually, these developments led to the construction of larger and larger greenhouses, which were used mostly to grow fruit out of season. Many of these huge structures were still the province of the very wealthy. By the mid- to late-1800s, however, large display greenhouses became an important trend in botanical science, with greenhouses being erected at many major botanic gardens in both Britain and America.

Nineteenth-Century Colossal Greenhouses

One of the best known of these large greenhouses was the Crystal Palace, a huge structure built in Hyde Park in London for the 1851 World's Fair. This building was close to 410 feet wide and 1,850 feet long, covered more than 19 acres, and contained almost a million square feet of glass in its walls and roof. It also had fountains that shot jets of water 250 feet into the air. After the fair, the Crystal Palace was moved to Sydenham Hill in North London. It was finally destroyed by fire in 1936.

The Palm House at the Royal Botanic Gardens, Kew, is another glasshouse built to similar mammoth proportions. The building was originally erected in 1848 and was recently restored. The Palm House is 363 feet long, 100 feet wide, and 66 feet high. Currently, its glass is supported

Noteworthy Glasshouses

The Crystal Palace in London,
built for the 1851 World's Fair

The main conservatory or 1868 House at
the Missouri Botanical Garden

The Palm House at the Royal Botanic Gardens, Kew, was built in 1848.

The Conservatory of Flowers in San Francisco's Golden Gate Park

by about ten miles of stainless-steel glazing bars, which have replaced the original bars.

England's early-Victorian-era conservatory craze largely passed by the United States. Shipping embargoes during the Civil War prevented importing these structures, and Americans at this time had more pressing concerns than investing in such an expensive hobby. It wasn't until the Gilded Age, which began in the late 1860s, that large American greenhouses began to come into their own.

One of the first examples was built by an Englishman named Henry Shaw in what is now the Missouri Botanical Garden. The building, known as the main conservatory or the 1868 House, enclosed exotic plants of many kinds. A few years later, in 1880, Shaw added another greenhouse near the main conservatory. This building became known as the Linnaean House and is still home to palms, citruses, and other tropical and semitropical plants.

Another beautiful old glasshouse is the 12,000-square-foot Conservatory of Flowers in San Francisco's Golden Gate Park. It was erected there in 1879, although most of it was reputed to have been made in Europe and shipped to San Francisco. This conservatory is listed as the oldest wood and glass greenhouse in the United States, with a significant portion of the structure being made of California redwood. It is now on the National Register of Historic Places and has recently been completely restored after high winds, structural damage, and the use of lead-based paints and other unsuitable materials threatened to close it permanently in 1995. Since these earliest American conservatories were built, many others have been constructed, including the Haupt Conservatory in the New York Botanical Garden, built in 1902.

The Hobby Greenhouse

These botanical garden greenhouses were heated by a combination of methods. One involved using hot beds made from manure and straw piled so that the compost heated up as it rotted. Once these beds were covered with loam, it became possible to grow plants on top of the heated compost. The number of horses in those days made it easy to get manure. Another method involved keeping the air warm with furnace-heated water that circulated through pipes around a greenhouse's perimeter. (The furnace was invented in England to heat greenhouses long before it was used to heat people's homes.) In addition, on clear days sunlight contributed to the level of heat in a greenhouse, often necessitating that windows be opened to vent the structure. The combination of these three heating methods allowed the season for citrus fruits and other warm-weather crops to be extended long enough for the fruits to be harvested even in cold climates.

The fresh fruit and flower market that such structures supported rapidly led to the building of commercial greenhouses all over Europe, especially in Britain, Holland, France, and Belgium. These were the days before trucks and planes carried fresh produce to market from far-off regions. Because everything had to be grown in local areas, greenhouses were a boon to growers. By around 1880, tomatoes were being produced in European greenhouses, mostly in France and Holland. The greenhouse industry looked set to thrive and expand.

But in World War I, millions of working men were killed on the western front. Many of these young men came from estates that had invested in the labor-intensive greenhouse market. Without these workers, the industry simply could not maintain its output, and it declined significantly as a result. The business of greenhouse growing did not recover fully until after World War II. In the United States, the Great Depression coupled with the high cost of capital investment required to construct greenhouses kept the greenhouse market from expanding much between the wars.

After World War II, aluminum and galvanized steel came into consistent use for greenhouse framing, eliminating altogether the need for wood, which nowadays is used only in smaller kit or hobby greenhouses. In addition, the use of lighter-weight polycarbonate, acrylic, or polyethylene glazing instead of glass made it relatively inexpensive to erect a greenhouse and easier to control the growing environment. Because of their higher insulation value, these lighter plastic materials also tended to make greenhouses less expensive to heat. As a result of these developments, the commercial greenhouse industry expanded worldwide, especially in Holland, which, with its rich soil and temperate climate, has the largest greenhouse area of any country in the world.

The growth of commercial greenhouses set the stage for a rapid expansion of the use of hobby greenhouses. Plastic and aluminum greenhouses became available to the home gardener for only a few hundred dollars. In addition, many new greenhouse add-ons such as hot tubs, spas, and fishponds, as well as new varieties of plants, also encouraged the growth of home gardening under cover. The result is that today, more and more keen gardeners are buying into the greenhouse lifestyle.

The hobby greenhouse market has been particularly explosive in many European countries. In Britain, for example, it seems that every garden plot has a greenhouse. In the United States the market is gaining momentum, with many people supplementing their gardening pleasure with a small greenhouse. Gardening is currently a very popular hobby in the United States: According to the National Gardening Association, one in four American families claims to have a garden. This can only strengthen the home greenhouse market in the future and help it to grow even more.

A commercial greenhouse

3 An Overview of Greenhouse Options

BEFORE YOU DECIDE TO purchase or build a greenhouse, you should understand that there are different types based on use and structural or building styles. What you want to do with your greenhouse can be wildly different from what your next-door neighbor wants to do with his or hers. Only by considering every aspect of owning a greenhouse — including what you'll be growing and how the structure will be used — can you determine what type and structural style it should be, as well as what glazing material to use and whether the greenhouse should have heating, plumbing, supplemental lighting, and misting or automatic venting systems.

Suppose, for example, that you want to grow orchids (one reason for building a greenhouse; many varieties require a great deal of warmth and humidity). Orchids like conditions that are similar to those enjoyed by many humans. Therefore, for an orchid house, you might consider a lean-to-style greenhouse that's an extension of your home but that incorporates supplemental humidity in winter. Unless such a structure is partially shaded by trees, however, it should not have clear glass glazing. Most orchids are understory plants and cannot tolerate high light levels.

If you want to grow vegetables for the dinner table, you can probably grow them in an orchid house, but most vegetables prefer slightly cooler temperatures, even as low as just above freezing, and they don't like the high humidity that orchids enjoy. In fact, high humidity and lack of air circulation for plants such as lettuce and tomatoes can increase the possibility of growth of fungal *Botrytis* (gray mold).

Of course, a particular structural style of greenhouse can have multiple functions. For example, here in Rhode Island my heated, attached lean-to greenhouse (see the illustration on page 18) contains citrus and banana trees, but I also grow vegetables and flowers there when I can squeeze them into the space. Likewise, my unheated freestanding greenhouse often contains a lemon or lime tree, as these plants transition to their summer home on the decks surrounding the house. In fact, for two months during the worst part of winter, the freestanding greenhouse may also become a repository for tools, wheelbarrows, and a few of the chairs that normally occupy the deck space. What greenhouses are used for often bears no relation to the specific style of the structure.

As another example, I built a polyethylene-walled greenhouse simply to keep away deer and rodents from my plants and to provide a controlled environment for my vegetables. Controlling the environment makes it easier for me to keep insects off plants, to precisely direct fertilizers, and to keep plants sheltered from the cool ocean air carried over the garden by southerly winds in spring. All these benefits add up to an improvement in growing conditions, healthier plants, and higher vegetable yields. For me, this is important. For other gardeners, it might be less so.

This overview chapter focuses on types of greenhouses based on use and particular structural or building styles that are available. When

This attached, heated lean-to greenhouse faces southeast and is located within a few feet of the fenced vegetable garden.

considering incorporating a greenhouse into your life, use the information in chapter 1 with that provided here and on the checklist on pages 100–109 to help in your decision.

What Type and Structural Style Do You Want?

Greenhouses come in many shapes and sizes, and are made of many kinds of materials. My first greenhouse was made of old windows still in their jambs. To open the greenhouse, I simply opened a window. This greenhouse wasn't very large — in fact, I couldn't stand up in it — but it satisfied my desire to grow plants out of season.

That early attempt was rather like the Romans trying to grow cucumbers out of season: It wasn't very successful, but it was a chance for me to push the envelope and try something new. Since that time, I've built a number of greenhouses. With each one, I've improved my knowledge of growing "under glass" and extending the growing season at both ends. Now I start a new growing season with seed germination in January in my basement germination chamber. In my heated greenhouse, growing season never ends; it merely slows during winter. Growing under

glass has become a hobby that provides exotic fruits and vegetables for my family's table, interesting flowers to perfume our house, and a place to relax when work gets too stressful.

The first step in the process of building your own greenhouse is determining how you might use the structure. You can use it only to grow orchids or specialty plants, vegetables, and fruits, or you can build a conservatory and eat meals there. If you like, you can put a pool or a spa in a greenhouse for year-round enjoyment. Some greenhouses are used for hydroponic growing — that is, for raising plants in a special soilless medium, a solution of water with various nutrients, to obtain optimum growth. Other greenhouses can provide added protection and heat to plants grown directly in the ground. Deciding on your goals for your greenhouse is the first step in designing or selecting it.

Five Basic Types

Following are some types of greenhouses conceived with specific uses in mind. Each is accompanied by a list of items required for optimal use of such a structure. The information in this section, while not comprehensive, is intended to help you consider the intended use of your greenhouse along with the possible equipment and materials (and their costs) that such a use necessitates before you commit to building it.

The Tropical Greenhouse

A tropical greenhouse is likely the most expensive type to heat during a cold northern winter. If you are going to heat your greenhouse to the levels required by tropical plants, you can install double- or even triple-pane glass or polycarbonate and accept the slight loss of light caused by the additional glazing. You'll need to be careful, however, when moving plants from a greenhouse with triple glazing to the outdoors; light levels in such a greenhouse are typically about 70 to 90 percent of those outdoors. Plant leaves tend to burn if they are placed in direct sunlight after being in such an environment for months. There are structural considerations as well: Tropical greenhouses can be quite humid, which can cause wood used in building to rot very quickly. Take care to construct the greenhouse of top-quality, rot-resistant materials.

Two other considerations of tropical greenhouses involve heat: They must be heated to high levels in winter (a minimum of 50°F to 65°F at night and 75°F to 80°F during the day) and they tend to overheat in summer, even when shaded with a cloth or by trees. I find that my greenhouse can easily reach 120°F on a day with little wind and bright sunshine, even though part of it is located under a large shady plum tree. A greenhouse that overheats must be equipped with sizeable vents or blower fans to move out the moist, hot air quickly or must combine an efficient method of shading with possibly an evaporative cooler. (Note that growth stops for most plants when the temperature rises to between 80°F and 85°F; anything above this can be defined as overheating.)

The Warm Greenhouse

You can grow some tropical plants in a warm greenhouse: I let my greenhouse cool to about 50°F at night, and the tropical plants seem to thrive. Their growth does slow in winter, how-

ever, and instead of growing bananas in a single season or two, in my greenhouse a single bunch might take from three to five seasons to grow.

Warm greenhouses must be heated at night during northern winters. Heaters can be fueled by propane, natural gas, electricity, or even wood. A wood-burning stove, however, emits dry heat that is not beneficial to plants.

You can supplement daylight in a warm greenhouse by adding lighting, thereby making the environment both warm and light for growing plants. This subject is covered in more detail in chapters 5 and 7. Your warm greenhouse's lighting, water, and heating can all be fully automated.

The Orchid Greenhouse

Because various orchid species require specific growing conditions, including unique light and temperature needs, before you specialize in growing orchids in a greenhouse you should know a fair amount about orchid growing so that your greenhouse structure and systems can match these special requirements.

The first step in the process of building your own greenhouse is determining how you might use the structure.

While this book is not the place to learn about growing orchids, there are basic considerations involved in the process that certainly play into greenhouse choices. For instance, some orchids will not flower in insufficient light, while others will not flower if the area is too wet or too cold. Some will not flower if the environment is too dry, preferring higher humidity, while other types thrive in dry conditions. Most orchids do not grow well in air laden with chemicals such as heater exhaust fumes and pesticides. Some require specific night and daytime temperatures at certain times of the year to set flowers.

Most orchid growers invest in a greenhouse after they have grown the plants for several years and have a pretty good idea what they require for optimum growth. With the easy-to-grow orchids available in many chain stores today, you can grow a variety and learn about them as you go. For example, *Phalaenopsis* orchids come from understory tropical forests in India, the Philippines, Indonesia, and northern Australia, which gives you a clue about the conditions they like. In your greenhouse they will require moderately bright light, typically on the order of 1,000 foot-candles (for more on lighting, see chapters 5 and 10). These lighting requirements will dictate the location and glazing of your greenhouse or necessary modifications to meet the plants' needs. If you've chosen to place your greenhouse in a location that gets full sun, for instance, you'll have to use some form of shading such as a roller shade or shade cloth, which you'll need to install or remove according to season.

For *Phalaenopsis* orchids, temperatures should not exceed 85°F during the daytime or drop below 55°F at night. These temperatures are typical of those in your home in front of a brightly lit window during the winter, as long as the window is insulated at night. *Phalaenopsis* orchids will also require some form of humidification system to maintain the conditions they favor. Other orchids such as *Dendrobium* and *Cymbidium,* can stand cooler temperatures, although some *Dendrobium* thrive best with warmer temperatures and require them at times. *Dendrobium* also require more light than *Phalaenopsis,* and *Cymbidium* need more light than both. In fact, *Cymbidium* should be given as much light as possible without burning them. Some orchid growers have a mini-greenhouse inside a larger greenhouse or a section of a larger greenhouse devoted to growing orchids that require either warmer or cooler temperatures or that have other special requirements.

To cut down on heating costs for orchids requiring warmer temperatures, you can build onto your home a wooden lean-to greenhouse with double- or triple-wall polycarbonate glazing. In this way, you can keep the greenhouse warm from the heat of your home.

What You Need for Tropical, Warm, and Orchid Greenhouses

GENERAL NEEDS FOR ALL THREE

- A good-quality heater with a thermostat. (For growing orchids, consider an electric heater to avoid problems with gas heater fumes.)

- Efficient waterproof lights to extend day length for plants and to allow you to work in the greenhouse in the evening. (Consider putting these lights on timers.)

- A power supply

- A fan to exhaust excess heat in summer and keep air circulating. (This helps prevent fungal diseases.)

- An automatic vent-opening system (optional)

- A misting system (optional)

- A water supply that will not freeze

- Low-temperature alarms

- Tool storage

- Fertilizer, potting soil, and orchid bark storage (in a separate shed, if greenhouse space is limited, or to ensure that the structure retains maximum heat; placing quantities of these in the greenhouse will lower the temperature of the environment)

ADDITIONAL NEEDS FOR A WARM GREENHOUSE

- A backup kerosene heater. (You can also use a small, canister gas heater, but in an enclosed greenhouse space you must be very careful when using any kind of heater with an open flame.)

ADDITIONAL NEEDS FOR AN ORCHID GREENHOUSE

- A misting or humidifying system for certain types of orchids (essential in winter, when the air is very dry, or in dry climates)

- Thermometer(s) and humidity gauges

What You Need for Unheated Greenhouses

FOR A COOL GREENHOUSE

- An automatic vent-opening system (optional)

- A water supply that can be turned off and drained for the winter

- Storage for your seeds, fertilizers, tools, and other gardening gear (in the greenhouse, in the greenhouse's air lock, or in a separate garden shed)

FOR AN ALPINE GREENHOUSE

- Screens around sides

- Windows that open and that may stay open all winter

- A fan to keep moisture off plant crowns

- Raised benches to allow air to circulate around plants

Some special orchid requirements may be met by the addition of a bigger water tank or pond to your greenhouse configuration. A larger tank can also act as a solar heat sink and can keep the greenhouse humidified during cold winters. Of course, you can also raise koi, goldfish, or tilapia in the tank or pond. In cold-winter climates, count on installing a heater with a thermostat. Most orchids like some variation in temperature, but no more than 20 to 30 degress from day to night.

The Cool (Unheated) Greenhouse

Most leafy green vegetables can stand much lower temperatures than orchids and grow best between 50°F and 70°F, and many vegetables will survive almost to freezing. A freestanding greenhouse without a heating system will allow you to grow vegetables for most of the year and will enable them to survive for most of the winter in areas up to Zone 5 or 6. If greenhouse beds are heated, either mechanically or by the creation of hot beds, vegetables may grow year-round in areas that reach temperatures as low as 25°F. (See chapter 10) If your only option is to add an attached greenhouse to your home, you may or may not decide to heat the structure separately.

An unheated vegetable greenhouse need not be full walk-in height. In fact, it will probably stay warmer nearer the plants if the greenhouse is only a little taller than the height of the plants.

In addition, the glazing need not be fancy: An unheated vegetable greenhouse requires less winter light to come through the glazing than does a greenhouse for flowers, and because the greenhouse is not heated, there is no need for double-thickness glazing. In fact, some growers rely on hoop houses or high tunnels with a polyethylene covering to enable them to grow for most of the winter.

A cool greenhouse will be warm enough to allow even artichoke plants to survive the winter — and last winter I left an olive tree in the cool greenhouse to see if it would survive. It lost its leaves, but it made it and is now growing happily.

The Alpine Greenhouse

Like many plants associated with specific climates or locations, alpine plants require unique conditions to survive: those that re-create the conditions found at high altitudes, where the plants are covered with frozen snow or ice for much of the year and bloom in the short, high-altitude summer.

In general, the growing season for alpine plants is extremely short. A greenhouse geared to their needs is designed to allow the plants to get very cold but to protect them from water or snow gathering on their crowns. Such a house might have a glass roof and open windows protected with screens to keep away insects and inquisitive animals. Often an alpine house has louvered windows that allow air to circulate but keep rain and snow outside of the structure. Inside it might have raised planting benches with mesh tops to allow air to circulate around the pots.

Basic Structural or Building Styles

Once you've determined how you will use your greenhouse and what special items this use may call for, you should choose the structural style that will best meet your needs.

Greenhouse styles generally fall into one of two categories: freestanding or detached (which can be sited in a number of places) or attached to an existing structure (usually the south side of a home). While your intended use may determine which one of these two categories you choose, in cases where you may select either, each comes with its own set of pros and cons. Of course, it may be that your growing needs do not require a formal greenhouse. If your intended use is to extend the gardening season, there are a number of options that require significantly less financial investment and building commitment. The following information outlines the pluses and minuses of freestanding greenhouses, attached greenhouses, and small season extenders and presents the specific advantages, and disadvantages associated with the building styles in each category.

Freestanding or Detached

A freestanding greenhouse is one that requires you to walk across the lawn or around the garden to get to it; it is not connected to your house or to any part of another building. It can be a preassembled, commercially manufactured model, a home-built greenhouse, or one that comes as a kit and is assembled by a contractor or by you.

Freestanding greenhouses come in a large variety of shapes and sizes, and are made of many different materials. Probably the most common type, sold in many seed catalogs and at many retail stores, is the rectangular hobby greenhouse with polycarbonate glazing and a lightweight aluminum frame. Home-built, freestanding structures are nearly as common. They vary in size, styles, and materials.

A-Frame

Most often, A-frame greenhouses are freestanding, although I have seen an A-frame greenhouse attached to an A-frame house. The biggest drawback to an A-frame greenhouse is that the floor space is small relative to the height. This is most disadvantageous in winter because heat rises, and in an A-frame it can rise well away from the plants. You can compensate for this by hanging a fan from the ceiling and aiming it toward the floor. (You can buy a plastic desk fan for $5 to $10, unscrew and remove the base, and hang the fan and motor from chains or screw them to the overhead framing.) It's important to use a fan when a greenhouse is closed to prevent sooty fungus and other fungal problems that develop on plants in stagnant-air conditions. In addition, a fan moves air around plants, helping them to "exhale" and get rid of toxic gases that hover over leaves in stagnant conditions.

On the plus side, an A-frame greenhouse is so simple to build that I'm surprised that this style is not much more common. Basically, it's constructed of two flat sides leaning against each other with end walls between them. An ideal glazing material for an A-frame is corrugated polycarbonate or acrylic, which can be screwed to structural beams. Simply cap the ridge and ends and voilà! You have a greenhouse!

With the tall structure of an A-frame, it's relatively easy to add a door at one end and shelves at the other, but the fact remains that the growing area is limited in this type of structure because of the lack of headroom over the sloping sides. This restriction in growing area is partly compensated for by an increase in height at the center of the greenhouse. For example, a 10-foot-wide A-frame greenhouse would be about 9 feet tall in the middle if the frames are sloped at a typical angle of 60 degrees. In contrast, a conventional 10-foot-wide greenhouse is 6 to 7 feet tall. The benefit to the extra height in an A-frame is that hanging baskets can be positioned well above a person's head to keep him or her from bumping into them (which is easy to do in a 6- or 7-foot-tall greenhouse). There is also room in an A-frame to grow taller trees or shrubs. An A-frame structure, however, does contain wasted space under the benches or at the foundation, where there is very little height. It thus does not allow for maximizing the planting of low-growing crops (which, space issues aside, would also be in the cool air left at ground level when warm air rises to the highest part of the greenhouse).

An A-frame greenhouse

Conventional (Vertical-Sided)

This is the most common style of greenhouse and can be found in most gardening catalogs. Because its sides are vertical, it's easy to set up shelves and benches inside. The roof is sloped toward a central ridge and the door is usually in one of the two peaked (gable) ends. Most conventional greenhouses have sidewalls about 5 feet high with a central ridge that stands 6 to 8 feet above the floor. The greenhouse has plenty of headroom in the central aisle. One of the easiest to make and operate, this greenhouse does suffer from one drawback: Because it has glazing on all four sides, the glazing on the north side allows heat to escape and may not get any sunlight to compensate for this. If you live in a northern climate in the northern hemisphere, you might want to fashion insulated panels to install on the north side of the greenhouse for the winter months to help restrict heat loss.

A conventional vertical-sided greenhouse. Many kit greenhouses are constructed in this style.

Gothic Arch

A Gothic arch greenhouse solves many of the problems of an A-frame greenhouse in that the arches are slightly curved, allowing for a larger base area than the A-frame, although not as much height. Commercial versions of this style of structure can be obtained from a company called Gothic Arch Greenhouses (see Resources, page 246). For people building their own greenhouses, however, it can be difficult to make the arches that are incorporated into the design. For methods of constructing them, see the Gothic arch greenhouse project in chapter 13. Another building difficulty is that

A Gothic arch greenhouse

TIP

When your greenhouse is closed, it's important to use a fan to help circulate air, which prevents sooty fungus and other fungal problems that can develop on plants in stagnant-air conditions. In addition, the circulating air generated by a fan helps plants to "exhale" and get rid of toxic gases that hover over leaves in stagnant conditions.

A slope-sided greenhouse

A gambrel-roofed model

glazing must be curved to match the arch. This eliminates glass as a glazing material, but any of the plastics (acrylics, polycarbonates) in bendable thicknesses are glazing options.

Slope-Sided

This type of greenhouse combines the best of both a conventional greenhouse and an A-frame for growing crops in the ground. In a slope-sided greenhouse, instead of the vertical walls of a typical kit-style greenhouse, the walls slope outward to give a greater growing area at the base. With the sloped sides, a large ground area can be covered, but because it has a conventional roof, the overall height of this type of structure is lower than that of an A-frame. If you plan to grow plants in pots on benches, this style is not as practical as a vertical-sided greenhouse because the sloped sides make it difficult to attach shelving and the shelving must be slightly smaller than the base area. For growing plants in beds, however, the slope-sided greenhouse covers slightly more area than either an A-frame or a vertical-sided greenhouse. To avoid the problem of moisture staying on the roof too long and contributing to the growth of algae and mosses, the roof slope should not be too shallow.

Gambrel-Roofed

This variation on the vertical-sided greenhouse has a roof with two pitches, like a Dutch barn. This provides more headroom near the walls, which is helpful if you stand up and work against the walls to tend in-ground beds, for example. If you put benches against the walls, however, the gambrel roof offers no advantage over a vertical-sided structure.

Quonset, Hoop, or High-Tunnel

For a relatively inexpensive freestanding greenhouse that extends the season for two or three months, a plastic-covered Quonset or hoop house is ideal. This type of greenhouse covers the largest area for the least cost, and building one is relatively simple, depending on the materials you use. A commercial hoop house is likely to be made of galvanized steel arches with a plastic covering. The length of a Quonset depends on the number of hoops it has. In general, the hoops are spaced 4 feet apart, and any greenhouse length in 4-foot increments can be accommodated.

The lightest covering for such a house is 6 mil, construction-grade polyethylene. The problem with this material is that it is not UV stable: It degrades in sunlight and usually splits along the folds. Further, it cannot stand up to high winds. I've found that my hoop house with a polyethylene cover will not remain undamaged in winds of 40 to 50 miles per hour. Small splits in the covering can easily be repaired with duct tape or, for a more attractive finish, clear plastic weather-stripping tape. This tape does tend to crack after a couple of months, however. Where I live, close to the seashore, strong winds usually result in having to purchase a new cover. Winds aside, the cover will last for two seasons, but some growers find that polyethylene covers last for only one season. Usually, after two or three seasons, the material becomes brittle and breaks. If you use a polyethylene greenhouse cover, it's best to replace it each season or at least every other season. The biggest benefit of polyethylene is its cost: A 14-foot by 40-foot-long hoop house can be covered for $50 to $100. There are some UV-protected plastic coverings that will last three or more seasons, but they're not easy to find.

The next best hoop house–covering material is called Tufflite. Available from most greenhouse suppliers, it comes in several styles, some with UV blockers and some with an additive to prevent condensation (which drips on plants and may contribute to overwatering or disease). Tufflite costs about 20 percent more than polyethylene.

If you want a more rigid hoop house, you can cover a metal frame with thin polycarbonate that is bent to the curve of the greenhouse. Installing such a cover requires greater effort and costs more, but the longevity of this glazing is extended to about 15 years. On the other side of the coin, the cover cannot be easily removed in summer and installing it on a greenhouse frame necessitates some form of ventilation and shading. Because hoop houses that incorporate

A hoop or high-tunnel greenhouse

this material are based on commercial structures, they usually feature large double doors at either end, which, when left open, provide a great deal of ventilation.

I've found that one of the least expensive ways to build a small hoop house is to make hoops from ¾-inch or 1-inch schedule 40 plastic water pipe and stretch polyethylene over this frame. (See the hoop house project in chapter 13, page 228.)

At the end walls of the greenhouse, I gather the polyethylene and staple it to old storm doors that I use for entryways. A tidier entrance at each end can be made from plywood sheeting fitted with storm doors. The total cost for a 14-foot-wide and 40-foot-long hoop house constructed in this way is about $150.

Geodesic Dome

Domes are interesting structures and have a terrific application as greenhouses, but they can be difficult to design and for glazing they require either custom-cut glass or plastic cut to size. Their overall advantages, however, often outweigh construction difficulties. A dome greenhouse can be a wonderful environment to enjoy just for its shape and area. The most common way to lay out a dome greenhouse is to set it up with growing beds around the edge; a wide, circular path about 4 feet in from the sides of the structure; and a central passive heat reservoir. This reservoir can double as a large fish tank to provide the benefit of fish waste to fertilize plants. For the height of the dome, the ground area is huge, but like slope-sided and A-frame greenhouses, bench area decreases with height and it's difficult to add benches and shelving to the sloping walls.

A geodesic dome greenhouse

A pit greenhouse

Freestanding Build-Your-Own

The great thing about building your own greenhouse is that you can create any design or style you like. You can design it to match the style of your home or you can follow one of the plans in chapter 13, modifying it to suit your particular needs or weather conditions.

Many self-built, freestanding greenhouses have an insulated north wall to help reduce the effects of cold winds. Others have three insulated walls with only the roof and the south-facing wall made of transparent glazing. Some have an air lock — a small entryway between the door to the outside environment and the door to the greenhouse itself that reduces the likelihood of cold, outside air entering the greenhouse in the middle of winter — while others have garage doors to allow for driving a lawn tractor or larger vehicle into the greenhouse for winter storage.

Freestanding build-your own greenhouses can be erected on bare ground, on a foundation, on a concrete slab, or even on a wooden platform. The possibilities seem endless, with the size and style limited only by your imagination, budget, construction skills, and site.

Pit Style

Below the frost line, soil temperature remains fairly steady at about 50°F. The floor of a pit greenhouse is set below grade to take advantage of this phenomenon. Of course, this temperature isn't warm enough to grow hothouse tomatoes or peppers or to germinate plants unless such a greenhouse is heated during the winter months. Most pit greenhouses contain benches or shelves to raise plants to a level where they can get a great deal of exposure to sunlight. Potting soil, seed flats, and tools are stored beneath these shelves.

Pit greenhouses, which may be freestanding or attached, can extend from 5 feet below grade to 3 feet exposed above grade but are most often 3 or 4 feet deep (below grade) so that tops of plant benches can be level with the bottom of the glazing. They tend to be expensive to build because their design requires excavation and the construction of a concrete retaining wall foundation to hold the soil in place. You can insulate the foundation, however, to help make it less expensive to heat. A pit greenhouse also requires the construction of a stepped entryway, and steps can be expensive to build, although I once built a pit greenhouse into a bank and used a conventional door at one end as an entryway.

Pit greenhouses can suffer from poor drainage, so you'll need to make sure that the greenhouse site you select can be drained easily. If your greenhouse is to have electrical power, it's not difficult to install a sump pump, although a natural drainpipe (see chapter 4, page 37) is much less expensive.

If you own property that slopes from north to south, perhaps you'll want to install a semi-pit greenhouse. With this design, the back of the greenhouse is at ground level and is constructed of concrete block or poured concrete, and the entire front of the greenhouse is glass. This style makes use of the terrain to insulate and protect the growing area.

Advantages and Disadvantages of a Freestanding Greenhouse

ADVANTAGES

- It can be any shape or style.

- It can be sited anywhere on your property where it is sheltered from the winter winds, where the soil is well drained, and where it is easily accessible.

- It can be expanded as required. If you need more space or outgrow your current space, you can often buy or build additional length. Hobby greenhouses can usually be expanded in 2- or 4-foot sections. (Keep this in mind when choosing a location.)

- If unheated, it can provide a place for off-season storage of wheelbarrows, tools, and plant pots. By choosing your site carefully, you can hide the "detritus" or unsightly apparatus of your gardening enterprise. Of course, you can also grow plants in your greenhouse in the off-season.

- It can be as large as you like, while the size of an attached greenhouses is constrained by the building to which it is attached.

- It can be less expensive to build than a greenhouse attached to your home.

- It can be placed near the garden, making it easier to move plants in and out of the structure.

- It receives light all day long and by orienting the ridge east to west, it can be placed to maximize available light.

DISADVANTAGES

- Power and water will need to be brought to the greenhouse. This may require digging a ditch to lay a water pipe below the frost line or toting water and using an extension cord for electrical power.

- Heat loss is higher with a freestanding greenhouse because all four sides are exposed to the elements. You can cut down on heat loss, however, by insulating the north side of the greenhouse. You can also insulate the structure using bubble wrap or layers of polyethylene sheeting, but this quite drastically cuts down on the light levels in the greenhouse, leading to your plants suffering sunburn when you bring them outside in the spring.

- If you live in a climate that is snowy in winter, you may have to dig your way to the greenhouse after a snowfall.

- It is readily accessible to intruders and is thus more susceptible to theft. For this reason, and if you store chemicals there, you should keep the structure securely locked.

- Because it can more easily be made of various scrap materials and often requires less refined construction techniques than attached greenhouses, it can look like a less-than-perfect work of craftsmanship.

An attached greenhouse with an exterior door can be used for plants alone or as part of the home and equipped with chairs and a table. This greenhouse has curved glass eaves and is built on a deck.

The roofline of an attached greenhouse should extend from the roofline of the house to which it's adjacent to prevent ice and snow from dropping onto the glazing.

Attached Greenhouses

An attached greenhouse allows you to work on gardening projects at any time — late at night or early in the morning, before you go to work, or, as I do when I need a break, in the middle of the day. You can regularly eat in such a greenhouse, install a hot tub or pool in it, or, in the middle of winter, use it as a solar space to help keep your home warm and moist. In the depths of winter you can grow and enjoy orchids or other flowers in an attached greenhouse or raise organic vegetables there. As with freestanding greenhouses, attached greenhouses have many advantages — but they have disadvantages too. (See Advantages and Disadvantages of an Attached Greenhouse, page 30, for a summary.)

The biggest advantage of an attached greenhouse is that it can be less expensive to build than a freestanding structure of the same size and quality. Of course, an attached greenhouse should match or complement the architecture of your home, which can add significant cost.

Such a greenhouse or solarium can be open to your home, allowing heat and moisture into your primary dwelling in winter. In fact, when it's frigid outside, the humidity that an attached greenhouse can supply is a definite plus. Because humid air always feels warmer to the skin than does dry air, your home feels warmer at the same temperature. One drawback to that humid air, though, is that it tends to smell a bit earthy. Many people don't mind this smell, but applying manure to the plants in your greenhouse might make it seem as though you're living next to a farm manure pit!

Though additional humidity in your home is a benefit in winter, it can be much less desirable in summer. To remedy this, an attached greenhouse can be separated from your home by doors that allow you to block it off in summer. Either blocked off or open to your home, an attached greenhouse should have an outside door to allow you to bring in potting soil, plants, and tools without having to carry them through the house.

If you live in a snowy area, before you build an attached greenhouse, ask about snow loads and learn how well the roof will support them. If you plan on a lean-to greenhouse, figure out how far snow sliding off the house roof will fall and whether it will land on the greenhouse glazing. A lump of frozen snow or ice can easily shatter glass or damage polycarbonate if it drops more than a foot or two. If you decide that you want a lean-to greenhouse, try to ensure that the roofline abuts the eaves of your home so that ice and snow will simply slide over the glass rather than drop onto it.

Attached greenhouses, including custom designs, can be purchased from a garden center, catalog, or online, or you can build one yourself (see chapter 13, project 5). There are many varieties to choose from in diverse materials and styles. Their frames can be wood, aluminum, or metal and their glazing may be glass, plastic, or fiberglass. They may be heated or unheated, curtained, separated from the home, or left open to the primary dwelling.

The Conservatory, Sunroom, or Solarium

As we learned in chapter 2, the term *conservatory* was coined around 1660 by the seventeenth-century naturalist John Evelyn at his Sayes Court Gardens in Deptford, England, where he preserved delicate plants during Britain's cold winter months. Evelyn's planned conservatory was a little more grand, perhaps, than our idea of a conservatory today: It was intended to have Corinthian capitals and wreathed columns supporting it and was set in an ideal garden of about 70 acres.

If you decide that you want a greenhouse attached to your home so that you can grow houseplants such as ferns, philodendrons, maybe an orchid or two, and a couple of pots of herbs, you might want to consider a conservatory or sunroom, which serves as an additional room in a home. Conservatories have glass walls and ceilings, while sunrooms and solariums have plenty of windows and conventional roofs. Some conservatory or sunroom owners love to eat breakfast and lunch in such a space, surrounded by plants and greenery. Others use the area as a living room, where they can relax and enjoy the ambience. Conservatories or sunrooms are also

A custom-built conservatory becomes an integral part of the home and can contribute to both the warmth and humidity level of the main house in the cold, winter months.

popular locations for hot tubs, and the plants certainly benefit from the extra humidity the hot water brings.

The biggest advantage of an attached greenhouse is that it can be less expensive to build than a freestanding structure of the same size and quality.

Conservatories, sunrooms, and solariums all allow for the free passage of heat and warmth between the structures and your home. In general, a conservatory tends to have a connotation that is slightly more upscale than a sunroom or a solarium. Part of the conservatory's appeal is that it can house both plants and people because of the increased glazed area, whereas sunrooms and solariums tend to be used more for plants than people. While conservatories are marked by a profusion of plants, they often include a dining or reading area. People do not usually perform the dirty work of repotting plants in their conservatory; they usually pot elsewhere and then bring the clean, potted plants into the room.

Advantages and Disadvantages of an Attached Greenhouse

ADVANTAGES

- It provides additional living space, incorporating several hundred square feet to your home.

- It's a source of additional heat during winter daylight hours. During the long winter nights, however, you'll need to use blinds or shades to slow heat loss through the glazing.

- It provides additional insulation for your home. Acting as a buffer between the walls of the home and the outdoors, an attached greenhouse can increase the insulation value of an exterior wall by 10 to 15 percent.

- It's a source of humidity for your home during dry winter months. If you suffer from aches and pains when humidity levels drop, you may find that an attached greenhouse alleviates such symptoms.

- The costs of building an attached greenhouse may be less than those of a freestanding one of comparable size and quality. The reason: An attached greenhouse requires that you build one or two fewer walls.

- The plants can be easily tended to at any time. Instead of watching television in the evening and in a few spare minutes before going to work in the morning, you can spend time in the greenhouse. And you don't have to shovel snow to get into the greenhouse!

- In most cases, it will increase the value of your home.

DISADVANTAGES

- Insects can find their way into your living space. If you spray insecticides in the greenhouse to get rid of these pests, the spray can also get into your home.

- It requires shading in summer. All greenhouses get hot during the summer months and attached structures often vent that extra heat into the home. A well-designed attached greenhouse includes ways to vent excess heat, shade the structure, and close it off from the home.

- Because plants transpire, a greenhouse will always be humid. This humidity can get into the walls of your home and cause rot. When installing an attached greenhouse, you will need to add a good vapor barrier over wooden walls of your home in the area where the greenhouse is attached to prevent humidity from getting to the wood.

- Its size may be restricted by the size of the space available for it adjacent to your home. This can limit future expansion or the size of plants that you can grow.

- Its orientation may be problematic. The most efficient greenhouses face due south or slightly southeast. If you cannot build on a site with southern exposure, you may not get optimal results with your plants. If you attach your greenhouse to a wall that doesn't face south, which may be good for certain types of plants, it will be expensive to heat in winter and may be much colder than one that gets southern exposure.

- Generally, it needs to be kept clean and tidy. Dropped potting soil can be cleaned up at your leisure in a freestanding greenhouse, but in an attached greenhouse, you'll need to clean it up fairly promptly lest you track dirt into your home. (It's true, however, that an unclean greenhouse of any type tends to increase the chances of disease spreading to your plants. It's always desirable, then, to keep any kind of greenhouse clean and neat.)

- It requires that you (or your builder) give special attention to the join between the greenhouse and your home to prevent it from leaking when the greenhouse expands and contracts.

On a sunny day, the temperatures in a conservatory can soar to 80°F or 100°F. You can raise the temperature of your entire house by circulating this warm air using a small fan or other method. On a dull, overcast day, however, the heat will move in the other direction, from your warm house out through the conservatory glass. To minimize this heat loss, many conservatories have insulated blinds on the walls and ceilings or doors to close off the area so that heat is retained in the core home.

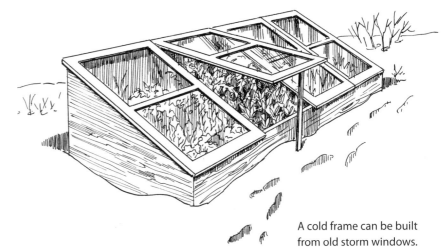

A cold frame can be built from old storm windows.

Small Season Extenders

Season extenders are typically lightly built using thin, often ½- or ¾-inch planking and old, single-pane storm windows. Most are small, for example, a simple 2-foot by 4-foot cold frame. In general, season extenders are not heated, but in one of mine I've installed a hot bed (a heated growing bed) and managed to keep broccoli, carrots, and other root vegetables growing for most of the winter here in Rhode Island (Zone 5). In general, however, season extenders add only 2 to 4 weeks at either end of the growing season.

A small season extender can allow you to use a window — see chapter 13, project 8, for plans to build a window greenhouse — or even a basement as a growing area, especially if you install fluorescent lighting in these spaces. (See chapter 5 for a full discussion of types of greenhouse lighting.)

Hot and Cold Frames

The difference between a cold frame and a greenhouse is size: You can walk into a greenhouse, but you can only reach into a cold frame. The small size of a cold frame has its advantages and disadvantages: It's easy to access and maintain plants growing in it and replace plants that have outgrown its area, but its relatively small volume means the cold frame both heats up and cools quickly, which is not very good for plants. In addition, its small size doesn't allow room for growing many plants.

To increase the heat in your cold frame, you can create a hot bed inside it: Remove the dirt from inside the frame and replace it with a load of manure or fresh compost, then cover this with 6 to 12 inches of soil. As the compost or manure rots, it increases the heat inside the frame, helping plants to grow in colder weather.

In spring, a cold frame creates a warmer microclimate that can help plants grow sturdier a few weeks before they can be moved into an unsheltered outdoor area. Cold frames can also be used to harden-off plants — that is, to acclimate to cooler temperatures any plants that you have grown indoors and are setting out for the first time.

Cold frames may be made of almost anything, but the most frequently used materials are old storm windows for the glazing and either dimensional lumber or plywood for the box, although I've also seen straw bales used for the frame.

Cloches, Bell Jars, Walls o' Water, and Fleece

A cloche can be simply panes of glass held together with either clips or specially made wooden blocks. These small structures are temporary and can be moved around the garden as plants need them. I find that they're helpful for plants that have just been transplanted outdoors and for melons, which require additional heat in my Rhode Island climate. Cloches don't raise the temperature by much, but they shelter plants from the wind and also keep predators away from new transplants.

I've tried traditional bell cloches or bell jars — real glass jars with a glass ball top — and find that because they're so small, they both heat up and cool down too quickly. Unless you're in your

A cloche is made of panes of glass held together where they meet with wooden clips or specially made wooden blocks.

A bell-jar cloche that sits on a tabletop provides a microclimate for tender plants.

garden full time and can monitor and adjust them constantly, in my opinion they're not of much use. If you leave them and the sun comes out, you can cook your plants in a few minutes.

Walls o' Water are topless and bottomless polyethylene plant covers with tubes of water around the sides. The theory behind them is that the water absorbs heat during the day and reflects this heat back to the plant at night. I've found that they aren't very useful in helping to establish plants. For example, putting out tomatoes protected by Walls o' Water allows the plants to get roots into the ground early, but the earth under the device remains cool and the plants don't grow much faster than those without the polyethylene covers. In my use, as soon as the ground warmed, the plants grew quite quickly, although I suspect they grew slightly faster not because the water provided extra heat, but because the polyethylene walls kept the wind off the plants. As for early tomatoes,

in my experiments, the tomatoes grown without the Walls o' Water were slower by a few days than those grown with them, but did not grow as fast as the ones situated in the greenhouse, probably because tomatoes don't set fruit unless the nighttime temperature is over 55°F.

Season extenders such as spun rayon fleece material and floating row covers keep temperatures slightly higher and keep veggies clean — no splashing mud. Most important, they keep insects, especially butterflies, off the plants, which prevents them from laying eggs that hatch into plant-eating caterpillars. I've found, however, that if such row covers are allowed to lie with no support, they can break tender young plants when the fleece flaps in the wind. I support fleece row covers with ⅜- or ½-inch bent PVC water pipe to form a tunnel over the plants. If you use the fleece in the greenhouse, however, it can simply lie on top of the plants because the wind won't disturb it.

4 Choosing the Greenhouse Site, Size, and Interior Layout

THE LOCATION AND SIZE of your greenhouse are extremely important. They can affect how much heat the greenhouse retains, the amount of sunlight it gets, the ease with which you can enter or leave it and carry things to and from it, and many other factors.

For example, different options and issues are presented by building your greenhouse against your home either as part of the structure or as a lean-to (typically, sunrooms and conservatories — see chapter 3, page 29 — are part of your home's structure, while a lean-to greenhouse is simply attached to the home) than by installing a freestanding greenhouse. If you are installing a freestanding greenhouse and heating costs are a consideration, you can locate the structure near other buildings or a hedge, where the topography may shelter the greenhouse from the wind and help to keep it warm.

No matter where you place the structure, however, it will require a great deal of sunlight during winter and not as much in summer, which should play an important role in determining where you site it.

Another important consideration in site selection is the greenhouse's desired proximity to various places and supplies on your property. Will the greenhouse be near the garden? Will the greenhouse be near electricity and water sources?

This chapter deals with all the factors that go into the decisions of where to site your greenhouse, what size it should be, and how to plan for use of its space. It also addresses the issue of

permits as they relate to size and location of the structure. For example, you may need to get a permit for a greenhouse built onto a permanent structure and you may have to pay additional property taxes on it once it's built, whereas building a "temporary" structure — one that does not have a concrete foundation — may require no permits and may cost nothing in additional taxes.

Site Selection

Factors in site selection for your greenhouse include the amount of available light and seasonal changes of this light; wind patterns and protection from/exposure to the wind as it blows on your property; the topography that can create frost pockets; drainage around and in the greenhouse; and proximity to power sources, water, and your home. Because a greenhouse is a structure that is usually more than temporary and may be permanent, you should weigh carefully each of these factors to ensure that you select the most effective site possible.

Light Considerations

The amount of light the greenhouse will receive is a key factor in determining where it will be located. In most cases, it will require a great deal of sunlight in winter and less sunlight in the warm summer months. This means that your greenhouse should face south rather than north (unless you don't mind spending a fortune

This greenhouse is shaded for part of the day by the nearby shrubs and trees. The shading can be helpful in summer, but evergreens and branches may block important winter sun.

Of course, any decision based on the amount of sunlight the greenhouse receives will naturally be affected by what times of year you plan on using the structure. If you will be using it primarily in winter, it should have a southern exposure and there should be few or no obstructions to sunlight reaching it — the object is for it to be heated by direct sunlight for as long as possible during the daytime without the shady obstructions of trees, shrubs, or other buildings. If you intend to use the greenhouse only during summer and plan on it remaining empty all winter, you can accept long shadows over the growing area when the sun is low, as long as they are not present in summer. From my experience, however, it can be difficult to get typical greenhouse vegetables such as tomatoes, peppers, and eggplant to grow in the filtered shade of deciduous trees.

Before you install your greenhouse, determine how many hours the sun will shine on it during the seasons in which you will use it. The illustration below shows the angle of the winter and summer sun, important factors in choosing an orientation for your greenhouse that allows it to get the most year-round light. The intensity of the winter sun is about one third the intensity of the sun in summer, so it is important that the glass is at nearly a right angle to the sun's rays and that the greenhouse is not shaded in winter. As the illustration shows, the sun will shine on the greenhouse during winter, but care must be taken to ensure that the tree in the foreground does not grow large enough to shade it. Having shadows from a tree may not be as big a drawback as you might think, however. One of my greenhouses is half shaded by a plum tree. In winter the tree sheds its leaves and the weak winter sun shines through its branches. In summer, the tree is fully leafed out and shades part of the greenhouse, preventing it from becoming too hot. After monitoring, I did prune the lower branches of the tree to allow some light to get to the greenhouse when the tree was fully leafed out. If a greenhouse is shaded by conifers, though, which keep their foliage all year along, they should be removed (or site the greenhouse to avoid their shade altogether).

on heat in the winter or you plan to grow ferns and other shade-loving plants in a cool greenhouse; see chapter 3, page 21 for more on requirements for a cool greenhouse). Southeastern or southwestern exposure is also possible, but each of these provides fewer hours of daylight and may require that you shade your greenhouse during the summer months and supplement the lighting during the winter.

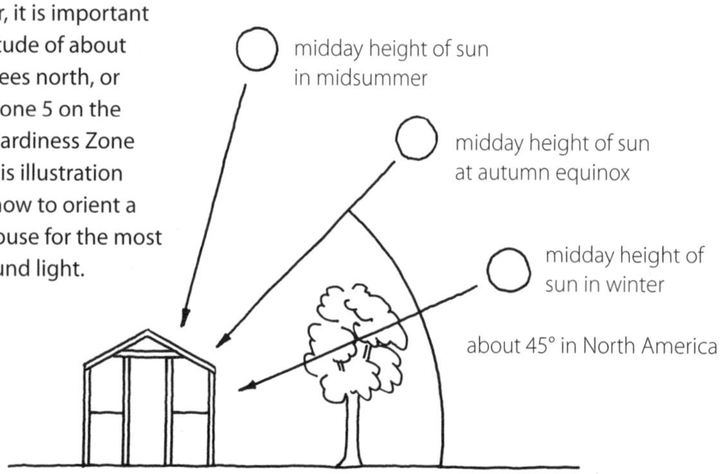

Although winter lighting is not so important in southern areas during summer, it is important at a latitude of about 35 degrees north, or about Zone 5 on the USDA Hardiness Zone map. This illustration shows how to orient a greenhouse for the most year-round light.

midday height of sun in midsummer

midday height of sun at autumn equinox

midday height of sun in winter

about 45° in North America

When selecting a greenhouse site, you should also check the location of buildings that might shade it and how the sun behaves with those buildings. For example, you may find that the sun shines over the top of a building in summer but that in winter it shines lower and is blocked by the building. Of course, if you are not using the greenhouse for winter growing, this configuration won't be a problem.

Consider the Wind

When you locate your greenhouse, you need to be aware of wind patterns as well as shade. Placing a greenhouse in a windy location, such as at the top of a hill, is likely to keep it cool and may significantly shorten the growing season. If you absolutely must locate your greenhouse in an area where the wind is strong, figure out how to protect the side that will get the most wind.

How Much Light Reaches Your Plants?

The amount of light getting to your plants depends on a number of physical, geographical, and time-related factors as well as the characteristics of the greenhouse itself. Among these are:

- **Latitude.** The farther north you are, the less sunlight your greenhouse is likely to receive in winter.

- **The day of the year.** December days have much less daylight than do days in June, July, and August.

- **The hour of the day.** Noon is close to the best time to get maximum solar radiation into the greenhouse, so orienting the glazing to suit the winter sun location at noon allows less reflection and more radiation of light. The glazing should be at a right angle (90 degrees) to the sun to enable light to easily penetrate it. If the glazing is not set at a right angle to the sun, a large percentage of light is reflected away from the plants inside the structure. For example, if you are using the greenhouse to grow vegetables during winter, orienting the glazing slightly more vertically will allow more sun to penetrate it.

- **The weather conditions.** On cloudy days there is less available sunlight.

A layer of snow on the glazed roof will also block sunlight from getting into the greenhouse, although snow will reflect more light through the greenhouse walls.

- **The power of southern exposure.** Orienting your greenhouse directly south is best, but it can be oriented about 45 degrees to the east or west of south as well. Early-morning sun is preferable to late-evening sun. A lean-to greenhouse should be attached to a south-facing wall of your home if at all possible.

- **The materials used to build the greenhouse.** Wood framing tends to be heavier than aluminum, and because of its size (2×4 or 2×6 rafters rather than 1-inch or 1½-inch aluminum rafters), it blocks more light — even when it is painted white to gain the maximum amount of reflection.

- **The size and type of glazing.** Some greenhouse glazing reflects or diffuses a great deal of light, while other materials allow a lot of light to enter the structure. For example, when set at right angles to the sun, glass allows over 90 percent of available sunlight to enter. By contrast, tinted polycarbonate allows only

about 75 percent of available light to enter. Dirty glass also cuts down on the amount of light that enters the greenhouse. Size matters as well: Small panes of glass allow less light to enter than do larger panes because more supports are required for the glass. While glass allows the most light through, certain types, such as argon-filled and tempered glass, allow less light transmission than others. Fiberglass allows less light through, but it diffuses light more than glass does, and for certain types of plants is beneficial. (For a full discussion of the light-emission qualities of glass, see chapter 7; for a chart comparing the light transmission of various glazing materials, see page 97.)

- **The height and style of the end walls.** Glazed end walls allow more light into the greenhouse than do insulated, opaque end walls.

- **The reflectivity of the materials used to build the greenhouse frame.** As already noted, a white-painted surface will reflect more light than does an anodized green, bronze, or black aluminum frame.

A hedge of arborvitae (*Thuja accidentalis*) develops into a dense wall that can protect your greenhouse from cold winds, and it can be trimmed if desired. You can substitute any trees from the cedar family that are indigenous to your area.

For example, if it is on the north, you can insulate that side or plant a windbreak of trees and shrubs. If prevailing winds are from the east or west, you can install double-pane glass on those sides to cut down on heat loss. You might also make an air lock, a small entryway between the door to the outside and the door to the greenhouse itself that allows the outside door to be closed before the inner door is opened. (You can use also the air lock as a cold room for wintering perennials and other dormant plants.) An air lock minimizes the amount of warm air lost when the greenhouse door is opened.

If you decide to plant shrubs on the north side of the greenhouse, choose your plants with care. They should be evergreen to shelter the structure year-round. They also need to grow fairly quickly — but be sure to select a species that you can trim if they grow too tall. Which plants fill the bill? I've used arborvitae (mem-

bers of the cypress family originally from northern China and Korea) to shelter my greenhouse, and after twelve years of growing, the trees are close to 15 feet tall and have been trimmed once. I like this plant because, unlike spruce and cedar, which have a cone-shaped growth habit and may get so wide that they must be trimmed at ground level to keep them from touching the greenhouse, arborvitae have a more columnar growth pattern. Depending on which part of the country you garden in, you might want to use some of the fast growing *Cupressus leylandii* or slower growing cedars and cypresses indigenous to your area.

Whatever you decide to plant, don't place the screening plants too close to the greenhouse. Even if a tree or shrub doesn't end up touching the greenhouse, its roots may gravitate toward the structure, especially if you are growing plants in beds and fertilize those plants regularly. When planting, think about how large the screen of trees and shrubs will be in 10 or 15 years. When you have determined a planting position based on this, move the trees an additional 10 feet from the greenhouse.

Finally, if you live in a climate with cold winters, note how snow builds up on the downwind side of the house or any other building when the north wind blows. Once your screen or hedge is more mature, there will be a similar area immediately adjacent to it where the snow piles high. You don't want your greenhouse to be in that area. I've found that a greenhouse should be 10 to 20 feet away from the screen you plant to place it outside the snow zone and to allow for the growth of the trees and their roots. If you have any doubts, move the greenhouse farther away from the screen (or, if you're planting the trees after the structure has been sited, set them farther away from the greenhouse).

A tree screen does make the wind more turbulent on the downwind side. This zone of turbulent air can extend beyond the barrier by as much as 15 times the height of the trees or barrier. In other words, if your trees are 10 feet tall, the turbulent area may extend 150 feet downwind of them. Locating your greenhouse in this area of turbulent air (generally 50 to

TIP

An air lock (a small area between the door to the greenhouse and the door to the outside environment) helps to regulate the temperature inside the greenhouse by keeping out the brunt of outside cold air in winter. It can also serve as a useful storage area and a cold room for wintering perennials or hardening-off plants in spring.

100 feet downwind of your screen) can help to keep it warmer because the air is not flowing as quickly over the greenhouse and cooling it.

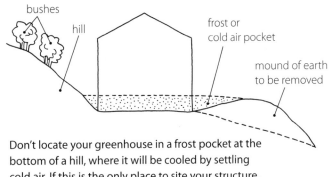

Avoiding Frost Pockets

As we noted, you should not situate your greenhouse on the top of a hill where it is open to the wind, but locating it in a sheltered spot can have its drawbacks too. The location shown in the following illustration may seem ideal. The hill on the left of the greenhouse shelters it from the worst of the wind. The rise on the right is slight so it doesn't prevent the sun from shining directly into the greenhouse year-round. The big problem, however, is that cold air flows downhill and rests in the low spot where the greenhouse is located. This air can be several degrees colder than the air higher up, and those few degrees may mean the difference between your plants surviving and dying. This type of area is called a frost pocket and should be avoided as a greenhouse site. If such a locale is the only spot for your structure, try to regrade the slope in front of the greenhouse, as shown in the illustration, to allow cold air to flow away from it.

Ensuring Good Drainage

Your greenhouse must be well drained. A greenhouse with poor floor drainage may contribute to the breeding of insects and force you to spend time getting rid of water rather than working with your plants.

If your property suffers from flooding during heavy rains, think about building your greenhouse on a platform or installing a drainage system when you put in the foundation. Note that most greenhouses have drainage systems, but in an area that is prone to flooding, the system must be more robust to get rid of water quickly.

Before you install a system like this, however, you must decide on the type of flooring and where the drainage system will be located. Position a center drain before the foundation walls are built and the structure is erected (see chapter 8, pages 114 and 124, for information on locating the drain when pouring a slab foundation). The greenhouse floor should slope slightly toward the drain so that water will flow toward

Don't locate your greenhouse in a frost pocket at the bottom of a hill, where it will be cooled by settling cold air. If this is the only place to site your structure, grade the space in front of the greenhouse (as shown by the dashed line) to allow cold air to continue down the slope.

One option for a greenhouse drainage system

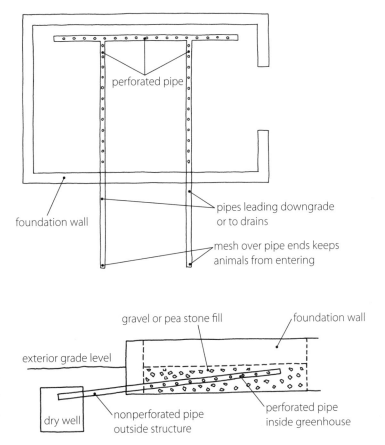

it and the drainpipe should be sloped so water will move through it away from the building.

Proximity to the Garden, Power, and Water

It's important to consider the proximity of the garden and a power and water source when you decide where to site your greenhouse.

Remember, you'll be spending a lot of time carting plants between the greenhouse and the garden. Locating your greenhouse near garden space makes this journey much shorter and quicker and allows you to get more done in less time.

If you intend to light or heat your greenhouse or use a fan or venting/air circulation system, consider how close the structure will be to a power source. And while a garden hose can suffice as a water supply if you don't plan on using the greenhouse during winter, if you do intend to use it in the winter months, you'll have to have access to a water source. This will involve digging a trench for power and water lines to the structure — and in colder climates, the trench will have to be deep enough to ensure that the water line is below the frost line. Unless you prefer to get your exercise by digging instead of going to the gym, it can be very expensive to prepare a long trench! Keeping the greenhouse close to both a power and a water source will make it far easier to bring these services to the structure. (See chapter 5 for more on greenhouse lighting, heating, and water.)

Determining the Size of Your Greenhouse

In conjunction with deciding where your greenhouse should be located, you must determine how large it will be. Earlier, I advised you to build the largest greenhouse you could afford — you will definitely grow into the space, especially if you're a serious gardener — but exactly how wide and how long you make it depends on several factors. Builders of greenhouse kits have developed standard-sized greenhouses that take these factors into account, but if you are going to build your own structure, they are presented here.

Width

The width of a greenhouse is critical to its success. It is much more comfortable to work in a wide greenhouse with wide walkways than it is in a narrow structure. That said, most garden-center or kit greenhouses tend to be a standard width, usually 6 or 8 feet. The benches in these greenhouses are 36 or 38 inches wide (because greenhouse manufacturers know that people cannot reach more than 3 feet into a bench or bed without knocking over plants).

Given that the minimum door width that a person can walk through is about 22 inches at the shoulder, the optimal greenhouse width is at least 8 feet. This would allow for a 2-foot-wide walkway and a 3-foot-wide bench or bed along each side. Of course, greenhouses that are wider than this have room for wider benches and walkways. Those with two aisles are usually 12 to 14 feet wide to enable you to have a center bench or growing bed. In a wider greenhouse, the growing bed or bench in the middle of the greenhouse can be up to 5 feet wide because it is accessible from both sides.

To accommodate wheelchair-bound individuals, a walkway should be about 45 inches wide. Therefore, a greenhouse for a person in a wheelchair should be much wider overall to allow for beds that are wide enough to hold many plants. Such a greenhouse should also have lower benches with no obstructions (such as support posts) beneath them so that a wheelchair can be easily navigated around the space.

Length

A greenhouse can be as long you want, but most manufacturers make greenhouse lengths in increments of 2 to 4 feet to suit standard glazing sizes. To figure out how much growing space you'll need, work out how many plant trays you want to put on the benches and use this figure to determine length. For example, many seedling trays measure 11 inches by 21 inches. Making the benches 21 inches or 42 inches wide means that one or two trays can fit on them set either widthwise or lengthwise. The length of the benches can be determined in multiples of 11 inches or 21 inches.

One of the major factors in determining overall greenhouse width and length is glazing size. Glass and other glazing materials come in certain widths, and a greenhouse that uses the widest glazing possible requires fewer supports between pieces and the glazing therefore admits more light. For example, I was given seven double-pane windows, each 34 inches wide, that I used to make a 20-foot-long free-standing greenhouse on an existing garage foundation 20 feet in length. The length of the windows in total was 238 inches, or 19 feet 10 inches. Each of the two 4-inch-wide end walls allowed for a 3-inch overlap of the glass, making the total greenhouse length 20 feet. The support between each pane of glass was a 2×6 joist, with the glass almost butting at the joint. I used a wooden strip with a rubber gasket to cover each joint, but the fit between the panes was tight and I needed to take care that the screws holding the covering strips did not touch the glass. I've found that with a tight fit, as the glass expands, it may crack where it touches screws or nails. One way around this is to set between the glass panes (and screws) rubber inserts that are wider than the screws or nails. Another method is to put a couple of hard rubber washers around each screw when you install it. (See chapter 7 and the individual projects in chapter 13 for further information on installing glazing.)

Polyethylene sheeting comes in 100-foot lengths, which means that you can cover a hoop house that is up to 80 feet long with plastic sheeting and have some left over to cover the end walls if they are not made of wood or some other solid material. If your hoop house is to have solid end walls, you can make it 100 feet long and have enough plastic sheeting to cover it. The width of the plastic becomes the governing factor in a hoop house. The material is available in widths from 4 feet to 16 feet in increments of 2 feet, and to 40 feet wide in increments of 4 feet. Figuring the radius of the hoop house semicircle, as shown in the following illustration, gives you an idea of how wide the sheeting should be to suit the width of the greenhouse. Also see the following chart for information on determining the required width of polyethylene sheeting from a hoop house's specific height and width.

Polycarbonate glazing is available in 4-foot-wide panels. Because these panels are lighter than glass, they can be supported on 2×4 raf-

Determining the Width of Polyethylene Covering for a Quonset or Hoop House		
WIDTH OF HOOP HOUSE (IN FEET)	**HEIGHT (IN FEET)**	**MINIMUM WIDTH OF PLASTIC (IN FEET)**
8	4	12
10	5	15
12	6	18
16	8	25
20	10	31.5
24	12	37.6

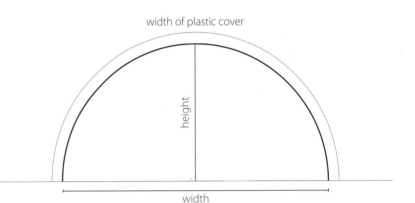

The height and width of a high tunnel or hoop house govern the width and amount of polyethylene sheeting needed for the cover.

ters or even aluminum angle bars, with a rafter along the middle of each panel to act as an extra support.

The length of a greenhouse glazed with 4-foot-wide polycarbonate panels can increase in increments of 4 feet, adding in the thickness of the end walls and the width of the spacing between the glazing: In a five-panel greenhouse, you might include ½ inch between glazing panels and a 6-inch-thick end wall to make the total length of the greenhouse 21 feet 2 inches. This assumes that the glazing is butted at each joint. If you used single-pane glass or corrugated glazing panels, you might have to overlap the joints to ensure that they were watertight. In that case, the total length would be shorter, depending on how much you overlap the panels. For example, if flat panes are overlapped 1 inch, as they might be in a single-pane, fiberglass-paneled greenhouse, the total length of the greenhouse would be 20 feet 8 inches.

It pays to figure out what you will use for glazing and how it will be installed before deciding on the length of a do-it-yourself greenhouse to avoid having to cut an extra panel of polycarbonate or fiberglass in order to completely cover the glazed surface. In the case of a glass-covered greenhouse, you might have to get a specially cut piece of glass to make up the length, and that could get expensive. When figuring out the length for the glazing, remember to include the thickness of the end walls. A 2×4 stud wall may be 3½ inches thick + ½-inch plywood outside + 1-inch rigid foam (polystyrene) insulation + ½-inch drywall for a total thickness of 6½ inches. Of course, you can eliminate the polystyrene insulation or the drywall to reduce the overall thickness.

Height

It really doesn't matter what the greenhouse height is where the roof meets the wall as long as it is high enough to give the plants enough headroom whether they are in the ground or on a shelf and for you to be able to tend to them comfortably in growing beds or if they're positioned on a shelf. If you are growing cabbages in the ground, for example, the height where the roof meets the wall of the greenhouse needs to be only a foot or two. But if you were to grow trees on shelving, you must add together the height of your plants and the height of the shelving to be sure there is ample headroom.

Of course, height of the structure is important in areas where you'll be walking. Less than 6 feet may be all right for shorter people, but taller people may hit their head or have to duck to get into the greenhouse. A low roof could limit the amount of time you'll want to spend in the greenhouse. If you grow hanging baskets, either place the baskets out of a walkway or, if they will be above a walkway, increase the height of the greenhouse to accommodate the baskets. With this in mind, the height over walkways should be at least 6 feet 6 inches, but at the side walls, the height can be 4 or 5 feet or even less. If the side walls are 5 feet high and benches are 3 feet high, you will be able to set plants that are 2 feet tall at the back of the bench against the glazing.

Roof Pitch

If possible, the roof should be steep enough to shed rain or snow easily. (Remember that any plants around the outside walls of the greenhouse may be damaged when the greenhouse heats up after a snowstorm and the snow slides off the roof.) Greenhouses with a shallow roof pitch do not shed water and snow as easily, making them susceptible to leaking with heavy rain or snow loads. In addition, you may find that a roof with a shallow pitch is difficult to clean because you cannot easily reach over the eaves. This couples with the fact that a shallow-pitched roof collects moisture that contributes to the growth of algae, which keep dirt from washing off the glazing, leading to reduced light levels transmitting into the greenhouse.

With some greenhouse styles, such as hoop houses, you may not be able to adjust the roof pitch. Snow will definitely build up on top of a hoop house unless it is heated. In some cases, the weight of the snow is enough to cause the hoops (especially if they're made of PVC) to collapse. I find the easiest way to get rid of unwanted snow on a hoop house is to walk through the inside and bang the underside of the plastic with my hand.

Making the Floor Plan

Your greenhouse floor plan will be affected by both the site and the size of the structure, so it's important to consider it early on. For example, if the only possible spot for your greenhouse is in a frost pocket, in addition to placing external insulation around the foundation, you can make some provision for raising the beds inside the greenhouse and designing the beds so that you can protect them against early frosts.

When configuring the floor plan, you should think about features such as a quarantine area, where you can put new plants for a few weeks to enable them to become acclimated to the greenhouse and where you can monitor them for early signs of insects or disease. You might also want to include a space to store tools, pots, and potting soil; consider different bench sizes and heights; plan for an air lock to make it easier to enter the greenhouse without letting in cold winter winds; and decide where to locate items such as heaters, fans, and watering and misting systems.

Making a floor plan is an essential part of getting the most enjoyment from your greenhouse. The right floor plan makes a greenhouse easy to enter and easy to work in and allows the plants optimal space and growing conditions.

Locating and Sizing Beds and Paths

The possible location and configuration of beds in a greenhouse are often determined by the greenhouse style and can have an impact on what you want to grow in it. With an A-frame greenhouse, the slope of the walls is very shallow and the greenhouse is very tall. Because it's desirable to keep warmer air around the plants, a tall greenhouse works best if you are growing trees, but is not optimal for starting plants or growing short plants in low beds and offers only limited space for hanging baskets. For growing plants in beds, a better solution might be a Quonset or hoop house or a conventional, slope-sided, or gambrel-roof greenhouse, which will offer you plenty of growing space without unwanted height.

Whether you plan on growing plants on benches or in beds, the width of each should be no more than 4 feet, which is about as far as you can reach without stepping in a bed. (Aside from the possibility of harming plants, when you walk on a growing bed, it compacts the soil, which slows water permeation and makes it difficult for plant roots to penetrate the soil.) In most cases, you will find that either 36 inches or 38 inches is suitable. Just remember that wide benches or beds, while increasing the growing area, also make it more difficult to tend plants. (For more on bench width, see Benches, page 44.)

If the aisle in the middle of the greenhouse is intended to accommodate a wheelbarrow or garden cart, it will need to be about 3 feet wide. But if you'll be using the aisle only for walking, you could decrease its width to as little as 20 inches.

If you are growing plants directly in the ground in your greenhouse, I recommend making the beds as wide as possible (up to 4 feet) and the walkways wide enough to accommodate a wheelbarrow. I often use the wider walkway for plants in pots and tubs. Keep in mind that some structures limit headroom. Consider the four possible greenhouse layouts illustrated on page 42. If we assume that the greenhouse is 8 feet wide and 12 feet long and the measurements are as indicated, the percentage of bed area to the area of the entire greenhouse is as follows.

Greenhouse A: 75 percent (3-foot-wide beds with a 2-foot-wide walkway)

Greenhouse B: 8.3 percent (same as A with a 4-foot-wide bed at the end)

Greenhouse C: 79.7 percent (3-foot-wide beds with a 2-foot-wide walkway and 3-foot-wide end beds)

Greenhouse D: 79.7 percent (same as C with an air lock)

I prefer a floor plan that offers as much growing area as possible, and originally used a simple rectangular plan similar to Greenhouse B, although I recently altered it to accommodate three 4-foot-wide beds and a double walkway only 12 inches wide to gain much more growing area. At times, however, I've had to walk in the beds to tend plants. My simple solution for this problem is shown in the illustration (top left, page 43): I placed concrete blocks in the beds and a block in the walkway to support a plank that rises above the plants in the beds. By resting the plank on various stationary blocks in the beds, I can move this plank from bed to bed simply by moving the block in the walkway. The plank easily supports my weight, and if the blocks in the beds are spaced right, all plants in the greenhouse beds are within reach.

Floor plans can vary enormously, depending on the greenhouse style. For example, a geodesic dome greenhouse (see illustration top right, page 43) might have 3- or 4-foot-wide beds around the perimeter of the dome with a large

Four Floor Plan Options for an 8' × 12' Greenhouse

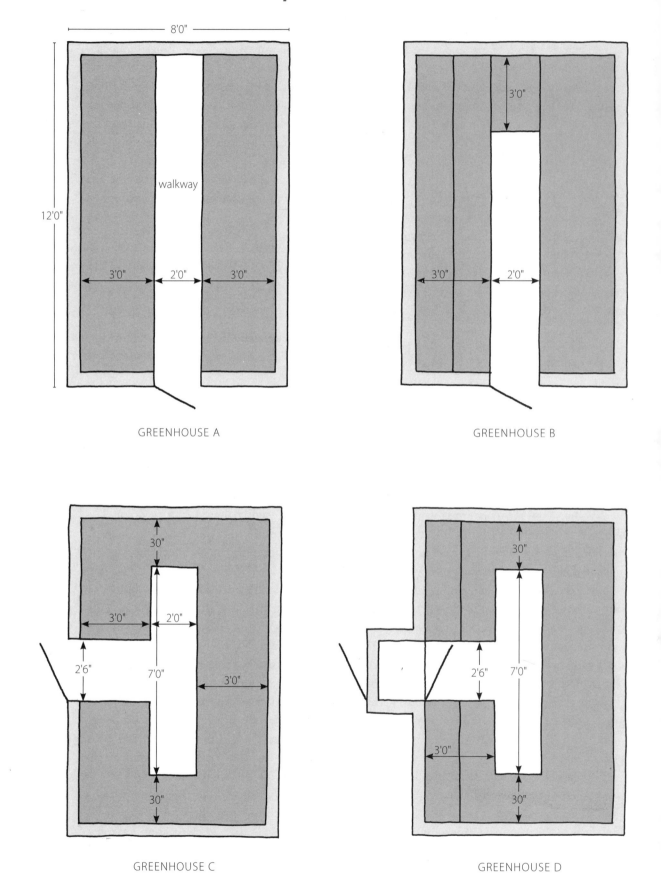

GREENHOUSE A

GREENHOUSE B

GREENHOUSE C

GREENHOUSE D

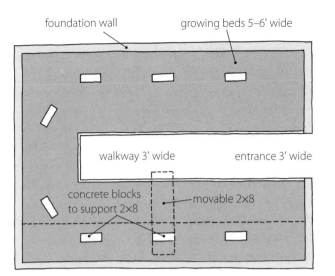

foundation wall

growing beds 5–6' wide

walkway 3' wide   entrance 3' wide

concrete blocks
to support 2×8   movable 2×8

You can solve the problem of tending wide perimeter beds without stepping in them by placing concrete blocks in the beds and the walkway and stretching a plank between them to stand on as you work.

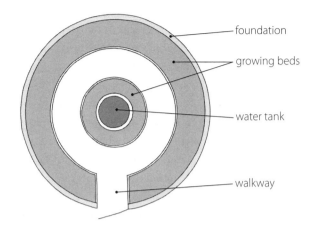

foundation

growing beds

water tank

walkway

A geodesic dome greenhouse can be designed with beds around the exterior walls and a central water tank.

water tank in the middle that serves as a heater for the space. If the structure is large enough, there could be additional beds around this central tank. If the path around the greenhouse is 2 feet wide, the central area could be 8 feet in diameter, allowing for a central tank that is 4 feet in diameter and 2-foot-wide growing beds. The larger ground area of a dome, as compared to the area in a square or rectangular, lean-to, or A-frame greenhouse, allows for much more flexibility in your floor plan. Some dome structures have waterfalls, fishponds, and all manner of exotic plants in the center area, and of course a water tank in the middle of the dome is optional; if it isn't included, the central area could become a raised bed.

You can be creative or conventional with your greenhouse floor plan (the illustration at right shows another option for an entryway), but one final consideration is whether or not you will be using a garden cart or wheelbarrow in the structure. For maneuverability of a wheelbarrow, straight lines work best, but if you don't plan on using such a cart in the greenhouse, curved paths and beds might be more attractive.

Along with considering the dimensions and locations of the walkways in the greenhouse, you should give some thought in the design process

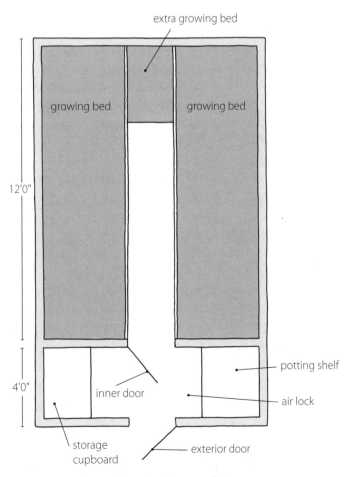

extra growing bed

growing bed   growing bed

12'0"

4'0"

inner door

potting shelf

air lock

storage cupboard

exterior door

This greenhouse floor plan has an air-lock entryway that can be used as a potting area.

to the material that will be used for the greenhouse floor and paths.

The first consideration should be drainage: Every floor and walkway should drain easily. In a greenhouse with a dirt floor, the walkway material should be able to absorb moisture or allow moisture to pass through it. Note that floors of dirt or sand can sprout weeds in summer. As discussed above, if the floor is made of concrete, it should slope slightly toward the drain (see chapter 8, page 124). In addition, in finishing the concrete (see chapter 8, page 124), you might want to make the walkways rough so they'll be less slippery and the other areas smooth so that it's easier to slide plant trays and pots around on them.

In my cool greenhouse, I use wood chips as a walkway. In a heated greenhouse pea stone, crushed stone, or gravel makes an attractive surface that is easy to walk on and drains well (see chapter 8, page 115). It tends to be difficult, however, to drag large pots or bags across a floor of wood chips or pea stone. Some of my fig and citrus trees are 8 feet to 10 feet tall and stand in 36-inch diameter pots! To get around the problem of dragging them across the floor to the outdoors in spring, I've made a flat dolly from an old wheelbarrow, which moves more easily over the walkways (with help from my sons, whom I press into service).

To put in a pea stone or gravel walkway in the greenhouse, first install wood or plastic or composite lumber support boards on either side of the path. Once you have delineated the pathway, lay a strip of black plastic sheeting on the surface of the soil in the walkway to keep weeds from growing through the stone. Punch a few small holes in the plastic to help with water drainage. Then lay the pea stone or gravel on top of the plastic.

If the greenhouse is attached to your home, you can install ceramic tile over the concrete slab to make the floor more attractive or decorative — especially if the room doubles as a dining room or family room. I wouldn't push a full wheelbarrow or heavy dolly over a tiled floor, however; doing so may crack the tiles. A concrete floor can be made more attractive by painting it with a water-resistant epoxy paint or sealer designed for concrete, or a pigment can be added to the wet concrete before it's poured. Remember that the floor will most often be covered with pots and potting soil!

You can also install what my grandfather, who fought in World War I, called duckboards. Originally used to cover the bottoms of waterlogged trenches during the war, duckboards are wooden slats that are laid over the width of the walkway. By making duckboards in sections (as opposed to fastening them together), they can be removed for cleaning or repair. While duckboards are usually wood, you could use plastic or recycled decking material, which will not rot. To make them, simply screw or nail ½-inch-thick, 2- to 3-inch-wide slats to a 2×4 cross brace. Make each section 4 feet to 6 feet long so that they are easy to remove. These boards can be painted as well. An added benefit is that the boards are much warmer to stand on for long periods in cold weather than is either concrete or bare ground.

If you decide to install a brick floor or walkway, you'll first need to dig out the path and put down a 2- to 4-inch layer of well-compacted crushed bluestone to provide a solid base. Next, lay 1 or 2 inches of sand over the bluestone and compact this material as well. Lay the bricks in the sand and then brush sand into the crevices between the bricks until the cracks are full. Finally, rinse the entire path with water to settle the sand before brushing more into the crevices. A brick path will last for years and looks beautiful.

Benches

Benches can be used as growing areas in place of or in addition to beds, easily holding pots and seed trays. In addition, you can use the area under a bench as storage space for plants, materials, or tools. You can also increase your growing area by installing grow lights under the benches and placing plants beneath them.

Benches can be arranged to allow all kinds of work to be done in a compact area. For example, they can be arranged to form a U-shape around the perimeter of the greenhouse to maximize their area with only a 20-inch walkway in the middle. The supports below the benches can be offset to allow easy access for a wheelbarrow. A small area at the end of one of the benches can be protected with additional glass and lighting to form a seed-starting bed.

Before choosing the kind of bench to install in your greenhouse, you should familiarize yourself with possible bench dimensions. As we've learned, the deepest bench you buy will most often be 36 or 42 inches wide, but for many people, 42 inches is too deep. Unless plants at the back of the bench are set a little higher than those in front, a 42-inch-wide bench may make it difficult to reach them. (*Note:* In the northern hemisphere, always set plants higher on the north side of the greenhouse to allow those farthest "north" on the bench to receive enough sunlight.) For the average person, the maximum bench depth should be between 32 and 38 inches if it's to be accessed from only one side, 60 inches if can be accessed from both sides.

The bench height should be determined by how tall you are. Look at the countertops in your kitchen. If you find that they are at a comfortable working height, measure them and duplicate their height in your greenhouse benches. If you are tall, feel free to make the benches higher. Bench height should be comfortable for the person who is going to work in the greenhouse the most. A bench that is too low will make your back and shoulders ache when you stand next to it, potting plants over a long period.

Plant size and type can determine bench height too: If you are growing taller bushes and trees, you'll want benches that are about 20 inches tall. If you are growing orchids, 30 to 36 inches is optimal height, so that the tops of the plants are at or just below eye level.

If you are building a greenhouse for a person in a wheelchair, you may have to raise the bench height to at least 31 inches, so that it clears the arms of the wheelchair, and make the benches narrower (22 to 24 inches) to allow easy access to the plants farthest back. Any benches or shelves lower than 31 inches from the ground shouldn't be more than 12 to 18 inches wide so as to allow access from a wheelchair to the plants farthest back, and any shelves above benches should be no more than 48 inches high and 12 to 15 inches wide. Remember to move bench supports inward to allow room for a wheelchair to maneuver partway under the bench tops. Of course, all these modifications can be adjusted according to the dimensions of individual wheelchairs, which vary substantially.

The Quarantine Area

Every time you introduce a plant into your greenhouse you could be bringing in a new insect or disease that will decimate your other plants. If you buy a plant in a store, for example, it has likely been sprayed with pesticide to kill insects, but insect eggs may not have been killed in the process, and when you bring the plant home and put it in your greenhouse, these eggs may hatch. Ridding your greenhouse of an insect infestation can be extremely time-consuming and difficult. Because it's always better to eliminate a potential source of trouble before it can do its damage, you should allocate a small area of your greenhouse — enough to hold one or two plants — as a quarantine area. This setup doesn't have to be elaborate: You can use a simple 20- or 30-gallon aquarium tank set on end with a tight-fitting cover or pane of glass (which you'll have to remove at times). The idea is to keep a new plant in the quarantine area for a few weeks, or until you've determined that it does not harbor a deadly disease or insects. Keep the quarantine area shaded so it won't get hot enough to damage a plant.

Storage Areas

As mentioned above, if you have benches in your greenhouse, the area beneath them is perfect for storing pots, pesticides, fertilizers, and all other paraphernalia, but if you plan on growing plants directly in in-ground beds, when you make your floor plan, you'll need to consider a place to hide all the unsightly debris of gardening as well as the tools and materials that you'll use. It's a good idea to install a lockable cupboard underneath a bench to store all the chemicals that you might use. This keeps them safely out of reach of both toddlers and animals if you let them into your greenhouse. For greenhouses with or without benches, an air lock either with or without shelving provides another option for storage. As with other elements in your plan, if a wheelchair-bound individual will be using the greenhouse, all storage cabinets and cupboards should have handles installed within easy reach of those who can't stand — between 27 and 45 inches from the ground.

Also consider where you'll store heavier or bulkier items such as bags of potting soil and fertilizer if you start plants from seed.

Work Areas

Along with figuring out where you'll store tools and potting soil, you should determine where you will fill seed trays and pots. If you plan on doing this type of work in the greenhouse, make sure you include a protected, warm space where you can work while winter's chill still grips the outdoors. It should include room for a potting table. A collapsible one allows you to remove it for more room when it's not in use. (For one type of potting bench, see project 11 in chapter 13.)

Switches, Faucets, Thermostats, and Electrical Outlets

Another factor to consider early in the design and layout process is where the switches, faucets, thermostats, and electrical outlets are going to be located. Often these items are an afterthought and end up being in less optimal places. (See chapters 5 and chapter 10 for more on this topic.)

For maximum effectiveness, switches should be located near the entry door, but you can position them so that they won't inadvertently be turned on or off when you are moving plants and materials into and out of the greenhouse.

For maximum effectiveness, switches should be located near the entry door, but you can want to position them so that they won't inadvertently be turned on or off when you are moving plants and materials around or into and out of the greenhouse. Remember that you will need to install them in a watertight outlet box for safety when you water your plants.

The location of the thermostat deserves careful thought. If you put it at chest height, the thermostat may be 4 feet above the plants, which means plants may freeze before the thermostat registers the cooler temperature down at their level and causes the heat to kick on. A better location for a thermostat is at the same level as the plants. If they are situated on a bench, the thermostat can be at bench height. If the plants are grown directly in the ground, install the thermostat less than a foot above the plants. Like the electrical boxes and switches in the greenhouse, the thermostat should be installed with a watertight cover. Additionally, it should be shaded from the sun; often, bright sunlight can raise the thermostat thermometer 10 to 20 degrees, which may not at all reflect the air temperature at the other end of the greenhouse. This increases the possibility that your plants will freeze before the thermostat turns on the heat.

Electrical outlets should be at bench level if you want to use heating mats, water pumps, foggers, or an automatic watering system for your bench plants. If you plan to use an electric heater placed on the floor, you may need an outlet lower in the greenhouse so that the heater's cord can reach it. Remember, however, to take into account the possibility of flooding in the greenhouse. In a future renovation of my greenhouse I plan to add a couple of outlets in water-resistant outdoor boxes and I'll locate them about 2 feet from the floor to ensure that they do not get soaked when the greenhouse is watered.

Also consider the height of switches, faucets, thermostats, and outlets if a wheelchair-bound individual will be using the greenhouse. In this case, these should be located between 27 and 45 inches from the ground, at a height easily reached from a wheelchair.

Designing the Entrance

In planning the interior layout of your greenhouse, you should carefully consider design of the entrance. For example, I once built a pit greenhouse into a bank, with the door located at ground level at the bottom of the bank and the garden located at the top of the bank, level with the top of the greenhouse. Acting as a retainer for the bank was a 4-foot-high stone wall. Though it was easy enough to bring the wheelbarrow to the door of the greenhouse, to bring it back to the garden I had to push it — often laden with plants — up a plank resting on steps in the brick wall. This effort to get plants into and out of the greenhouse became one of the factors that ultimately led to the demise of the structure. Of course, the groundhog that tunneled under the foundation, the rotting of the non-pressure-treated wood used for the framing, and the lack of enough headroom in the greenhouse were other factors that started me down the path toward building a much taller, larger, better-designed structure.

Ideally, a greenhouse's entrance will allow you easily to reach the garden and will be wide enough to allow you easily to move a wheelbarrow or garden cart into and out of the structure. An added feature is that it will enable water to run away from the greenhouse.

As for the actual design of the entryway, my preference is to have a tight-fitting door that swings open rather than a sliding door. Unless a sliding door is an expensive, heavily insulated model from a top-quality manufacturer, it's not likely to make a tight seal when it's closed. Garage-style retracting doors don't seem to seal tightly either, and often allow rodents into the greenhouse. If you intend to heat your greenhouse, a tight-sealing entry door is very important to avoid heat loss. If you do decide on a sliding door, you'll have to make extensive use of weather stripping and other sealants to ensure that you keep out the worst of winter's cold.

I prefer to install a storm door outside the entry door. In winter, this door helps to keep warm air in the greenhouse, and in summer, the glass panels can be replaced with screens and the inner door can be removed or left open to permit ventilation without letting insects inside.

Remember that you may have to shovel snow to get to a freestanding greenhouse in winter; you may have to tote heavy bags of manure or potting soil to the greenhouse; you may have to carry plants, equipment, and tools to and fro; and you may need to ensure that the greenhouse is accessible to those who are physically challenged. For these reasons, your greenhouse door must be easily accessible and wide enough to negotiate through it with larger objects in hand.

Where Should You Locate the Entrance?

In most greenhouses, the door is placed on one end and reaches to the highest part of the roof to enable people to enter without bending over. But this location may not be best for certain greenhouse types or for certain sites. For example, an entrance might be located in a greenhouse's rear wall to allow for construction of an air lock/storage or for easy access to the garden behind the structure.

The ideal entrance will be at least 6 feet high, simply to help prevent head knocks. You can bet your life that if you make the door header any lower, someone will hit his or her head on it — and will spill a huge wheelbarrow load of manure or loam as well. For width, the door need be no wider than the walkway inside the greenhouse, although if your walkway is only 20 inches wide, you can make the door wider, and if you are going to push wheelbarrows and garden carts into the greenhouse, the door will need to be at least 3 feet wide. If you are planning a handicapped-accessible greenhouse, most experts say the door should be at least 34 inches wide; 45 inches is the recommended width.

Air Locks

Another feature that you can consider is an air lock, especially if you plan to heat the greenhouse and grow plants during winter. The idea of an air lock is to provide a space where the warm air of the greenhouse cannot flow directly to the cold outside and the colder outside air cannot directly enter the warmer greenhouse. As mentioned, with careful design, an air lock can also become a potting shed as well as a storage area for tools and materials.

Accessibility

The path outside of the greenhouse leading to the entrance ideally should have no sharp curves, to make it easy to wheel a garden cart or wheelbarrow directly into the structure. If the greenhouse is on a slab or is raised in any way, consider constructing a ramp instead of steps. This will make it easier for everyone to use and access the greenhouse. If your ramp will be accommodating a wheelchair, a 1:12 slope (1 inch of rise per 12 inches of run) is the maximum allowed in both the United States and Britain. If the ramp is long, a level section midway is an important addition, as are rails along one or both sides. The ramp width should be at least 4 feet and should allow room for a wheelchair to turn around. It should have no sudden shifts in direction, and there should be no steps or sills between the ramp and the entrance to the greenhouse.

Getting Permits

Before building, while your greenhouse is in the planning phase, it's important to check with the local building department to learn if a building permit is required to install a greenhouse. In most cases, if the structure is to be built on a permanent foundation, you'll need a permit. In addition to providing permits, your town or city building office can tell you what types of glazing have been approved for use in your area. Note that if you do have to obtain a permit, you'll need a drawing or plan of the greenhouse so that the building official can verify that the structure will be built to current code.

Recently, in certain areas such as Florida and Rhode Island, there has been a trend toward requiring installation of hurricane-proof glass in all buildings. This extremely expensive laminated glass is able to withstand (without shattering) the stress of impact from a 2×4 flying through the air and striking it like a missile. If you are installing an attached greenhouse with glass glazing in a hurricane-prone area, you may have to install this glass.

If you plan to install lighting, water, or a heating system or plan to incorporate any kind of open flame or furnace, you may also need an electrical, plumbing, and heating permit. A heater that has an open flame may also require a fire code inspection. All these permits will add to the cost of your project and should be considered early on.

In addition, you may need a zoning or site plan showing the location of the greenhouse on your property so that building officials can verify that you have obeyed all the setbacks (especially if the greenhouse is to be situated close to one of your property lines) and have, for safety's sake, taken into consideration the location of the septic system and all power lines. If you have buried power lines on your property, it would be best to call your utility company early in the planning stage and have it locate these for you. Most companies provide this service for free. (For the Dig Safe Web site, which provides information and phone numbers to call if you plan on digging for a foundation or power and water installation anywhere on your property, see Resources, page 248).

Check with your city or town to determine whether there are any other requirements to meet before you build. Some requirements, such as setbacks, can involve a public hearing, and in many areas such hearings are scheduled only on set days of the month, which can affect the building schedule if you wait till the last minute.

Planning where you will situate your greenhouse, how large it will be, and its layout or floor plan certainly takes some time. It's best to tackle these issues on a cold winter night, next to a roaring fire, long before the growing season begins, when you have the time to make sketches until you get it right. Planning these elements is essential to erecting a greenhouse in which everything functions smoothly. Remember that making changes once construction has begun can be very expensive, but it costs little or nothing to make changes during the planning stage.

5 Controlling the Greenhouse Environment

PLANTS, LIKE MOST PEOPLE, don't care much for variation in their immediate surroundings. They dislike extremes of temperature and moisture; thus, ventilation, cooling, and heating systems are an essential part of any greenhouse operation if you want to grow plants year-round. These systems maintain a reasonably constant greenhouse temperature and humidity, but they manage only part of the environment. Maintenance of water, lighting, and soil (through the use of insecticides and possibly fungicides, for example) also plays a part. Keeping the plant environment stable is a major consideration in owning a greenhouse. Without a controlled environment, plants may dry out or freeze, they may grow poorly because they are being fed chlorinated water or are not getting enough light, or they might be overrun by insects.

To create a beneficial environment in your greenhouse, you can set up ventilation, cooling, heating, lighting, and misting systems. Some of these may be precise and automated — such as thermostatically controlled cooling and heating systems, automatic spray and misting controls, and electric or gas heaters with thermostats — while others, such as solar-powered vent openers, portable foggers, heat sinks, and nighttime blinds are less precise and rely on less automated methods of operation.

While some of these systems will be in service year-round, the operation of others will be determined by the climate in your area, seasonal changes, and differences in temperature and light from day to night. For example, if you live in a climate with great variations in temperature from summer to winter, you will probably switch from a summer cooling system to a winter heating system sometime during the fall, and vice versa, using only sprinklers and a watering system year-round. Of course, whatever systems you employ, you'll need to add a large dose of TLC to keep everything growing well during the entire year.

Water in the Greenhouse

Year-round you'll need access to water in your greenhouse to water the plants. Soil moisture must be maintained at a fairly constant level because most plants do not fare well in a desert environment or in soil that swings wildly from bone dry to wet and back again. I find that I need to water the plants in growing beds about once a day during the dog days of summer, but this tapers to once or twice a week during fall and early winter. If you have any doubts as to how often you should water your plants, use a moisture meter to check soil moisture levels. You'll find that plants in pots need frequent watering during summer, but in winter the pots should be allowed to dry out almost completely between waterings.

Maintaining moisture levels means that you'll either have to tote water into the greenhouse almost every day during the growing season or install an underground water line to the greenhouse and a spigot in the structure (which can add considerably to the expense of building, especially if certain requirements are specified in the local zoning code). To avoid any varying of moisture, you may want to install an automatic watering system, a sprinkler system, or a misting system. To supply water to a greenhouse, some people run a garden hose from an outdoor spigot to the greenhouse, but this works only as long as the hose does not freeze, and, as has happened to me a number of times, you always run the risk of the hose breaking and leaking.

The Water Line to the Greenhouse

To install a water line, you'll need to dig a trench from the house to the greenhouse for either copper or plastic water pipe, depending upon the type required by your zoning code. If you live in a part of the country that experiences freezing temperatures, pipe should be set below the frost line (approximately 3 feet in most areas) to ensure that it will not freeze during the coldest winters. If you use plastic pipe, lay sand in the bottom of the trench and cover the pipe with sand so it will not be damaged by stones in the fill for the trench. (See chapter 10, page 161 for more information on installing a water line.)

When planning the design for your greenhouse, you should determine the location of spigots and outlets.

Once the line is installed, it must be plumbed into the house line. At either end there should be a valve to allow you to turn off the water should the line burst or leak (see page 161, for information on these valves). At the greenhouse end there should also be a nonreturn valve to ensure that any chemicals that are used with a hose-end sprayer cannot get back into the house water line.

Of course, chemicals from the house line can also be harmful to what you grow in the greenhouse. For instance, most municipal household water is highly chlorinated, which can be harmful to plants, restricting their growth. For under $50, however, you can purchase a water filter such as the Chlorgon filter sold by Charley's Greenhouse and Garden (see Resources, page 246), which will remove chlorine from municipal water. If you want to be certain that you have removed all chlorine from the water, you can install a water purifier system at the house end of the line. Of course, if you tote water to the greenhouse, you can let the water sit overnight to allow the chlorine to evaporate, but this method of watering usually requires many buckets; it is either impractical or impossible to fill enough extra containers for overnight chlorine evaporation.

To avoid the problem of chlorinated water, I prefer to use roof runoff water for plants in my greenhouse rather than water from a water line. I've shortened several downspouts and installed collecting tanks under them. One 60-gallon tank of runoff water will maintain the needs of the plants in my 28-foot by 14-foot greenhouse for ten days to two weeks if I water every other day. In summer, this may not be enough water, but because a heavy shower can easily fill the water tank, I look forward to thunderstorms in July and August. The only drawback to this system is that the tank attracts mosquito larvae and must be treated regularly with granules of *Bacillus thuringiensis* subspecies *israelensis* to eliminate them.

To use the water in the tank, I either pump it into the drip irrigation system using a small, electrically powered pump (a fishpond pump is suitable) or I dip from the tank with a watering can. Some collecting tanks have a small spigot at the bottom to allow you to drain off water into a watering can or bucket as required, but when I raised my tank to accommodate such a spigot, I found that once the tank was a foot or two off the ground, it had the potential to topple over. With water weighing about 8 pounds per gallon, I didn't want to contend with the possibility of 480 pounds of water falling on children playing nearby. In addition, leaves falling into the tank via the gutter downspout tended to clog the spigot. While dipping water with a watering can is the most tedious way to bring moisture to plants, it does enable me to target specific areas that are in need of moisture.

When planning the design for your greenhouse, you should determine the location of spigots and outlets because these often dictate where your water line passes through the foundation. (See Installing the Water Line to the Spigot, page 161.) In addition, if you are going to be washing pots in the greenhouse, you might want to install a sink or tub. Its location will also help to determine where to run the incoming water line and where to put the greenhouse drain.

Misting Systems

You may not think about using a misting system in a small greenhouse, but it can help keep plants cool during summer and contribute to their growth. The primary application for misting systems, however, is for plants that are being propagated. Misting the leaves of these plants keeps them from respiring too much, allowing starter plants and cuttings time to grow roots before the leaves shrivel. Through the process of evaporation, misting and fogging systems can also be used to lower the temperature of the surrounding air as long as the humidity is low.

Misting systems are usually installed on the underside of the roof of a greenhouse or on poles that situate the misting heads just above the plantlets. From these, water vapor drifts down over the plants just as rain would. Most such systems have misting nozzles, and unlike fogging systems (see Fogging Systems, below), which are connected to a water reservoir, are connected by pipes to a water line. In general, misting systems are less expensive to install than foggers and clog up less often. Nozzles cost from $2 to $5 each and water piping costs a few dollars for a 10-foot length.

If you do invest in a misting system for propagating plants, remember that you'll also need to keep temperatures around the plants fairly high (72°F–80°F) to ensure that the plantlets will grow roots, and you'll have to keep the air circulating around the plants to avoid fungal problems.

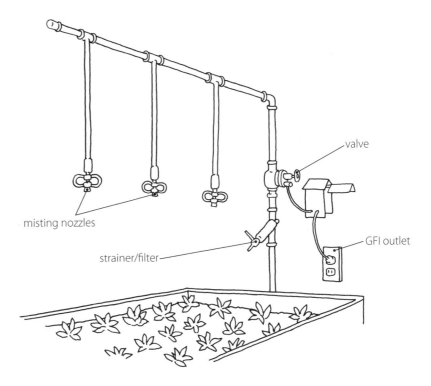

The elements of a misting system include misting nozzles, a filter, valves, and, of course, a GFI outlet.

Fogging Systems

Fogging systems spray smaller particles of water than do misting systems, injecting a fine fog of water into the air. Both can be used for cooling and both provide moisture to help reduce heat stress on growing plants. Although a fogging system is not that important for growing vegetables, it is helpful for growing orchids and tropical plants, which prefer a great deal of humidity. Fogging systems can cost from $100 to well over $1,000, depending on the size of the greenhouse and the amount of moisture you want to pump into the air. Small, portable foggers with a 2- to 5-gallon-per-day output can cost as little as $100 to $300, while larger foggers, which use an installed water line and several outlets throughout a large greenhouse, can cost $2,000 or $3,000. The water tank on a portable fogger must be kept filled for the unit to work properly. For most automatic fogging or misting systems, you will need a water line and electricity in the greenhouse.

Most foggers work by raising the water pressure from normal tap level pressure to several hundred pounds per square inch (psi). At this pressure, the water is atomized and sprays out of the machine like a cloud of water vapor. A high-pressure fogger with a large number of outlets may use up to 1 gallon of water per minute, although a smaller fogger for a greenhouse that is about 300 square feet may only use one tenth that amount.

If you use a built-in system, you'll also need a humidistat, and probably a timer to regulate the flow of moisture. You should fog or mist only early in the day to ensure that the plants are kept moist during the day but can dry out before night. If they are fogged or misted at night, when there is no warmth to dry them or no air circulating, they could succumb to disease. You may also want to install a filter in the water line to eliminate heavy metals and chlorine in the water system. In areas that have high calcium deposits in the water, you can install a calcium inhibitor filter for under $20.

Drip Irrigation

Unfortunately, a greenhouse prevents rainwater from moistening the soil around plants. Because studies have shown that plants benefit tremendously from a constant source of moisture, with some plants watered in this way putting on huge amounts of growth when compared to plants that are watered only regularly, having the means to keep beds moist at all times is a real plus. A drip irrigation system keeps the soil moist, can be directed at particular plants, does not wet the leaves of plants, and allows for adding fertilizers to the water at any time.

> The beauty of a drip irrigation system is that the water can be directed very precisely to each plant's root zone.

The system is quite simple. A hose is connected to a regular water outlet and special pressure-compensating drippers or emitters are fitted into smaller tubes joined to the main hose.

Each dripper is placed on the soil near a plant or on the soil surface of a potted plant, where it emits a constant drip of moisture. Note that to avoid the problem of the first emitter soaking the first few plants in line before the last plant gets any water, you must buy pressure-compensating emitters or drippers. The system can be designed to turn on or off by a timer.

Drip irrigation systems are not very expensive. Charley's Greenhouse and Garden sells a kit for under $150 that can water up to 55 plants and larger, 100-plant kits for under $200. Most drip irrigation systems work at pressures from 0.5 to 2 gallons per hour and can be easily attached to your home water line. (Large commercial greenhouses may use 5 gallons per hour.) If you want, you can also install chlorine, sediment (which tends to clog the emitters), and carbon filters at the hose end of the water line. Some systems also have in-line filters that allow you to add fertilizer tablets to feed plants automatically. As long as the pressure is maintained in the line, you could attach a pump to a standing water tank, though you'd need to experiment a bit to get the right pressure and make sure that the pump doesn't burn out by trying to force water through the system.

The beauty of a drip irrigation system is that the water can be directed very precisely to each plant's root zone. Special emitters are designed for potted plants, and you can put ground emitters and pot emitters on the same line. If you garden exclusively in hanging baskets, simply place your drip irrigation system high in the greenhouse and use short, small-diameter tubing to feed water to an emitter in each basket. Note that drip irrigation systems are separate from misting and fogging systems.

Soaker Hoses

Soaker or "leaky" hoses are a practical way to water in-ground beds. These porous hoses are made of recycled rubber material and can be connected to your home's water line. Usually buried in the bed from 4 to 6 inches deep or placed on the soil's surface and covered with mulch, soaker hoses are fed by a hose connected to the main water line. Having used them in my raised beds, I find that they water a strip of soil about 12 to 18 inches wide, depending on how long the water is left on. This means that for a 4-foot-wide bed, you will need two hoses placed about 10 to 15 inches away from the edge of the bed. While they worked reasonably well, I found that the beds at the farthest end of the extensive system received less water than the ones nearest to the water outlet.

Remember to remove the hoses from a bed before digging in it! I have stuck a fork through one on a number of occasions. (To repair a soaker hose, simply cut the hose, trim the two ends square, and reconnect them using a hose-repair connector.) It eventually became such a chore pulling the hoses out of the beds each spring before I could dig over the winter rye that I gave up on using them outdoors and now use them only in the greenhouse.

While the actual hose in a soaker hose system costs only a few cents per foot, the cost of other necessary parts, though only a dollar or two each, can add up. With the required one or two garden hoses, T-joints, L-joints, and connectors, you can end up spending $200 by the time your system is complete. I recommend that you carefully plan your soaker hose system and locate each joint and connector unit before you start so that you'll have to make only one journey to the hardware store.

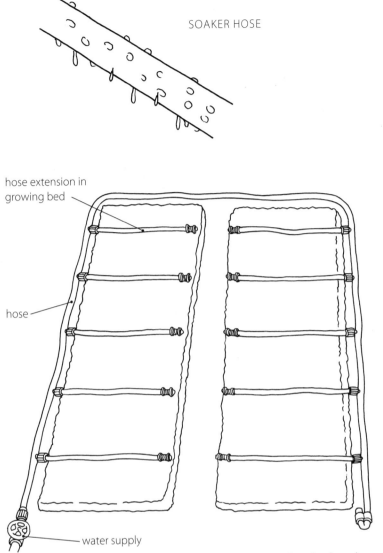

SOAKER HOSE

hose extension in growing bed

hose

water supply

A soaker hose layout for a cool greenhouse

Lighting and Electricity in the Greenhouse

Have you ever wondered why plants you see in garden centers each spring are short and stocky and look like they are ready to grow fantastically well in your garden while your greenhouse plants are long and leggy? You may be surprised to learn that part of the reason is lighting. The right wavelength and amount of light are critical to growing the healthiest plants (though even the right lighting will probably not produce the short, stocky plants grown by commercial growers because many of these are also sprayed with chemicals to contribute to stockier growth).

Without light, photosynthesis — a plant's conversion of sunlight to carbohydrates (complex sugars) — cannot occur. Sunlight, along with supplemental lighting, drives photosynthesis. Without the right amount of light, a plant may not flower or set fruit, but with just the right amount, a plant is triggered to react — for instance, flowering at a certain time of the year.

Plants grown from seed, such as impatiens, may need up to 20 hours of sunlight in one day in order to germinate; certain onions require a long day length (up to 14 hours of daylight, equivalent to the daylight in midsummer) to set bulbs; and spring-flowering plants bloom in reaction to warming temperatures and increased day length. At the other end of the scale, some plants, such as chrysanthemums and Christmas cacti, react to shortening days to flower, and poinsettia will grow red leaves only when the day length is less than 12 hours. Commercial greenhouse operators adjust lighting to achieve the desired day length in order to trigger certain reactions, known as photoperiodic responses, and home gardeners can use these techniques to grow flowers out of season.

TIP

When setting up any electricity in the greenhouse, remember always to install any on/off switches in a watertight box to protect them should they inadvertently get wet, and always put all greenhouse circuitry on a ground fault interrupter breaker to ensure that it will quickly trip should water permeate the system. In addition, all light fixtures should be rated for outdoor use. Take care not to get water on light fixtures or hot bulbs, which may explode if water contacts them.

There are a number of scenarios in which plants will require supplemental lighting in the greenhouse: In spring and fall, when plants are still actively growing, you may need supplemental lighting, and if you plan to keep your plants growing through the winter or want to grow warm-weather plants during colder seasons, you will need plenty of supplemental lighting. This could take the form of a few fluorescent lights or might involve a more complex system of high-intensity lighting on tracks to illuminate an entire growing bed.

General Lighting

The first step in lighting your greenhouse is to install lights so that you can see your way around if you want to work inside at night. Usually this means hanging 4-foot fluorescent lights from the ridge of the greenhouse directly over the central walkway. These lights should be waterproof and are best operated from a switch at the door. (The FarmTek catalog has reasonably priced waterproof lights for around $25 each; see Resources, page 246.) Most shop fluorescent lights are not waterproof, meaning that

if you install them, you must take extra care not to spray them when watering in the greenhouse. Remember *always* to install any on/off switches in a watertight box, however, to protect them should they inadvertently get wet, and *always* put all greenhouse circuitry on a ground fault interrupter (GFI) to ensure that the breaker will trip quickly should water permeate the system (See chapter 10, page 158, for more information on GFIs).

The second step in greenhouse lighting is to determine where you will be performing various gardening tasks so that lighting can be placed accordingly. For example, you might want a bright light over the potting bench and another over the quarantine area to allow you to inspect for insects.

Finally, there is the consideration of supplemental lighting for your plants. Remember to determine each lighting circuit before wiring begins (see page 156) and immediately after you have decided where everything will go in the greenhouse.

Lighting Your Plants

Determining exactly how much light your plants need depends on the distance between the fixtures and the plants, the type of lights, and the type of plants you are growing. Fluorescent lights must be very close to the plants (almost touching the leaves of seedlings, for example) to help them achieve the best growth. Because of this proximity, however, the lights' reflectors tend to block out natural sunlight. The lights and reflectors should therefore be designed to be raised and lowered as necessary. I use fluorescent lights in my germination chamber (see page 172, for an illustration) to give seedlings a strong start. You can make your own germination chamber under a greenhouse bench, or grow other plants under a bench with supplemental lighting. The best type of fluorescent lights are the more expensive, twisted tubes developed especially for gardeners (grow lights) and sold under such names as Nurture-lite and Floralight. After years of starting seeds, however, I've found that regular inexpensive shop light fixtures with cool white fluorescent tubes will do the job, provided the plants are moved out of the germination area within 4 to 6 weeks. Ordinary cool white fluorescent tubes tend more toward the blue end of the spectrum with some red wavelengths, which helps seedlings and foliage plants grow but doesn't do much to promote flowering. A cool white light and a warm white light in the same fixture give a pretty good imitation of the entire natural light spectrum. When my plantlets are about 3 inches tall, I transplant them to larger pots and move them from the germination chamber into the main greenhouse, where additional lights supplement natural daylight.

You can also consider where you locate plants under fluorescent tubes. I've been told that light is stronger in the middle of the tubes than at the ends, although in my propagation chamber it doesn't seem to make a difference. I've also been told that the tubes should be changed annually, which seems to be an unnecessary expense. I use my fluorescent tubes for two or three years before changing them. Using fluorescent growing lights for only two to three months at the start of each season probably means you don't have to change the bulbs each season.

Other types of lighting, such as halide, mercury vapor, and sodium lighting, can be located farther way from plants, but they also have large reflectors that can block natural light, a problem you can circumvent by installing lights and reflectors that can be raised and lowered as required. For a hobby gardener, this small adjustment can save a great deal of energy.

When considering a lighting system, you will need to decide whether the light will supplement natural lighting (in other words, you will raise and lower the reflectors and turn the lights off and on) or whether your plants will be in a totally controlled environment, with all their lighting supplied artificially. If you decide on the latter system, you can probably do without a greenhouse and grow everything in your basement. (See chapter 10 for more information on installing plant and task lighting.)

Warning: If you use supplemental lighting, you will need to be extremely careful when watering plants. Do not get water on the light fixtures or on hot lightbulbs, which can cause the bulbs to explode. If you can, purchase fixtures with protective glass over the bulbs. You should also make sure that all fixtures are watertight or are rated as outdoor fixtures and that all circuits are to code and fitted with a GFI breaker.

The Quality of Light

Because lighting is so important, it behooves the greenhouse gardener to understand a little about light quality and quantity before investing in a lighting system. First, not all lightbulbs (or lamps, as bulbs are called in the lighting trade) are created equal. Some emit light oriented toward the blue end of the light spectrum, while others operate at the red end of the spectrum — that is, the wavelength of the light emitted by the bulb is different depending on the type of bulb. For example, metal halide lights tend toward the blue (ultraviolet) end of the spectrum and high-pressure sodium lights tend toward the red (infrared) end.

Light that plants use best is in the visible range — typically from around 380 nanometers to 720 nanometers. Light at the blue, or ultraviolet, end of the spectrum tends to promote plant growth and helps to keep plants compact. Because natural light has plenty of light from the blue end of the spectrum, it results in the growth of leafy green plants. Using a light from the red, or infrared, end of the spectrum will help to bring plants into bloom faster and promote flowering. In the middle of the visible spectrum are the violet, blue, green, and yellow bands that help to promote strong plant growth by maximizing the absorption of sunlight to promote photosynthesis.

Photosynthetically Active Radiation (PAR)

For the greenhouse grower, finding a lightbulb that emits the right wavelength of light can help to promote either growth or fruiting. But how do you find the best bulb for your purpose? Experts express the quality of light in several different ways. As discussed in chapter 7, which focuses on greenhouse glazing, photosynthetically active radiation (PAR) is a measure of

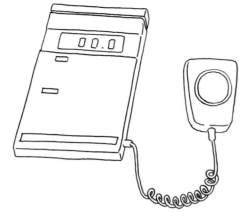

A digital light meter measures foot-candles to determine how much light is shining on a particular area.

how much light transmits through the glazing to drive photosynthesis. We can also use this figure to describe light from lightbulbs, but other terms are used more effectively.

Lumen is the light output from a bulb or other light source. A look at the packaging for a typical lightbulb tells you how many lumens that bulb produces. For example, a 60-watt tungsten bulb — one that you might use in a lamp in your home — emits 820 to 840 lumens.

Foot-candles measure how many lumens are shining on a particular area — one foot-candle is equivalent to one lumen per square foot — and can be measured with a simple foot-candle light meter, or photometer, such as the Gossen Mavolux, which is used by commercial growers. For about $30 through Charley's Greenhouse and Garden (see Resources, page 246), home gardeners can purchase a photometer that measures foot-candles. Some photometers come with a booklet listing how many foot-candles are required by various plant species.

> For healthy plant growth, you should use an incandescent light specially made for growing plants.

Holding a plant light meter above shelves, upper and lower benches, and even in-ground beds will provide information to help you determine which plants will grow best in those locations: For example, *Cattleya* orchids need 3,000 foot-candles (full sun is 5,000 foot-candles) and should grow best on the top shelf in the greenhouse; phalaenopsis orchids require 1,500 foot-candles and may do best on a middle shelf; and begonias and ferns, requiring about 800 foot-candles each, will prosper most on lower benches. Properly placing plants according to foot-candle requirements prevents sunburned leaves and helps them avoid spindly growth. A light meter can also tell you how far from plants grow lights should be positioned in order to provide the right number of foot-candles for blooming and fruiting.

Illumination intensity is a measure of the number of foot-candles that actually hit a surface. For example, if a 60-watt lightbulb is shining 820 lumens over a 1-square-foot surface, the illumination intensity is 820 lumens per square foot. If you have two 60-watt lights shining on the same surface from the same distance, the illumination intensity is 1,640 lumens/square foot. (In the metric system, a *lux* is one lumen per square meter and can be calculated by dividing the number of foot-candles by 10.76.)

Light levels may also be expressed in terms of *radiant flux, radiant emittance, irradiance,* and *quantum flux density.* Radiant flux is measured in watts and is the energy emitted by a light source over a period of time. Radiant emittance is measured in watts per square meter and is the amount of light emitted over 1 square meter. Irradiance is the amount of energy received by 1 square meter of surface (but this measure is rarely used by nonprofessionals.)

Incandescent Lights

If you want to grow only a few plants, a simple incandescent lamp such as the ones you use every day in your home can do the job. Use the highest intensity your budget can afford (taking into account the cost of the unit and the cost to run it), with a 100-watt lamp as the minimum. Because incandescent lamps generate a great deal of heat and tend to dry out the soil fairly quickly, you will have to place the lamps at a distance from the plants (usually at least 18 inches, but the actual distance will vary according to the amount of light you want the plant to receive) to avoid burning them, and check the soil-moisture levels frequently. Note that incandescent lamps provide light from the red end of the spectrum, which tends to promote flowering.

An incandescent lamp is suitable for starting seedlings but does not do much for plant growth. For healthy plant growth, you should use an incandescent light specially made for that purpose. You can also purchase incandescent fixtures (grow lights) that allow you to change the lightbulbs to either full-spectrum fluorescents or high-intensity discharge lighting without resorting to new and more expensive fixtures. FarmTek sells such fixtures for $20 to $30. These incandescent lights emit much of their light at the blue end of the spectrum, helping to maintain foliage growth. They are, however, much more expensive than regular incandescent lights.

Fluorescent Lights

If you want to start seedlings or grow a greater number of plants, you'll probably need to use fluorescent lamps. Cool, white, workshop-style fluorescent lights are quite inexpensive (a few dollars a tube) and emit light toward the blue end of the spectrum. There are also warm white fluorescent lights that emit more toward the red end, and full-spectrum lights, although these tend to be more expensive. By using a cool white tube and a warm white tube in the same fixture, you can obtain a reasonably balanced light for much less than the cost of a full- or balanced-spectrum tube. A typical 4-foot-long, two-tube fixture emits enough light to start two flats of seedlings, each 11 inches by 22 inches long, if the fixture is placed about 2 inches over the tallest plants. Once the plants are about 3 inches high, they should be transplanted and placed under stronger, more balanced lights.

The minimum bulb wattage you should use in your workshop light fixtures is 40 watts. Be aware that shop lights have weaker ballasts (transformers containing capacitors to start the light) that tend to burn out more quickly than more expensive fluorescent light fixtures. This usually means that they give out less light and that the light level tends to weaken over time. In general, more expensive light fixtures emit more

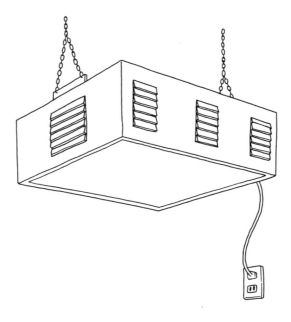

Two examples of incandescent growing lights, which are conducive to plant growth. Remember to purchase fixtures that allow switching the bulbs from full-spectrum fluorescents to high-intensity discharge lighting.

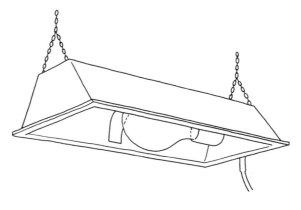

Holding a plant light meter above shelves, upper and lower benches, and even in-ground beds will provide information to help you determine which plants will grow best in those locations.

foot-candles per tube than do shop light fixtures. Measuring the light levels of a number of different types of tubes 12 inches from the light source yielded the following readings (by way of comparison, direct sunlight in a Rhode Island August measured 825 foot-candles):

New shop light with cool white tubes: 40 foot-candles

New shop light with warm white tubes: 40 foot-candles

Older shop light with older cool white tubes: 35 foot-candles

A more expensive lamp with new cool white tubes: 44 foot-candles

A more expensive lamp with new warm white tubes: 42 foot-candles

A 100-watt grow light bulb: 95 foot-candles

A regular 100-watt lightbulb: 75 foot-candles

A 60-watt lightbulb: 45 foot-candles

A 15-watt fluorescent spiral lightbulb (equivalent to a 60-filament bulb): 65 foot-candles

A halogen light: 100 foot-candles

If you don't have space for 4-foot fluorescent lights, you can buy high-output fluorescent lamps (known as full-spectrum compact fluorescents, or CFL bulbs) that fit into an ordinary lightbulb socket. Such bulbs encompass the full light spectrum but tend to be expensive when compared to conventional incandescent bulbs (from $20 to $100 per bulb). CFL bulbs use between 55 and 95 watts of power and have a life of about 10,000 hours.

You can also consider spiral fluorescent plant lights that cost from $10 to $15 apiece. These lights are also full spectrum, have a low heat output, and use a lot less energy (about 25 to 30 watts each). But again, they must be placed close to the plant to optimize their light output. The color rendering index (CRI) can help you

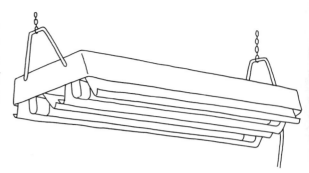

This high-output fluorescent lamp produces low heat so, it can be placed close to plants.

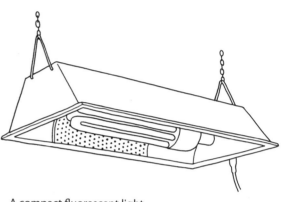

A compact fluorescent light

find the full-spectrum bulb to meet your needs. A CRI value of 100 is the same as natural sunlight. The nearer the index number is to 100, the more like sunlight the bulb will be. Most compact fluorescents have a CRI between 70 and 90, with some as high as 95.

High-Intensity Discharge Lights

If you decide to go beyond the basic fluorescent and incandescent light systems, you may want to consider high-intensity discharge lights (HID), which run from a ballast. The two main types of HID lights are high-pressure sodium (HPS) and metal hallide (MH). HPS lights are used most effectively where you want to supplement natural daylight. They tend to emit light from the red end of the spectrum, which makes them efficient at encouraging plants to flower. Metal halide lights tend toward the blue end of the spectrum and complement sodium lights. They can also ease your fuel bill somewhat if you plan on heating the greenhouse during nighttime hours because they generate a great deal of heat. When using HID lights, the lower wattages — up to 250 watts — work best if placed 1 to 2 feet above the plants. Higher wattages should be located farther away from the plants to avoid leaf burn. (For example, a 1,000-watt fixture should be placed about 3 feet above the plant.) A small, 100- to 250-watt HID light will illuminate an area about 4 square feet (2 feet by 2 feet), while a 1,000-watt fixture will light an area about 64 square feet (8 feet by 8 feet). The cost of these lightbulbs ranges from $20 to $80 each or even higher, depending on power output. Remember, though: One drop of water on the glass may cause the lightbulb to explode.

Sodium lights are used to induce heat-loving plants such as tomatoes and corn to grow during seasons with short nights. Keeping the lights on for up to 18 hours continually helps the plants to set fruit during winter. In this kind of light and with no insects to plague them, the plants thrive, although they must be hand-pollinated. Growing corn and tomatoes in this way, however — that is, under lights in the middle of winter — is expensive and the results are not as good as those obtained during summer. After experimenting with lighting my greenhouse plants, I've found that here in Rhode Island, I can keep the previous year's tomato plants going until late February, when I'm able to pick one large tomato every few days. Without more light, however, the yield gradually falls off. I've picked the last fruit on February 26, at which time the plants appeared weak, with few leaves.

You can also buy convertible light fixtures that allow you to start seedlings with sodium vapor bulbs and convert to metal halide bulbs once the plants are established.

Films and Reflectors

In addition to lighting the greenhouse, if your greenhouse has an insulated wall on its north side, you can also install a reflective mylar film there to reflect even more light onto your plants. For example, garden catalogs and centers may sell shiny film on rolls (a bit like rolls of wrapping paper) or a reflective, foil-faced bubble insulation called TekFoil that can be used in this way. You can also use insulated foam board or

HPS lights are used most effectively where you want to supplement natural daylight.

rigid insulation with aluminum facing to both insulate and reflect more light onto the plants.

Most lighting fixtures come with reflectors to direct the lighting toward the plants. Be aware, however, that reflectors may block natural sunlight from reaching your plants, requiring that you keep plant lights on longer to provide the necessary cumulative light plants need. Some of the large lights may both illuminate an 8-foot-by-8-foot bed and block natural sunlight from reaching the plants. This problem can be solved by installing the reflector so that it can be raised out of the way during the day and lowered at night, when the light is turned on.

Deciding Where to Locate Lights

Once you have familiarized yourself with the various types of lights available, you can determine which you are going to use in your greenhouse. The following diagram shows a 10-foot by 16-foot greenhouse that incorporates growing beds throughout and a small seed-starting area in the rear left corner. In this corner germination chamber is installed a bank of four fluorescent shop lights. Each fluorescent light holds two 40-watt tubes (either twisted fluorescents or cool white tubes), adding up to 320 watts illuminating the 4-foot by 4-foot area. Because the germination chamber will be used only at certain times of the year, this bank of lights has its own on/off switch. In the large growing area (the rest of the greenhouse), over the growing beds there are four HID lights, each using 400 watts of power and illuminating a 4-foot by 4-foot area. These HID units are used in winter from 4:00 P.M. to about 10:00 P.M. and from 6:00 A.M. to about 8:00 A.M., but may not be used at all during summer. Refer to chapter 10 to learn how to calculate the amperage of these lights to see whether they can all be installed on one circuit or if two circuits are required. (Also see chapter 10 for more information on creating a wiring layout diagram that includes locations of lights.)

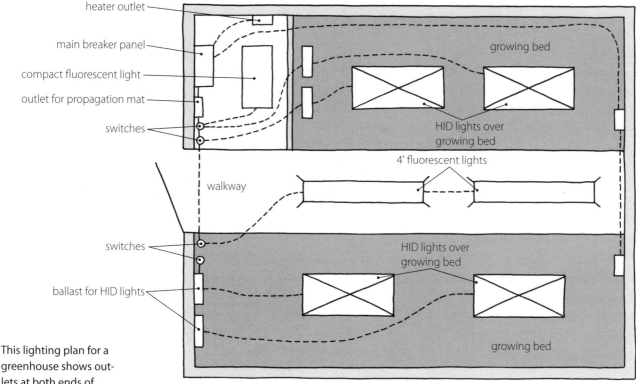

heater outlet

main breaker panel

compact fluorescent light

outlet for propagation mat

switches

growing bed

HID lights over growing bed

4' fluorescent lights

walkway

switches

HID lights over growing bed

ballast for HID lights

growing bed

This lighting plan for a greenhouse shows outlets at both ends of the structure, four HID lights over the growing beds, fluorescent lights over the walkway for general lighting, and outlets for a heat mat and tools. All fixtures and outlets are waterproof.

Heating, Cooling, and Ventilation Systems

Besides controlling the water and light in your greenhouse environment, you'll have to control the temperature and air movement. The glazing on the structure allows sunlight to enter but prevents heat from escaping, which means that temperatures can change dramatically in the greenhouse in a very short time. During the summer months, heat will build to such a level inside that plants will wilt and can eventually die. When I have inadvertently left the windows and doors closed in the greenhouse in summer, temperatures in the structure soared to 140°F.

To counter this, you'll need to install some method for allowing the heat to escape — some

form of ventilation. This can be as simple as configuring a roof vent that can be manually controlled or involve more complex vents that open automatically at a preset temperature or vents that allow hot air to be expelled by electrical fans controlled by a thermostat. Cooling can also be accomplished by a thermostatically controlled fan that circulates air within the structure or by a misting system or evaporative cooler that lowers the temperature of plants in regions where or times of the year when humidity is low.

But while you may want heat to escape during the day, at certain times of the year you may need to either heat the greenhouse at night or devise some method of retaining within the structure the heat generated during the day. Here we explore the methods and issues around heating and cooling a greenhouse to maintain an optimum temperature for the kinds of plants you want to grow and when you want to grow them.

Controlling the Greenhouse Environment in Summer

On sunny days in summer a greenhouse is prone to overheating and must be cooled. The

TIP

To lower the temperature fast in an overheated greenhouse, open all the windows and doors and spray water throughout the structure. As the water evaporates from the floor and from the leaves of the plants, the plants are cooled.

simplest and most common method is simply to vent the hot air out of the greenhouse by opening doors, windows, or roof vents. The problem with this system, however, is that these openings are often not large enough to allow heat to escape, or they may suffice on windy days but not on calm ones. Opening windows and vents also requires a person to do the job, which means that you must be attentive to the weather and the greenhouse when plants are in it to avoid having the plants cooked on a hot, sunny day. (Conversely, you must remember to close what you've opened: If you leave the windows open at night, animals may get inside the greenhouse and eat your plants and set up housekeeping.) To avoid any chance of cooked plants, venting systems should be automated.

Shading

If you do not have an automatic vent opener or a fan system in your greenhouse, you should shade the structure. One way you can achieve this is by locating the greenhouse where it will be shaded by deciduous trees in summer. Yet sun-loving plants don't grow well in the shade of trees all day; you must get at least 4 hours of direct sunlight into your greenhouse every day.

Other ways of shading a greenhouse are applying water-soluble paint directly to the glazing or using shade cloth, canvas or fiberglass, or bamboo matting over the top of the structure. You can even provide shade in the form of a fast-growing vine. One year I used a passionfruit vine for shade by training it out of a roof window in the greenhouse and letting it cover the glazing on top. As a bonus, the flowers were visible and the vine even bore some fruit. The drawbacks were that the shade the vine offered was not immediate and in fall, when I cut back the vine, the roof glazing required a good cleaning.

Any shade cloth or premade covering imparts more control and offers immediate results. You can purchase them in different densities or use movable shades. A word of caution applies when installing any shade cloth or covering: Do not walk on the greenhouse roof. It may seem strong enough to bear your weight, but looks can be deceiving. Don't take that chance.

Note that when installing any shade cloth or covering, do not walk on the greenhouse roof, even if it seems strong enough to bear your weight.

The light-blocking ability of shading is measured in terms of the percentage of light it allows through. For example, some shades allow 75 percent of the available sunlight to enter the greenhouse, while others block up to 75 percent of the sunlight (allowing 25 percent of available light to enter). Be sure you read the label or specs correctly before buying shading materials. In most cases, gardeners living in hotter parts of the country need shading rated to block higher percentages of light. Professional growers use shading to optimize the growth of the plants in which they specialize.

Shading Paint Shading paint is an old-fashioned material still used by plenty of gardeners. I think it can look a little sloppy, however, and it tends to wear off over time, especially during a wet summer. Its advantage is that the paint can be thinned to give just the right amount of shading.

Reflective Shading This is a shading material that reflects light away from the greenhouse. It is best used where and when there is great exposure to sunlight but is most effective used outside the greenhouse, on top of the glazing.

Shade Cloths Some shade cloths roll up like blinds and others fold to allow you to adjust the amount of shading in the greenhouse. Knitted green or black polyethylene shade cloth, which can be purchased from greenhouse suppliers, is sold in various levels of density that block as little as 25 percent of light to as much as 75 percent of light. Shade Rite polyethylene cloth is available in various densities ranging from 30 to 90 percent. The cost varies from around 10 cents to 25 cents per square foot, depending on the density.

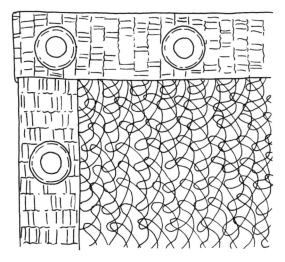

Shade cloth is available in different woven densities to block from 25 percent to 75 percent of available light.

ACF Greenhouses (see Resources, page 246) offers a knitted polyethylene shade fabric that blocks 50 to 60 percent of available sunlight. The fabric is 12 feet wide and costs a few dollars per linear foot. The same company offers tie-downs for shade fabric — which you'll need if you don't want to find your shading in the neighbor's yard as soon as the wind gets up!

Shade cloths are much more effective when installed on the outside of the greenhouse, where they can keep heat from building up inside the structure. If installed inside, solar heat tends to build up between the shading and the greenhouse glazing. In fact, some sources suggest that the shading will be up to 40 percent more effective when installed 3 or 4 inches *above* the greenhouse glazing. Installing shading with a gap between it and the glazing allows air to pass between the two surfaces and keeps the glazing cooler. On the other hand, shade cloths on the outside of the greenhouse can be blown around by the wind and may be damaged or moved in the process, which will render them ineffective.

Other Shade Options You can, of course, install blinds outside the greenhouse, but these move a great deal in the wind and the aluminum ones may leave marks on the outside of the greenhouse. In addition, aluminum blinds are more expensive than shade cloth (they can cost dollars per square foot as opposed to cents per square foot for cloth). If you use blinds, they're probably best installed on the inside of the greenhouse, where they can be used to block sunlight in summer and keep the structure a little warmer in winter. Inside installation, however, does allow heat to build up between the blinds and the glazing.

Ventilation Systems

When deciding what type of ventilation system to use, ask the following questions: How much air do you need to move? Where do you want to move it? How do you want to move it? Remember that air leaving the greenhouse must be replaced with new air from outside. This means that you must install an intake vent (or window) as well as an exhaust vent.

As mentioned in the previous chapter, in winter the additional advantage of an attached greenhouse is that it can be vented into the home. My heated lean-to greenhouse is adjacent to the wall of my studio. In winter, I open the window and door to the greenhouse and allow the warm, moist air into the house. On a sunny winter day, this air is 70°F to 80°F, which allows me to turn off the studio heating system, thereby saving the cost of a good deal of energy. An attached conservatory or solar greenhouse can be used for the same purpose, supplementing dry, winter indoor air with moist, warm air. At night, however, unless the greenhouse or conservatory is heated on its own, you will need to close it off from the house in order to avoid using your home heating system to keep the greenhouse warm. If the greenhouse must be kept warm at night, look to installing its own heating system so that your home system doesn't run continuously in an effort to warm the greenhouse space. (For information on methods to heat a greenhouse in winter see page 66.)

How Large Should Vents Be? To my knowledge there are no hard-and-fast rules for sizing greenhouse windows or vents. I suggest that the vents (both intake and exhaust) be at least 25 percent of the total glazed area. Your greenhouse will stay cooler if you increase this area to 30 percent. Others suggest that intake vents (usually located near the floor; see Where Should Vents Be Located? below) and exhaust vents each be equal to at least 10 percent of the floor area. Charley's Greenhouse and Garden, a gardening catalog and Internet company, recommends that roof vents be equal to at least 20 percent of the floor area. As for the vents themselves, they should be sized so that the greenhouse neither cools excessively nor overheats — an area equal to between 20 and 25 percent of the floor or glazed area accomplishes this. If this percentage cannot be reached with vents alone, opening the greenhouse door or using a screened door and running an exhaust fan will get rid of extra heat. If you fit vents or other openings with insect screens, the area taken up by vents should be increased by about 20 percent to allow for the restricted airflow through the screen.

Where Should Vents Be Located? Because hot air rises, exhaust vents should be placed high on an end wall or, in the case of my cold greenhouse, at the apex or ridge of the roof. In many store-bought hobby greenhouses, exhaust vents are set over the door or may be part of the door.

Intake vents are often also located high, but I prefer to position them in the glazing nearer the floor so that the cool air can pass over or circulate through the leaves of the plants in growing beds. Air passing through plants such as peppers, tomatoes, roses, orchids, and other ornamentals helps to prevent disease and mildew from disfiguring and potentially killing them.

Locating intake vents close to the ground does, however, pose a problem. Unless they are screened, insects, birds, and other animals can enter the greenhouse through them. Once, a groundhog came into my greenhouse through a low vent opening and I had a terrible job trying to get it out. Along with screening these openings, hinging these windows at the bottom (so that they open from the top) makes it more difficult for animals to access them (though a determined animal can navigate this arrangement). Screens of metal hardware mesh (half-inch mesh should do the job) and closing the vents at night are the only surefire ways to prevent pests from entering your greenhouse.

In a relatively inexpensive hoop-style greenhouse, the polyethylene plastic covering may be stapled to a thin wooden furring strip or a large-diameter bamboo pole at the sides. On hot days, this furring strip or pole can be raised to open the cover at ground level and allow fresh air to cross the growing beds, but this method offers no protection against animals and insects.

Making Vent Openings Watertight If they are not installed properly, vents or windows will leak and allow rainwater to drip into the greenhouse. When I had to design a watertight vent for my greenhouse, I took a page from my boat designing experience and fashioned it after the hatch on a boat. (See Making Overhead Windows, page 147, for illustrations of overhead roof vents and information on building them.) In the vent I designed, the inner lip projects upward from the inside of the opening and the vent lid closes down around this lip to make a tight seal. This seal can be made even tighter, preventing rain and snow from entering, by installing foam-rubber caulking around the top of the inner lip. An automatic vent opener can be set to determine the temperature at which the vents are opened (see Automatic Solar Vent Openers, page 64).

Vertical vents are built in a similar way: They are hinged at the top or bottom and butt against an inner flange intended to stop water and air from flowing through the vent when it's closed.

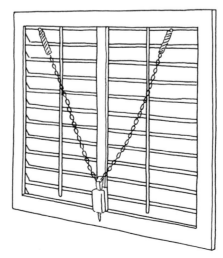

A vertical vent is one way to encourage air circulation in the greenhouse, though it will allow in cold air during winter.

Animal-control vertical intake vents are hinged at the bottom and are secured with chains to prevent the cover from opening all the way and falling to the ground.

Louvered Doors or Windows In southern climates, where winter temperatures don't get too cold, a glass-louvered door allows air to move into the greenhouse at any time. Such a door, however, is not a good idea in the North; on days that are very cold, frigid air can enter the greenhouse through louvers that seal poorly. A louvered vent that you can seal by taping plastic sheeting over it during the coldest months of winter is a good way of maintaining cooler air in the greenhouse during summer.

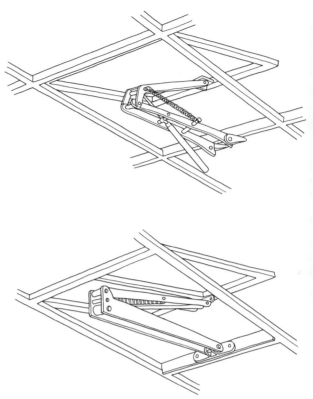

Two examples of automatic solar vent openers

A louvered window is another good option to allow air into the greenhouse at all times, including winter.

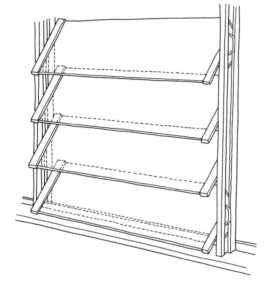

Automatic Solar Vent Openers There are a number of solar vent openers available. Most have a cylinder filled with liquid that expands as surrounding temperatures rise, forcing a ram out of the cylinder, which opens the vent. As temperatures cool and the liquid contracts, the ram drops back into the cylinder, pulling the vent shut. These simple devices come in several forms, and are rated to open vents of varying weights. The direct-acting cylinder can handle vents weighing up to 15 pounds. A heavy-duty, scissors-action auto-vent from Bayliss is capable of lifting vents weighing up to 35 pounds.

Be aware, however, that solar vent openers don't function at precise temperatures. They can be adjusted to open at a specific temperature, but it takes a lot of fiddling to get the adjustment just right. This means that your greenhouse may be vented at a temperature that is not precisely what you'd like it to be. These vent openers also wear out over time; monitor them and remove them during exceptionally cold spells to make sure that the greenhouse heating system doesn't cause them to open. For more precise vent control, you should turn to an electrically operated ventilation system.

Internal Air Circulation

When your greenhouse is closed up, circulating the air will help to keep mold and mildew from growing on your plants. This is accomplished by positioning fans inside the structure. Commercial growers usually situate fans high in the apex of the roof at either end of the greenhouse, where they are out of the way and can move a large amount of air. Hobby growers can use smaller fans for the same purpose. Because these fans are electrically powered, you should consider their location when determining where to locate electrical outlets and switches.

Vent Fans Vent fans can be used to blow air into the greenhouse or "push" air from it — but as a heating and air-conditioning expert once told me, air doesn't push very well; it is more easily pulled. For this reason, a vent fan should be located where, as long as a vent is open elsewhere in the structure, it can pull air from the space and send it outside. Ideally, the intake vent should be open on the end or side of the greenhouse, opposite the fan, to allow air to flow across the entire space.

Vent fans should be operated by a thermostat and should have shutters mounted on the outside to prevent cold air from flowing into the greenhouse when the fan is not running. Most shutters operate simply by being blown open when the vent fan is on. Vent fans can cost from $100 to $400 depending on their size and capacity. Of course, you can design your own system by installing a fan that is turned on by a thermostat inside the greenhouse.

When purchasing a fan, you should look at the amount of air it can move measured in cubic feet per minute, its weight, and the noise level it generates (you don't want to wake the neighborhood every time it operates). If you are concerned about power consumption, also be aware of the amperage draw of the fan. Bigger fans use more power than smaller fans, and because the cost to run a fan for long periods can substantially increase your electric bill, this cost should be built into your greenhouse operating budget. I find it ideal to have a less powerful fan running for longer periods, rather than a high-powered fan that cycles on and off. A high-powered fan requires high amperage to overcome inertia each time it kicks on, and uses more power when running. Once a fan is running, its power consumption drops from that used to start it; thus, keeping a less powerful fan running for longer periods lowers your overall electric bill.

If you want to get even more sophisticated, you can control the speed at which the fan operates: Rather than a fan starting up and dropping the temperature quickly, it can start slowly and increase speed to lower the temperature more gradually. A fan can also run at a slower speed to maintain a constant temperature, instead of running at high speed for a short time to cool the temperature, then turning off to allow the heat level to build up before turning on again. These kinds of systems are newly developed, however, and often required computer-aided controls.

Another way to more precisely control the greenhouse temperature is to use a thermostatically operated shutter control. This control ensures that the shutter covering a fan closes tight on cold days and opens only when the fan runs, rather than blowing open every time the greenhouse door is slammed.

Thermostat for Vent Fans Electrically operated fans must be controlled by a thermostat to enable you to maintain an optimal greenhouse temperature. Ideally, the thermostat should be waterproof because it is likely to get wet when you spray plants in the greenhouse. Because a fan thermostat should be turned on when the greenhouse temperature rises and a heater thermostat is turned on when the temperature drops, the two will be wired differently. (See chapter 10 for more on wiring a greenhouse for various systems.)

Automatic Solar-Powered Fans As I have mentioned, when it came time to vent my greenhouse, I turned to my boat design experience. After completing one project on my boat, I found I had an unused Nicro Marine solar vent. I realized that this 7-inch circular fan with a solar cell in the middle of the fan body would serve perfectly installed in my greenhouse. When the sun is out (and the greenhouse is being heated), the fan runs. When there is no sun, no solar power is available and the fan doesn't operate. This fan fits into a 4¾-inch hole that can be cut into an overhead panel. When my fan died of old age, it was a simple job to replace the entire unit. Interestingly, I suggested to the former owner of Nicro (now owned by Actuant Recreational Group, Inc.) that these products be offered to greenhouse gardeners, and I now see that they are indeed available from some greenhouse suppliers (see Charley's Greenhouse and Garden, Resources, page 246).

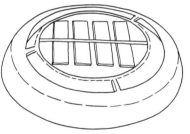

This Nicro-Marine solar vent is operated from a 7-inch fan that runs automatically on solar power. Originally used in marine applications, it's perfect for a greenhouse setting.

Controlling the Greenhouse Environment in Winter

Winter is a stressful time for plants. In many parts of the country it is a cold, dry season with little humidity in the air. In others, it is a chilly, wet season. Is it any wonder that perennial plants go dormant at this time of year? You may want to grow greenhouse plants in winter to bring a few blooms into the dreary days, or perhaps you want to grow vegetables out of season rather than buy supermarket produce. Or winter may provide you with a break from gardening chores and during this season you simply need to keep plants warm enough to prevent them from freezing (though some plants such as rhubarb and strawberries need to freeze to help them set fruit the following season) and give them time to rest. Any of these reasons requires that, in addition to providing extra light and moisture to reduce dryness if you decide to keep plants growing (see Water in the Greenhouse on page 49, and Lighting and Electricity in the Greenhouse, page 53), you'll also need to generate heat in your greenhouse.

Given that winter in some parts of the country can be five to seven months long, providing a warm environment for your plants can be an expensive undertaking, but there are ways to limit the costs. The first is to understand how heat is transmitted and use that knowledge to increase the efficiency of the greenhouse environment. The second is to use a combination of the least expensive methods to maintain heat at a level that plants can accept and to install some form of heat storage device to help keep heating costs under control.

It's important to remember that there are a number of ways to achieve heat in the greenhouse. For instance, if you live in a very cold area, you may have to heat the soil in the greenhouse to keep plants going. This can be accomplished by installing soil heating cables in the beds, or by running warm water pipes through the soil below the level of plant roots, or simply by locating a compost pile under a bed.

How Much Heat Do You Need?

Before installing a heating system, you must determine how much heat you need, the differ-ence between the temperature outside of the greenhouse and that inside the structure, and the type of heating system you want.

Heat in a greenhouse is lost in four ways: radiation, convection, conduction, and infil-tration or exfiltration (cold air coming into the greenhouse or heat escaping from it through cracks around doors and other openings). Only a small amount of heat may be lost by each, but added together, they significantly lower the over-all temperature inside the structure. You must choose a way or ways to make up for this lost heat so that the overall heat available remains balanced:

heat lost = solar heat (from the daytime) + additional heat provided (from greenhouse heat source[s])

Obviously, reducing the amount of heat lost from the greenhouse lowers the cost of supply-ing heat to balance what is lost, which lowers the overall cost of operating a greenhouse.

You can calculate precisely the heat lost through convection, radiation, conduction, and infiltration or exfiltration and can also specifi-cally determine the amount of solar heat gen-erated on a clear day, which will allow you to determine the amount of additional heat you must supply, but these calculations are long and tedious. Most people prefer to use a quick and easy formula, and one of the simplest is offered by the catalog and Internet company Charley's Greenhouse and Garden:

(wall area + roof area) × temperature differential between outside and inside of greenhouse (inside temperature – outside temperature) × 1.1 = the number of required British thermal units (BTU)

For my lean-to greenhouse, the wall area is 270 square feet and the roof area is 280 square feet. The outside temperature in winter aver-ages about 20°F and I keep the interior of the greenhouse at about 55°F. This gives a temperature differential of 35 degrees. (Note that if you grow tropical plants, you'll want to keep a higher greenhouse temperature.) Thus:

$$(280 + 270) \times 35 \times 1.1 = 21{,}175 \text{ BTU}$$

According to the calculation directions, because my heated greenhouse has double-pane glass throughout, I can subtract 30 percent from the overall BTU required to heat my greenhouse. (You can also subtract 30 percent if it is a lean-to greenhouse against a heated wall, as in the case of a greenhouse attached to a house.)

21,175 BTUs − 6,352.5 = 14,822.5 total BTU required

Considering that I have heated the greenhouse for a number of years with an 18,000-BTU portable propane heater and that the opening windows are only single-pane glass, the number resulting from these calculations is fairly accurate.

Now that you've determined how many BTU you must provide to heat your greenhouse, let's look more closely at the four ways in which heat can be lost from a structure so that you can minimize these and perhaps lower your overall heating costs.

Radiation Losses Radiation is the flow of heat from a body or source without the necessity of a medium for its transfer. In our case, greenhouse glazing either absorbs this radiated heat, reflects it, or transmits it (the most desirable option). Radiation losses occur when heat travels through space (e.g., the sun's heat is diminished as it is radiated to us through space). In winter the weather report might say that radiational cooling will take place on a clear cold night — that is, objects on earth are giving up heat to colder air.

Convection Convection is the circular flow of air prompted by a temperature differential or nonuniformity. For example, hot air rises from a heater because colder air is drawn in at the bottom, which in turn is heated and rises from the heater.

Conduction Conduction is the movement of heat through an object or material or from one medium to another. In a greenhouse, heat is transferred from the interior to outside by conduction through the frame and glazing of the structure.

Infiltration or Exfiltration Cracks in the seals around the edges of greenhouse glazing, windows left slightly ajar, cracks under doors — all of these openings allow cold air to enter the greenhouse (infiltration) and warm air to escape from the greenhouse (exfiltration). Usually, following the rules of convection, warm air escapes from openings high in the greenhouse, drawing cooler air in through openings lower down, typically from under doors or through low vents or windows that haven't been closed or sealed.

Reducing the amount of heat lost from the greenhouse lowers the cost of supplying heat to balance what is lost, which lowers the overall cost of operating a greenhouse.

While each instance of infiltration or exfiltration may not amount to the loss of more than a percent or two of the volume heat in the greenhouse, the cumulative effect can be quite substantial. Therefore, it behooves you to make your greenhouse as airtight as possible, to use high R-value material for glazing, and to supplement insulation to north walls to provide added protection on cold winter nights. This extra insulation can take the form of straw bales stacked against the wall or clear bubble insulation or a layer of IR (infrared radiation) film over the greenhouse and additional layers of polyester fleece inside the greenhouse (a method used by many commercial growers). Just adding IR film or bubble insulation can reduce heating costs by about 10 to 20 percent. It is also possible to add window insulation to opening south-side windows and sections of rigid foam insulation cut to fit windows on the north side. When building a greenhouse with heating costs in mind, it also pays to use a less conductive building material such as wood rather than aluminum or steel. More expensive greenhouses often have thermal breaks (an insulating material is placed between two conducting materials) built into the structure to cut down on heat loss.

Providing and Retaining Heat

Along with determining exactly how much heat to provide in your greenhouse and how to prevent heat loss, you must decide how to save or store any solar heat gained. Passive systems such as a solar wall or a rock or water heat collection and storage systems are inexpensive to install and store heat without requiring any action on your part. Yet these systems take up a great deal of space, allow great fluctuations in greenhouse temperature, and may be unreliable in very low temperatures or on cloudy days. An active system such as a propane or electric heater needs less space but requires a thermostat and the expense of electricity or gas to keep it operating.

Some gardeners use a combination of several types of heating. For example, a growing bed may be set up as a hot bed, with a black-painted concrete wall adjacent to it, rock storage or water tanks set behind it for heating, and a supplementary electric or propane heater provided for the days when the sky is cloudy or temperatures are very low. These combination systems reduce heating costs by spreading the heat load over several devices and provide backup should there be a power outage or should temperatures really plummet. Note, however, that the amount of heat you can store in rocks or water is limited unless you have a very large system (see the following section on Passive Heating Systems).

Certainly, a more sophisticated active heating system can be installed to precisely monitor and maintain an even temperature in the greenhouse. Such a system may incorporate a heating unit powered by electricity, propane, or natural gas and operated by a thermostat that electronically reads the greenhouse temperature at all times. It may also have an emergency backup system in case the power goes off or the main system develops a fault. Such a system can be wired to a computer or a phone line to inform you instantly if the heater has gone off and if temperatures are dropping to levels at which plants will be harmed.

For the hobby greenhouse owner, the type of heating system installed is likely to be determined by money and space available, the amount of work entailed for installation, ease of operation, and a consideration of the extremes in temperature that plants can endure.

Passive Heating Systems

Once a passive heating system has been installed, it requires little or no work to do its job. Such systems do keep the greenhouse warm, although with a greater temperature fluctuation than may be desirable. In fact, passive systems may allow greenhouse temperatures to fluctuate by 50 degrees or more in a 24-hour period.

Most passive systems rely on sunlight to gather warmth during the day and then radiate stored heat back into the greenhouse at night. (The hot bed is the one exception to this; it maintains a constant temperature until the material in the bed decomposes sufficiently.)

There are two main types of passive solar storage media: water and rock or stone. To be moderately efficient, rock systems must take up huge amounts of space. A water system also requires a great deal of space, but not quite as much as rock. As we've learned, instead of using solar heat, a hot bed, much like a compost pile, uses the heat generated by the decomposing matter within the bed.

Water Storage Tanks If your greenhouse is big enough, you can use water storage to heat it. This involves installing water-filled 55-gallon drums that have been painted matte black or a large plastic or fiberglass tank (which you can find on the Internet as an aquaculture or agriculture tank). The water in the drums or tanks is heated by sunlight during the day, and because of its mass, it slowly radiates this heat into the greenhouse at night. My experience is that in the area immediately around the drums or tank, temperatures do not fall below freezing at night after a day's sunlight has heated the water. Yet a water system should not be considered a complete replacement for an active heating system. A full day of sun exposure in the greenhouse heats the water in a large tank only a few degrees. While this may be enough to ward off freezing, it is not enough to promote plant growth and to keep the entire greenhouse heated.

Keeping the areas farthest from the drums warm is problematic; I found a considerable temperature differential between the beds next to the drums and those farthest away, despite the fact that I ran fans to circulate air. Another drawback to this system is that plants do not like to grow next to a black surface; exhibiting phototropism, they lean away from it toward lighter surfaces.

In addition, by design the water storage system is not as efficient as it could be. The greatest amount of heat is released from water when it thaws or turns to steam. Comparatively, then, using water as a mass that releases stored heat does not take advantage of its greatest potential as a heat-releasing material.

The most serious drawback of the system is that the tanks can freeze in the winter after a few days without direct sunlight. It takes a fair amount of heat and sunlight to unfreeze a large tank of water, and while it is thawing, cold air comes off the tank and affects your plants. Installing a small, electrically powered water heater (such as a large aquarium heater that costs under $100) in each of the tanks or drums can eliminate freezing, but operating this heater continuously during the coldest part of the winter can become expensive.

Certainly, you can position a large water tank near the middle of the greenhouse, well away from freezing walls. This system works best for a circular-style greenhouse, such as a geodesic dome. You might even us the tank for fish such as tilapia, koi, carp, goldfish, crayfish, or even trout (if you keep the water moving), and you can water plants with waste water from the fish tank (it's high in nutrients) and recycle the used water back into the tank after it has filtered through the soil drains into a sump. A tank of this kind, however, results in water evaporation in the greenhouse, which leads to large amounts of condensation and moisture on the plants. With low greenhouse temperatures and lots of moisture, your plants can grow gray mold and rapidly die in spite of circulating air.

Another way of using water to heat your greenhouse involves building a solar water heater mounted to one side of the structure. But again, it works only when the sun is out. This unit comprises a large insulated box with copper tubing inside. The interior is painted black and the copper pipes absorb solar radiation. Antifreeze is circulated through the solar water heater and into a heat exchanger located inside the water tank. It's important to note that if the antifreeze line develops a leak so that the solution enters the water, any fish or animals in the tank will die. By keeping the water moving through the solar heater, a great deal can be heated very quickly. This system can be backed up by a wood-fired stove or a small furnace that heats a fin tube water pipe that circulates around the greenhouse and through the tank heat exchanger.

Rock Heat Storage This system traps and stores heat using moderately sized rocks (fist-sized or a bit bigger) in an insulated rock bin. When the sun is shining, hot air is blown through the storage medium. The major drawback to this system is the volume of rock needed for effective heating: 3 to 4 cubic feet for every square foot of south-facing greenhouse glazing. When I investigated installing a rock heat system in my heated greenhouse, I found that for the 280-square-foot space, I needed 280 × 3 = 840 cubic feet of rock. In order to accommodate such a large quantity, I'd have to locate a 3- to 4-foot-deep bed of rocks beneath an insulated greenhouse floor. The cost of the medium, however, was reasonable: less than $100 a ton for a few tons of rock. (One ton of rocks is roughly equivalent to the amount that fits into the bucket of a backhoe.)

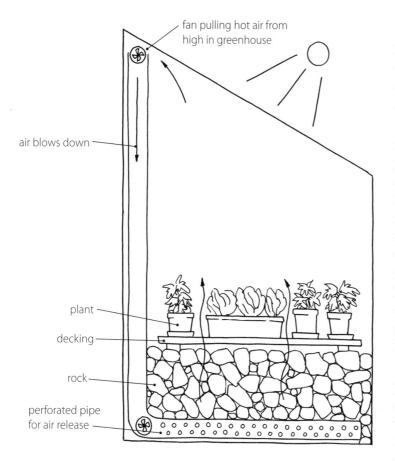

fan pulling hot air from
high in greenhouse

air blows down

plant

decking

rock

perforated pipe
for air release

Heat from a rock heating system is produced and
circulated in a greenhouse.

One other problem posed by this system is
that in order to get the full benefit of it, a fan
is required to blow air constantly through the
greenhouse, sending heated air into the rock pile
when the sun is shining and taking heat from the
pile at night or on overcast days. Should there be
a power outage, then, the heat stored in the rock
is virtually useless.

It's possible to make a rock system more efficient by passing heated water pipes through the
medium to maintain heat levels — but if you are
installing heated pipes, it might be superflu-
ous to bother with the rocks. Like water storage devices, this passive system raises and lowers the greenhouse temperature by only a few
degrees and may not ward off freezing.

TIP

Remember that electricity and water do NOT mix.

Hot Beds As described in chapters 1 and 2, a
hot bed uses decomposing manure or compost
to keep the soil warm beneath growing plants.
(Any odor is eliminated by a 12-inch layer of garden soil on top of the compost.)

Hot beds are simple to build and operate and
require very little work to maintain once the
plants are growing. To set up a hot bed, remove
all the soil from your growing bed to a depth of
3 or 4 feet and refill the excavated area with a
mixture of horse manure, fertilizer-free lawn
clippings, wood chips, leaves, and other vegetable compost material to within 1 foot of the
maximum bed height. Top the bed with a 1-foot
layer of sifted loam, then seed or plant the bed
with bedding plants. It's important to note that
moving such volumes of compost and manure is
backbreaking work.

As the organic matter decomposes, the temperature of the core of the hot bed will rise to
about 160°F, which usually takes from 4 to 6
weeks. It will remain at this temperature for
about 2 months before gradually cooling down
to about 80°F, warm enough to keep plants growing for a long time after they've stopped growing
outdoors.

I've used a hot bed to grow cool-season vegetable plants such as broccoli, greens, and leeks
almost to maturity before winter fully sets in
(from October to January). In January and February I harvested these plants at close to full
size, with the warmth of the bed preventing
them from freezing or dying.

One way to create a hot bed without the labor
of digging is to heat the bed with buried heating
cables. Note that heating cables can be expensive to operate, however, depending on how
much electricity costs in your area, and seem to
give limited results.

In orangeries of old, water pipes were run
through growing beds to keep them warm. If
you have a water heating system in or near
your greenhouse, this may be an option for you,
although you will have to monitor the water
temperature carefully.

If you want to germinate or propagate plants,
a waterproof, rubber warming mat or cables
located on the growing bench are one of the

most effective and controllable options for delivering heat. This method is also a useful and cost-saving way to keep tropical plants growing and blooming in an otherwise cool greenhouse. (See Local Heating Devices, page 74.)

Active Heating Systems

Systems that require energy sources other than the sun — that is, electricity, gas, oil, coal, wood pellets, and wood — are known as active heating systems. These systems offer control, allowing you to adjust the temperature and the time during which the heater will run. They can also raise the greenhouse temperature much higher than that of any solar storage system. With an active system, you might not need to change the thermostat setting for the course of the winter, but you have the option of turning the heat up a notch or two on a very cold night. Almost all active systems are expensive to run, however; if you plan on installing one, spend time increasing the greenhouse's insulation.

Electrical Heating Electricity, easy to use and clean, is one of the most common methods of heating the home greenhouse when the sun is not available. If your greenhouse is wired for electricity, you can plug a heater into a wall outlet. Electrical heating systems are not cheap to run, however, especially if your greenhouse is not well insulated. If you plan to implement this type of system, you'll also need to determine what temperature you'll maintain inside the greenhouse. Too much heat may cause the vents to open, allowing heat to escape, while too little heat may cause plants farthest from the heater to freeze unless you install another energy-consuming fan to circulate air around the greenhouse.

During the coldest months of the winter I set my electric heater at 50°F — high enough to keep the plants from freezing and the citrus trees from losing their leaves but not so high that I'm warming the place too much or incurring enormous bills. Ten years of heating the greenhouse has shown me that this temperature is the best compromise to keep the greenhouse warm without it costing an arm and a leg to heat it. If you

don't have warm-weather plants in your greenhouse, you can allow the temperature to drop to about 40°F at night, though a temperature that's any lower may mean that some areas of the greenhouse will freeze while the space nearest the heater (or thermostat) stays warm.

You can also use an electric heater to heat the entire greenhouse. Gardening companies such as FarmTek offer a variety of heaters with prices ranging from $50 to $2,000. There are 220-volt and 110-volt heaters available; you'll need to consult an electrician to determine whether you can install a 220-volt line to the greenhouse. You probably already have a 220-volt line in your home (many cooking stoves and air conditioners work on 220 volts), so running such a line to the greenhouse for a heater may not be an impossibility. Remember, however, that electric heating can be expensive without good insulation.

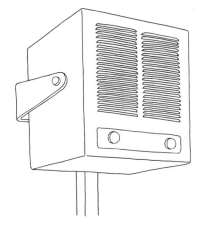

A Modine-type electric heater, operating on 220 volts, is permanently installed in a greenhouse. You'll also need to install an automatic thermostat with such a heater. Below you can see the type of airflow produced from a heater mounted near the ceiling, depending on the type of benches you have.

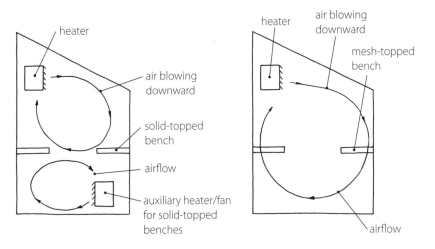

AIRFLOW WITH SOLID-TOPPED BENCHES

heater
air blowing downward
solid-topped bench
airflow
auxiliary heater/fan for solid-topped benches

AIRFLOW WITH MESH-TOPPED BENCHES

heater
air blowing downward
mesh-topped bench
airflow

(See chapter 10 to find out more about insulating your greenhouse.)

In my opinion, the best type of electric heater for the greenhouse is a ceramic disk heater such as the Pelonis furnace. It's portable and can be set under a bench so that the heater's built-in thermostat can react to the temperature in the lowest part of the greenhouse or can be moved to the potting shed when the greenhouse is watered. (Turn off the electricity and remove the heater from the greenhouse until you have finished watering, and protect the heater from drips or condensation until the greenhouse has dried out.) It is not very expensive to run, provided you make sure that heat losses in the greenhouse are minimized.

Wood-Burning Stoves There are several types of wood-burning heating systems on the market that are suitable for greenhouse use. Simplest is a wood-burning unit in the greenhouse with a flue that extends out of the structure. This requires that you regularly tote logs into the greenhouse to fill the stove. Heat radiates from the stove and flue. Running the flue from one end of the greenhouse to the other may provide more heat, but be aware that this is a potential fire hazard: Creosote builds up in the flue, which requires frequent cleaning to prevent fire.

Larger greenhouses may be heated with a 55-gallon drum stove that can take a 3-foot log. These wood-burning stoves do give off a lot of heat, but the smoke they produce must be vented out of the greenhouse via a chimney. Smaller hobby greenhouses can be heated with a regular wood-burning stove, but the heat from these is very dry and, if blown directly into the greenhouse, can quickly dry out plants and soil, especially in winter's low-humidity conditions.

This type of system might work best if you have a large water tank in the greenhouse. The humidity from the tank might temper the dry heat from the wood-burning stove. Without any humidity source, however, unless a fan circulates air around the greenhouse, you'll find that there is a hot zone next to the stove where plants are dried out quickly, an area where the temperature is just about right, and the remaining area of the greenhouse in which temperatures stay fairly cool. The major drawback of a woodstove for greenhouse heating, however, is that the unit needs constant feeding, which means that the greenhouse door will be opened frequently as you haul in wood, each time causing heat to be lost. In addition, dragging cold logs into the greenhouse and allowing them to warm up before you put them on the fire can introduce unwanted insects. Finally, because even large logs take only an hour or so to burn on the coldest nights, the fire in a stove can go out without a night feeding, causing the death of all your plants. As a backup system, though, a wood-burning stove can prevent the loss of all your plants should you experience a power outage.

Some wood-burning stoves come equipped with blowers that turn on when a stove is heated to a certain temperature. These can help to efficiently distribute the stove's heat. I've found that these fans are a good way to warm the greenhouse just before dawn after a very cold night, when the stove has burned through most of the wood during the night and the greenhouse is fairly cool. By stoking the fire with smaller pieces of wood and opening the damper as much as possible, you can quickly raise the greenhouse temperature.

Better than a woodstove in the greenhouse itself is an outdoor wood-burning furnace. In this setup, the furnace heats water that is circulated around the greenhouse through finned tubing, keeping the entire building warm. You can also run heating pipes through an insulated concrete floor slab to keep the greenhouse floor

An outdoor furnace allows you to heat with wood without having to tote wood into the greenhouse or contend with the kind of drying that can occur with a woodstove inside the structure. The furnace heats the water in pipes that circulate around the greenhouse.

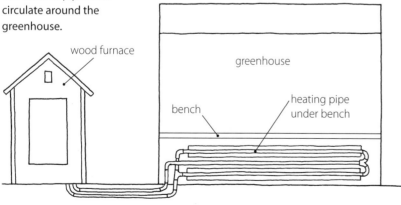

wood furnace

greenhouse

bench

heating pipe under bench

warm throughout the winter. Outdoor furnaces are available from a number of companies and can also be fueled by propane or oil. FarmTek sells a line of outdoor furnaces made by Royall in prices ranging from $5,000 to $14,000. These sit on legs above the ground and can handle logs up to 5 feet in length.

There are a number of factors that make an outdoor furnace an attractive choice for heating the greenhouse: Wood never has to come into the greenhouse, you don't have to go in and out of the greenhouse to load the stove, the stove's heat is not concentrated at one end of the greenhouse when the fire is left for the night, there is no chance of carbon monoxide gas accumulating, and some systems can operate up to 72 hours without refilling. In addition, according to the Environmental Protection Agency, an efficient and clean wood-burning stove has very little negative impact on the environment. One drawback: the cost of plumbing the furnace to the greenhouse and the location of a bulky outdoor furnace shed near the greenhouse.

In addition to the cost of the unit itself and of plumbing it to the greenhouse, you may have to install a slab for the furnace to sit on and you will have to purchase other parts for plumbing such as piping, a heat exchanger, a high-volume pump, an insulated water line, and various valves and insulation.

Coal Stoves A coal stove heating system has drawbacks that are similar to those of a wood-stove system. While they can emit a great deal of heat and can be closed down to burn slowly overnight, they do need to be filled and watched to make sure that the heat level in the greenhouse remains fairly constant. Another negative is that you must find a place to store the coal before using it. A woodpile can be stacked anywhere, but a coal pile leaves a mess that should be contained in a bin of some kind. In addition, you'll have to find a place to safely dispose of the coal ashes.

Pellet Stoves Another alternative for heating a greenhouse is a pellet stove, but while the cost of the stove itself is fairly reasonable, the cost of the

pellets is quite high compared to that of wood or coal. With the stove come the familiar problems of filling it and keeping it going overnight. There are some automatic-feed pellet stoves, but they are quite expensive.

Liquified Propane Gas (LPG) or Natural Gas (CNG) Gas greenhouse heaters are moderately safe and reliable and most are available to run on either propane (LPG) or natural gas (CNG) — the only marked difference between the two sources is that propane has a slightly higher heat output. When looking for a greenhouse heater, try to find one that does not have a pilot light if the heater is going to be located in a drafty area. The pilot-light versions that run without electricity, however, can save your plants if there is a power outage during a winter snowstorm. Two drawbacks of which you should be aware: Propane leaks can kill your plants and a unit without proper ventilation or air intake can result in burning up all the oxygen in the greenhouse, making the space hazardous to you and others who enter it.

I have been using a portable under-bench propane heater for more than ten years with no difficulty, however. It's a specially designed greenhouse heater from Southern Burner Co., in Chickasha, Oklahoma (see Resources, page 248), that has worked effectively all along, although I did have to replace the control unit when it ceased working after the heater had been left unused for the entire summer. Requiring no electricity, it's controlled by a pilot light and comes with a thermostat that I set at 55°F.

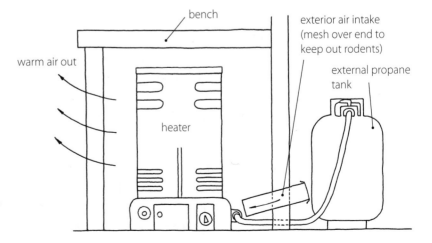

A handy, portable under-bench propane heater with a built in thermostat can be a very cost-effective and safe way to heat a structure.

bench

warm air out

heater

exterior air intake (mesh over end to keep out rodents)

external propane tank

With a supply of twin 40-pound propane cylinders located against a wall outside the greenhouse, the system works on its own, requiring no outside power source. This particular heater is available as a vented or nonvented unit, though the vented unit is better, exhausting combustion gases outside the greenhouse. If you install a similar unit, you'll need to install an air line leading from outside into the greenhouse somewhere near the heater. I don't worry about getting this stove wet when I water, but the control unit should be protected. (I've cut off the top of a gallon milk jug and, after making a couple of notches in it for gas lines, inverted it over the control unit to cover it.) Of course, during the coldest two months of the year (late January to early March) I do have to change the propane about once a week.

Many greenhouse vendors offer several propane heaters, some of which look like they could be used in your home as well as in the greenhouse. They come in sizes as small as 5,000 BTU and as large as 25,000 BTU. When deciding which type to purchase, note the heater's gas consumption, the amount of BTU it produces, and where it can be located. If you are growing gas-sensitive plants such as orchids and other tropicals, you should install a vented heater with an electronic ignition so that the pilot light cannot give off fumes that might harm your plants. For less sensitive plants such as citrus, fig, and banana trees, you can install a nonvented heater, but both types require a rodent-protected air vent to allow air into the heater combustion chamber. If you do not provide an air intake, the heater will burn all the oxygen in the greenhouse, which could kill you and could lead to sickly plants.

Backup Heating Systems In England, where winters are not as extreme as they are in the northern parts of North America, kerosene and paraffin heaters are popular. These make effective backup units, but are not suitable for continued long-term use unless they are certified. For a while, I used a British-style kerosene heater (one with a lighted wick) in the greenhouse, but the kerosene tended to add moisture to the air

and this extra moisture made an ideal breeding ground for *Botrytis* (gray mold). If you decide to use a kerosene heater as a supplemental or main heater, buy high-quality kerosene that burns with a cleaner flame than ordinary kerosene.

Local Heating Devices If you decide that you're going to propagate plants or bring on new seedlings, you'll need some form of additional heating in a local area where the plants will be germinating, such as a workbench. A source for this heating can be a small, clear plastic tent or similar enclosure over the bench with heating cables or a waterproof heat mat beneath it.

For a localized heating system, large commercial operations use heating pipes and electrical cables that run underneath a bench to warm the plants sitting on it. For your smaller operation you can purchase a waterproof propagation mat that sits under a seeding or propagation tray and can keep it at the desired temperature. These mats come in sizes ranging from 22 inches by 14 inches to 22 inches by 96 inches and cost about $40 for the smallest size to about $140 for the largest.

For grand-scale seed starting, mats are available in sizes ranging from 11 inches by 22 inches for one seed tray to 11 inches by 25 feet. Standard lengths are 8, 10, 12, 16, 20, and 25 feet and their cost is from $4 to $6 per foot. The wattage of these mats varies with their length and generally costs about the same as a lightbulb per foot of mat.

You can also build a simple heated germination box or propagation chamber in a small

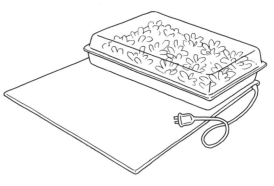

A seedling propagating mat provides localized heat for starting plants. Sizes range from 22 inches by 14 inches to 22 inches by 96 inches.

area of the greenhouse (see chapter 11 for more information on building a germination chamber). In most cases, a single lightbulb is all that is required to keep a propagation chamber warm enough for plantlets to take root.

Underslab Heating In some garages and commercial work spaces, heating cables or tubes that carry hot water are installed under or within the concrete slab foundation to keep the slab warm so that it can radiate heat. There is no reason why this type of heating system could not be used in a greenhouse, although it may be expensive to install and operate.

Hydroponics

Using hydroponics to grow plants gives you ultimate control over greenhouse growing conditions, from the medium the plants grow in and how much daylight the plants receive to the exact formula for plant nutrients. The simplest method of growing hydroponically is to put a growing medium into a pot and once or twice a day add plant nutrient solution. The most complex method involves using computer-controlled pumps to automatically flush plant roots with nutrient solution as often as required for maximum growth. This does show to what extent a grower can control the entire plant environment. Growing in this manner keeps unwanted organisms from entering the greenhouse and keeps growing tables clean of dirt and potting soil.

In hydroponic growing, plants are set in a well-drained, inert (sometimes called soilless) material that can be polystyrene balls, expanded clay pellets, gravel, pea stone, perlite, vermiculite, rock wool, or coconut fibers. Plants might also be started in potting soil and then transplanted to the growing medium.

Once in the medium, they're watered with a nutrient solution. Two of the most common, made by General Hydroponics, are Floragro and Florabloom, with their use depending on whether you want your plants to grow or flower. The company also manufacturers kits with both solutions so that you can start relatively inexpensively. Other products from this company are intended for hard-water areas or for mixing to grow specific plants. Because the solution is concentrated, it must be diluted according to package instructions, then poured into the aggregate and allowed it to drain. Most nutrient solutions are listed as having many trace elements, but you'll need to check the specific product you choose to see exactly what's in the solution before you buy it. As it passes through the aggregate, it wets the plant roots, with enough moisture staying in the medium to keep the roots just damp until the next watering. The solution can be collected and reused several times.

You can grow almost any plant hydroponically, but fast-growing plants such as lettuce, tomatoes, peppers, herbs, and greens are most often grown in this way.

For my homemade hydroponic growing facility, I installed a gutter throughout the greenhouse

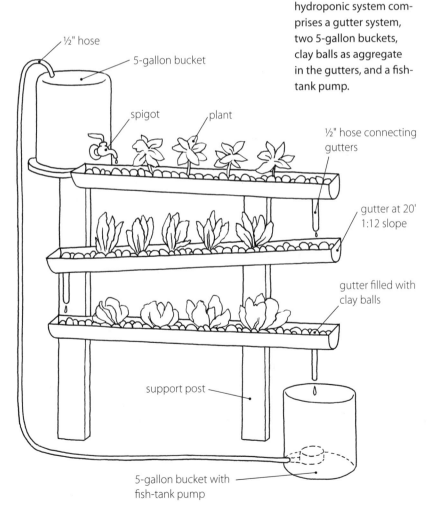

This simple homemade hydroponic system comprises a gutter system, two 5-gallon buckets, clay balls as aggregate in the gutters, and a fish-tank pump.

½" hose

5-gallon bucket

spigot

plant

½" hose connecting gutters

gutter at 20'
1:12 slope

gutter filled with clay balls

support post

5-gallon bucket with fish-tank pump

that held expanded clay balls. A small hole in a 5-gallon bucket located on a shelf near the ceiling of the greenhouse allowed the nutrient solution to run into the sloping, aggregate-filled gutter, where it wet the roots of each plant. At the end of the system was a second 5-gallon bucket, which collected the solution after it had run through the gutters. This pail contained a small fish-tank pump and an automatic shutoff valve. When the lower pail was full, the solution was pumped back to the upper bucket, ready for reuse. I turned on the pump when I went out to the greenhouse in the morning and did the same thing in the evening to circulate the solution. The water could be heated automatically to keep it moderately warm. This system produced a supply of fresh hydroponic lettuce and herbs. The biggest problem I found with growing hydroponically was that when I harvested plants, the roots pulled out so many clay balls from the gutter that I was constantly replacing them.

Store unused insecticides well away from any area a child may have access to.

Of course, you can create a much more elaborate hydroponic system than my simple gutter-growing method. You can devote an entire greenhouse to growing vegetables and flowers hydroponically. In fact, you can purchase specialized sloped growing tables in which the nutrient solution flows into the higher end and out the low end, where it is collected for the next application. You can also adjust the nutrient solution to suit the particular plants that you want to grow. For example, for those plants that like a more acidic soil, you can make the nutrient mix slightly more acidic, and for those that like a lot of nitrogen, you can adjust the solution accordingly. All of these additives can be purchased from a hydroponic supplier.

Along with the hydroponic system's reputation for an insect-free, controlled greenhouse environment, the vegetables produced from such a system often command high prices at supermarkets and other outlets should you decide to sell your produce.

Insecticides in the Greenhouse

I prefer to garden organically and to use organic controls to eliminate pests in the greenhouse, but because plants "under glass" are spaced much more closely than plants outdoors and there is no wind to blow insects from their leaves and buds, you may well have to resort to sprays at some point.

If you decide to spray pesticides to control insects in your greenhouse, read the labels very carefully and make sure that you conform to all the application requirements. Always store unused insecticides well away from any area that a child may have access to. In addition, note which insecticides are most harmful to humans; I prefer not to use these in my greenhouses, where I spend so much time.

The only spray that I use in a greenhouse is Safer's insecticidal soap — and I try to avoid spraying it on plants such as herbs that I plan to eat. If weather permits, I first take an infected plant outdoors and spray it with plain water. Using this method, you might find that you don't need an insecticide at all; spraying the plant with the fine mist of a hose is often good enough to remove aphids and most whiteflies. Hanging sticky yellow cards in the greenhouse can also help control whitefly and aphid infestations.

Avoiding overzealous use of insecticides may mean coexisting with some pests. I know there are some insects in my greenhouse and that I'm never going to get rid of them completely — and for me, this is acceptable.

A greenhouse also offers a totally controlled, largely enclosed environment for the release of beneficial insects that can take care of pests. I once released 3,000 ladybugs (the smallest amount I could purchase) into the greenhouse to control aphids, and even today, seven years later, there are a few dozen ladybugs wandering around inside, doing their job of helping to keep down the pest population.

6 Greenhouse Building Materials

BEFORE YOU BEGIN building your greenhouse, it's important to understand and consider the variety of materials that can be used in its construction. Only by learning more about these materials will you be able to make the best choice for your greenhouse style and location and for the conditions in your region.

In this chapter you'll find information on materials for construction of the structure itself. At the same time that you plan your greenhouse, you should make decisions about building materials, the foundation (materials for the foundation are discussed in chapter 8), the glazing (addressed thoroughly in chapter 7), and the wiring and plumbing (information on wiring and plumbing can be found in chapter 10).

Included in this chapter are discussions of wood, aluminum, and steel as building materials; an assessment of sheathing and various external finishes for walls such as those on the north that may not be glazed; and a look at the kinds of insulation you might incorporate into your structure. Also considered are alternative building materials and the various paint finishes you can use.

In choosing building materials, it's important to take into account the temperatures in your region and specific area and the effects of wind at various times throughout the year. Cooler temperatures or cold seasons (such as you'll find in the northern United States) dictate the need for insulation, especially on the northern wall of your structure. Also consider building an unglazed wall on the north side that's higher than the knee wall

you might build on the south side. Note, however, that if the north wall is the tallest wall of the structure, the greenhouse is liable to flex in high winds, which can pound the structure from the north, even when it's constructed according to the best building practices. To avoid this, build lower and reinforce the wall with an air lock or potting shed, which provides some structural rigidity to the wall.

Wood as a Construction Material

Any decision to construct a greenhouse from wood should be made with some understanding of wood species and properties. It's important to select the right wood for your construction. A nondurable wood can quickly rot, endangering you and ruining your greenhouse investment. For example, a heated greenhouse I built early on of regular kiln-dried pine lumber purchased at the local hardware store lasted seven years in total, but in the heat, some of the pine lumber rotted after only five years. Even though the lumber was painted with exterior paint, the constant humidity and heat of the greenhouse simply led to rot.

Understanding Wood

Wood can be divided into two categories: hardwood and softwood. Softwoods are usually evergreen conifers and hardwoods tend to be leaf-dropping species, but there are exceptions to this rule. For example, larches (tamaracks) and bald cypresses, which retain their leaves year-round, are hardwoods. Some hardwoods such as basswood and balsa are very soft, while some softwoods, such as long-leaf pines, are very hard, so don't make the mistake of thinking that the classification of tree or lumber is always indicative of the toughness of the wood.

In general, hardwoods tend to be more resistant to rot and most are classified as durable — that is, they last a long time in the moist, humid conditions of the greenhouse. Durable woods such as ash, beech, elm, greenheart, hickory, locust, mahogany, maple, white oak, teak, walnut, and poplar can all be used for greenhouses, but in most areas they are likely to be expensive and difficult to obtain. You should find out which durable woods are available in your area before you start estimating and designing your project.

Though durable, hardwoods can be difficult to work. If you've ever tried to drive a finish nail into a maple board, you know how hard these woods can be! Some hardwoods require that you drill a hole slightly smaller than the nail before hammering the nail into the wood. Gluing these woods is also difficult. Teak and maple are notoriously hard to glue or epoxy because the wood is so dense. In addition, the oils in teak require that you wipe down the wood with a solvent such as acetone before you apply epoxy.

Rot-resistant softwoods are less expensive, more readily available (though some are scarce relative to pine and the woods more commonly used for dimensional lumber), and easier to work with than hardwoods. That said, the cost of naturally rot-resistant woods such as some cedars, cypress, and redwood has skyrocketed in recent years (due mostly to their endangered status). If you can find them, you're unlikely to obtain enough lumber to build a greenhouse. Other woods such as tidewater cypress, western red and Alaskan cedar, and eastern larch (tamarack or hackmatack) can also be used for greenhouse structures in that they all have a moderately high resistance to decay.

You can use other, less durable woods, but you'll need to protect them with an impermeable layer to prevent moisture from getting into the wood and causing rot. (See Painting Your Greenhouse, page 88.) You can use ordinary exterior oil-based paint or epoxy resins or marine paints designed to withstand very humid conditions, though these tend to be quite expensive. Just remember this trade-off: Using a less expensive wood means that you need to use a more expensive paint. It might be worthwhile, then, to invest in better-quality wood at the outset.

Finding the "Right" Part of the Wood

Along with the kind of wood you choose, how the wood is cut and what part of the tree it comes from are important factors. Heartwood, as may be expected, comes from the middle of the tree, while the sapwood comes from the area nearer the bark. The rings in the wood give an idea of how fast the tree has grown and offer a clue to how durable it is. For example, widely spaced sapwood rings often indicate that the tree grew quickly and that the wood is less durable. Conversely, annual rings that are very close together indicate a wood that has grown slowly and that is very dense and likely quite rot resistant. Obviously, this is the kind of wood that's most desirable to use for your structure. Heartwood, formed when the cells in the sapwood die and the tree's pores get plugged, is the strongest wood available. Sapwood is the living part of the tree trunk and is usually not very resistant to decay.

This cross section of a tree shows from which tree part different kinds of building lumber are produced. Elements such as annual rings, sapwood, and heartwood determine a lumber's strength and thus use.

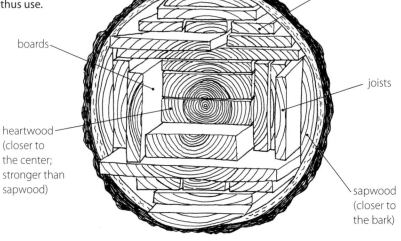

planks

boards

joists

heartwood (closer to the center; stronger than sapwood)

sapwood (closer to the bark)

Another characteristic to consider when choosing wood for your greenhouse is the grain: Make sure the grain flows along the wood as opposed to across the wood. A grain across the wood may cause the lumber to snap or fracture under the weight of any load. In addition, remember to pick the pieces with the straightest grain.

If you yourself are selecting the lumber for your project, don't be afraid to dig through the pile at the lumberyard to select the best pieces available. Reject any pieces that have gouges or are split or that come from the outer edges of the log and have rough grain along one side. Look over the entire piece of lumber to make sure that it's straight. If the lumber is warped, you may have difficulty building with it and installing straight-edged glass or other glazing after you've framed the structure.

Knots

Knots are formed where branches develop from the trunk of a tree. As the tree grows, the branch remains attached to the pith in the middle of the tree and a knot forms where the sapwood grows around the branch. From a builder's point of view, knots are undesirable because they cause irregular shrinkage and compromise structural integrity; the knot usually shrinks at a different rate from that of the surrounding wood and may drop out of the wood after it has been cut, leaving a hole and weakening the lumber. Knots are also difficult to paint over: They tend to allow resin to seep through the paint layer.

When selecting wood for your greenhouse, try to choose pieces with few or no knots. If you must accept some knots and you plan on painting the greenhouse, paint them with two coats of oil-based sealer before you start work to ensure that they will not bleed through the paint layer.

Building Lumber

Regular building lumber, mostly pine, can be obtained at your local hardware or building supply store. It comes in standard sizes, as described.

Standard Lumber Sizes

Standard lumber widths and thickness are known as either 1× ("one-by"), as in 1×6, 1×8, 1×10, or 1×12; or 2×, as in 2×3, 2×4, 2×6, 2×8, 2×10, or 2×12. Heavier lumber may be 4×, as in a 4×4 post or a 6×6 post. Landscape timbers are 8×8. Typically, 1× lumber is used for trim and edging, while 2× is used for joists, rafters, framing, and other structural elements. Note that all dimensions cited are in inches. Lengths increase in 2-foot increments starting at 6 feet, although you can often get a lumberyard to cut shorter lengths. Longer lengths, up to 18 and 20 feet, usually must be specially ordered.

Pressure-Treated Wood

As I mentioned, I used regular lumber for my first greenhouses, but found that spores, heat, and humidity caused the lumber to rot after four or five years, even though it was protected with an undercoat and topcoat of paint and I repainted it after several years. By contrast, the lean-to greenhouse attached to my studio was built with pressure-treated lumber and has lasted for more than 15 years without any signs of rot.

TIP

In considering what building materials and methods to use for your greenhouse construction, you must consider wind speeds to which the structure will be exposed. As the wind speed increases, the pressure it exerts on a tall wall increases exponentially: In a 5-mile-per-hour wind the pressure is 25 units, in a 20-mile-per-hour wind the pressure increases to 400 units, and in a 40-mile-per-hour wind the pressure reaches 1,600 units. Take wind pressure into account and adjust your structure's design and materials accordingly.

Pressure-treated lumber is created by bathing the wood in a water solution of chemicals (arsenic, chromium, or copper) and then pressurizing it so that the chemicals impregnate the wood. Generally the chemicals do not penetrate very far into the wood, but they bond with it to make it reasonably impervious to rot and insect damage. Uncoated chromated copper arsenate (CCA) pressure-treated lumber can, however, leach arsenic into the soil when the lumber gets wet. Plants grown in soil where high levels of arsenic are present can take up the element, and when these plants are eaten by humans, the arsenic can be absorbed into the body. Although arsenic is found in the body in tiny trace quantities, in larger quantities it is a known carcinogen. The Environmental Protection Agency (EPA) therefore announced that as of December 31, 2003, no wood for residential use may be treated with CCA.

Varieties of pressure-treated lumber sold today include those treated by copper azole (CA), ammoniacal copper quat (ACQ), and ammoniacal copper zinc arsenate (ACZA), although ACZA lumber is most often used in the marine environment. Use of CA-treated lumber and ACQ-treated lumber has replaced CCA lumber. Note that you cannot dispose of CCA-treated wood in landfills. Nor should you burn it. Even the sawdust from this wood can be toxic.

Because various scientific studies have shown that the elements in pressure-treated wood can leach into the soil, if you choose to use this wood, all pressure-treated lumber should be painted before installation and kept painted while the greenhouse is being used. According to test studies, no leaching occurs when pressure-treated lumber is painted regularly. If, however, the prospect of painting (and repainting) your lumber is not appealing, you might want to think of lumber treatment alternatives that produce rot and insect resistance. These include zinc and sodium borates and the organic pesticide copper 8-quinolate. These chemicals don't remain in the wood, though, and may also leach into surrounding soil.

If you do choose pressure-treated wood for your structure, take care in the building process. According to a recent alert issued by the federal Consumer Product Safety Commission, ACQ wood may cause faster corrosion of fasteners that come in contact with it. The commission recommends using stainless-steel brackets and nails instead of galvanized fasteners.

A safer, greener alternative to pressure-treated wood is a new product called TimberSIL, which utilizes a brand-new mineralization process to both preserve wood and eliminate all the problems of CA- or ACQ-treated wood. According to the company, TimberSIL uses sodium silicate technology to produce a nontoxic, noncarcinogenic, and noncorrosive preserved wood that can safely be in contact with the ground for up to 40 years. The product earned a BuildingGreen Top 10 award for 2004 (see Resources, page 248, for information on this product).

Sheathing

Any part of the outside of your greenhouse that is not glazed will be sheathed before siding is installed. The most common (and most expensive) sheathing is ½-inch plywood made for this purpose. Most greenhouses require only a few sheets of plywood, and the extra expense of this material is well worth it. The American Plywood Association (APA) uses a grading system for such wood (see Plywood Manufacturing and Grading, below) and you should familiarize yourself with it before you make any purchases.

Install plywood horizontally so that it spans the vertical structural supports and stagger each row of panels if the wall is more than 4 feet high. When nailing plywood, use 6d nails spaced at a minimum of 6 to 9 inches apart. Nailing the plywood properly to the stud walls makes the entire structure more rigid and stable.

Plywood Manufacturing and Grading

Plywood is made by first peeling a thin veneer of wood from a log as it is rotated. Once the wood has been separated in this way, the veneer is cut to size and dried to give it a uniform 2 to 4 percent moisture content. Each dried piece is then sent to a gluing machine, where sheets are glued together in panels, and a press. When exposed to heat and pressure, the glue dries in a few minutes and the plywood panel moves to another

TIP

The actual measurements of dimensional lumber differ from those that are used to label the lumber. For example, an 8-foot 2×4, known as a stud, is actually 8 feet by 1½ inches by 3½ inches and a 2×10 joist actually measures 1½ inches by 9½ inches. The labeled dimensions reflect the size of the piece of lumber before sawing, while the actual dimensions reflect the lumber size after sawing and planing.

station, where it is trimmed. At this time, the better-quality pieces are sanded.

The plywood is then graded according to the quality of the veneer. According to the American Plywood Association–Engineered Wood Association, these standards are voluntary and may follow one of two systems: The first rates panels according to the thickness or span rating, with the span rating being the measure of the plywood stiffness and strength parallel to the face grain. The number on the left side of the stamp on a sheet of plywood gives the span rating of the wood — that is, the load it will carry when placed across a given span.

The second method rates plywood according to the veneer quality. N and A are the highest grade levels. Veneers with these grades have no knots or patches. A is intended for paintable surfaces, while N is the rating for plywood intended to be left with a natural finish. Both grades are sanded very smooth, though grade B plywood has small surface knots and may be plugged where larger knots occur. All the knots in grade C plywood are plugged; it is intended for use as an underlayment or for subfloors. Grade C, with its small knots, is the lowest grade of exterior plywood. Grade D plywood often has voids or unplugged knotholes.

If you see an entire sheet of plywood graded AB, this means that the face grade veneer is A quality and the back veneer is B quality. In AC plywood, the back veneer is grade C.

Plywood that is manufactured to be used where it will be exposed to more than 18 percent moisture content (meaning it will get rained on!) comes with an X designation. This means that it was assembled with a waterproof glue or epoxy and is suitable for use in wet areas such as a greenhouse. A number of projects in chapter 13 call for using CDX plywood (grade C on one side, grade D on the other, with an X designation meaning it is suitable for moisture exposure). See Resources, pages 247–248, for more information on plywood use and grading.

Preservative-treated plywood is also available should you decide that you need to protect your structure. The APA suggests, however, that the only plywood suitable for greenhouse use is that treated with copper 8-quinolinate, an organic preservative, though plywood treated with this chemical may not be readily available in most areas.

Fiberglass-Sheathed Plywood

Also available is plywood made with fiberglass plastic as its veneers. In a situation where the inside face of the plywood will be exposed — for example, in a lean-to greenhouse with varnished rafters and a partial white ceiling or rear wall — you might investigate using this material. Its fiberglass overlay keeps the CC-grade plywood dry. Its applications include use for truck bodies.

Oriented Strand Board

Oriented strand board has become a replacement for plywood in many areas. It is made from smaller trees that are chopped into pieces from 2 to 6 inches long. These wood chips are dried and coated with a glue before being oriented longitudinally in a machine. As the panels come from the machine, heat and compression are applied to form them into a large "master" panel, which is then cut into the appropriate size. Like plywood, oriented strand board has a span rating to give the builder an idea of its structural applications. When fastening this material, use 6d 2- or 2½-inch nails spaced 6 to 8 inches apart. See Resources, page 245 for more information on oriented strand board.

House Wrap

Sheathing is usually covered with either Tyvek house wrap or a similar commercially available material. House wrap over sheathing helps to prevent air infiltration (and exfiltration); allows moisture to pass through the wall; and helps

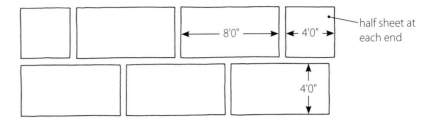

half sheet at each end

When you install two rows of plywood sheathing on a greenhouse, be sure to stagger the pieces to avoid continuous seams, which make for a weak surface.

prevent mold, mildew, and wood rot. Other materials such as building paper, tar paper, and roofing felt can be used in its place, though these don't have all of the properties of house wrap. Building paper and tar paper, for instance, don't allow much moisture to pass through the wall, and if it gets wet on a regular basis, building paper can deteriorate.

For installation, Tyvek is stapled or nailed in place and the seams are sealed using a special tape that adheres to the wrap. Building paper is nailed in place with large-headed roofing nails or nails fitted with large tin washers.

Exterior Siding

Siding, installed on top of house wrap, can take many forms. So that my greenhouse would harmonize with the look of the other structures on my property, I shingled its north, west, and east sides. If your home has wooden or vinyl siding, you can use the same material on your greenhouse so that it will blend in with the house. Following is a short review of a few siding materials, though there are many others from which to choose.

Side-Wall Shingles or Shakes

Wooden side-wall shingles or shakes come in either red or white cedar. Sometimes they've been dipped in an oil-based preservative such as bleaching oil (and sometimes you must dip them yourself) or you can install them and then coat them with a similar preservative.

Wood shingles or shakes are an attractive and long-lasting siding for a greenhouse.

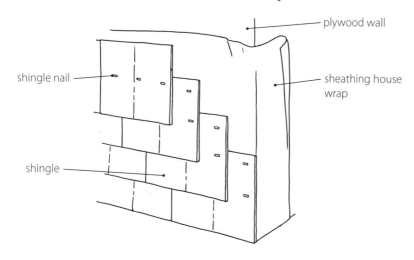

shingle nail

shingle

plywood wall

sheathing house wrap

Shingles are nailed or stapled directly to the sheathing. When shingling, measure the height of windows and doors above the bottom of the area to be shingled and divide the resulting area into equal sections of 6 to 7 inches. This will give you the number of inches of each shingle that will be exposed to the air or, as a builder might say, "to the weather." For example, if a windowsill is exactly 3 feet above the ground and the top of a door frame is 6 feet 6 inches, each course of shingles will be spaced 6 inches apart. In that way, the bottom of the window will coincide with the seventh row of shingles. If you decide to space the shingle courses 5 inches apart, you will end up with a course of shingles 1 inch wide under the windowsill. Shingles that are this small tend to split and drop off a wall quickly and easily.

When setting up the first course of shingles, nail or staple the first row directly over the Tyvek or tar paper. About every 3 feet, set one shingle 2 inches to 3 inches below the others. This hanging shingle is used temporarily to hold a piece of straight furring whose top edge is level with the bottom edge of the shingles. Next, nail a row of shingles onto the first course fastened to the sheathing. Make sure that joints between shingles on the top course do not lie directly over joints on the bottom course. Also make sure that your nails are more than 6 inches above the base of the shingles so that the nail heads will be hidden under the next course of shingles.

When the second course is complete, remove the furring strip from the temporary low shingles, reset it at a level 6 inches higher, and trim the low shingles level with the bottom edge of the course. Next, nail the furring strip so that its top edge is 6 inches above the bottom edge of the first course and begin fastening the second course of shingles in place. Repeat this process until you have shingled the entire area.

When shingling corners, on one course the end shingle from one side of the structure overlaps the end shingle from the other, and on the next course, the overlap is reversed. Of course, if you don't want to make corner overlaps, you can install 1×4 or 1×6 wood trim on the end of the walls, overlapping the trim where the corner meets.

Lap Siding

As its name implies, in horizontal lap siding, one board of siding overlaps the board below it. This type is probably the most common and perhaps most popular in the United States today and comes in a variety of materials: wood (usually cedar), vinyl, and fiber cement, which is resistant to rot and cracking. Like shingles, lap siding is installed by working upward from the bottom of the building.

If you plan on using cedar siding, the first step is to make sure the material has a low moisture content (by allowing it to dry or keeping it under cover) and that it's either stained or painted before installation. If you use a clear stain or bleaching oil, the wood should be coated on all sides. If you plan on painting the boards with siding paint, they should first be covered with an oil-based primer coat (either on both sides or on the fronts alone while the backs are painted with a clear water sealer).

Before installing lap siding, nail a furring strip to the bottom of the greenhouse wall to set the first piece of siding away from the wall. Lap siding is nailed in place at 24-inch intervals using 6d ring or siding nails for siding measuring ½ inch or ⅝ inch, 7d nails for ¾-inch siding, and 10d for ⅞-inch siding. Siding nails have a blunt tip that tears into wood without potentially splitting it. The nails should be either stainless steel or galvanized. Note that if you must nail near the edges of siding, you should predrill nail holes to avoid splitting the board. When nailing siding, always make sure the top course overlaps the one below it by about an inch and that the nails pass through only a single piece of wood. (If you nail through two pieces, there is little room for the wood to expand and the siding will probably split.)

Barn Board Siding

Barn board is an exterior-grade, plywood-like material that comes in 4×8 sheets that are stained or painted and nailed to the sheathing. If you wish, you can bypass sheathing and nail barn board directly to studs. It also makes an easy-to-install wall covering.

Board-and-Batten

With this method of siding, boards between 1 inch and 2 inches thick are nailed vertically to the sheathing, then a thin strip about 1 inch by 2 inches is nailed over the seams between the boards to cover the joints. Boards that are 16 inches wide can be nailed to the studs in lieu of plywood sheathing, but any width other than 16 inches will require the boards be fastened to sheathing or furring strips. Installing board and batten siding on furring strips may necessitate using caulking to eliminate any gaps and construction adhesive to be sure each join is firm. Construction adhesive can be used instead of or along with nails, but if your greenhouse will need to be moved or disassembled for any reason in the coming years, using nails will make this process far easier.

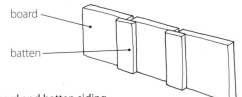

Board and batten siding

Other Greenhouse Framing Materials

Other materials besides wood can be used in greenhouse construction. The most commonly employed are aluminum, plastic, and steel. Aluminum and plastic are used mostly for kit greenhouses and steel for larger commercial greenhouses. While steel is less expensive (aluminum costs about three times as much), its use in hobby-sized greenhouses has largely been eliminated as lighter aluminum and plastic extrusions have become available.

Aluminum

Aluminum-frame greenhouse kits may come assembled or may require assembly, which usually consists of simply bolting together the various parts. Aluminum for greenhouses is

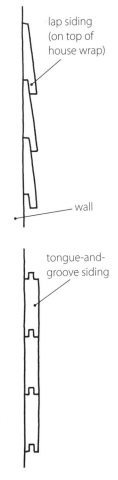

Lap siding and tongue-and-groove siding

extruded, meaning the metal is heated until it is just molten and is then squeezed through a die to give it its shape. When the metal emerges from the die, it is rapidly cooled to ensure that it keeps this shape. The extruded metal is made with a channel of a specific size that is designed to accept a glazing material based on the material's thickness, which means that if you use an aluminum frame for your structure, you may not be able to substitute glass glazing for polycarbonate. If the fixed channel size of the metal is large, it can accept double or twin wall glazing, or you may install a rubber or plastic insert if you plan on using a thinner glazing material. A rubber insert can also serve as an expansion joint and a thermal break between the glazing and the aluminum.

One of the pluses of working with aluminum is that it can be cut with the same tools that you would use for wood. Another benefit of the metal in a greenhouse application is that it has a natural oxide layer that makes it corrosion resistant. On some greenhouse extrusions, the oxide layer is enhanced by anodizing it, or treating the surface of the material to help it resist corrosion. In more upscale greenhouses, the aluminum extrusion is painted with a urethane- or epoxy-based paint that adheres strongly to the alloy. This type of paint should last the lifetime of the greenhouse, but in severe conditions it may require repainting every 10 years or so. In addition, unlike one of wood, an aluminum structure, with its consistent dimensions, rarely leaks.

Aluminum-framed greenhouses typically cost more to heat because the metal is a poor heat conductor and allows heat to pass through easily. If you plan to heat your aluminum greenhouse during a northern winter, you can decrease heat loss by suspending a layer of plastic or bubble wrap insulation inside the structure to prevent warm air from touching the cold metal framing.

Steel

As we saw in chapter 2, the earliest greenhouses were often made with cast- or wrought-iron frames and supports, but the use of cast iron has gone the way of the dinosaur. It was replaced with steel for structural supports in larger greenhouse applications.

When used in commercial structures, this metal is protected from rust and corrosion by either galvanizing or painting it, though galvanizing (coating the metal with zinc) provides a more durable finish. The zinc is electroplated to the steel after the metal is bent (bending steel after it has been plated often results in cracking the zinc layer and eventual corrosion). Non-galvanized steel will eventually rust if it is not painted regularly. In addition, steel must be protected from the humid environment of a greenhouse, which usually requires paint that must be refreshed about every 10 years. Note that if you plan to weld together your steel frame, you will have to use ungalvanized steel; welding galvanized steel emits hazardous fumes.

In home greenhouses today, steel (in the form of galvanized steel pipe) is used most frequently for framing hoop houses. The pipe frame is covered with plastic greenhouse sheeting or with thin layers of flexible polycarbonate or acrylic. (See chapter 7 for more information on these and other glazing materials.) Because steel frames, like those of aluminum, tend to lose more heat than structures framed with wood, hoop house covers made of two layers of plastic with warm air blown between them can help to reduce the heat loss of the metal structure.

Plastic

Like aluminum, plastic frames can be extruded (pushed through a die) or pultruded (pulled through a die) to produce a shape suitable for holding polycarbonate or acrylic glazing. Because most plastics cannot carry heavy glazing, however, kit greenhouses with this framing are usually small (from 2 feet by 4 feet to 6 feet by 8 feet), although some of the latest styles using heavy-duty plastic for the frame and lightweight polycarbonate glazing can reach dimensions of 8 feet by 10 feet. Benefits of plastic construction are that it will never rot, it has reasonable UV resistance, it can retain heat fairly well, and frames using it tend to be inexpensive. If you can afford a wood- or metal-framed greenhouse, it will hold up longer, but if you are not sure that you want to embrace the greenhouse gardening lifestyle, a plastic-framed greenhouse is a good starting point.

As I mentioned earlier, an alternative to a plastic kit greenhouse is a homemade hoop house made from schedule 40 PVC pipe. For a cost of less than $150, I made such a house that was 40 feet long and 14 feet wide as a temporary garden structure to keep plants slightly warmer and to keep deer out of the garden. For the cover I used a 100-foot roll of construction polyethylene at a cost of less than $100. Manufacturers of higher-quality greenhouse coverings do NOT recommend using them for plastic hoops, specifying that they should be used only with metal frames. During summer, I remove the polyethylene and install deer netting on the plastic frame to protect the garden from deer and rodents. See chapter 13 (project 7) for specific information on building this type of do-it-yourself hoop house.

Insulation

Properly insulating your greenhouse can cut down enormously on heating costs should you choose to operate the structure year-round. There are a number of types of insulation available to get the job done. Specific applications may depend on where and how the insulation is to be used. Following are explanations of some of the most common, along with the pluses and drawbacks of each and some tips for installing them.

Fiberglass Insulation

Fiberglass insulation usually comes in precut batts, or you can buy it in a long roll and cut it to size. Its width is designed to fit between studs that are either 16 inches on center or 24 inches on center. If you are going to lay a vapor barrier on the inside of the greenhouse, you do not need to buy paper-backed fiberglass insulation, though the backing does make it easier to staple it into place. If you do install paper-backed fiberglass between the studs, cover it with a nonflammable material such as drywall (waterproof drywall, sometimes called greenboard, is best). In addition, don't leave the fiberglass batts or paper exposed because tiny particles of fiberglass can fall and contaminate the growing beds.

Installing Fiberglass

Installing fiberglass is probably one of the most unpleasant jobs you'll ever undertake. Installation day always seems to be hot, especially in a greenhouse, when you least want to wear a Tyvek suit, respirator or dust mask, and any of the other gear that you use for this type of work. To install fiberglass insulation, I first apply a barrier cream on my arms and face, then a Tyvek suit with a hood (both the cream and Tyvek suits are available in good hardware stores). Next, I put on a pair of boots, rubber gloves, and a respirator. You can also wear goggles, but they steam up very quickly, eliminating visibility. After I'm finished with the installation, I usually toss the Tyvek suit in the trash because it is covered with so many fiberglass particles. Finally, I wash off in a cold shower (hot water opens the pores in your skin and allows the tiny needles of fiberglass to enter). I also rinse the respirator, boots, and gloves to get rid of any fiberglass shards.

Once the fiberglass is in place, you can cover it with a polyethylene film vapor barrier or install waterproof drywall directly on top of it.

Polystyrene or Rigid Foam Insulation

Polystyrene is the pink or blue rigid foam insulation that you see at your local lumberyard or home center. It comes in panels that are 1, 2, or 4 inches thick. Extruded polystyrene has an R-value of 3 to 5 per inch, depending on how it is made, and expanded polystyrene, which is white, has an R-value of 2 to 4.

Each polystyrene panel is 2 feet wide and 8 feet long and, with the exception of white expanded polystyrene, has tongue-and-groove edges. When using this material, make sure the tongues and grooves lock properly to eliminate air gaps. On the inside of a building, the panels are generally nailed or screwed directly to the studs using large tin washers to prevent the fastener heads from breaking through the insulation. Remember that it's easy to damage polystyrene when hammering nails into it, even if you use large washers. Furring strips can be installed horizontally along the walls at 16-inch centers so that you can screw the drywall to them. The additional air gap created by the strips between the drywall and the polystyrene ensures that the insulation is not crushed, and imparts a little more insulation value.

You can also install polystyrene on the outside of your greenhouse walls using the same method along with ¼-inch or ⅜-inch exterior-grade plywood or oriented strand board sheathing. Lay the polystyrene on the plywood, using furring strips between each sheet for nailing, and then cover the entire furring/polystyrene layer with a second layer of ⅜-inch plywood. This makes for a very rigid structure, but obviously costs more than a single layer of plywood sheathing. Of course, if you plan to leave the exterior wall exposed, use barn board or plywood rated for exteriors as your outer layer.

Polyisocyanurate

Often known by its trade name Celotex, this material looks like rigid foam insulation but has aluminum foil on both sides, with the manufacturer's name printed on one side. The printed face should be installed against the wall. Polyisocyanurate costs slightly more than regular polystyrene insulation, but in my opinion it does a better job. I've used it on the inside of my cool greenhouse, where, along with its insulating properties, the foil face reflects sunlight onto the plants. After you have installed this type of insulation, tape with ordinary duct tape all seams or, for a few dollars more, use foil tape designed to adhere to the foil surface of the insulation. The foil tape certainly looks much better than duct tape and also makes a better vapor barrier.

The drawback to polyisocyanurate is that it is highly flammable, and when it burns, it gives off toxic fumes. If you plan to use this material in a greenhouse attached to your home, most fire codes call for it to be covered with a nonflammable material such as drywall. Of course, you should also install smoke detectors in the greenhouse area.

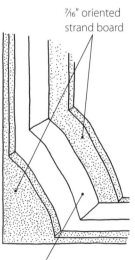

The anatomy of a stress skin panel

⁷⁄₁₆" oriented strand board

3¹¹⁄₁₆" polyisocyanurate core

Stress Skin Panels

If you decide that your greenhouse will incorporate an insulated north wall, you might want to install newer-to-the-market stress skin panels, which have an insulated core material sandwiched between two layers of plywood or drywall or, in some instances, higher-quality wood veneers. Such panels are made by several manufacturers (among them Winter Panel Corp. and Eagle Panel Systems, Inc.; see Resources, page 248) and have an R-value of between 4 and 5 per inch of thickness. Along with offering more insulation value than conventional stick-built construction, these panels make for easier building. Structurewall panels, made by Winter Panel Corp., have a layer of foam insulation between two layers of oriented strand board (OSB) and are intended to carry the load of mounted shelving or cabinets. Curtainwall nonstructural panels, also made by Winter Panel Corp., have an interior surface of gypsum wallboard that can be finished to have an R-value of 25, making them ideal for the north wall of a double-glazed greenhouse. At a slightly lower cost, you can use panels with an expanded polystyrene (EPS) core, such as those made by Eagle Panel Systems. The layers of the panels are tightly bonded, so you will never have to worry about them coming apart.

If you decide to build a free-form, insulated greenhouse using either of these products, you will need to design the structure to accommodate their sizes. The panels come in lengths up to 16 feet for Curtainwall and 24 feet for Structurewall and are 4 feet wide. The framing carries the structural load and the stress skin panels provide additional rigidity. You should install the panels with 1½-inch nails spaced 12 inches apart on hardwood frames or 2½-inch nails on softwood frames, and each panel should be fully supported on all edges. Unlike regular plywood, they can be installed horizontally or vertically simply by nailing or screwing them to the structure. Panel edges are joined with splines set just inside the exterior layers to ensure good insulation and strong joints.

According to the Winter Panel Corp. Web site, because ants and termites may get into the insulation between the external layers of stress skin panels, you should install a termite shield on the sill plate before installing the panels.

Note that one drawback to stress skin panels is the installation of wiring, which can't be run through the panels themselves. If you locate outlet boxes at or near joints, however, you will be able to run the wiring through the middle of the joint and have nothing but the outlet box showing.

Vapor Barriers

If your greenhouse is attached to your home, you should install a vapor barrier between the greenhouse wall and the house wall, which will keep moisture from entering the walls of your home. Water in the walls combined with the heat of the greenhouse will quickly cause rot.

Foil-faced insulation can serve as a vapor barrier, especially if it is taped at each seam, but most people use 4- or 6-mil polyethylene plastic sheeting. The thicker version is more durable and, because of its extra weight, is easier to install without tearing.

I have found that a vapor barrier is best installed on the side of the studs facing the interior of the greenhouse so that air outside the vapor barrier can flow away from the walls. Because the air in the greenhouse is usually more humid than the air in your home, installing the vapor barrier on the greenhouse side of the studs keeps moisture out of the walls. I do not recommend that you put a second vapor barrier on the outside of the greenhouse, because it will hold in any moisture that made it through the inside barrier and could cause the walls to rot.

Doors

The size of the greenhouse door you install depends on how you plan to use it. If you will be mainly weeding and moving trays of seedlings in and out of the greenhouse, the door can be as narrow as 30 inches, but if you want to be able to get a wheelbarrow or lawn tractor through the door, you will need to make it much wider. Some gardeners fit garage doors to their greenhouses to facilitate moving large volumes of plants and to allow easy vehicle access, though these are more commonly seen in commercial structures as opposed to hobby greenhouses.

Greenhouse doors should be as airtight as possible if you plan to use the structure year-round, to keep cold winter air and wind from blowing on your plants. Install a good-quality door with weather stripping. Wooden or foam-filled doors have the best insulation values. In addition, as we've learned, a screen door installed outside the main door is very useful. Not only does it provide an extra layer of insulation in winter, but in summer it can serve as a means of allowing air to circulate through the greenhouse and keeps insects off plants when the main door is open as well.

Alternative Building Materials

There are a number of alternative building products you can use for greenhouse construction. Many of these combine structural properties with insulation value, often using principles of thermal mass to ensure heat absorption during the day and radiation of this heat back to plants at night. In addition to possibly incorporating the more "formal" alternative methods described below, you might use the ideas of thermal mass in your more traditional greenhouse structure by painting large cans black, filling them with antifreeze, and stacking them on a north-facing wall, where they can absorb and radiate heat. Or you might make a thermal mass "wall" of old tires packed with sand or gravel to provide nighttime heat.

Note that some alternative materials do not offer the structural longevity of those materials in common use.

A Straw-Bale Greenhouse

Straw bales are used more and more for construction, but if you use this method and decide not to wrap or plaster them in any way, you may find that critters like to nest in them and eat the products of your hard work.

If you plan to build a large structure using straw bales, you should support the roof with wood framing so that the straw walls are not bearing the entire load. A typical straw bale has an R-value of 2.5 to 3 per inch of bale; thus, a normal 18-inch bale has an R-value of about 48, which is more than adequate for most greenhouses. Straw bales that are protected by plaster or a kind of stucco applied over chicken wire can last for many decades in some parts of the country.

A temporary straw-bale greenhouse made of three walls with panes of glass or translucent glazing on the front and roof can be used to protect plants in spring. The simplest such structure has a sloping glass front. Old storm windows or old patio doors work perfectly for the front or roof of such a greenhouse.

An Adobe Greenhouse

Adobe, used primarily in the southwestern United States, is a time-tested material for home construction. Original adobe bricks are made from sand and clay with straw or grass added to bind the material. Bricks are allowed to dry in the hot sun and are then cured for several weeks before they are used. Because adobe bricks can absorb moisture and slowly deteriorate, they are often stabilized with the addition of cement or asphalt to the sand and clay. In construction, adobe bricks are joined with a mud mortar, although many builders use regular mortar mix with stabilized bricks to get the same effect. An adobe brick wall can be further stabilized with a coating of mud, lime plaster, or stucco. An adobe wall in a greenhouse provides an excellent thermal mass that may be up to 18 inches thick. The humidity of the greenhouse, however, may expose the wall to moisture, thus causing its deterioration.

Rammed-Earth Walls

Rammed earth is ordinary soil with a high clay content that is compacted in a special machine and made into bricks. Unlike adobe bricks, which are sun-cured, rammed-earth bricks may be baked in a kiln. These bricks can

then be used to build a wall similar to the way concrete blocks or house bricks are used. One pronounced difference: Unlike concrete blocks, rammed-earth bricks tend to be wide and flat, producing a wall that can be 18 to 24 inches thick. An alternative to using bricks is building forms into which you pour the earth mixture, which is then compacted.

The problem with a rammed-earth wall made entirely of compacted soil is that it will be compromised by rain. Consequently, today rammed-earth walls are made with a mixture of earth, clay, sand, gravel, and up to 10 percent cement. Even with this more impervious material, however, rammed-earth greenhouses usually have large eaves. On the plus side, repair of rammed-earth construction is relatively easy and the material does not burn and is vermin-resistant.

Painting the Greenhouse

Unfortunately, greenhouses combine the three elements that most often cause rot in wood and corrosion in metal: heat, moisture, and fungal rot spores. No matter how hard you try to eliminate these, they will almost always be present in your structure. The only option is to protect against them in some way. If your greenhouse frame is made of wood, this is most commonly accomplished by painting, oiling, or staining it. (As discussed on page 80, you must coat even pressure-treated wood or cedar to promote long life or protect chemicals from leaching into the soil.) Painting is not required if the greenhouse frame is made of aluminum, which is naturally protected through the oxidation of the metal, or of anodized aluminum, which has been treated for additional protection.

As for the paint you use, it should be durable because it will be exposed to heat, moisture, solvents you'll use to clean glazing, and the overspray of fertilizers, pesticides, and herbicides (if you use them). This means that you should use oil-based exterior paint both inside and outside the greenhouse. The moisture levels inside the greenhouse will cause indoor paint to peel in a short time. Don't rely on a coat of latex paint to prevent the wood from rotting. Moisture can penetrate latex paints. Home exterior oil-based paints tend to prevent rot for a little while longer, but these do not form an impermeable layer on the wood either. Much as you need to repaint your home every few years, you'll need to repaint your greenhouse — if the wood doesn't begin to rot first. (Note that a heated greenhouse rots faster than an unheated one).

One way to protect wood is to encapsulate it in an epoxy resin such as that available from WEST System or Epiglass from Interlux, and then apply paint or varnish over it. The epoxy prevents moisture from entering the wood but it does not protect against UV radiation, so after applying it, you'll have to paint the wood with a few coats of polyurethane with UV blockers. The best varnishes with the highest levels of UV blocking are Epifanes and Schooner.

If you really want to protect a less expensive wood, I recommend cutting all lumber to size and, before assembling it, undercoating it with a marine epoxy paint such as 545 base (gray) from Awlgrip or Interprime (available in white or gray) from Interlux, and then coating it with a marine topcoat such as brushed or sprayed Awlgrip, Brightside from Interlux, Toplac, or Perfection. (Make sure you use a respirator when spraying paints, and read the manufacturer's safety data.) Brightside and Perfection are polyurethane paints that protect wood from rot; Toplac is a silicone-based paint that is easy to clean and also helps to protect wood. These marine paints are intended for use on wood that will be in a hot, humid environment and they do the job quite well, although they are expensive. Surfaces painted with them can be easily cleaned with the wipe of a sponge.

In my warm greenhouse, I used a conventional oil-based house paint undercoat and topcoated it with an outdoor latex paint. I find that this type combination lasts from 3 to 5 years. It can be cleaned, but eventually the paint gets dirty or the humidity gets to it and causes it to peel.

Note that using white paint ensures that all surfaces reflect the maximum amount of light onto your plants. White also reveals where dirt and condensation are collecting.

In a finish coat, you may prefer the warm look of natural wood as opposed to paint. My experience is that finish products of this kind made for the home stand up to the moisture and humidity of a greenhouse for only a year or two before requiring another application. For a natural look, seal the wood with epoxy and then paint it with a good polyurethane varnish with plenty of UV block for a finish that will last for a number of years without the need for recoating. In my opinion, the best high UV varnishes are Epifanes and Schooner, both boat varnishes that have the best reputation for protecting wood over the long term. The beauty of using epoxy for the first two coats is that it bonds to the wood (it can be removed only by sanding) and it dries within an hour or so.

Some Notes of Caution about Epoxy

If you use epoxy over teak, it will not adhere because of the oils in the wood. It's necessary to wipe the teak with a solvent to remove oils before applying epoxy. According to one manufacturer, the makeup of epoxy is very close to that of polyurethane varnish, thus the varnish, which has UV inhibitors, can easily be applied over the epoxy. To do this, simply lightly sand the epoxy (wear a dust mask), wipe the surface with a solvent, then brush on the varnish. When it comes time to recoat, simply sand the top layer of varnish and varnish it again.

When working with solvents, epoxies, and paints, remember ALWAYS to wear rubber gloves, a dust mask when sanding, and other appropriate protective gear.

TIP

Ideally you should paint building lumber before you assemble the greenhouse and before you install any glazing so that the wood is protected on all sides and surfaces.

7 Glazing

THERE ARE A VARIETY OF materials you can use to glaze your greenhouse: glass, plastic (acrylic, polycarbonate, or polyethylene sheeting), and fiberglass. The best choice for you depends on factors such as the specific material's properties, the amount of light that must be transmitted through the glazing, cost, weight, frequency of glazing maintenance, and the location of the greenhouse. For example, you might intend to use your greenhouse to grow orchids, which favor bright light but not full sun. Consequently, clear glass may not be the best choice. A slightly more opaque material such as tinted fiberglass or a material that diffuses light such as polycarbonate would be more suitable for your plants. Of course, if you really want to use clear glass, you can use one of the shade cloths that block 10 to 75 percent of the light entering the greenhouse. These cloths are available from commercial greenhouse suppliers. (See chapter 5, page 61, for more on shade cloths.)

The frequency of necessary maintenance of glazing also factors in to your ultimate choice. If you have to clean the glazing weekly (because of smoke or other environmental pollutants, or because of falling leaves or bird droppings or other substances that might affect how much light gets to your plants), your greenhouse may become too much of a chore and you may neglect it in a short time. If your glazing requires frequent cleaning, it may acquire small scratches (as is the case with polycarbonate), which may affect the transparency of the product. Of all the glazing products available, glass is the easiest to clean. Next are polycarbonates (given the scratching caveat), but unless it is coated, fiberglass tends to collect dust and dirt, and when it is cleaned, tiny particles dislodge from the material.

How to choose between glass and plastic? Each material has unique properties that make it suitable for certain applications and not for others. For example, though glass is one of the best materials for light transmission, it is heavy and can shatter relatively easily. In an area where large hailstones are likely or in some greenhouse frames, polycarbonate or fiberglass is a better choice than glass for sloping surfaces and roofs.

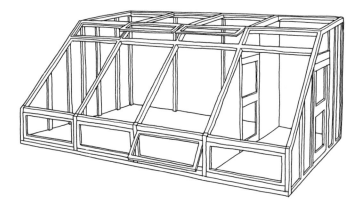

A south-facing, glass-fronted greenhouse incorporates a combination of 1-inch-thick single-pane glass panels supported on rafters laid flat on the vertical walls for the front roof. The north side has an insulated wall and the north roof section is covered with double-pane-glass panels on rafters for insulation and light. The end walls are insulated to retain heat when the cold northeasterly wind blows.

Understanding Light Transmission

While you can supplement greenhouse light with electric light, most of the light in your greenhouse will come from the sun. Solar radiation comes in many wavelengths, but plants use only the wavelengths between 400 and 700 nanometers for photosynthesis, which are approximately the same wavelengths that the human eye sees. Radiation in this wavelength is known as photosynthetically active radiation (PAR). A prism will divide light into the colors of the spectrum, ranging from violet to red. The wavelengths from the blue to the red end of the scale are the ones most used by plants. Certain wavelengths affect growth, while others promote flowering and fruiting. In general, wavelengths toward the red end of the spectrum encourage flowering, while wavelengths toward the blue end of the spectrum tend to make plants shorter and stockier. This is because the amount of energy in a wavelength is inversely proportional to the wavelength. Thus blue, a longer wavelength, doesn't have quite as much energy as red light and doesn't promote a plant's robust growth. Studies have found that plants prefer light from the red end of the spectrum. If you want to grow plants under lights, then you need to look for bulbs that emit wavelengths from this end.

Studies have found that plants prefer light from the red end of the spectrum.

Light loses some of its radiation as it passes through glazing material. The plants may also experience partial shading from greenhouse benches and shelving and other structural elements. Some light is also reflected off the structure and some is absorbed by objects inside the greenhouse. A wood-framed home-built greenhouse may lose as much as 30 percent of the available light from shadows cast by the structure and the glazing. If you have any doubt about how much light is getting into your greenhouse, buy a light meter and take readings both inside the building and outside. The difference between the two figures is the loss of light as it passes to your plants in the structure. Because of the lower light levels inside the greenhouse, take care when moving plants from inside to outside. Because they become used to the lower light inside the structure, outside they cannot develop enough chlorophyll to protect themselves. If moved too abruptly or for too long a period of time, they will often drop leaves or suffer sunburned leaves when exposed to full-strength sunlight. When you bring your plants out of the greenhouse in spring, place them in a slightly shaded area for a month or so, until the leaves have had time to adapt to full sunlight.

Types of Glazing Materials

The initial design of your greenhouse should take into account the type of glazing material that you will be using. As I have pointed out, because it is heavy, glass requires fairly strong structural members that also tend to block more light. Polycarbonate and fiberglass, however, can be installed on a lighter frame of wood, aluminum, steel, or PVC. Polycarbonate allows up to 85 percent of light through the material (the specific amount depends upon the thickness and color of the material), while fiberglass may allow through only 75 to 85 percent of available light. (For direct comparisons of light transmission of various materials, see the chart on page 97.)

You must also consider the expansion and contraction of glazing materials when designing your greenhouse. All glazing materials will expand somewhat as the greenhouse heats up, but the rate of expansion varies dramatically. Glass, for example, expands only a little, but polycarbonates can expand significantly.

Glass Types

For most people, glass is the obvious choice as a glazing material. It is plentiful, can easily be replaced, and has a long life span (some Victorian glasshouses are still in operation with most of their original glass in place). It is resistant to UV degradation and maintains excellent light transmission (as long as you keep it clean). Glass comes in different thicknesses, can be cut to suit a specific application, comes as either clear or with built-in shading, and can fit many aesthetics — you can even get rounded glass panels to make a greenhouse with curved eaves or walls.

Its weight and fragility, however, are important considerations. If you want to use glass in your greenhouse, check your building codes carefully; in many areas, walls and overhead panels are required to be of tempered or laminated glass. I find that the biggest problem with breaking a pane of glass is not so much replacing the pane as it is picking the broken glass out of the plants and growing beds. Of course, if a pane of glass breaks in the middle of winter, you will have to repair the damage as quickly as possible or you could lose plants. Until it's replaced, cover the hole with plywood or plastic right away.

Glass comes in many types. You can choose from regular single-weight or single-thickness, double-weight or double-thickness, tempered, laminated, or double-pane or Thermopane low-emissivity (low-E) or low-resistivity (low-R) glass. Low-E glass has a thin layer on the exterior that allows short-wave solar energy through but blocks long-wave infrared and UV energy. This allows most of the sun's energy through but restricts heat energy from escaping. A low-E coating can give a double-pane window efficiency near or equal to that of a triple-pane window. Generally, about 70 percent of solar heat and about 75 percent of solar light are allowed through low-E glazing. Low-R glazing cuts down on the amount of heat escaping from the greenhouse. (The R-value is the resistance of a material to heat flow.) A window with a high R-value has greater resistance to heat flow. Typically, a single-pane window has an R-value of 2 or 3, while a double-pane window has an R-value of 4 to 6. A triple-pane window may have an R-value as high as 8 or 9. By filling the space between the panes with a gas such as argon or krypton, the R-value can be increased to about 10. This is almost the value of a stud wall (about 11 in older homes and as high as 19 in well-insulated newer construction).

The intended use of your greenhouse should govern the type of glass you select. For example, a greenhouse used for growing understory tropicals in the winter might have triple glazing to keep down heating costs. The lower light levels of triple-pane glass will probably not affect the plants — in fact, more shading may be needed. If your plan is to grow vegetables to market, however, you might decide to use a glass that keeps in heat and allows the transmission of plenty of light.

One problem you should be aware of when you install any type of clear glass is that birds tend to fly into it, even when windows are marked with decals or ornaments to warn the creatures. Necessarily, the glass in a greenhouse must be kept clean, and the green plants inside the greenhouse naturally attract wildlife. Because vertical panes in a greenhouse can take their toll on birds, install a few pieces of reflective tape or other defensive features on many panes to discourage as many avian impacts as possible.

Single-Weight or Single-Strength Glass

The most common glass is single-weight window glass that comes 3/32 inch thick and can be cut to almost any size. From the early days of their construction until the late 1950s, greenhouses were built with fairly small panes of glass that overlapped no more than 1 or 2 inches. Single-weight glass can now be purchased in sheets up to 48 inches by 84 inches, but such large sheets are very fragile and should not be used in a typical greenhouse. The biggest panes that can safely be used are about 24 inches by 24 inches, but again, check local building codes before using panes of this size.

Double-Weight or Double-Strength Glass

Double-weight glass is 1/8 inch thick and can be used for slightly larger spans (it is made in sheets of 72 inches by 120 inches, but this size is generally available only to specialty glass users and may be hard to find). As with single-weight glass, you should check the local building codes to see if it is permissible to glaze a greenhouse with ordinary glass and to learn what pane size is considered too large. The best reason to use double-weight glass in a greenhouse is that it is easy to cut to size, though even if codes do allow it, I do not recommend using it in overhead greenhouse applications.

Plate Glass

Plate glass comes in large sheets and is usually ¼ inch thick, although it can be obtained in thicknesses up to 1 inch. Quite often, you can get plate glass directly from the owner of a store that is being dismantled or from a builder specializing in dismantling old stores. Plate glass doesn't cost much more than double-weight glass and will stand up to much more impact. In addition, because it is stronger than single- or double-weight glass, the panels can span greater distances between supports, which allows more light through, even though the individual supports must be stronger to support these heavier panels. Note that plate glass is quite heavy; just one plate glass sheet may require two or more people just to lift it.

Laminated Glass

Laminated glass consists of two layers of glass bonded on either side of a plastic layer to create a single glass panel. The plastic layer is usually polyvinyl butyral (PVB), but it can also be a resin. This type of glass is also called safety or shatterproof glass because if the glass is shattered, the plastic layer between the panes holds the fragments together to prevent them from falling.

Laminated glass can be made earthquake-resistant, hurricane-resistant, and resistant to the impact of rocks and hail. It can be obtained in a variety of colors and is also fabricated with reinforcing wire running through it. Laminated glass is expensive — three to four times the price of single-pane glass — but must be used if your building codes call for it in overhead structures.

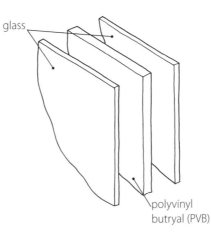

glass

polyvinyl butryal (PVB)

Laminated glass has a layer of PVB (polyvinyl butyral) in the middle of two pieces of glass to minimize damage if the glass shatters.

Tempered Glass

Tempered glass is created by carefully controlling the conditions under which the glass is cooled. It can resist about four times the impact of regular glass and when it fractures, it shatters into tiny fragments, known as *dicing*. If tempered glass falls on you, it is unlikely to cause serious injury because the glass fragments are so small; nevertheless, it can give you some nasty nicks. Because of its unique structure, you cannot cut tempered glass, and it must be ordered sized to fit. It is best used for overhead glazing and for areas that are subject to high winds.

If tempered glass shatters, it goes everywhere and will need to be carefully picked out of beds and off benches. I've found the best way of removing shattered tempered glass from a bed is simply to shovel it away along with a layer of the topsoil. Light transmission of tempered glass is only slightly lower than that of conventional glass of the same thickness, but installation requires great care: If it's bent or catches in any way, it can shatter.

Double-Pane Glass

Often known by the trade name Thermopane, double-pane glass is composed of two layers of glass with an air space between them. The panes are held apart by a beading that contains moisture-absorbing chemicals to keep the space between the panes dry. Light transmission of double-pane glass is lower than that of single-pane glass. Note for installation that the panels are extremely heavy and must be handled very carefully to avoid breaking the seal around the edges that keeps the panes dry. Any amount of bending during installation will break this seal, resulting eventually in moisture entering between the panes and fogging them. If the seal is not replaced, the inside of the glass will become etched and gray, cutting down dramatically on the amount of light it transmits.

You can order double-pane glass in any size, but two standard sizes — 34 inches by 75 inches and 46 inches by 76 inches — are readily available because they are used in 3-foot and 4-foot patio doors, respectively. These standard panes are sometimes referred to as patio glass. The 46-inch by 76-inch panes in my heated greenhouse allow me to heat a 3,000-cubic-foot space with a small, 18,000 BTU propane heater during the worst of winters.

The biggest drawback of double-pane glass is that the seals may eventually break. In my heated greenhouse I have found that the roof panels lose their seals after about 8 to 10 years, while the vertical panels have been installed for 12 years with no failure except as a result of a hurricane. In fact, the vertical panels of double-pane glass used in my house construction have lasted for more than 20 years; only three windows have required seal replacement.

When installing double-pane glass, take care to allow the glass to expand and contract freely. Usually this means mounting vertical panels on small pieces of hard rubber and leaving an expansion gap around the edge of the mounting. Each panel is held in place with quarter round or tapered wooden molding that you can paint to keep the greenhouse looking neat and tidy. Do not allow any nails or screws on the greenhouse structure to touch the glass. This contact can form a pressure point that will eventually break the glass. This means you must build precisely so that the glass does not butt against bare wood or fasteners. I have discovered from experience that a pane of glass resting against a screw in the greenhouse will crack during the first winter, if not earlier.

Triple-Pane Glass

Not only is triple-pane glass expensive, but it also reduces light transmission to half or a third of natural light. In addition, as a drawback to installation, triple-pane glass is extremely heavy. The seals between the panes are also broken very easily. Yet the R-value of triple-pane glass is high, often up to 8. Considering that 3½ inches of fiberglass has an R-value of 11, in some climates triple-pane glass could be used on the north wall of a greenhouse instead of a wood-framed insulated knee wall without the huge heat loss of single- or double-pane glass.

Low-E and MC Low-E Glass

Tempered low-emission (low-E) glass is often recommended for walls of solariums (which have glazed roofs) and sun spaces (which have solid roofs) because it is a safety glass that allows heat into the greenhouse but keeps out UV radiation and cuts down on heat escaping from the structure. More expensive than regular, tempered low-E glass are MC low-E glass and super MC low-E glass. Both of these are UV-resistant and tempered and are recommended for use in roof areas of solariums. Light transmission of low-E glass is 75 percent and that of MC is 65 to 70 percent. Super MC low-E glass is available from Florian. Be aware, however, that low-E glass tends to block the rays that plants need, leading to slow or stunted growth.

Hurricane Glass

With the incidence of hurricane destruction on the rise in a number of areas, various coastal cities have enacted building codes that require the use of hurricane glass in new construction. Before you build, you'll need to determine if these codes are in place in your area. Hurricane glass consists of two layers of glass sandwiching a polycarbonate laminate. The glass is capable of withstanding a blow from a 2×4 stud fired at it at 40 miles per hour. Hurricane glass is very expensive and reduces light transmission.

Storm Windows

If you, like me, are a pack rat, you may have a collection of castoff storm windows that you've saved for use in a greenhouse or cold frame. You can, indeed, build a greenhouse using old storm windows, but most of these windows leak (probably why they were replaced). Rather than using the windows in their casements, it might be better to remove the glass panes from the wooden frames and use them in a frame you construct from scratch.

For many years I've successfully used a cold frame built of storm windows. In it I keep greens growing most of the winter. (See page 31 for an illustration of a cold frame built from old storm windows and project 10 of chapter 13 for building instructions for a cold frame.)

Glass Alternatives

There are a number of alternatives to glass glazing. Most of these come in the form of rigid plastic panels made of polycarbonate, acrylic, PVC (polyvinyl chloride), or fiberglass, or flexible membranes of polyethylene (PE) sheeting, PVC, or ethylvinyl acetate (EVA). Flexible materials may also be reinforced with threads to reduce damage from tearing. All these materials are used in commercial greenhouses and have advantages and disadvantages for use in home greenhouses.

Fiberglass

Fiberglass comes in two forms, flat and corrugated, which is more resistant to flexing. There are hundreds of grades of fiberglass. For a greenhouse, you need the clearest that you can buy (usually not the kind you'd find at your local lumberyard). Because of the glass fibers embedded in the material, it diffuses light well, but it can also yellow with age.

Fiberglass sheets are made either by laying chopped fiberglass pieces, known as a fiberglass mat or chopped strand mat (CSM), on a flat or corrugated surface that has been sprayed with a clear gel and then wetting the fiberglass mat by spraying it with a polyester resin, or by spraying chopped strands of fiberglass coated with resin directly onto the gel coat by using what is known as a chopper gun. The clear resin sets up hard within a few minutes. The fiberglass sheet may be coated with gel on one or both sides and may be squeezed between rollers to make it smooth on both sides. Some types of fiberglass are smooth on only one side. If you buy this type, make sure during installation that the smooth

side is facing the elements. If the rough side faces out, it will trap dirt and be extremely difficult to clean. Eventually the material will hold enough dirt to affect the transmission of light. About the only way to clean old, rough fiberglass is to use a vacuum cleaner to remove the dust and loose particles of fiberglass. During this process, wear a Tyvek suit and a dust mask to keep from getting the particles on your skin and clothes and to keep from inhaling them. Fiberglass that is coated and pressed smooth on both sides is much easier to clean, but it tends to be more opaque.

To its credit, fiberglass is moderately flexible and quite strong. In general, it will last 8 to 10 years and its light transmission is 75 to 85 percent, though Charley's Greenhouse and Garden (see Resources, page 246) offers fiberglass through which up to 93 percent of the available light can pass. Because it is flexible, fiberglass requires more support than glass, but it does have high impact resistance, is easy to handle during installation, and is relatively inexpensive. The biggest drawback of fiberglass is that unless a flame-retardant resin is used in its fabrication, the material is highly flammable. Flame-retardant resins, however, tend to make the material darker, thus reducing light transmission.

If you need an unusually shaped panel for a custom greenhouse, it can be created from fiberglass. To do this, buy chopped strand mat, make a mold from a sheet of glass or wood, spray it with mold-release wax or lay plastic sheeting over it, and lay the mat over the mold. Once the mat has taken the required shape, wet it with polyester resin or epoxy and allow it to set. You can also attach structural reinforcing such as plywood, steel, or plastic supports directly to fiberglass by bonding it to the surface with resin or epoxy. (See chapter 7 for information on installing fiberglass panels.)

Acrylic

Acrylic is known best by trade names such as Plexiglass and Acrylite. The material can be bent using heat (a professional installer will have specialized heating tools for this purpose), stays reasonably clear for many years, is more flexible than glass, and repels the impact of small hailstones (though large rocks or hailstones can crack it). Acrylic is also easy to cut with a slightly blunt saw and can be shaped with ordinary hand tools. Triple-wall acrylic saves up to 25 percent more energy than double-wall while allowing about 80 percent light transmission. Less expensive types of acrylics can yellow and craze, but more expensive types usually come with a 10-year warranty against discoloration and will last up to 30 years. Before buying acrylic panels, check the warranty.

Polycarbonate is reasonably lightweight and can be installed by one person.

One drawback to acrylic is that it can easily be scratched. When installing it, leave the covering paper on the material until all the work is done. You should also be very careful when drilling acrylic during installation. A slight twist or jamming of the drill bit can crack the material. When drilling, it is best to use a slightly blunt drill bit and to cut slowly. Additionally, acrylic is highly flammable. If you use an open-flame heater in your greenhouse, you should not choose this glazing material.

Acrylics for greenhouses come as single panels or double- or triple-wall panels in a variety of thicknesses. The layers of double- or triple-wall sheets are separated by a rib placed roughly every 3 to 6 inches. A ³⁄₁₆-inch sheet is often used for commercial hoop houses because it can easily be bent to suit the arch of the greenhouse frame. When purchasing acrylic panels, look at the R-value and the amount of light the material transmits. (This information can usually be found on the manufacturer's Web site or in the brochure available where you'll be buying the product. See Resources for acrylic panel manufacturers.) In choosing the thickness of the material, take into consideration this data as well as the application. For example, on a greenhouse roof you can install ½-inch or ¾-inch glazing to prevent

too much heat loss but use only ¼-inch or ³⁄₈-inch on the walls to allow more light transmission. Acrylic is a great material to use for larger greenhouses because sheets can be obtained in 4-foot widths and up to 40-foot lengths.

Polycarbonate

Like acrylic, polycarbonate comes in either double- or triple-wall panels. There are many brand names for polycarbonate, such as Suntuf, Palgard, and Macrolux. Double-wall panels can save about 30 percent more heat than single-wall panels while allowing through about 85 percent of the available light. Also available is a white double-wall, sometimes called opal polycarbonate, that blocks about 50 percent of direct sunlight and diffuses the light that does get through. This glazing is good for greenhouses where plants need to be protected from any strong, direct sunlight. Standard sheet sizes are 48 inches long by 72 inches wide, but you can obtain lengths up to 36 feet. The R-value for double-wall polycarbonate is about 1.6 and for triple-wall it is 2.1 — close to the value for glass.

Polycarbonate is reasonably lightweight and can be installed by one person. If you install it yourself, however, you must take care because the material expands and shrinks a good deal more than glass. In addition, the ribs that separate the two or three layers of the material must run vertically to allow moisture to drain from the panels. With polycarbonate that has been coated with a UV blocker, you'll need to make sure that the panels are installed so that the blocker faces the elements. There are also hidden costs with polycarbonate installation: You'll need to cap the ends of the panels, install glazing tape and sealant to seal all joints, and install bar caps on the ends of the sheets.

Some extremely strong polycarbonate sheets such as Suntuf, Palgard, and Palsun have greater impact resistance than glass. These allow more than 90 percent light transmission, are almost unbreakable, and weigh less than half as much as glass and only 43 percent as much as aluminum. Macrolux, a polycarbonate manufactured by Co-Ex Corporation, has the highest impact

The Properties of Various Glazing Materials

MATERIAL	LIFE SPAN IN YEARS	MAINTENANCE	STRUCTURAL VALUE	INSULATION (R-VALUE)	DEGRADATION	LIGHT TRANSMISSION (PAR)
Glass (single pane)	Indefinite	Low	Strong	2 to 8	Low	About 90%
Polycarbonate (6 mil double-wall)	10–15	Low to Moderate	Medium	3–6	Low to Medium	About 80%
Acrylic (double-wall)	8–12	Low to Moderate	Medium	2–6	Low to Medium	About 85%
Fiberglass (single-wall)	8–12	Moderate	Light	1–4	Medium	About 90%
Polyethylene sheeting (single layer)	1–2	Moderate to High	Light	1-3	Medium to High	About 85%
PVC sheeting (single layer)	3–5	Moderate	Light	1-2	Medium to High	About 85%

resistance of any co-extruded thermoglazing. Consider these materials if you live in an area where your glazing is exposed to hailstones, golf balls, small tree limbs, small animals, or other sources of potential breakage.

Plastic Sheeting

Flexible sheeting such as polyethylene (PE) sheeting and polyvinyl chloride (PVC) has a relatively short life span, often as little as one season, although most sheets will last at least two seasons before UV radiation breaks down the material beyond use. If you purchase commercial-grade PVC intended for greenhouse use, it will last longer than industrial grade PVC, but as I mentioned earlier, it is for use only on metal-framed structures. The biggest drawback to flexible sheeting is that snow loads and wind can destroy the material in a few weeks. My experience with both building polyethylene and greenhouse PVC is that they tend to split along the folds, but you can use either duct tape or a commercially available repair tape to make a serviceable repair and extend the life of the covering. Another negative is that it doesn't have a very high insulation value. In fact, it raises the inter-

nal temperature of a greenhouse by only a few degrees. Benefits of polyethylene sheeting are that it transmits plenty of light, it is inexpensive, and it is easy to install. A 100-foot roll can be purchased for less than $200 and comes in various widths up to 50 feet.

For greater longevity and heat retention of the material, you can install two layers of polyethylene sheeting on your greenhouse with an air space between them. In fact, some commercial growers who use hoop houses blow warm air between the layers. Not only does this insulate the greenhouse, but it also creates more stability for the plastic and requires just a small blower fan, although, due to air leaks, the fan will run almost continuously. To create two layers, fasten one sheet to the inside of a wooden frame with wooden strips cut to size and the other layer on the outside of the frame. Typically, two layers of plastic sheeting as compared to a single layer cut light levels by about 10 percent but increase the energy savings by up to 40 percent. One problem with a dual-sheet system is condensation between the layers, which can reduce the energy savings and cut light levels even further.

Combining Glazing Materials

Combining glazing materials can address specific weather conditions in various areas and can add insulation value. In regions where winters are especially severe, for instance, you might install double- or triple-wall polycarbonate with an inner liner of polyethylene sheeting. You can also use an inner layer of sheeting beneath single-pane glass. The air space between the panels or panes and the sheeting helps insulate the plants. In Britain, many gardeners install a layer of bubble wrap inside their greenhouse to help reduce energy losses. Bubble wrap can readily be purchased from many packing suppliers, shipping stores, and office supply stores in widths up to 4 feet for under $20 per 50-foot roll. As I mentioned earlier, clear polyethylene or weatherproofing tape can be used to tape bubble wrap to the greenhouse structure to eliminate drafts. While bubble wrap slightly lowers light transmission levels, the additional insulation it provides protects plants from freezing and helps to promote growth in cooler conditions.

Caulking and Weather Stripping

Using the right caulking and weather stripping material will prolong the life of your greenhouse and glazing, prevent water from entering the structure and heat from escaping it, make it easier to paint, and make it much easier to remove and insert a new pane of glass or sheet of plastic should one get broken. Varieties of caulking (whether from a tube or a roll) are most often applied directly onto the wood or metal frame and the glass or polycarbonate glazing is then pressed into it. It's important to note that caulking is not glue and should not be relied upon to hold the glazing.

There are many types of caulking. Selecting the right one for the job is important to getting good adherence and a good seal. For your greenhouse, the best type of caulking is butyl or polybutyl, which allows you to install and easily remove glass for repairs. A bead of adhesive caulking will certainly do the job, but should you have to replace or repair a pane or sheet of glazing, it will be impossible to remove the piece without breaking it. If you use butyl or polybutyl caulking and mechanical fastenings to secure the glazing, making repairs will be simple.

Before you caulk, wearing rubber gloves, wipe the area with a solvent or degreaser such as acetone or 3M's general-purpose adhesive remover to eliminate grease, dirt, and other residue. This will give the caulking better adhesion. Apply tube caulking from a caulking gun or unroll a strip before you install the glazing. (Strip caulking is most convenient to use in areas where glazing must be lowered onto caulking.) When the glass is in place, use tube caulking from a caulking gun to seal the gap between the glass and the greenhouse structure. Caulking guns can be purchased for a few dollars from any hardware store. Before fitting the tube in the gun, cut the tip of the tube nozzle at a slight angle so that the caulking will come out of the tube in a bead. You may have to use a spatula or a finger to smooth a bead once you lay it. If you decide to use your finger, wear a rubber glove for easy cleanup or, as Don Mather, a glazier and building contractor in Middleton, New Hampshire, says, wet your finger and smooth the bead. Be warned that there is a knack to this and if you don't do it right, you can end up with sticky fingers!

After you have applied the caulking, use a rag and solvent to clean up the area. Try to clean up the caulking before it dries, or you may have to remove it with a knife or razor blade, which could scratch the paint job, the frame, or the glazing.

Types of Caulking and Sealants

Silicone is the most often used adhesive caulking primarily because users are not aware of other types of caulking that could be more suitable. When choosing a type of caulking for your greenhouse, look for one that stays flexible, does not yellow, and can be painted (if you paint your greenhouse).

Silicone

Silicone caulking has high UV resistance and because they are water-cured, most silicones emit no volatile organic compounds (VOCs) when they are applied. Silicone applied on very humid days will cure faster, and in most environments it will dry to a tack-free stage in 3 hours, but you should allow at least 24 hours for the caulking to cure completely. The benefits of silicone sealants are that they are clear and noncorrosive and they provide a good seal without a great deal of effort, though their adhesive strength is low compared to other types of caulking, such as polyurethanes and polysulphides. Silicone caulking cannot be painted, however; it must be applied to painted surfaces or purchased in a color similar to that of anodized aluminum. Note that the strength of the seal of silicone applied over a painted surface often relies on the strength of the paint surface itself, which may be low. When it comes time to remove a silicone sealant, often the paint surface peels away with it.

Silicone stays flexible for a long time, but brands that are less expensive can allow mold growth, which may cause rot in wooden surfaces. Some more expensive marine silicones are usually made with fungicides and UV inhibitors. While there is no real silicone remover, a lacquer remover will get it off hard surfaces or a razor blade can be used to remove it from glass after it has cured.

Polyurethane

Polyurethane sealants have strong adhesive qualities and great strength. Typically, they are used where a permanent seal is required. Polyurethanes cure to tacky in about 24 to 48 hours and set up fully in 4 to 7 days. One drawback is that they may yellow when exposed to sunlight.

Polysulphide

Sulfur-based with high adhesive properties, this is one of the most commonly used sealants available. Polysulphides come in a variety of colors and are priced in the middle of the spectrum of caulking. They stay flexible over their lifetime, are not affected by most liquids, and can be painted and sanded. Because they are sulfur-based, however, polysulphides can degrade some plastics and acrylics. (If you have any doubts about its effects on your greenhouse plastics, make a test in an inconspicuous place or on a spare piece of polycarbonate or acrylic glazing. Allow it cure for several days before you apply it to your structure.) Polysuphides reach the tack-free stage in times that vary from 30 minutes to 3 days, depending on the brand.

Butyl

This low-adhesion, rubber-based material is used mostly as a sealant rather than as caulking. It comes in a variety of colors and prices.

Compounds

Typically, compounds try to combine the best qualities of different caulking and sealants and eliminate the problematic qualities of each. One such compound is Bostik Marine 940 Fast Set, a nonyellowing polymer sealant blended from sylilated polyethylene, silicone, and urethane. Compounds made from silicone and polyurethane are designed to be low in odor and to have moderately strong adhesion.

Two-Part Sealants

For any greenhouse that might move with heat or wind pressure, you should use a two-part polysulphide sealant that cures to a rubbery stage. Many manufacturers make such a product. The sealant remains flexible; resists cleaners, oils, and petroleum products; and is designed to adhere well to wood surfaces and to bend or flex with the wood. These sealants were developed for marine use, where flexibility in the face of heat, wind, and water is important.

Weather Stripping

If you intend to heat the greenhouse, it pays to apply weather stripping around window and door openings. This will stop stray drafts and help cut your heating bill. The most common type is a spongy material with adhesive on one side. Pressed into place in a door or window frame, it allows the door or window to be closed tightly against it. Weather stripping costs very little in relation to the amount of energy that it saves.

Checklist for a New Greenhouse

The questions here are intended to help you determine what you want in a greenhouse, what will serve your needs, and how building your greenhouse might be realized. Think of this as a worksheet that can be filled out early on to help guide you in the process of achieving the best greenhouse for you and that can help you determine costs for a variety of scenarios.

1 Determine Your Greenhouse Use

You will use your greenhouse for:
- ☐ Hobby growing
- ☐ Growing for a roadside stand
- ☐ Growing and propagating plants for sale

Besides using it for growing, you will use the greenhouse:
- ☐ To house a swimming pool
- ☐ As a recreational area
- ☐ To heat your home

Note: *For these uses, a greenhouse attached to your home, rather than a freestanding structure, will better meet your needs.*

What will you grow in your greenhouse?
- ☐ Flowers
- ☐ Orchids
- ☐ Other tropical plants
- ☐ Vegetables
- ☐ Fruit

Note: *Your answers to these questions will determine not only the kind of greenhouse you build, but also whether it will be heated and what systems you will need to install to control the greenhouse environment.*

2 Assess Your Site

Size of site (in feet):

length: _____

width: _____

possible height: _____

Note: *For an attached greenhouse, the site may be limited by your house. Sometimes windows, trees, wires, or eaves limit the possible height of a structure.*

Greenhouse access (in feet):
- ☐ To the garden
- ☐ To the house
- ☐ To easily navigated paths, walkways, or driveways
- ☐ To power and water lines

Light available at site:
How much daily sun does the site receive and at what times of day?

_____

_____

_____

_____

In which direction does the site face (north, northeast, south, east, northwest, other)?

_____

How much sun will the site receive around July 20 (the longest day) and December 20 (the shortest day)?

_____

_____

Condition of site:

Is the site in a frost pocket?

☐ Yes   ☐ No

If so, how can you ameliorate this?

_____

_____

_____

Is the site likely to get flooded?

☐ Yes   ☐ No

If so, can you prevent flooding with landscape or other changes?

_____

_____

_____

_____

Does the site have good drainage?

☐ Yes   ☐ No

Is the prevailing wind direction from the north?

☐ Yes   ☐ No

Note: *If the site receives cool north winds, you may have to consider a greenhouse with an insulated north wall to save on heating costs.*

3 Determine Whether You Will Order a Kit, Build It Yourself, or Hire a Builder

Once you have a clear idea of how you will use your greenhouse and where it will be located, it's time to decide either to order a greenhouse kit or to draw up plans and a materials list, and to determine whether you will build the structure yourself or hire a builder. Of course, part and parcel of this decision is cost. The following portion of the checklist will guide you in your decision. When making up a materials list or kit greenhouse list, try to be as specific as possible about materials you will use or the model you will order so that you can make the most realistic cost estimate possible.

If you plan to order a kit:

Create a list of local retailers and Internet companies for research and cost comparison. Use Resources (pages 246–248) for some source information. Determine how long each vendor has been in business.

_____

_____

_____

_____

_____

For each model you are considering, is the **glazing** glass (single-, double-, or triple-pane), polycarbonate, acrylic, or fiberglass? Is an alternate glazing package available?

_____

_____

_____

_____

_____

Checklist for a New Greenhouse *(continued)*

For each model you are considering, determine what materials are used for the **frame** and how sturdily it is constructed.

_____

_____

_____

_____

_____

Note: *Metal structures tend to lose heat faster than do wooden ones. Make sure the structure is sturdy enough so that it will not twist or rack in high winds and so that it can be taken apart should it need to be moved or should you need to repair it.*

For each model you are considering, determine the **size of the structure** and the available storage in each.

_____

_____

_____

_____

_____

Note: *If a particular structure does not have adequate storage, you may need to build a potting shed or find another place to store tools, pots, wheelbarrows, and so forth.*

For each model you are considering, determine the **kind of benches** included and what sizes they are.

_____

_____

_____

_____

_____

Note: *Freestanding benches are preferable to ones that attach to the greenhouse structure because if a bench collapses, it won't bring down the greenhouse with it. When siting the greenhouse, the highest benches and shelves should be on the north side so they won't interfere with light transmission.*

What is each greenhouse's **warranty**? Is it warranted for at least 1 year after installation? Is an extended warranty available?

_____

_____

_____

_____

Note: *Before erecting a kit greenhouse, check your insurance to see if the structure is covered if the glazing or structure breaks after the warranted period of time. Also check to see if your plants are insured and if any of your tools are insured if they're stolen.*

Can **damaged or broken parts** for each greenhouse be replaced easily?

_____

_____

_____

If you, the consumer, are supposed to construct the greenhouse, determine for each if **adequate manuals, directions, videos, tools, and support** are provided; how difficult assembly is; and how long it takes an average owner to assemble.

_____

_____

_____

_____

_____

Note: Particularly check the glazing installation process. The glazing should be relatively easy to install.

Determine if vendors for each greenhouse offer after-construction **support and help** with greenhouse operation.

_____

_____

_____

If the vendor's team is to construct the greenhouse, are the **workers bonded and insured**?

_____

_____

_____

For each structure you may order, what are the **shipping requirements and costs**?

_____

_____

_____

_____

_____

Note: Make sure that somebody will be home to check for damage or an incomplete delivery when the greenhouse arrives.

For each greenhouse you may purchase, determine if it requires a **foundation** (and what type) or **anchors** and note the cost here (see step 4, page 104).

_____

_____

_____

_____

_____

For each greenhouse you may purchase, determine what **levels of winds and severe storms** it is made to withstand.

_____

_____

For each greenhouse you may purchase, determine from vendor information approximate **heating and cooling costs** and what systems these costs are based upon.

_____

_____

_____

_____

_____

For each greenhouse you may purchase, **add together** the kit cost; the cost of a foundation (if required); and the cost of purchasing and installing electricity, plumbing, and heating (if required or you choose to include them).

_____

_____

_____

_____

TOTAL COST OF THE KIT GREENHOUSE YOU WILL PURCHASE: _____

Checklist for a New Greenhouse (continued)

***If you plan to have a greenhouse built
or plan to build your own:***

Will you hire the services of an architect?

☐ Yes   ☐ No

A. Total cost of architect's services: _____

*Note: If you are going to hire an architect, you will need to get
estimates for the cost of drawings, determine precisely what the
architect will provide, determine how the architect will work
with the contractor, and work up a contract.*

Will your greenhouse require specialty work and the plans
that go with such work?

☐ Yes   ☐ No

Collect names and contact information for builders you may
use.

_____

_____

_____

_____

Does each builder act as a contractor who hires any sub-
contractors (e.g., electrician, plumber) that may be necessary
or will you be responsible for acting as contractor and hiring
subs?

_____

_____

_____

Will you need a building permit?

☐ Yes   ☐ No

B. Total cost of building permit: _____

Will you need a zoning permit and what are the specific
glazing and structural materials required to comply with
building and/or zoning codes?

_____

_____

_____

_____

_____

_____

C. Total cost of zoning permit: _____

*Note: You can usually obtain information on permits and the
permits themselves from city or town offices.*

---

4 Determining Costs If You Plan to Have a Greenhouse Constructed or to Build One Yourself

Cost of the foundation and floor:

☐ No foundation

☐ Wood frame (include size and cost of landscape timbers)

_____

☐ Concrete slab (include size, cost of materials and formwork, and volume/cost of concrete)

_____

☐ Concrete foundation wall (include size, cost of materials and formwork, volume/cost of concrete, and cost of
stucco or brick facing if you will use either)

_____

☐ Concrete block wall (include size and number/cost of
blocks and mortar)

_____

☐ Stone wall (include size of wall and cost of mason)

_____

☐ Brick wall (include size and cost of bricks and mortar)

_____

☐ Adobe (include size and cost)

_____

☐ Straw bale (include size and cost)

_____

☐ Other (recycled or alternative materials; include size and cost)

_____

☐ Cost of rentals and tool purchases (e.g., concrete mixer, tools)

_____

Floor of greenhouse
  ☐ Dirt
  ☐ Concrete slab (include size and cost; see above for figures)

_____

  ☐ Crushed stone/gravel (include quantity and cost)

_____

  ☐ Brick or stone (include size and cost)

_____

D. Total cost of foundation and floor: _____

Note: *Be sure to add in cost of insulation and cost of installation of electrical lines and plumbing (e.g., drainpipes) that pass through the foundation, if these are required.*

Cost of preparing the site:
Cost of marking and grading site _____

Cost of excavating the site _____

Cost of excavating for water and electricity lines _____

E. Total cost of site preparation: _____

Note: *If you are in an area that gets frost (see the USDA Zone map on page 249), you will need to install a greenhouse foundation that extends below the frost line. This will increase the excavation and foundation costs.*

Cost of glazing:
In areas where temperatures are likely to fall below freezing for a week or more during winter and where the greenhouse will be heated, glazing might be double-pane glass or double- or triple-wall polycarbonate. In areas where you have a month or more of subfreezing weather, consider triple-pane glazing to reduce heating costs.

Type of glazing
  ☐ Glass (choose from single-weight, double-weight, plate, tempered, laminated, double-pane, triple-pane)
  ☐ Polycarbonate (choose from single-wall, double-wall, triple-wall)
  ☐ Acrylic (choose from single-wall, double-wall, triple-wall)
  ☐ Polyethylene sheeting (choose from 4 mil, 6 mil, or commercial sheeting)

Area to be glazed _____

Size of glazing (size of panes, sheets) and total amount needed (allow 10 to 15 percent extra for cutting and trimming)

Checklist for a New Greenhouse *(continued)*

Note: *Small panes of glass are easier to install but they usually overlap, which sets up the scenario for moisture to enter and algae to grow. Large panes of glass require more support but offer a greater clear area for light transmission. Large pieces of polycarbonate bend rather than break when hit by golf balls and hailstones.*

Cost of glazing material _____

Cost of caulking (include type) _____

Cost of trim bars or strips _____

Cost of rubber wedges _____

Cost of screws and nails _____

F. Total cost of glazing: _____

Cost of building the structure:

Type of structure

☐ Steel

☐ Aluminum

☐ Wood (choose from pressure-treated, cedar, oak, regular dimensional lumber to be painted)

☐ Plastic

Materials (confer with your builder or gather yourself based on plans; include specific dimensions)

_____

_____

_____

_____

_____

Amount and dimensions of lumber/other frame material

_____

_____

_____

_____

_____

Cost of lumber/frame materials: _____

Number/dimensions of windows and doors

_____

_____

_____

Cost of windows and doors _____

Fasteners (includes nails, screws, bolts, etc.)

_____

_____

_____

Cost of fasteners _____

Other hardware (includes backing plates, knobs and pulls, hinges, etc.)

_____

_____

_____

Cost of hardware: _____

G. Total cost of structure: _____

Cost of heating the structure:

Note: *If you will not be heating your greenhouse, skip this section.*

Determine the number of heating degree days for your area. (Heating degree days are determined by the National Weather Service.) _____

What type of heating system do you plan to use?

☐ Electric
Cost of heater and installation _____

Cost to run heater_____

☐ Propane
Cost of heater, storage tank, and venting system and installation _____

Cost to run heater _____

☐ Natural gas
Cost of heater, storage tank, and venting system and installation _____

Cost to run heater_____

☐ Wood-burning stove
Cost of heater and installation _____

Cost to run heater _____

☐ Solar mass
Cost of tons of rock or water and setting up system _____

Cost to run fan or water heater _____

Do you plan on installing a backup heating system?
☐ Yes ☐ No

If so, list the type and cost _____

Do you plan to install thermostats and temperature-control systems?
☐ Yes ☐ No

If so, list the cost (include wiring and piping costs, breakers, etc.) _____

Cost of heating safety inspection _____

H. Total cost of heating _____

Cost of ventilating the structure:

What type of vents will you install?

☐ Natural vents (windows that can be opened; cost included in total cost of structure)

☐ Windows with automatic openers
Cost of automatic window openers: _____

☐ Fan (to circulate air through the greenhouse)
Cost of fan _____

Cost of installing fan (wiring, etc.) _____

Cost of running fan _____

☐ Blower (to blow hot air out of the greenhouse)
Cost of blower _____

Cost of installing blower (wiring, etc.) _____

Cost of running blower _____

I. Total cost of ventilation: _____

Checklist for a New Greenhouse *(continued)*

Cost of plumbing the structure:
Note: *If you will not be plumbing your greenhouse, skip this section.*

Cost of digging a trench for a water line from your house to the greenhouse (if your area freezes, you must install the water line beneath the frost line) _____

Cost of drilling through house's existing basement wall

_____

Length and cost of piping to be installed

_____

Cost of additional materials (such as sand to cover pipe)

_____

Cost for plumber to hook up valves at both ends of the pipe

_____

Cost of plumbing work inside greenhouse (sink, spigots, etc.) _____

J. Total plumbing cost: _____

Note: *If you will have a fixture such as a pool or hot tub in your greenhouse, include cost of fixture and plumbing.*

Cost of electrifying the structure:
Note: *If you will not be using electricity in your greenhouse, skip this section.*

Cost of breaker or breaker panel _____

Length of outdoor wiring required and cost _____

Cost of conduit to protect wire _____

Number of greenhouse outlets and cost _____

Number of fixtures in the greenhouse and cost
☐ Incandescent lights _____

☐ Fluorescent lights _____

Electrical installation cost _____

Cost to run lights and other electrical appliances _____

K. Total electrical costs: _____

Note: *If you will have a fixture such as a pool or hot tub in your greenhouse, include cost of electrifying fixture.*

Cost of Greenhouse Accessories/Furnishings
What types of benches will you use?
☐ Wire-topped wooden
Number and dimensions: _____

Cost of wire-mesh topped: _____

☐ Wood-topped
Number and dimensions: _____

Cost of wood-topped: _____

☐ Hydroponic
Number and dimensions _____

Cost of hydroponic _____

☐ Plastic
Number and dimensions _____

Cost of plastic _____

What other accessories will you install?

☐ Shelves
Number of shelves _____

Cost of shelving and brackets/mounting hardware _____

☐ Potting bench
Cost of building (see chapter 13, page 245,
for a materials list) _____

Cost of purchasing bench _____

☐ Storage cupboard or locker
Cost of building _____

Cost of purchasing _____

☐ Propagation mat
Cost of propagation mat _____

☐ Growing chamber
Cost of building _____

L. Total cost of greenhouse accessories: _____

Finish landscaping around the greenhouse:
☐ New shrubs and plantings
Cost of shrubs and plantings _____

Cost of installation _____

☐ Path to greenhouse
Cost of excavating (if necessary) _____

Cost of materials (crushed bluestone and bricks or
stone and sand or cost of concrete) _____

M. Total cost of finish landscaping: _____

TOTAL COST OF BUILDING A GREENHOUSE
(add A–M plus 10–15 percent for contingencies
and any overruns): _____

8 The Foundation

A NUMBER OF GREENHOUSES are built on some form of foundation, slab, or base to anchor them and provide a level area on which to build. Other, less permanent greenhouses are sited directly on the ground and are anchored by reinforcing bars or U-shaped rods driven into the soil or they are set on wooden beams installed in the ground. Typically, greenhouses in areas where the ground freezes are built on a foundation, while those in areas where the ground does not freeze can be anchored to the ground.

Before installing a foundation with or without a slab, *you must determine where the water line, electrical lines, and any drains will pass through the foundation wall.* These items may have to be roughly installed before concrete is poured and construction begins. For example, you might decide that the greenhouse will have a center floor drain. Because the floor should slope slightly toward the drain in order for it to work optimally, a contractor (or you, if you are doing the work yourself) should keep this requirement in mind before work is begun. Likewise, if you intend to bring electrical lines into the greenhouse through an underground line, the conduit for the line must be built into the foundation.

This chapter first focuses on describing the various types of greenhouse foundations and masonry walls that can be constructed, then provides more detailed explanation of the building process for each.

Types of Foundations

Foundations can be made of a variety of materials: concrete, wood, brick, concrete block, rock, and even straw bales. Before you start building, you must determine what type of base or foundation is best for the greenhouse you want to construct and any requirements specific to your area (such as the depth the ground freezes to in the winter). If you plan on growing in the ground, your foundation may be simply a wooden perimeter of 4×4s either partially buried or lying on grade level. Other, more permanent or substantial options include a poured concrete footer with or without a poured or masonry knee wall and a poured concrete slab.

The Least Expensive Option

Using the ground itself is the least expensive option for a greenhouse base or foundation. This type works best if you are going to grow directly in the ground as opposed to on benches. Without a reliable anchoring system, however, a strong windstorm or hurricane is likely to damage or destroy the structure. A friend of mine placed a small hobby greenhouse on a growing bed and anchored it with bent metal rods hammered into the ground. In a gale the greenhouse blew off, leaving a trail of plastic and broken metal parts strewn across the neighbor's property.

One quick and simple way to anchor a hoop house is to hammer short lengths of rebar deep into the ground and fit the pipes of the greenhouse frame over them.

Another method is to hammer the straight portion of J-shaped bars into the ground (these bars can be made by bending each piece of ⅜-inch rebar into a J) with the hook of the J bent over the base plate of the greenhouse. You may want to drill holes in the base plate of the structure to accept the J-bar so that the base plate doesn't split or rout out a shallow strip in the wood for the hook of the J-bar. The number and spacing of these anchors will depend on how windy it is in your area, how solidly you want to anchor your greenhouse, and the size of the structure.

Another option is to cut 4×4 or 6×6 posts to suit the perimeter of your greenhouse and bury them to grade level so that your greenhouse can be bolted to them. Before you decide to use treated lumber, you should note that the chemicals used to preserve it are known to leach into the soil. This is true of both landscape timbers (whose ends have been soaked in preservative) and pressure-treated wood. (See chapter 6, page 79, for more on using pressure-treated wood.) If you decide to build a wooden foundation of any kind for your greenhouse, use the somewhat safer ACQ (alkaline copper quaternary) or CA (copper azole) pressure-treated wood, both of which have replaced the banned CCA pressure-treated wood in most home centers. Or, to avoid the issue of leaching altogether, you can use cypress (available mostly in the South) or any of the naturally durable, rot-resistant woods discussed in chapter 6.

The best anchoring system involves digging a hole at each corner of the greenhouse (and in the middle if the structure is more than 8 feet long), setting a 6- or 8-inch-diameter fiber form tube (such as a Sonotube) about a foot to 18 inches into each hole, and filling it to grade level with concrete. (The amount of concrete required is so small that a few bags of ready-mix concrete should do the job.) While the concrete is still wet, embed a bolt in the center top of each filled tube. The greenhouse can then be safely bolted to these concrete pilings.

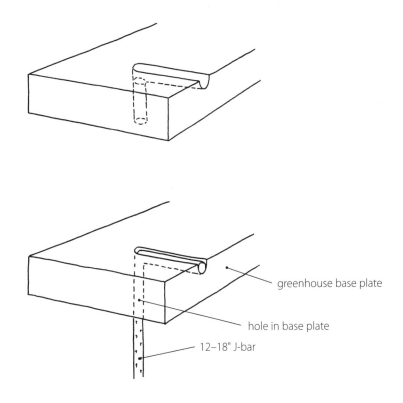

greenhouse base plate

hole in base plate

12–18" J-bar

A simple greenhouse such as a hoop house can be anchored to the ground by securing the base plate to the ground via J-bars hammered into the soil.

Some drawbacks to setting a greenhouse directly on the ground are that animals can easily tunnel under the sides; if you live in a colder climate, the ground inside the greenhouse will freeze just as it does outdoors; and you will need to install some form of walkway in the greenhouse between growing beds to avoid trudging back and forth in the dirt and mud. To help prevent animals from getting into your greenhouse, you can bury a row of hardware mesh or chicken wire at the edges of the structure.

The Concrete Footing and Foundation Wall

A simple poured-concrete footing about 4 inches to 6 inches wide is an easy greenhouse foundation to build and serves as a necessary base for a concrete or masonry greenhouse knee wall, which often extends from it. In areas where the ground freezes, you can set the footing below the frost line and erect a foundation wall to grade level or even higher. Some greenhouses are built with a 2- or 3-foot-high concrete, stone, or brick wall set on a footing or with a wall as high as the tops of the interior benches to enable out-of-sight under-bench storage. Remember that before you pour any concrete foundation and/or slab, you must locate and install your water line and drain line(s).

Poured-concrete posts (using fiber form tubes as molds) can serve as footers of sorts on which is set a deck or a wooden platform or beams that act as a base for the greenhouse (see project 6, chapter 13).

Adding a poured-concrete wall to the footing increases the expense of the foundation but gives your greenhouse a sense of permanence. In many cases a concrete foundation wall is simply an extension of the greenhouse footing and, like it, is usually 4 to 6 inches thick. It may extend anywhere from 6 inches above grade to the height of the benches installed in the structure, though higher walls are usually not left as exposed concrete but are instead covered with

brick or stone to make them more attractive or are made entirely of masonry construction. If you plan on facing a poured-concrete footing and wall with brick, remember that the foundation will have to be stepped to create a shelf on which the brick face will rest (see the illustration on page 129). This is an important consideration in building your forms and pouring the concrete. (For more information, see Masonry Foundations and Walls, page 114, and Constructing a Brick Foundation, page 129.) By installing a greenhouse on a foundation wall, you can increase its overall height.

Make sure a foundation wall is well insulated before the area is backfilled. On my greenhouse I used 2 inches of polystyrene insulation on the walls, and the beds inside have yet to freeze. Just remember that polystyrene insulation requires flashing along the top to prevent water from getting down between the insulation and the concrete.

Concrete Amounts for Fiber Form Tubes

TUBE DIAMETER IN INCHES	CUBIC YARDS OF CONCRETE FOR 1 FOOT OF HEIGHT
6	.007
8	.013
10	.020
12	.029
14	.04
16	.062
18	.065
20	.081
22	.098
24	.116

Thus, for a 4-foot-long fiber form tube 12 inches in diameter, you will need 4 × .029 = .116 cubic yard of concrete and if you have six supports in all you'll need .69 yard of concrete. Such a small amount of concrete will probably not be available from a concrete supplier, meaning that you'll probably have to mix it yourself. Many builders remove the tubes after the concrete has set, although they can be left in place. It depends on whether you want to look at concrete or cardboard until the cardboard rots off. Note that each concrete piling should have a post anchor for the wood sitting on top.

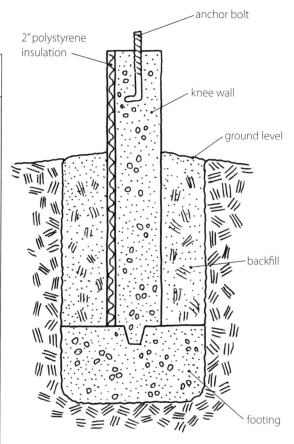

A concrete knee wall is poured as an extension of a concrete footing and, like the footing, is usually 4 to 6 inches thick.

What Is Concrete?

Concrete is composed of sand, Portland cement (a mixture of limestone and clay or marl), water, and aggregate (varying from fine to coarse — sand is a fine aggregate and gravel or crushed stone as large as 1½ inches per piece is coarse). For a greenhouse base or concrete slab, sand or gravel is most often used as the aggregate. Mixed with these four basic materials are additives such as calcium chloride (which helps the concrete to cure more quickly), fiberglass strands (which help to bind the concrete when it is curing), and other materials to increase its strength or to help it to set in colder weather. The ratio of the three primary ingredients is one part cement, two parts sand, and three parts aggregate, with water added to obtain the desired consistency.

The function of water in the mix is to hydrate the ingredients and allow them to be worked. Too much water produces a sloppy mix that will pour easily but will take a long time to cure and will be weaker than a thicker mixture. The ideal mix is one that is close to the consistency of nutty peanut butter. When adding water, use enough to wet the mixture without leaving dry patches. If your dry mixture is perfectly dry, you'll need about 6 gallons of water for each 94-pound bag of concrete; usually, however, the sand or aggregate may be a little wet, meaning you'll need less water to get just the right mixture.

If you buy ready-mixed concrete or a bagged concrete mixture, there are five basic types, referred to as types 1 through 5. For a greenhouse, you'll need type 1 unless the greenhouse foundation or base is being poured during winter, in which case type 3 will provide a faster set with some protection against colder weather.

Some of the pluses of a foundation wall are that animals cannot get into the greenhouse, it's a permanent and secure base for your greenhouse, and setting a greenhouse on a taller foundation wall increases headroom in the structure.

The Concrete Slab

If you're not going to grow directly in the ground in the greenhouse, consider installing a poured-concrete slab either inside a poured footing and foundation wall or simply on its own as a base for your structure. Slabs are usually from 4 to 6 inches thick and are poured on a base of gravel to allow for easy drainage. They can also be insulated with rigid foam insulation or plastic. Typically, a slab will have bolts embedded around its perimeter to which the structure is attached.

Because greenhouses are fairly light structures, only the largest slabs are poured over reinforced bars (rebar). Whether or not you pour a footing with your slab depends on the weather in your region. Kevin Reed, of J.A.M. Construction Co., in Newport, Rhode Island, says that in the Northeast and in most colder parts of the country, an owner would be advised to install a knee wall or footing extending below the frost line to prevent shifting and cracking of the slab from frost heaves. "Typically, the knee wall would be about 4 or 6 inches thick and go down about 4 feet," he said. "That would prevent any problems with frost. The knee wall, slab, and corners for a light structure are usually poured all at once, but for a larger structure, the knee wall would be poured first and then the slab is poured. The slab itself is about 6 inches thick and sits on a 6- to 8-inch bed of gravel. If you want to insulate the floor, use a 2-inch layer of rigid foam insulation between the gravel and the slab."

Drains and conduits for electrical outlets should be installed before any gravel, rebar, or concrete is poured. If you are installing a small hobby-style greenhouse, installing a drain is not critical, but you might want to slope the floor slightly to let water drain out the door or to one side or the center (see Setting the Drainpipe, page 124, and the illustration on page 114).

Please note that if you intend to build a concrete block or masonry wall on your slab, you must decide before you pour it whether this wall will be built on the edge of the slab or 2 inches to 3 inches inside the edge. If the latter, the slab dimensions will have to be larger than the greenhouse that will be attached to the wall to

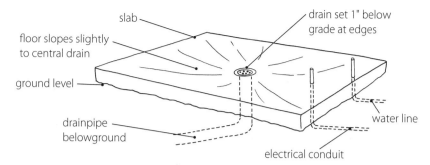

slab

floor slopes slightly
to central drain

ground level

drainpipe
belowground

drain set 1" below
grade at edges

water line

electrical conduit

When adding a drain
to a concrete slab,
remember to slope
the slab toward the
drain after the pour.

allow for the wall to be set in from the edge of
the slab.

Building a concrete slab involves excavating
for the slab and building forms for the concrete.
For more specifics on the preparation and construction process, see Constructing a Concrete
Foundation and Slab, page 118.

Masonry Foundations and Walls

You greenhouse wall doesn't have to be made
of concrete. It can also be constructed of blocks,
bricks, fieldstone, or slate. Usually masonry
walls are built on a poured footing, but alternatively you can pour a concrete half-thickness
wall and face it with half-thick bricks or slate
to give an attractive masonry look to a strong,
smooth-topped wall.

The Concrete Block Wall

Standard concrete blocks measure 7⅝
inches by 15⅝ inches by 7⅝ inches — 8 inches
by 8 inches by 16 inches when set in mortar,
making it easy to lay out a wall in multiples of
8 inches. In your planning, remember that you
can get half blocks and that each course must be

leveled before adding the next one. If you want
a thinner wall, you can also get blocks that measure 3⅝ inches thick. If you plan on using these
half-thickness blocks, however, you should not
build a wall more than two or three courses high
without adding some form of reinforcement to
prevent the blocks from toppling. Other available concrete block sizes are 7⅝ inches by 15⅝
inches by 3⅝ inches and sizes similar to those of
an ordinary brick. Blocks are also available with
rounded corners (known as bull nose) and with
a double corner (known as concrete masonry
units, with both ends square so that you don't
need to cut them). See Constructing a Mortared
Block Foundation, page 126, for more on building a concrete block wall.

Dry-Laid Block with Reinforced Parging

If you are not skilled at mortaring concrete
block, you can lay the blocks without using
mortar between them. Once the blocks are in
place, you can pour concrete into the voids in
the blocks to solidify the wall (you can insert
rebar in the holes in the blocks before pouring
the concrete if the wall is high). For this type of
application, the concrete should be as loose as
possible (made with as much water as possible
without becoming a sloppy mess) so that it will
fill all the voids.

Another method involves coating the exterior
of a dry-laid wall with a thin layer of concrete
— a method known as parging. Generally, this
thin material is reinforced with fiberglass and is
applied in one or two coats, with each coat being
about ¼ inch thick. This method works well for
walls that are only three or four courses high and
that will not have to hold backfill. It does have
one drawback, however: In areas where there
are heavy frosts or severe weather, the wall may
buckle or bend, though this doesn't occur often
beneath a structure as light as a greenhouse.

Brick

Bricks are baked blocks of different shale
and clay mixtures. They come in many colors,
shapes, and styles, but the basic size of a brick is
2½ inches by 3¾ inches by 8 inches (although
the dimensions may vary slightly as a result of the

What Is Mortar?

Mortar is made from Portland cement, sand, and water and comes in
two types: A and B. Type A is stronger than type B and is the one to use
for brick and stone walls. Typically, mortar is mixed on-site in a barrow,
mortar box, or a mixer. As with concrete, it is critical to add the right
amount of water to the mixture. If mortar is too runny, it will slide out of
joints between block, brick, or stone. If it is too thick, it will not adhere
properly to the wall material and the resulting wall will be weak.

baking process). Those used for walls are called face brick because they have a side (or face) that is meant to be exposed. Face brick costs a little more than paving brick and is slightly more uniform in color. Face bricks are the best kind to use if you are building a brick knee wall for your greenhouse.

Other types of brick are building bricks (used for walls), fire bricks (used in fireplaces), glazed bricks (one or two faces are glazed white or some other color), and pavers (used for paving walkways).

You can pour a concrete knee wall for your greenhouse and face it with a brick veneer. Veneer bricks are only half the thickness of standard bricks and are set against the wall in mortar. This building method combines the strength of concrete with the attractiveness of a brick exterior wall.

Stone

You can also use stone to build the greenhouse knee wall. In fact, the entire back wall of one greenhouse I saw was built of mortared stone with a waterfall that ran into a pond at the base of the wall. While this is more than most people would want in their greenhouse, it gives you an idea of what can be done with a little imagination. If you decide on a stone knee wall for your structure, you will probably do best to hire a mason to build it. Be prepared for it to be expensive; stonework is time-consuming.

There are many types of stone that can be used for a knee wall. If possible, choose one that is indigenous to your area, rather than one that needs to be shipped from elsewhere (which, besides adding to the cost, might make it difficult to get more to match should you decide to expand the greenhouse or build another one). In New England, granite, Connecticut bluestone, slate, and many other varieties are easy to find. In fact, you can even use stone as the floor of your greenhouse, provided it is reasonably flat. (See Types of Floors, at right.) When deciding on a mason for the job, make sure you see samples of his or her work before making your final choice and selecting the look you're after. (A mortared wall, for instance, might be built

with an inch or more of mortar visible around the stone or with no mortar at all visible.)

Alternative Foundations

People have used adobe bricks, wood, old tires filled with sand or rubble, concrete-filled tin cans, straw bales, old telephone poles, and recycled building parts as foundation materials — especially on the north walls of greenhouses, where there may be no glazing and insulation value is important. If you don't have a lot of money to spend, look around nearby; you can probably find materials for a foundation or wall without having to resort to the expense of concrete or brick. Use your imagination!

Straw bales can provide plenty of insulation for a temporary greenhouse. They can be stacked to form a wall and then staked to bind them together. Once coated with plaster or a mud mixture, they provide thick, solid insulation as a north wall. Filled tin cans or orange juice cartons filled with sand or concrete and buried to grade can serve as a solid foundation for a temporary greenhouse. Again, the use you intend for your greenhouse will also dictate which alternative materials will work as its foundation.

Sometimes an existing foundation on your property may be dedicated to a new use. The foundation for my cold greenhouse started life in the late 1920s as a garage foundation, with two tracks for the car wheels. I broke up the tracks, dug out the old oil-contaminated dirt, and built a greenhouse of recycled materials on the foundation, complete with beds filled with fresh loam.

Types of Floors

A larger greenhouse (a 12-foot by 20-foot structure is substantial for a hobbyist) is likely to have, along with a poured foundation, a floor that is either a poured-concrete slab (see The Concrete Slab, page 113), a floor of brick or slate pavers laid in crushed bluestone or sand, or simply raked pea stone (a mix of stones that are ¼ inch to ½ inch in diameter).

A Brick, Paver, or Stone Floor

For specific information on pouring a concrete slab, see the following section, Constructing a Concrete Foundation and Slab. For creating a brick or slate floor, the first step is to lay the base, which can be either sand or crushed bluestone. I prefer crushed bluestone because it packs down hard and forms an almost impenetrable layer against weeds. The base should be 3 to 4 inches thick. Lay the material and tamp it down using a heavy flat-ended tamper—a 4-foot length of heavy log will do in a pinch, although you can make a tamper by mounting a heavy piece of lumber on the end of a pole with a hand-grip circumference. The point is to produce a surface that is well compacted and firm. Next, wet the bluestone to help compact it. On top of the bluestone, distribute a layer of sand 1 to 2 inches thick. The bricks, slate, or stone will be laid onto this surface, allowing you to adjust the grade level without disturbing the bluestone base. If the floor is fashioned of brick or stone, brush sand into the cracks between the bricks or stones and then water everything down again. You will probably have to brush more sand into the cracks after you have watered it, until the cracks between the individual bricks or stones are filled.

As a base for a brick, stone, or slate greenhouse floor, first layer crushed bluestone 3 to 4 inches thick, then add 1 to 2 inches of sand. After the floor material is placed, fill spaces with sand or bluestone dust.

fill space between with sand or bluestone dust

brick

sand (1–2")

crushed bluestone (3–4")

The Pea Stone Floor

A pea stone floor, unlike a concrete slab, does not require installation of a drain because water drains easily right through the stone. Pea stone, like bricks and flat stones, is also added on top of crushed bluestone in a 3- to 4-inch layer. If you install benches in the greenhouse, you will have to either pour a small concrete base for each bench or dig through the pea stone to rest the benches on the firm foundation of the bluestone base.

Constructing a Concrete Foundation and Slab

Following are basic step-by-step instructions for building a greenhouse foundation and/or slab made of concrete. As with all building projects, to ensure optimal results, before undertaking any aspect of the construction, it's important to work out specifically what you are going to do and when you are going to do it and to have the materials on-site ready for use. You may also need people to help mix and pour concrete, set rebar, and level the concrete after the pour. Make sure that they are ready to go before any work starts.

Laying Out the Foundation

Before beginning the foundation installation, you must carefully mark the dimensions of the foundation and ensure that it is perfectly square. If the foundation is slightly out of plumb, your greenhouse will be slightly out of plumb, which means it will be difficult to install glazing. In the case of glass and plastic panels, glazing is perfectly square. You'll want to make the least number of adjustments at the glazing stage of building.

Stake Out Rough Corners

The first step in laying out a foundation is to decide where the four corners will be located. Choose and stake the location for one corner. In one direction from this corner, lay a 3-foot length of wood. Perpendicular to it and meeting at the corner lay a 4-foot length of wood. Between the ends of these two lengths, set a 5-foot length of wood as a diagonal. This will give you a 3-4-5 triangle that will be square (see the illustration on page 117, top). The two perpendicular sides form the first corner of your greenhouse.

Now measure along one side of the greenhouse from the corner edge of the 4-foot length of wood. Let's assume this side will be 8 feet. Hammer a stake in the ground 8 feet from the first stake and use the 3-4-5 triangle to square this corner. If your greenhouse will be 12 feet long, measure 12 feet from each corner and hammer in stakes. Now check the diagonals between the stakes (see the illustration on page 117, center).

For the foundation to be perfectly square, the diagonal measurements should be equal. If they are not, you will need to adjust the stakes until they are. Once the diagonals are equal, check all the other measurements (length and width) again to ensure that you have not inadvertently shortened one side.

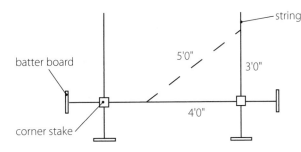

Erect Batter Boards

Next, on each side of the foundation outline you'll have to place batter boards—that is, boards located a few feet outside of the margins of the foundation. Attach string to these to mark the outline of the foundation, which will allow the foundation to be excavated while the measurements you've determined are kept accurate. You'll need a pair of stakes and a crossbar screwed to each batter board. I prefer to use 2×4s as stakes and a 1×6 or 2×6 as a crossbar. This produces a sturdy batter board that allows the string to be pulled fairly tight.

The batter boards are set up as shown in the illustrations at top right and bottom right, hammered into each corner about 2 feet from the corner stakes, with the location of the string marked by hammering a nail or making a saw cut in the batter board. You can also use a second string attached to the batter boards to mark the inner edge of your foundation.

Mark the First Side

Tie a length of mason's twine across opposing batter boards to delineate one side of the foundation. Make sure the line passes directly over two of the stakes.

Establish the First Corner

You'll need two helpers for this step: Tie a length of string perpendicular to the first string, between batter boards, to delineate one corner of the foundation. From the corner, measure 4 feet along the first string you tied and make a mark on the string. From the same corner, measure 3 feet along the second string. While one helper holds the end of a tape measure on the 4-foot mark on the first string, the second helper holds the other end of the tape measure diagonally on the 3-foot mark on the second string.

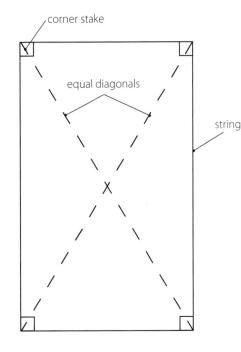

After you've established the site for your foundation, stake out rough corners and check that your diagonals are equal by measuring a 3-4-5 triangle.

Place batter boards at the corners of your foundation and attach string to them to help in ensuring that your diagonals remain square during the excavation and after.

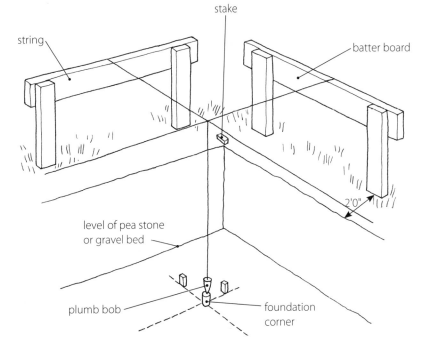

This diagonal should be 5 feet. If it's not, adjust the second string on the batter board until you've once again established a 3-4-5 triangle, which will allow you to rough out the rectangle. Attach and adjust the remaining two strings the same way, forming the other corners of the foundation. When you have the rectangle marked out, make sure you check the diagonals. They should be exactly the same. If they aren't, adjust the strings until they are.

Excavating the Foundation

Depending on the type of foundation that you intend to install — footing and foundation wall, slab alone — the depth of the area to be dug may vary considerably. Following are measurements to be used as guidelines for digging for both a slab and a slab with a knee wall.

Excavating for a Slab

If you're constructing a slab foundation, the top of the finished slab should be at or maybe an inch or two above ground level. Making it a bit higher than ground level allows water to drain off easily. A slab that is above ground level should be 4 to 6 inches thick in total (depending on the size of your greenhouse) with 6 to 8 inches of gravel beneath it. To accommodate these measurements, you should excavate 10 to 14 inches below grade.

Excavating for a Footing and Knee Wall

If your region's winter temperatures require that you install a foundation below the frost line, you will need to excavate a trench around the perimeter of the greenhouse to the depth of about 4 feet. A backhoe can usually finish this work in an hour. This trench will be twice as wide as the knee wall, although it is usually made even wider (typically, the width of the backhoe bucket) to allow a worker to get into the trench and set up forms after a preliminary footing has been poured. The footing will also hold the concrete slab in place without the need for formwork. Note that the knee wall may extend to the level of the top of the slab or may rise as high as 4 feet above the slab, depending on the type of greenhouse you are going to build.

When excavating the foundation, remember to place the topsoil in a pile separated from the subsoil. If you plan to grow plants in beds directly in the greenhouse floor without pouring a slab, you can reuse the topsoil. If a contractor does the job for you, ask him to keep the subsoil and topsoil separate.

The footing, poured first, serves as a base for the forms and poured knee wall. Depending on local zoning, you may be required to install concrete reinforcing bars (rebar) upright in the footing. The concrete knee wall is poured around the bars to tie together the knee wall and the footing.

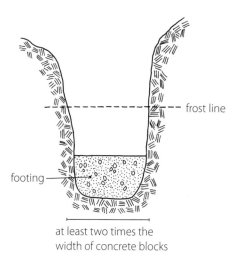

frost line

footing

at least two times the width of concrete blocks

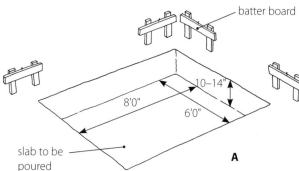

batter board

10–14"

8'0"

6'0"

slab to be poured

A

Excavation for a slab foundation (**A**) and for a footing and knee wall (**B**). For the slab, the excavation extends down a foot or so, which will later be filled with up to 6 inches of gravel or pea stone. The 4- to 6-inch-thick slab is poured on top of the gravel. For the footing and knee wall, excavate a trench. This will extend below the frost line, up to 3 feet in colder areas.

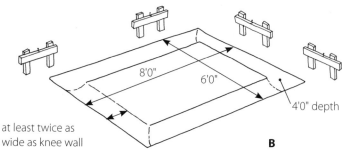

8'0"

6'0"

4'0" depth

at least twice as wide as knee wall

B

Setting Formwork

Wet concrete is runny stuff. In order to pour it successfully, you'll need to contain it inside formwork, which is removed after the concrete is set. Commercial operators use the same forms from job to job; they oil the inside of the wood to prevent the forms from sticking to the concrete. If you make the forms yourself, you can disassemble them and reuse them as lumber in another part of the job where they won't be seen. For example, if you are building a custom greenhouse with an insulated north wall, you might reuse the lumber from the forms for this wall.

Note that if water lines, drainpipes, and electrical conduits are to pass through the foundation walls and the slab, you'll need to drill holes in the forms for the piping. After you install the piping through the hole, you must determine how you'll remove the form with the pipe set in the concrete. One way to do this is to drill the hole for the conduit or pipe and then cut a vertical slot the width of the hole from the hole to the edge of the board. The wood that you cut from the slot can be temporarily nailed in place to hold the concrete and removed later.

Forms for a Slab Foundation

The forms for a slab foundation should be tall enough to reach from the bottom of the excavation to grade level or an inch or two above it (depending on how much above grade level your slab will rise — usually from 2 to 14 inches). For one slab foundation, I made forms from recycled 2×8s and held them in place with stakes driven into the ground on the outside of the planks. It did the job and I was able to use the planks elsewhere afterward. If the forms don't need to be tall, it is relatively easy to use planking like this.

The type of forms you construct varies according to the thickness of the slab you will pour, but usually 2×10s on all four sides suffice for a slab up to 6 inches thick. If the formwork is to extend below the frost line, you'll need forms that are at least 4 feet high and will possibly want to pour a footer to provide a flat base for the forms before setting them up.

It's important that the formwork be absolutely level or that it slope consistently about ⅛ inch per foot from side to side to allow water to drain off the slab. If you slope it slightly toward the doorway, you can simply brush the water out the door. As shown on page 114 and in Setting the Drainpipe, page 124, if you install a drain in the floor, set it ½ to 1 inch below grade and float the wet concrete to slope toward the drain. Note that if your forms are out of plumb and you count on using as a guide for leveling your slab a line that you mark on the inside of the formwork, the resulting slab will not be level. What's more, during a pour, concrete often splashes on such a line, obscuring it and making it very difficult to use as a guide.

Forms for a Knee Wall

If the formwork is to be more than 20 inches high, it is more economical to use ½-inch plywood rather than planks or lumber to build. Attach 2×4s every 16 inches to the outside of the plywood to support it and brace plywood forms with 2×4s to ensure that the plywood does not bulge under the weight of the foundation's cement. Cement is heavy — about 180 to 200 pounds per cubic foot, depending on aggregate type and moisture content — so tall forms must be substantial.

As we mentioned before, if you plan on pouring a slab in addition to the knee wall, the forms might be set up only around the outside perimeter of the wall and everything can be poured in one go. Otherwise, you'll need forms for both the inside and the outside faces of the knee wall.

If you have multiple forms for the entire greenhouse foundation (sometimes they are made in 4-foot lengths), they should be tied together, and if they are more than 30 inches

TIP

Figure about 4 to 6 hours to excavate the foundation for a 10-foot by 12-foot greenhouse. This should allow enough time for a backhoe to set up and dig the area. Be aware, though, that this time may increase if the excavator encounters large rocks or ledge. Ask the excavator for a cost estimate and compare it to the cost of doing the job yourself.

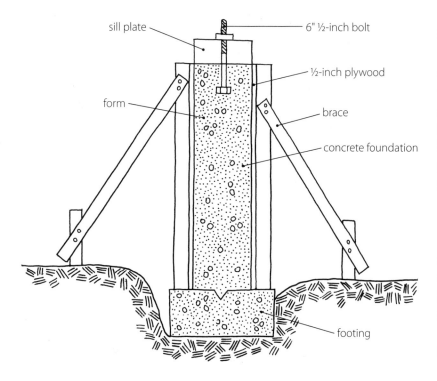

sill plate

6" ½-inch bolt

½-inch plywood

form

brace

concrete foundation

footing

The 4-foot by 8-foot forms for a knee wall are braced with short pieces of lumber driven into the ground behind them. When in doubt, add more bracing. Wet concrete is heavy and you don't want the forms to collapse.

tall, they should be braced so that the weight of the cement doesn't cause them to collapse. For added strength on taller forms, you should install rods (also called snap ties) across the foundation and run some rebar in the center of the form channel, though rebar is not altogether necessary for a greenhouse, which is much lighter than a habitable structure. Check local building codes for the final word. Rebar may be required, especially in earthquake-prone areas. You can forgo snap ties if you fasten the forms together with short 2×4s across the top of the formwork. In my experience, however, these nailed braces seem to be located right where you want to pour or trowel the wet concrete.

TIP

It should take 2 to 4 hours to set up formwork for a 8-foot by 12-foot greenhouse footing and another 2 to 4 hours to pour the cement. Often the slab and the knee wall are poured as one piece, especially if the foundation is for a smaller greenhouse.

Building Custom Forms

If you are building a greenhouse on a rocky surface that requires specially cut forms, you will save a considerable amount of money if you do it yourself. As already pointed out, for most forms, you can use ordinary plywood and lumber or pressure-treated lumber and incorporate the material into the greenhouse structure once the building starts.

Where to Get Concrete for Your Job

There are three ways to get concrete: Order ready-mixed concrete from a supplier, rent a mixer and mix your own, or buy bags of dry ingredients to which you add water and then mix.

Ordering Concrete

Concrete can be ordered from a supplier ready mixed by the cubic yard. To determine how much yardage you'll need, measure the length, width, and height of your foundation in feet, multiple the three figures (length × width × height) and divide the result by 27 to get cubic yards. Most suppliers will deliver a minimum of 5 cubic yards (or charge for the full 5 if you order less).

If you decide to order the concrete, you must completely prepare the site for the pour: Formwork must be in place and you must provide access to the site for a large heavy truck. If your site is inaccessible, you may have to hire what is known as a boom truck to pump the wet concrete mixture to the greenhouse excavation. These trucks can cost $1,000 to $2,000 per day. You could organize a wheelbarrow brigade to move concrete to the site, but this means the truck will have to wait while the concrete is moved and you may get charged extra for waiting time. *Note:* When ordering concrete, order an additional 10 percent to ensure that you have enough to finish the job, but be aware that ordering too much often results in concrete being dumped at the job site. Measure carefully so that you accurately determine your needs!

Mixing Your Own Concrete

A less expensive option if you need a smaller amount of concrete is to rent or buy your own concrete mixer and prepare the stuff yourself. An electric or gas-powered mixer can cost under $500, or you can get one from your local rental store for less than $100 a day. Be aware, however, that you may need a truck to get the mixer from the store to your site. Of course, you also need to know how to make concrete. (See the box What Is Concrete? on page 113.)

Another option for small jobs is to buy pre-mixed bags of concrete, pour the mix into a wheelbarrow, add the required amount of water, and stir with a hoe or shovel. In my experience, this is the most expensive way to get concrete. If your job is larger, it is much less expensive to purchase the ingredients separately as opposed to premixed. In addition, making your own is time-consuming and the concrete is often not mixed properly. The most cost-effective method is to buy or rent a mechanical mixer. The time saved, not to mention the wear on your back, is significant as well.

To make concrete from separate ingredients, mix one 94-pound bag of Portland cement, 2½ cubic feet of coarse builder's sand (do not use beach sand), and 3 to 4 cubic feet of aggregate. To this mixture add from 5 to 6 gallons of water. Add the water carefully to avoid making the concrete too wet and sloppy. If it's too wet, the mixture will slump, or sag, and will dry with an uneven surface. A shovelful of concrete should stay on the shovel when you lift it. If it runs off the edge, it is too wet. To correct a too wet, sloppy mix, simply add more sand and Portland cement in the appropriate proportions. *Note:* When you have finished mixing the cement, remember to hose off the mixer so the cement doesn't have a chance to set up on it. Hardened cement can be removed from a mixer by lightly tapping the metal casing with a hammer.

Tools and Supplies for Mixing Concrete

- Shovel
- Measuring bucket (5-gallon bucket)
- Wheelbarrow
- Water supply (usually a hose)
- Concrete mixer (electric or gas-powered)
- Trowel
- Float
- Edger
- Mason's hoe
- Bags of Portland cement (you may need a two-wheeled dolly or wheelbarrow to move them)
- Sand (purchasing by the cubic yard is less expensive than buying by the bag)
- Aggregate (gravel or small pea stone)
- Water

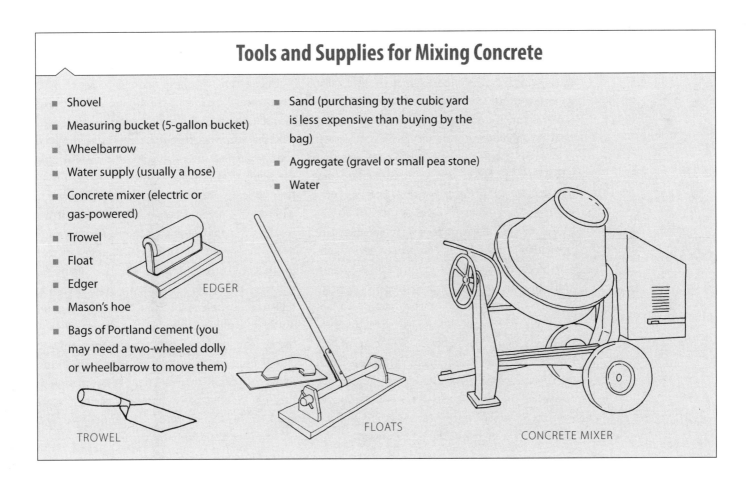

EDGER

TROWEL

FLOATS

CONCRETE MIXER

Pouring the Concrete Footing and Foundation Wall

For a commercial greenhouse installer, the job of excavating the hole, setting up forms, and pouring concrete is relatively easy, though these services may be expensive. Of course, you can do the work yourself, but pouring the concrete can be the trickiest part of the whole process.

When the concrete is poured, it should be consolidated or compacted while wet to make sure that all air spaces and holes have been eliminated: If you are doing the work at the pour, drive a concrete bar, a hoe, or a spade into the substance until you hit the bottom of the form, then work it up and down to settle the mix. After this process, carefully level the surface of the concrete using a trowel. This will ensure that the greenhouse structure can sit on the foundation without any gaps. (If you do have gaps between the foundation and the greenhouse after you install the sill plate on the sill insulation, you can fill them with spray foam insulation, available at any hardware store.) Let the concrete set for a half hour or so before going over the top again to ensure that it is perfectly level. After this time, much of the water in the concrete will come to the surface. In addition, during this time the concrete may slump (if it is going to) or an air bubble may pop on the surface, making it necessary to level it.

After the concrete has set for an hour and it is still damp, you can insert in it the bolts that will be used to hold the greenhouse to the foundation. The sill plate or bottom plate of a prefabricated greenhouse may be predrilled for bolts, so you'll have to take spacing measurements from these holes and space the foundation bolts precisely. If the greenhouse is custom and you plan on using a 2×6 or 2×8 sill plate in your construction, space the bolts 2 to 3 feet apart, pushing them into the top of the foundation and leaving 1½ inches to 2½ inches of bolt exposed above the concrete. In the future, you'll thread each of these bolts with a washer and nut to anchor the greenhouse to the foundation. If you intend to recess the bolt into the sill plate, leave only 1½ inches of the bolt exposed.

Poured concrete should be allowed to cure in the forms for at least a week before you remove the forms and begin building, but if you can leave it longer, do so. Concrete continues to cure for a long time after it has hardened. While it is curing, it is best to cover the concrete with damp sacking or plastic sheeting to keep it moist. Note that the strength of the concrete is affected by the temperature at which it cures. In general, it takes concrete much longer to cure in cooler temperatures, and pouring concrete in temperatures below freezing is not recommended.

Insulating the Poured-Foundation Knee Wall

In colder areas, it will be very beneficial to insulate your greenhouse foundation wall. Typically a poured wall for a greenhouse will be 4 inches to 8 inches wide, which allows for using 1-inch-thick rigid polystyrene foam insulation around the outside of the foundation and a 2×8 or 2×10 sill plate. If you live in a really cold region, you might want to use 2-inch thick insulation. If you are assembling a kit or premade greenhouse, you can still use insulation, but you'll need to cover the top with flashing that extends from the top of the sill plate over the outside of the insulation.

Polystyrene insulation comes in 1-, 2-, or 4-inch-thick 2-inch by 8-inch panels. Before the foundation is backfilled, paint the knee wall with black tar waterproofing and install the polystyrene against this material, which will hold the insulation in place. Then cover the insulation above grade to about a foot below grade with a gray, cementlike coating such as Structural Skin from Conproco (see Resources, page 248). This will prevent it from being damaged by animals or tools that might bang against it and keep it from breaking down in the weather. It also helps to eliminate pink or blue foam chips on the ground outside the greenhouse. Trowel the coating onto the polystyrene, then smooth it to a final finish. Attach reinforcing mesh to joints between foam panels before covering with this material to ensure that the covering doesn't crack in these spots when dry. Some insulation coatings are also fiber reinforced.

Estimating the Cost of a Concrete Foundation

Foundation costs will vary according to the cost of the concrete, but the calculation is simple, allowing you to plug in your own numbers and come up with a fairly accurate price for your part of the country.

The following cost estimate is for an 8-foot by 10-foot greenhouse with footings that are 18 inches wide poured 1 foot below the frost line; foundation walls that extend 2 feet above grade level; and a slab floor with a drain, electrical conduit, and water line.

First, calculate the volume of the footing (the length of the footing all the way around the foundation × the width of the footing × the depth of the footing): 36 linear feet × 18 inches × 12 inches. Remember not to mix feet and inches; convert inches to feet: 36 × 1.5 × 1 = 54 cubic feet. Divide 54 by 27 (the number of cubic feet in a square yard) to arrive at 2 cubic yards, which is the amount of concrete needed for the footing.

Next, calculate the wall volume (length × width × height). The walls are 4 feet high and 6 inches thick, from the top of the footing to sill plate: 4 × .5 × 36 linear feet = 72 cubic feet. Divide 72 by 27 to arrive at 2.67 cubic yards.

Finally, calculate the volume of the slab. It will be 7 feet wide by 9 feet long by 6 inches thick: 7 × 9 × .5 = 31.5 cubic feet. Divide this by 27 to get cubic yards: 31.5 ÷ 27 = 1.2 cubic yards.

To determine the total amount of concrete for the job, add together the amounts you've determined: 2 + 2.7 + 1.2 = about 6 cubic yards. Call a local concrete supplier to find out how much concrete mix costs per yard and multiply this figure by 5 to arrive at a final cost.

To reach a total cost for the pour, factor in the cost of formwork (which can be reused in construction), rebar, anchors for the greenhouse, and any associated piping, including electrical conduit from the hardware store or home center. These costs vary and may add only a few dollars to your total depending on how many conduits you need.

The coating I used has lasted more than 12 years with only one small area of damage where an animal tried to burrow into the greenhouse. The covering is easily patched where it is necessary.

Pouring a Slab

A slab is the simplest concrete foundation to make for a greenhouse, but it may move or crack if you live in an area of heavy winter frosts. To help prevent cracking or moving, before you pour the concrete lay down a bed of gravel or crushed stone at the bottom of the excavation. This bed will help the area around the greenhouse to drain, effectively keeping water away from the concrete pad. Because the gravel moves, it also eases the expansion of the concrete slab, allowing it to "float" as the ground freezes and thaws, thereby preventing cracking. A gravel base can be between 4 inches and 6 inches thick. (See Insulation at right for more information on options for insulating between the gravel and the pad.)

Reinforcing Mesh

As Kevin Reed suggests, to further prevent any shifting in the slab floor and to keep the slab from breaking should it shift, lay wire mesh 6 inches on center before pouring the slab. Reed says, "The mesh comes in 4×8 sheets and is easy to handle and manipulate. We set it on small stones to keep it off the gravel and to allow the concrete to flow around it." Note that the mesh should be 1 to 3 inches from the edges of the slab to prevent any metal from protruding from the finished slab.

Insulation

If you are building a slab foundation and you live in an area where winters are very cold, you might want to insulate beneath it. After the hole for the foundation is excavated, deposit a layer of sand or crushed stone at the bottom and tamp it down to provide a smooth, even surface for insulation. Next, lay rigid foam insulation directly on the sand or crushed stone, making sure to butt the panels together tightly. You may even tape them to keep them in place when the concrete is poured. Try not to step or walk on the panels during this process; your weight could break them. After the panels are laid, creating a flat surface, you can install the wire mesh on top of them.

Note that after you have poured the concrete for the slab, you cannot step into the concrete at all to screed or smooth it; all work must be done from the edges of the slab to avoid disturbing the insulation. Once the concrete has hardened, you can strip away the forms and install insulation around the edges of the slab before backfilling the area. This ensures that the concrete slab is "floating" completely on insulation, which helps to prevent heat loss from the bottom and sides. Insulating the slab in this manner is very helpful if you intend to use under-floor radiant heating to keep the greenhouse floor warm. When the greenhouse is completed, avoid driving into the structure or introducing other exceptionally heavy weight to the slab to keep the insulation beneath it and on the sides from breaking.

Setting the Drainpipe

If you are to install a drain in the slab, use a flush-mounted shower-style drain that is set about a ½ inch or 1 inch below the top of the concrete and then slope the concrete down to the level of the drain. A ½-inch slope for a 10-foot-wide greenhouse and a 1-inch slope for a 20-foot-wide greenhouse ensures that the greenhouse floor will not collect puddles. Remember to cover the drainpipe with duct tape or a similar material when pouring the concrete so the drain doesn't become plugged. At the other end of the drainpipe you can install a dry well — that is, a hole filled with gravel to give draining water a place to go. (See The Dry Well, page 163.) If you don't install a dry well, make sure that the drainpipe is sloped sufficiently, about ¼ inch per foot is adequate, to allow water to run away from the greenhouse — preferably not onto your neighbor's property!

Pouring the Concrete

If you are mixing concrete in a mixer, do so at the job site and tip it straight into the formwork.

If you have concrete delivered, the truck will simply back up to the site and run the concrete into the formwork. Make sure you don't disturb the rebar or mesh when pouring, and work the concrete to remove air pockets or bubbles.

Screeding

After the pour, the next job is to remove excess concrete and level the slab. This process, known as *screeding*, involves using a straight board, usually a 2×6 or a 2×8 set on edge. The lower edge is pulled across the wet concrete in a sawing motion to level the top while the other end of the board rests on the forms on the perimeter of the slab. Effective screeding is another reason why the formwork must be completely level.

As the screed board is moved across the concrete, some concrete may build up in front of it. That's fine. The excess will fill any hollows as the board travels along the forms.

Be extra careful if you have installed a central drain. To accommodate the slope toward the drain, one end of the screed board is placed on the drainpipe and the other end rides on the forms. This keeps the entire greenhouse slab sloping slightly toward the center drainpipe.

If you intend to build a brick wall on your slab, note that the bricks may be set at the edge of the slab or 1 or 2 inches inside, with the edge of the slab outside of the wall sloped slightly away from the wall to allow water to drain off it.

Smoothing the Slab

When screeding is finished, the slab will have a slightly ridged surface. From here you have two choices. If your greenhouse is large, the slab is "floated": A wooden float is moved over the concrete to smooth the surface by removing bumps and voids, pushing any lumps below the surface and compacting the concrete. Floating a slab is usually done when a slight roughness is desired in the final concrete surface.

If you want a very smooth hard surface for your greenhouse floor, you will need to trowel the slab. To get the smoothest surface, you should let the concrete dry slightly until it has hardened enough so that water ceases rising to the surface of the slab. If there is water on the surface, it should be squeegeed off or allowed to evaporate before the concrete is troweled. To trowel effectively, press the tool against the surface of the concrete and work in a large sweeping motion, gradually smoothing the concrete. Try not to dig the trowel into the concrete or you'll have to go back over it to get it level and smooth. If the slab is large, some masons walk backward through the concrete smoothing it as they go (not an option if you've used polystyrene insulation beneath it); others build staging over the job and kneel or lie on it. If your slab is not too large, you can set a board over it with the board ends resting on two concrete blocks on either side of the slab and, making sure it will hold your weight without bending or breaking, kneel on it to trowel. If you sign your name or write your initials and the date in the corner of the slab with a trowel, forever after people will know that you did the foundation work.

Inserting Anchoring Bolts

As the concrete cures, insert anchor bolts into the edges of the slab to serve as fasteners to hold down the greenhouse if it is to be mounted directly on the slab. If you don't insert bolts while the concrete is wet, you'll have to drill into the hardened concrete later to fix the greenhouse structure to the slab, which can lead to cracks and breakage on the edges of the slab.

When inserting anchor bolts, take care to place them where they will not interfere with studs or glazing supports. Some builders prefer to set the anchor bolts on a footing and foundation wall with only 1½ inches showing so that they can be recessed into the wooden sill plate, though it's also possible to set the bolts with 2½ inches exposed and secure them on top of the sill plate. Note that if you'll be fastening them on the top of the sill plate, you'll need to make sure they aren't located where you'll be installing studs and supports. If your greenhouse has a base plate on top of the sill plate, you can hide the tops of bolts under the base plate.

Another way to install a sill plate is to insert the bolts into a 2-inch by 8-inch plate and push the sill plate down into the concrete so that its surface is level with the top of the concrete, as

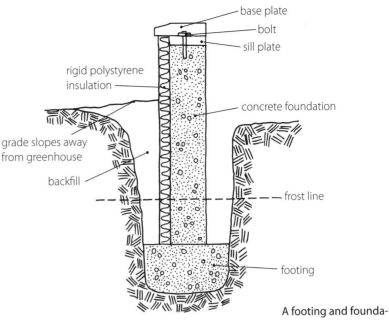

A footing and foundation wall is insulated before being backfilled. You can set the sill plate into the concrete to ensure that your structure will sit solidly on the foundation.

shown in the illustration above. This should be done just after the concrete is screeded and before the concrete starts to harden. After pushing the plate into the concrete, the edges of the foundation wall will probably need to be reworked to make them smooth. Note that pressure-treated wood reacts chemically to contact with concrete and, as a result, can rot very quickly. Because of this, it's preferable to make this embedded plate out of a durable wood such as cedar.

Remember that if you are planning to build a kit greenhouse, the bolt location may be predetermined by existing holes in the greenhouse base. In such a case, you'll have to use the base plate of the greenhouse as a template to locate and mark the bolt positions. You may want to support the base plate slightly above the concrete and use it to hold the top of the bolts in position.

If you intend to build a concrete block or brick wall around the edge of the slab, you must insert metal brick ties into the wet concrete to help anchor the blocks or bricks and then add more ties as you build the wall. As mentioned above, typically, a brick wall will be set either right at the edge of the slab or 1 or 2 inches inside the edge of the concrete slab, with the edge of the slab outside of the wall sloped slightly to allow water to run off.

Edging and Prepping the Slab for Curing

To give the slab a finished look, you should go around the edge with an edger or a pointed edging trowel, which rounds off the concrete corners and helps to prevent them from breaking.

Once the slab has been finished, cover it with plastic or damp sacks and leave it for several days to a week to allow it to harden slowly and cure. Do not walk on it until it is hard. Stepping on the slab before it has hardened can lead to cracks, chips, and marks in the surface.

Finishing the Foundation

Once the slab or slab and foundation wall has been poured and is hardened, you can begin the work of finishing the foundation. This may mean that you (or your contractor) will need to build an above-grade knee wall using concrete blocks, brick, or stone (if you have not poured a concrete wall). Even in the case of having poured a concrete knee wall, you may now need to surface it with brick or stone veneer. Along with referring to the following information, see Masonry Foundations and Walls, page 114, for suggestions on ways to finish a concrete foundation.

Finishing a Concrete Knee Wall with Stucco

Mortar consists of Portland cement, sand, and water (see What Is Mortar? on page 114). Adding hydrated lime to the mixture produces stucco, which is used to coat the exterior surfaces of poured concrete or concrete block walls to waterproof them and give them a consistent, finished look that will not deteriorate and will retain its color without requiring any painting. You can also add plasticizers to make the stucco more workable and pigments to color the material. The amount of hydrated lime added varies according to the coat of stucco to be applied (scratch coat, brown coat, or finish coat). The material can be purchased premixed, however, much like concrete.

Stucco must be applied on a roughened wall; if you have a smooth concrete surface as a result of contact with forms, stucco will not adhere to

it. You should rough up the surface with a wire brush or a scoring tool before applying the surfacing material. If your formwork was coated with oil, this will also make it difficult for the stucco to adhere to the concrete. In this case, you might have to pressure-wash the wall with soap and water to get rid of the oil residue.

To apply stucco, use a plastering trowel and smear the first coat (called a scratch coat) over the wall ¼ inch to ⅜ inch thick. Apply the coat with some force to ensure that it sticks. Before it hardens, scratch the surface with a special saw-tooth-edged trowel to give the second coat a good base to which to adhere. Allow it to dry thoroughly, then wet it down before the next coat is applied.

The second coat, known as the brown coat, should also be applied using a trowel, about ¼ inch to ⅜ inch thick. It is then smoothed before it too is scratched so that the third and final coat can be applied.

The third coat, known as the finish coat, is applied after the brown coat has dried thoroughly. If possible, start and finish the entire coating job in one day to eliminate any joints (places where you stopped troweling one day and started again the next). Once the final coat is in place, there are varying techniques to obtain different finishes. Wearing a rubber glove, you can apply hand or finger textures on the wet final coat, or you can use a hard bristle or wire brush for a different finish texture. To produce a smoother texture, use a large sponge or a wooden float on the wet surface. Try different techniques on a small test piece of concrete or a small corner of the wall to see which you like best before applying a technique to the whole project.

Constructing a Mortared Block Foundation

If you decide to make your foundation from concrete blocks, you'll still need to lay a footing similar to one for a concrete foundation wall: a concrete base twice as wide as the wall. A footing provides stability and a flat base on which to build the concrete-block wall. Concrete blocks offer a reasonably inexpensive and fast way to build a greenhouse knee wall if you don't want to pour concrete, but to some, concrete block is less attractive than brick or plain or surfaced poured concrete.

If you decide to build a concrete-block wall, you should plan the wall to accommodate the overall length of the individual blocks. Essentially, the dimensions of your greenhouse will be dictated by the length of the concrete blocks. This means that for a custom greenhouse, you will use multiples of the block length to determine its dimensions, which will allow you or the builder to construct the wall without cutting or breaking blocks.

Standard concrete blocks are 7⅝ inches wide by 7⅝ inches tall by 15⅝ inches long. Adding a ⅜-inch layer of mortar between the blocks makes each 8 inches by 8 inches by 16 inches once positioned. It is not too difficult to design your greenhouse to suit this unit to eliminate the need to cut blocks. For example, locate the door 32 or 48 inches from the corner rather than 36 or 38 inches. Purchase 7⅝-inch-long half-blocks to use in every other course ending at the door opening. If you plan to build a greenhouse from a kit, make sure that door openings in the kit suit the use and location of the concrete blocks.

The mortar most commonly called for in construction with concrete blocks is type M: 1 part Portland cement, 4 parts sand, and ¼ part hydrated lime or 1 part type 2 masonry cement, 1 part Portland cement, and 6 parts sand. Type M is specifically recommended for foundations and belowground applications. Other types of mortar are type S, type N, and type O. Types M and N are the best for brickwork.

(For more information, see What Is Mortar? on page 114.)

Marking Out Blocks

The first step in building a concrete-block wall is to mark out where the blocks will be laid. Snapping a chalk line is the best way to enable you to lay the blocks straight. The line can be placed 2 inches to 3 inches inside the edge of the concrete slab, but you can also set the bricks right at the edge of the slab. Determine where you'll place your blocks before the slab is poured because if the slab is built to the same dimensions as the greenhouse, you'll have no choice but to build the wall at the edge of the slab.

Making a Mortar Bed and Laying the Block

Next, put down a mortar bed on which the blocks will be laid. *Note:* Do not apply mortar too far in advance of setting blocks. Doing so will allow the mortar to dry out, making it less likely to adhere properly to the blocks. The mortar bed should be 8 to 10 inches wide and about ½ inch to 1 inch thick. When you set the blocks into it, you will compress the mortar to about ⅜ inch. Set the corner block in the mortar and tap it down carefully until it is lined up with your strings or chalk line. Use a level to make sure the block is perfectly horizontal and vertical on the top and sides. Every other block will be lined up according to this first corner block, so you'll need to be sure it's positioned perfectly.

Then put a trowel full of mortar on each of the two vertical ends of the second block and push the block down into the mortar bed to align it with the corner block. Be aware that if

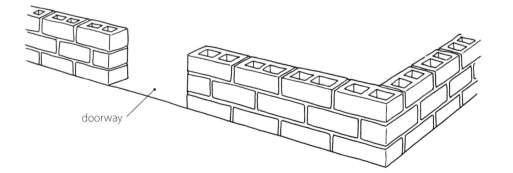

doorway

A mortared concrete-block wall is first built up at the corners and is then filled in, with a space left for the door. This space can be 37½ inches wide to allow for two ¾-inch jambs or 39 inches wide to allow for two 2×4s on either side of the opening.

your mortar is dry or not well applied, it may fall from the end of the block as you set and align it. As you lay the second and third blocks, try not to move the blocks already in place, however easy it is to do so.

After you have set the first four or five blocks, check them with a level to be sure they are straight. This first row of blocks is the most important and should be laid very carefully. If it is not straight and level, the next layers will probably not be level either. Work from the corners toward the middle of the wall. If you doubt the accuracy of your eye, place string lines across the face of the wall to ensure that the courses

of block are going up straight. Use the level frequently to make sure that the wall remains true. First build four or five courses of blocks on the corners, then stretch a string between each corner to help you keep the middle blocks level when you lay them.

If the wall is curving or leaning or if the mortar is seeping out from between the blocks, stop and figure out what you are doing wrong. It may be that your mortar mix is too runny. It should be the consistency of thick, gritty peanut butter. If it's too dry, it won't adhere to the blocks very well. If it's too wet, it will run out from between the blocks. If some mortar squishes out from between the blocks, after you've tapped them down to level them, wipe it off flush with the blocks.

Experienced builders can put up most of a tall wall in a day, but until you gain experience, don't build more than a few courses at a time. Be sure you check that the wall is straight and level before leaving the mortar to harden.

When the mortar has become hard enough to just press a thumb into it, it should be tooled or pointed: All the joints should be sloped or made concave or V-shaped to allow rainwater to run off the blocks. Use a diamond-shaped trowel held at a slight angle to cut the mortar into a slight slope, or if you prefer a concave or V-shaped joint, slide a special pointing tool along the line of mortar.

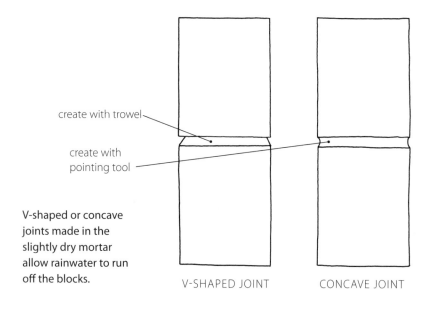

create with trowel

create with pointing tool

V-shaped or concave joints made in the slightly dry mortar allow rainwater to run off the blocks.

V-SHAPED JOINT   CONCAVE JOINT

Installing Anchor Bolts

Install anchor bolts in the top of a concrete wall by filling one of the hollow cores in the concrete block with mortar and inserting the bolt into the mortar while it's still wet. Fill the holes in the blocks about halfway with crumpled paper to hold the mortar in place while it sets.

Constructing a Dry-Laid-Block Foundation

An alternative to laying a concrete-block wall with mortar is dry-laying a wall using concrete blocks and then filling the voids in the blocks with poured concrete. An important consideration in this type of building is the dimensions of the blocks: They will not be the same as they are

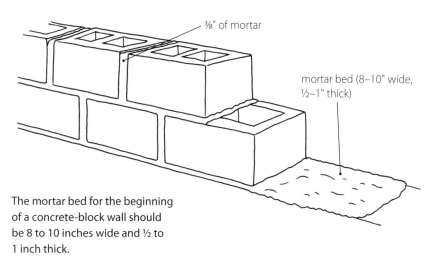

⅜" of mortar

mortar bed (8–10" wide, ½–1" thick)

The mortar bed for the beginning of a concrete-block wall should be 8 to 10 inches wide and ½ to 1 inch thick.

if you mortar the blocks in place (because you will not be able to count the mortar in between the blocks). For a novice builder, however, this method is a very easy way of building a strong wall. After the wall is finished, you can coat it with stucco or parge it (see Dry-laid Block with Reinforced Parging, page 114).

Constructing a Brick Foundation

You can use brick veneer on a concrete or block foundation to improve its appearance or you can build a low foundation wall of solid brick. Generally a brick veneer is started just below grade level on a step in the concrete wall known as a brick shelf. If you plan on building a wall entirely of brick, the wall is usually started on a footing poured into the ground below the frost line. Another possible combination is a poured footing with a concrete-block wall to just below grade with a brick wall built above the grade.

If you want a fancy foundation wall or if you'll be facing a poured concrete or concrete-block foundation, you should use face brick, which is of higher quality than common brick. There are a number of other types of brick that you could use, some designed for paving, others

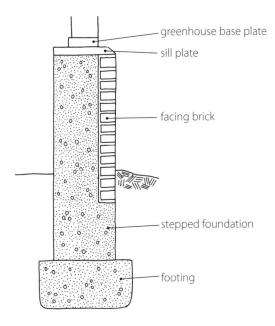

This concrete foundation has a step to allow application of brick facing, or brick veneer, on the knee wall. The concrete carries the load of the greenhouse while the brick face adds a pretty touch.

for ornamental work. Make sure that you ask for the right type of brick for your project. Remember that a standard brick measures 2¼ inches by 3¾ inches by 8 inches. Allow ⅜ inch of mortar between courses and sides to determine the dimensions that will work for your wall so that you won't have to cut brick.

Because freezing and thawing are virtually the only things that affect brickwork, you must be sure that you are using the right type of mortar mix, that the joints are made properly, and that the wall is flashed and caulked properly. You should install flashing at any point on the wall that is penetrated by an opening or capped with the sill plate. Flashing is simply a piece of metal or lead sheeting that is placed under the mortar layer 1 inch to 2 inches in from the outer edge of the brick and extends ¾ inch to 1½ inches beyond the bricks. It is usually bent downward to allow moisture to run off its surface. A well-laid brick foundation wall will keep most of the rain out of the greenhouse.

The outer face of the mortar should be tooled or pointed to a concave surface, which will prevent water from getting into the joint. After the foundation wall is completed, you might want to apply some form of sealer to the bricks to help prevent moisture from penetrating the wall. Any brick or concrete sealer painted on either side of the bricks will help to provide resistance to rain (on the outside) and sprayed water (on the inside).

If you decide to make your entire foundation wall of brick (as opposed to facing a concrete wall with brick veneer), for a small greenhouse the wall can be the width of one row of bricks (called a single-wythe wall). But if the greenhouse size is to be larger, the wall must be more substantial: Two walls parallel to each other with an inch between each, known as a two-wythe wall, may be required. The base of your greenhouse will give you a good idea as to which type of wall you'll need. A base that is less than 4 inches wide requires one wythe. If the greenhouse base is 6 inches to 8 inches wide, you should plan on two wythes. A good mason will give you a better idea of how wide your wall should be.

The Terminology of Bricklaying

Course: Each level or row of bricks

Header: A brick that bridges the gap between the two sides or wythes of the wall. A bull header is a brick standing on its side between the two sides of the wall. A brick that is not used to tie together both sides of the wall but is set like a header is known as a blind header.

Soldier: A brick that is set on end with the narrow face out. If the wide face is out, it is known as a sailor. This type of application is most often used for decorative applications.

Flashing: Sheeting made of lead or tin that is used to divert rain and snow from a wall or other surface. Flashing should be used around all windows, doors, and other openings in a brick wall and beneath the mortar layer where it meets the sill plate.

Bond: The pattern used in a brick wall. Common bond, running bond, English bond, Flemish or Dutch bond, running bond, and stack are some of the most common. Each pattern gives the wall structural strength and ties together both sides.

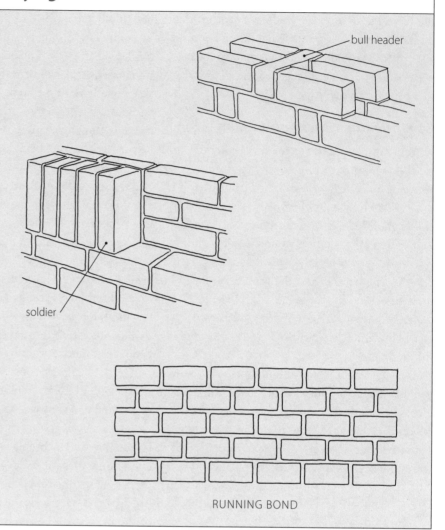

RUNNING BOND

Laying a Brick Wall

A greenhouse foundation wall is a good project for learning to lay brick. Most greenhouse knee walls are only five or six courses high — not so high that an amateur can get too far along without being able to correct any mistakes, even if they require dismantling the work to correct them.

If you want to lay a brick foundation wall properly, it's very important, as with a concrete-block wall, that each course be kept perfectly level. The first step in achieving this is learning how to handle the trowel. A trowel should be held with your thumb on the top, which makes it easier to pick up mortar and lay it on the bricks or the foundation. If you hold the trowel with your thumb wrapped around it, it is difficult to turn your wrist to apply the mortar in the right place. If you hold the trowel in your right hand, work from left to right.

First deposit a ¾-inch layer of mortar three to five bricks long on top of the concrete slab to form a mortar bed. Trim the mortar from the front face of the slab and then lay the first brick at a corner. Tap this brick into place and check it with your level to make sure it's perfectly level and square with the greenhouse corner. "Butter" the next brick on the end and set it against the first placed brick, ensuring that there is a good bond between the mortar and the brick. It's important that you don't move the first brick as you lay the second one. Typically, a beginner does not sufficiently butter the end of the second brick, meaning there's not enough mortar between the bricks to fill the joint. Pushing mortar into the joint from above makes for a weak joint that allows moisture into the wall. It's better to rebutter the brick and lay it again.

When laying a brick wall, as with a concrete-block wall, it's best to build the corners first and stretch a mason's twine between them to ensure that each course is straight and level. Work carefully and lay the bricks tight, with about ⅜ inch to ½ inch of mortar between each. If you've been careful in your greenhouse design and dimensions, you may not have to cut bricks. If you do need to cut a brick, however, there are several ways to do it. You can score around the brick with a brick set, then rap the brick along the cut line on each face. A brick may have flaws that cause it to break in places other than the cut line, however; if this occurs, either discard the brick or chip away the damaged part until you get the half-brick that you need.

A more accurate and foolproof method for cutting brick is to use a masonry saw or an old circular saw fitted with a masonry blade. I've used this method when laying a brick path. I had to cut bricks as the path narrowed from ten bricks across to eight or seven. Be aware that cutting a brick using a masonry blade creates lots of dust and flying debris, so you'll need to wear a dust mask and eye protection.

When you've finished laying a course or two in your wall and the mortar is still plastic, tool or point the joints of the brick so that they shed rain. (See Making a Mortar Bed and Laying the Block, page 127, and the illustration on page 128.)

Constructing a Stone Foundation

For an old-fashioned, rustic look, you can want to build a stone foundation for your greenhouse. Stonework is an enormous subject and working with stone requires a great deal of skill. The first step is to decide what type of stone you want to use. Visit a local landscaper to see what's available. A landscaper or mason can also advise you on the best type of wall for your area and the best way to construct it. Though I offer a basic overview here to help you understand the process, if you decide you want a stone

Buttering Brick

To butter a brick, place about half a trowel of concrete on the end of the brick. Then, using the trowel, cut off the concrete edges at about a 30-degree angle on all four sides of the brick. Now you will have a short, pyramid-like pile of mortar on the end of the brick. Push this pile of mortar against the previously set brick and the mortar will squish to fill the entire joint. Use the trowel to lop off any mortar that has been squeezed out of the joint beyond the edge of the brick. Butter each brick before pushing it against the previous one. If you don't get enough mortar between the bricks, lift away a brick, scrape off any mortar, and butter it again before laying it in place. Don't try to push more mortar into the brick because doing so creates a weak joint.

Holding a trowel with your thumb on top makes it easier to pick up mortar and lay it on a brick.

foundation and/or wall, you should talk to a qualified mason. These and stone veneer work are not usually jobs to be taken on by an amateur.

Building a stone foundation is much more difficult than building with brick. For a start, stones come in many sizes and are not uniform. Second, a greenhouse requires a low stone wall with a top that is flat and smooth. Laying a stone veneer on a concrete wall requires even more skill. No matter which route you take — full stone wall or veneer — the result will tend to be quite thick and massive and you may well end up with a good-size stone shelf inside the perimeter of the greenhouse.

If you plan to build with stone, you (or the mason) should inspect each rock carefully, looking for a flat side that can be used for the outside face of the wall. The theory is to build with smaller rocks around larger ones so that there is no gap in the face of the wall. A stone wall can be dry-laid or built with mortar that either shows or doesn't show (giving it a dry-laid look).

The top of a stone foundation or wall should be impervious to water. This can be accomplished by finishing the wall with a mortar cap to smooth and level the surface. A stone wall can serve as a good heat-retaining rear wall of a passively heated greenhouse set into a hill. Such a wall can be up to 4 or 5 feet tall. If you decide to build a wall of this nature, you may want to insulate the exterior face to ensure that it stays warm after it has been heated by the sun.

Of course, if you want a really fancy greenhouse, you could build a stone wall with a fireplace in it and a flue that circulates through the wall to retain more heat. Or you could build a stone wall with ornamental features such as a waterfall built directly into it.

Constructing a Wooden Foundation

In general, a wooden foundation is most often made of pressure-treated wood, but I don't like to use pressure-treated wood where vegetables are going to be grown in the ground. The chemicals may leach into the soil and can potentially be absorbed by vegetables; the deeper the timbers extend into the soil, the more leaching

can occur because of increased exposure of the soil to the wood's chemicals. (See chapter 6, page 79, for more on this.) Remember, too, that a wooden foundation, like other kinds, will shift with heavy frost and freezing. If you do decide to use wood as a foundation material, you may have to install it below the frost line. Animals can also tunnel under a wooden foundation at ground level.

Using Landscape Timbers for the Foundation

If want an easy method of building a foundation without the hassle of pouring concrete or using cement blocks or bricks, you can lay down landscape timbers to suit the size of your greenhouse and set the greenhouse on top of them. The advantages of this method are that it is fast and easy and you can buy the timbers at most home and garden centers. The disadvantage is that you'll have to use treated lumber.

If you decide to use this method, place 8×8 timbers in a shallow trench so that the tops of the timbers are level with the ground. You may want to lay two or three timbers one above the

For an easy-to-construct foundation, you can use 8×8 landscape timbers buried in a trench and pinned together (A). For areas where the ground freezes, install layers of timbers (B) deeper in the ground to avoid heaving with freeze-and-thaw cycles.

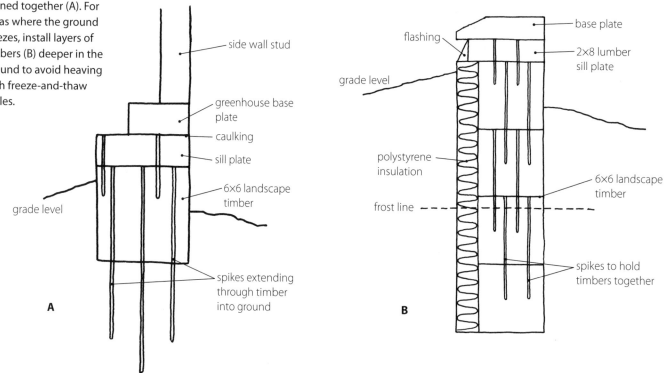

A — side wall stud / greenhouse base plate / caulking / sill plate / 6×6 landscape timber / grade level / spikes extending through timber into ground

B — flashing / base plate / 2×8 lumber sill plate / grade level / polystyrene insulation / frost line / 6×6 landscape timber / spikes to hold timbers together

other in a deeper trench so that the foundation is set farther down in the ground. In this case, the two timbers should be attached by drilling ½-inch-diameter holes through both timbers and hammering rebar through the holes. The length of your rebar will, of course, depend on the number of 8-inch-thick landscape timbers you are using.

Corner joints can be made quite simply by cutting lap joints and pinning the two timbers with rebar as described above. A lap joint is a section cut from the corner of the wood so that it will lie flush with the wood meeting it at 90 degrees. If your landscape timber is 8 inches thick, to mark where the lap joint will be cut, measure 8 inches from the end of the wood and mark a line across the wood 4 inches in toward the center of the timber on both sides. Next, draw a line from the tops of the 4-inch lines to the end of the timber and across the face of the end to mark the piece that will be removed. You can cut it out with a handsaw or a chain saw. Mark in the same way the timber that will be joined with the first. Fit together the two timbers, drill two or three holes through the lap, and pin the two together with rebar. If you are

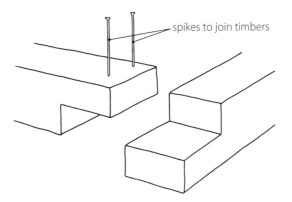

spikes to join timbers

Lap joints create a secure fit at the corners.

building a timber wall that is three or four timbers high, drill and pin all the corners at once rather than doing them individually.

The sill plates of the greenhouse will be fastened on top of the landscape timbers and are best attached using 16d galvanized nails or 3-inch galvanized or stainless decking screws. Caulk before laying the sill plate to ensure that there are no spaces between the lumber and the sill. With the sill plate in place, you can build your greenhouse on top of the wooden foundation using any of the methods described and illustrated in chapter 9.

9 Building Techniques

BEYOND ALL QUESTIONS OF STYLE AND intended use for your greenhouse (see chapter 2 for more information on these), your choices for greenhouse construction are quite simple: You can, like many people, buy a kit, or you can design and build a structure yourself (or with a contractor), incorporating an eclectic style, perhaps, and making use of materials close to hand. If you decide to design and build a greenhouse on your own, you'll need an understanding of basic building techniques ranging from framing and hanging doors and windows to installing insulation.

Building a Kit Greenhouse

If you decide to purchase a kit greenhouse, the structure may come partially or completely assembled on the back of a truck or it may be delivered in boxed parts. For some greenhouses, you might have to assemble the jigsaw puzzle of aluminum struts and braces for the frame, bolting together pieces of the predrilled frame or even drilling the holes yourself and cutting parts to length. For other kits, the walls, roof, and ends come preassembled; all you may have to do is bolt together the sides and top. In still other cases, all that is required is installing the glazing. Most kit greenhouse suppliers have clearly illustrated building manuals to help you, and some include videos, a hot line, or even access to a local expert to help you assemble the project.

Before you start building any kit greenhouse, read the instructions carefully, watch any instructional videos provided, and do not cut anything unless the instructions tell you to do so. Before you begin any fastening, lay out the parts on a flat surface according to their placement in the finished structure, checking the part numbers carefully as you do so. Snapping together or fastening any parts before you've identified and organized all pieces may result in a join that is difficult to undo.

In general, for kit greenhouses you'll probably need to lay a special polyfoam sill moisture barrier/insulation on the foundation. Then you'll have to install the sill or base plate over the polyfoam and the bolts in the concrete foundation and bolt the sill plate to the foundation, which sandwiches the insulation and moisture barrier between the frame and concrete. After this, you'll have to assemble the walls and stand them on the sill or base plate. Some kits require assembling the wall first because the bottom of the frame acts as the sill plate. On larger greenhouses, you may lay the base plate and erect each framed wall one at a time, tying the entire unit together with longitudinals and a ridge bar.

As you assemble, remember to check that the structure is square and to install any bracing as you work. If you spread out your construction over two days and tighten bolts on day one, you'll usually find that the following morning you can go back and get another half-turn on each bolt — but be careful not to tighten bolts so much that you risk crushing or damaging the structure.

In many kits, the door is pre-hung. For some, however, you may have to hang the door(s) or install sliding doors. In general, sliding doors are made to run on tracks and if you install them properly, they should provide years of trouble-free operation if you lubricate the bottom track and roller bearings occasionally.

Assembling larger greenhouse structures may require you to set up supports and support posts fastened to the foundation plate. You should determine the location of these before the foundation is poured so that you can insert bolts or tubing into the wet concrete in the correct places for the supports to be attached to them. Note that if your kit is for a large greenhouse, you may need the help of four or five people to erect the structure, one frame wall at a time. The largest greenhouse structures may require a crane to hoist the frames into place. If you are building a sizeable structure, determine these needs well before you start construction.

Building a Conventional or Do-It-Yourself Greenhouse

Unless you are an avid woodworker who will get as much pleasure out of making a greenhouse as you will out of working in it, you may decide that building your own conventional greenhouse is not for you. Yet many benefits can come with building your own structure. For example, you might make decisions and adjustments for your particular situation: You can decide to install triple-glazed glass or polycarbonate on the north wall for better insulation or make a snug-fitting door to keep winter drafts at bay, or you can construct better and lighter vents that can easily be opened automatically. If you build the structure yourself, you can modify plans along the way or, preferably, decide to introduce particular elements at the outset. Refer to the plans for conventional greenhouses in chapter 13 to find a structure that suits your growing needs and think of the ways that you could modify the one you decide to build.

As stated in chapter 6, if you decide to build a conventional greenhouse yourself using red

Tools to Build a Kit Greenhouse

The specific number and type of tools will depend on the greenhouse kit, but will likely include:

- Assorted wrenches
- A portable battery-powered or electric drill and assorted bits, including a Phillips head bit and hex bolt driver heads
- Screwdrivers: flathead and Phillips head
- A saw or two (a hand ripsaw, a hacksaw, a circular saw, and a saber saw)
- A ladder or two, depending on the size of the greenhouse
- Pliers and vise grips
- Clamps
- Gloves (optional). These can make it difficult for you to cut accurately, but they might make building and assembly more comfortable
- Safety glasses and ear plugs

cedar or a high-quality wood, you'll have to decide on the glazing long before you start work on the greenhouse because the glazing will determine what type of framing you'll need. Glass, for instance, must be set into the greenhouse frame and fastened in place. Polycarbonate, on the other hand, can be fastened over the framework. Remember that some design modifications beyond glazing require that you make adjustments in the framework. For a precision job such as building your own structure with extensive variations or modifications on a conventional design, you'll probably need a good woodworking shop with quality tools and plenty of time (see the box above). But you can build a conventional structure such as a Gothic arches greenhouse or make small modifications to a conventional greenhouse using standard tools.

If you asked a plumber, a mason, and a carpenter to design and build a greenhouse from scratch, it is most likely that each would build it from the materials that he or she knows best. The plumber might build a Quonset-style or hoop house out of metal or PVC pipes. The mason would build a house that incorporates a lot of brickwork or stonework, and a carpenter would build it out of wood. Because many home-owners are most familiar with working in wood, it often becomes the material of choice.

Framing Techniques Using Standard Lumber

To design and build a wooden structure, you need to know standard lumber sizes (see chapter 6 for more information on standard lumber) and you need to incorporate these sizes into your design and construction.

For example, suppose your design calls for a 4-foot-9-inch-tall wooden structural wall. You can cut studs to 4 feet 4¼ inches and use a sill plate and double cap to get 4 feet 9 inches, but this wastes 3 feet 7½ inches of each stud. If you modify the wall to 4 feet 4½ inches, you can cut a stud in half and use a sill plate and double cap plate to arrive at 4 feet 4½ inches. For any wall height under 4 feet 4½ inches, you can get two pieces of support lumber from every stud. By sizing your structure for standard framing lumber lengths, you will reduce the amount of waste and keep down the cost of the construction.

If you are very careful to install vapor barriers, regular building lumber is adequate for a greenhouse given the caveats regarding longevity and rot resistance outlined in chapter 6. It is easily available and reasonably priced, and can be worked with few tools. But you must know how to build a wall, frame a door, and square the structure properly before you can successfully build a greenhouse.

Building a Lumber Wall

If you plan to build a 4-foot by 12-foot wall, you could go to the lumber store and buy a bunch of 2×4s and have at it. But if you work out your framing and lumber needs on paper first, you can figure out exactly how many pieces of lumber and what lengths are required. If the wall is to be 12 feet long, the top and bottom plates will be 12-footers, so you can put two (or three if you are using a double cap plate) 12-foot-long 2×4s on your list. Next you'll need to figure the spacing of studs on the top and bottom plates. By putting together both 12-foot 2×4s and using a square, you can quickly mark out the location of all the 4-foot-long vertical studs. Each stud is placed 16 inches on center; you'll need 11 of them. (Cut six 8-foot studs in half to get what you need and use the scraps for doubling the corners.) Where walls join at the corners, the framing of one of the walls must be three studs (4½ inches) thick because the adjoining wall will overlap by 3½ inches (the width of a stud)

Tools to Build a Custom Conventional or Do-It Yourself Greenhouse

If you intend to build the entire green-house yourself (especially using a wood such as redwood, cedar, or teak), you may require specialized power wood-working tools such as a planer or table saw to cut the lumber accurately to size. You can often rent specialized tools or have a commercial woodworking shop make the special parts for you. Lengths can be cut with a handsaw in a miter box or with a chop box.

SPECIALIZED POWER TOOLS TO MAKE THE JOB EASIER
- Table saw
- Router
- Planer
- Miter or chop box
- Power nail gun for framing and finish nailing. You will also require an air compressor to operate the nail gun.

ESSENTIAL HAND TOOLS
- Tape measure
- Hammer

- Assorted screwdrivers
- Wrenches for bolting the sill plate in place
- Saws: circular and various handsaws
- One or two planes
- Framing square
- Straightedge at least 4 feet long
- 4-foot-long level
- Assorted chisels and a mallet
- Portable electric or battery-powered drill and assorted bits
- Caulking gun

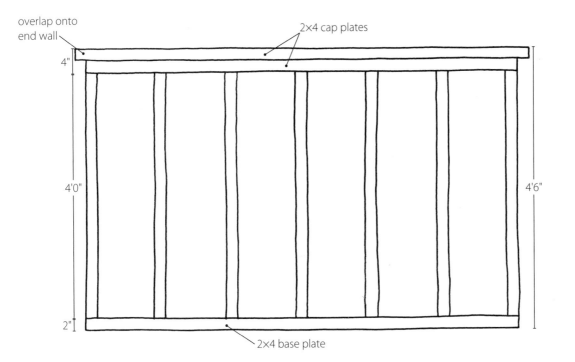

overlap onto
end wall

2×4 cap plates

This wall has one base
plate and two cap plates.

4"

4'0"

4'6"

2"

2×4 base plate

and you'll need the remaining 1 inch to provide a nailing surface for the interior sheathing. While you can actually frame the ends to be overlapped with three studs, it is more economical to use two studs with 2×4 scraps sandwiched between as shown in the illustration at right.

Some walls, especially those that are to be heavily insulated, may be made of 2×6 lumber. A wall will then be 6 inches wide instead of 4 inches wide (of course, the actual dimension of the lumber is 5½ inches wide). This will allow for 5½ inches of insulation. If you decide to make your walls 6 inches thick, you can space the vertical supports 20 inches on center rather than 16 inches on center.

Framing Doors and Windows

In your lumber calculations, account for window and door framing if a wall is to have them. Lay out the rough opening for these — that is, the space the door and its frame will occupy in the wall. Most 3-foot doors have a rough opening width of 37½ inches, allowing 36 inches for the door itself and ¾ inch on either side of the door for the frame. When you lay out the wall to include a door, notice that the two studs inside the door frame are cut shorter than the two outside of it. These studs, known as jacks, filler, or

blocking

corner stud

Frame a corner using two or three studs to ensure that the interior sheathing can be nailed to the corner. You can use blocking made from scrap pieces of lumber to space the studs the correct distance from the corner.

trimmer studs, support the door header, which is secured on top of the jacks to offer structural integrity to the opening so that the weight of the wall is supported. The header is made of two 2×8s or 2×10s, with ½-inch plywood sandwiched between to match the 3½-inch width of the studs.

A window is framed similarly, but in addition to a header, it has a sill, a piece like the header attached to the bottom of the window opening. The sill is supported by lumber called cripple studs. If a window to be installed is 3 feet wide,

A door is framed by making a rough opening 37½ inches wide. Two jacks (shortened studs) support the door header. A window has beneath it a piece similar to a header, which is supported on cripple studs.

the rough opening will be 37½ to 39 inches wide, depending on the type of window.

Note that when the wall is laid out, the bottom plate, known as the base or sole plate, is not cut from the doorway until the door is framed

in and the wall is erected. This ensures that the wall and doorway remain square. Note also that inserting a window or a door in a wall does not disrupt the continuity of the 16-inches-on-center stud spacing from end to end.

Building End Walls

Generally, the end walls of a greenhouse are peaked, though the peak may be located toward one side of the structure (at the back of a lean-to greenhouse, for instance) or in the middle of the roof. Many home-built greenhouses have a vertical wall and ridge at the rear and the glazing sloping from the back wall almost to a knee wall at the front. This type of design makes building the roof a bit easier.

If the ridge is to be in the middle of the greenhouse and the greenhouse is to be taller than 8 feet, you should construct stud walls for the end walls (see Building a Lumber Wall, page 136) and build the triangular roof section on top of it. If your greenhouse is to be less than 8 feet tall, you can build the entire end wall section from 2×4 studs.

To build an end wall with insulation for a lean-to-style greenhouse (see the illustration at bottom left), first set a base plate and lay out your studs at 16 inches on center. Next, lay out the height of the front knee wall and the tall rear wall and cut two studs to these measurements. You can then estimate the slope of the roof and cut all the rest of the wall studs. An end wall with a center ridge is built in a similar manner, although I like to ensure that the ridgepole is supported on doubled 2×4s.

Building a glazed end wall is a little more difficult. First, you'll have to determine what type of glazing you are going to use. Glass can be recessed into the wood supports. Polycarbonate can be bolted onto the outside of the wood supports. You'll also need to determine the width of your glazing and set your vertical studs to accommodate this width. For example, if your glazing is 2-foot-wide polycarbonate panels, you will set your studs 20½ inches on center. The additional half-inch allows for an expansion gap between the glazing panels. At the corners the first support might be set a little nearer to the

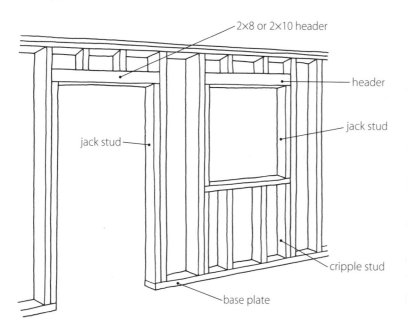

2×8 or 2×10 header

header

jack stud

jack stud

cripple stud

base plate

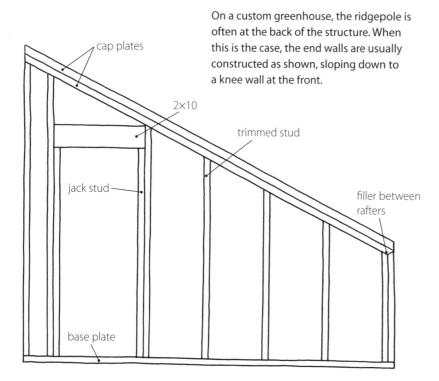

On a custom greenhouse, the ridgepole is often at the back of the structure. When this is the case, the end walls are usually constructed as shown, sloping down to a knee wall at the front.

cap plates

2×10

trimmed stud

jack stud

filler between rafters

base plate

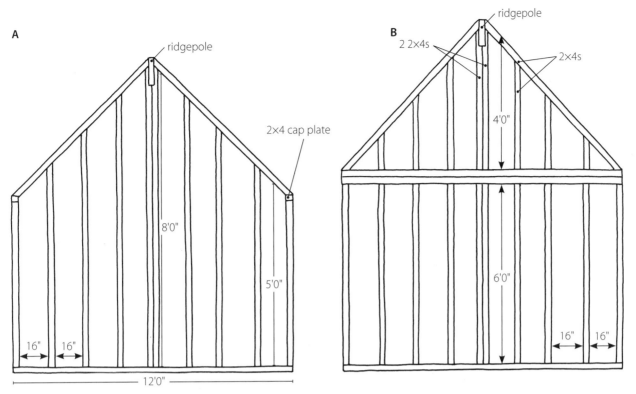

A

ridgepole

2×4 cap plate

8'0"

5'0"

16" 16"

12'0"

B

ridgepole

2 2×4s

2×4s

4'0"

6'0"

16" 16"

If the structure is 8 feet tall or less **(A)**, end walls can be constructed entirely of 2×4 studs. If it's taller than 8 feet **(B)**, construct stud walls with a triangular roof section on top.

edge of the greenhouse so that the glazing can cover the wood right to the corner.

The Ridgepole or Ridge Beam

Once your end walls are in place, the next step is to install the ridgepole or beam. It can be a 2×6 for a small greenhouse that is 8 feet to 10 feet long, but for larger greenhouses, it should be a 2×8 or 2×10. If your greenhouse is very long (more than 16 feet), you may have to install a center post to support the ridgepole or use a long laminated beam or maybe a steel I-bar. I've installed a center post in my 20-foot-long cool greenhouse.

Roof Construction

Building the roof is challenging because you want to be sure the glazing fits tightly on the roof so that there's no risk of it sliding off the edge. This means that both ends of each rafter beam must be carefully shaped. Typically, if the roof has an overhang or eave, a builder will cut a triangular piece, called a bird's-mouth cut, from the lower end of the rafter to ensure that the rafter will sit more firmly on the vertical support wall. If there is no overhang, the bottom of the rafter will have to be cut level, sometimes

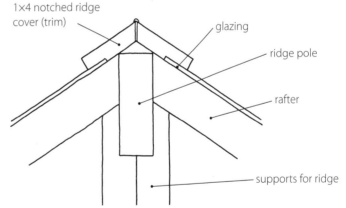

1×4 notched ridge cover (trim)

glazing

ridge pole

rafter

supports for ridge

Construction of the ridgepole

known as a seat cut. Most greenhouses do not have eaves and use a level cut at the bottom.

For a lean-to greenhouse (as shown in the illustration on page 138), the top of each rafter will need to be cut vertically with a bird's-mouth cut to allow it to sit on the rear wall. If the ridge is in the middle of the greenhouse, the top of each rafter should be cut vertically and butted against the matching rafter on the opposite side of the greenhouse. When installing rafters, always install the two opposing rafters before moving on to the next pair. If you install all the rafters on one side before installing those on the other side, you may end up bending the ridgepole slightly, causing misalignment of your greenhouse roof.

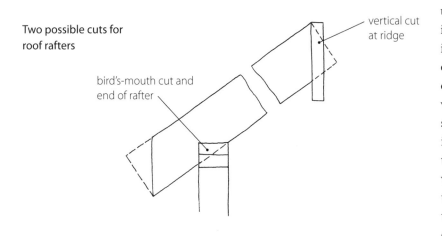

Two possible cuts for roof rafters

vertical cut at ridge

bird's-mouth cut and end of rafter

Laying Out Rafters

Laying out rafters takes a certain amount of knowledge and skill. You'll need to measure and cut carefully or, as Mr. Worrall, my old woodworking teacher, used to say, measure twice, cut once. The best way to cut each rafter is to determine all measurements while the rafter is on the ground. First, determine the pitch of the roof. Pitch is expressed in terms of 12 horizontal inches. Thus, a 4:12 pitch (read "four twelve") rises 4 inches for every 12 horizontal inches. Next, determine the span of the roof (the horizontal distance from the wall to the ridge). The above illustration, which shows a 6:12 slope (6 inches of slope for every 12 inches), let's us visualize the pitch of a roof.

To arrive at rafter measurements for a roof with a 4:12 pitch, measure the width of your greenhouse. Let's say the width is 12 feet with the ridge in the middle of the span. You can lay out the rafters in two ways. The first method uses the Pythagorean theorem, which holds that the square of the length of the hypotenuse of a right triangle is equal to the square of the base plus the square of the height. In other words, if the base is a, the height is b, and the hypotenuse is c, $a^2 + b^2 = c^2$. If the base is 6 feet and the height is 4 feet, the hypotenuse is $6^2 + 4^2 = 52$.

The square root of 52 = c = 7.211 inches or 7 feet 2½ inches. You can measure this on the rafter and then determine where the vertical cut at the ridge should be made and where the bird's-mouth or seat cut should be made.

Another method for laying out the rafters is to use a framing square. For a 6:12 slope, the square is placed on the upper end of the rafter with 12 inches along the base and 6 inches on the vertical. To find the right length, the framing square can be walked down the rafter to the bottom, where you can mark for either a bird's-mouth or seat cut. Note that because it slopes, the rafter is longer than the horizontal distance along the top of the wall and part of it will butt against the wall. For a greenhouse, I like to cut the seat so that it fits flush with the vertical edge of the wall to ensure that the glazing can fit without a large overhang or a gap between the wall glazing and the roof glazing.

Joints

Most of custom greenhouse construction is straightforward stud-and-nail or screw construction using butt or lap joints. At times, however, it calls for incorporating other joints. One such case is the construction of a window. For the corners, you can use a lap joint or a miter joint with or without a biscuit depending on your expertise as a carpenter. A biscuit is a flat, oval piece of compressed wood about 2 inches long and ⅛ inch thick that is inserted in matching mortises in the two pieces of wood to be joined. Once the pieces are joined, the biscuit is invisible. Glue is usually added to the biscuit and the mortises before inserting it so that when the two pieces of wood are brought together, the wet biscuit will expand and the join will be even stronger. Using biscuits helps to form a perfectly aligned joint.

In most situations, joints for a greenhouse structure can be simple lap joints. But in some cases — for example, where three pieces of wood need to be joined — a lap joint may be difficult to make or it may leave very little material on the original wood. In these cases, you'll have to modify the lap joint and perhaps glue it to increase its strength. Screwing or nailing corner joints is always fraught with potential difficulties when

Four Types of Joints

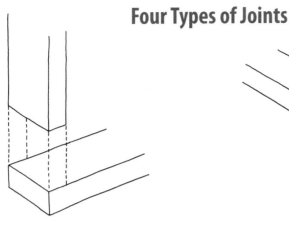

BUTT JOINT

LAP JOINT

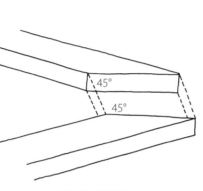

MITER JOINT

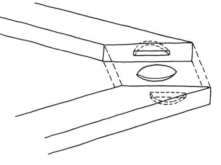

MITER JOINT WITH BISCUIT

large sheets of glass or other glazing must be fitted. Some common problems are glass slipping and breaking and glass not fitting in corners that aren't exactly square.

Using Epoxy

Instead of nailing or screwing your greenhouse together, you can glue it together with epoxy. This allows you to build the greenhouse without worrying about whether nails or screws will touch the glazing. You can also use epoxy as a coating to protect the wood. Once set, it is virtually waterproof. Epoxy does not contain any UV inhibitors, however, so if you decide to coat the wood with this material, you should apply a couple of layers of UV-resistant varnish such as Epifanes or Schooner to protect against UV degradation.

Epoxy construction is not used only for wood. It will bind fiberglass, aluminum, steel, many plastics, cement, and even granite, and can be an invaluable tool in greenhouse construction.

What Is Epoxy?

Epoxy is a glue that is usually colorless, although some epoxies appear to have a slight sheen. The source of its spectacular strength comes from the cross-linked molecular chains that are formed in the course of mixing in specific ratios its two parts, resin and accelerator (from one can or tube) and a hardener (in a separate can or tube). While it can be a wonder glue, it's important to note that epoxy is often difficult to work with.

Most manufacturers make a "fast" hardener that sets up within 10 minutes or so and a "moderate" or "slow" hardener to be used for bigger jobs that might take 20 to 30 minutes or more to set up. Typically, epoxy with a fast hardener is sufficient for small jobs, allowing you to put together the parts, clamp them, and walk away. If you are mixing large batches of epoxy, you should use the slowest hardener to allow you the time to use the mixture before it sets up in the pot. Some hardeners such as Epiglass from Interlux are designed to allow you to adjust the cure rate by mixing fast, moderate, or slow hardener. By mixing them carefully, you can get a cure rate that varies from about 10 minutes to 30 minutes or more.

Mixing

Always mix resin/accelerator and hardener in the proportions recommended by the epoxy manufacturer. These proportions vary by brand. One of the most significant causes of epoxy failure is incorrect mixing of these two ingredients. Most manufacturers supply mini-pumps for measuring with their gallon or quart cans, but if you don't have a pump, you can use a measuring cup or a measuring stick dipped in a cup of resin/accelerator measured against another stick dipped in a cup of hardener. *Important:* Don't mix resins and hardeners from different manufacturers — don't combine, for example, Epiglass resin and MAS hardener. These may have different properties and may not work together. Along with combining the two ingredients in the correct ratio, you'll need to make sure they are thoroughly mixed. In the process of stirring, scrape down the sides of the pot and make certain all material from the bottom is incorporated before adding thickening agents to help prevent the epoxy from running out of the joints. A thoroughly mixed resin will be an opaque, whitish color. If the epoxy is poorly mixed, it won't set up properly and you'll have to scrape it off the surfaces you wanted to join before you can apply a new mixture.

Sanding epoxies can be bad for your health because of the dust it produces. At the minimum, wear a dust mask.

Before you begin mixing, determine how much epoxy you'll need and mix only that amount. Mixing big batches often leads to tossing out unused resin. Note that the interaction of the resin and hardener produces heat, and if the mixture gets too hot, it will begin to harden in the mixing container before you get a chance to use it. In some cases, the heat generated will melt the mixing cup or container and has even been known to start a fire. For this reason, never toss unused, unset epoxy into the trash. Set it outside on a nonflammable surface until it has set up, then dispose of it properly.

Surface Preparation

Before mixing epoxy, ensure that the surfaces to be glued are clean and free of dust and sanding residues, waxes, and oils. Professionals generally wipe surfaces with a solvent such as Dupont's Prep-Sol or acetone. If the solvent beads up, it indicates that additional contaminants are present and the surface should be cleaned again. Use 40- to 60-grit sandpaper on wood to roughen the surface for a good bond. If you are gluing teak, wipe the surface with a solvent such as acetone to remove any teak oil before gluing.

Applying Epoxy

If you are using epoxy for a simple wood joint, coat both surfaces you want to join, wait a minute or two to allow the glue to penetrate the wood, and press together the two surfaces. Clamping or screwing the pieces after you've applied the epoxy will further strengthen the join as the glue sets; however, beware of clamping it too tight; if you squeeze most of the epoxy out of the joint, it is likely to fail. After the epoxy has set, use a chisel to clean excess glue off the surfaces of the wood.

It's all right if your application skills produce a job that's a bit sloppy. Epoxy works best in sloppy joints where the glue is plentiful. To mask errors, simply mix a little wood filler or fine sawdust into the epoxy and set up the joint in the usual way. The beauty of epoxy is that it both fills small holes and gives a strong joint. In fact, experiments have shown that the wood will fail before the epoxy in a joint does.

Curing Epoxy

The hardener speed and the temperature at the time of using the glue govern the cure time of an epoxy, although the amount of epoxy used and humidity also come into play. By using a fast hardener — the fastest I know of are MAS Fast Hardener and the newest variety of Epiglass hardener, both with a pot life of 7 to 10 minutes (*pot life* is the time it takes for the epoxy to set up in the container in which you mix it) — and allowing the epoxy to set in a temperature of around 75°F to 80°F, the cure time can be so short that you may not have time to set up the job properly. Remember that pot life is shorter than the amount of time it takes spread epoxy to set. A mixture tends to "kick" sooner in a deep pot than it will when spread thinly over a flat area. To extend the pot life of your resin, pour the epoxy into a shallower pot. You can also extend the pot life by half an hour or more by using a slower hardener and working in 50°F to 60°F temperatures. The amount of time the resin mixture stays in liquid form is known as the *open time*. This is the total amount of time that you have to work with the glue. Trying to use resin after it has started to cure produces a result that looks like a painted surface that has been disturbed when partly dry. In addition, the partially dry epoxy will not create a strong bond.

Sanding

Sanding epoxies can be bad for your health because of the dust it produces. When undertaking the job, at the minimum wear a dust mask, though it's best to wear a respirator. Epoxies can be sanded with normal sanding tools, but you must be careful not to over-sand the soft wood around a hard epoxy finish, which is easy to do. In most cases, epoxies should be left to cure for about 24 hours before they are sanded, although some fast-curing epoxies may be sanded after 6 or 8 hours.

Greenhouse Construction Details

There are myriad details in the design and building of a greenhouse, particularly concerning the roof construction, the way glazing is attached to the rafters and ridge, the way the greenhouse is attached to the foundation, and the construction of doors and windows. Although some of these may be specific to a certain design, many are common to most greenhouses.

Epoxy Safety

When working with epoxy, you should protect your eyes with safety goggles and avoid breathing the vapors. If you're not working in a well-ventilated area, wear a respirator. Some epoxies contain volatile organic compounds (VOCs) and phenols, which can make you quite ill. If you are doing any sanding, wear a respirator to ensure that you do not breathe in sanding dust. If you get any epoxy in your eye, most manufacturers recommend immediately flushing it with running water for at least 15 minutes. Epoxy fillers such as microballoons used to thicken the glue mixture (which can be fairly runny) are stirred into mixed epoxy. Because these fillers usually come in the form of powders, to prevent inhaling them, you should wear a respirator (or, at minimum, a dust mask) when working with them.

Epoxy is nasty stuff to get on your skin. In fact, it can be so sensitizing to your skin that you break out in a rash as soon as somebody opens a can of the material. When working with it, always use a barrier cream on any exposed skin and wear disposable gloves. Avoid direct skin contact with resin and hardener and wash thoroughly with soap and water after the job is done. Even though many professionals wash with solvent, I don't recommend doing so because the dilution of most solvents allows them to penetrate the skin very easily. Instead, use plenty of soap and water — and I've found that Hand and Tool Towels from Bostick are ideal for removing any resin that does get on the skin. Packaged in a can, these towels are handy to have around your workplace and home.

After the job, wash tools with acetone or white vinegar or (carefully) use the manufacturer's suggested cleaner. Don't discard containers of unused epoxy mixtures until the epoxy in them has completely set. Remember that heat is given off when epoxy sets up and if the mixture sets up in a container, it can emit smoke or even combust. Containers of unused, unset epoxy mix should be set on the ground outside the shop (never in a trash can) until the mixture cures and you can safely dispose of them.

If you have questions about the toxicity of any materials that you are working with, you can obtain a Material Safety Data Sheet (MSDS) from the manufacturer. MSDSs are required for all epoxies and provide details on all toxic materials in the resin and hardener.

The Roof and Ridgepole

There are a number of details related to the construction of the rafters. If the rafters call for cutting a joint so that each rafter comes flush to the top of the vertical wall, some way must be devised to keep the glazing from sliding right off the framework. In between the rafters you'll need to set a filler piece for the glazing to rest on before adding the blocking to keep the glazing in place. On top of the blocking and glazing, add a trim piece with a bead of caulking near the top to keep water out of the joint. In addition, some edging is required at the bottom of the glazing to keep out rainwater.

Keeping the water out of your greenhouse starts at the top of the structure, with the roof and ridgepole assembly and the covering that overlaps the glazing. At the bottom of the roof glazing, the cap pieces are tapered to allow water to run off and all joints are horizontal. Caulking and flashing are used extensively to ensure that water stays on the outside of the structure.

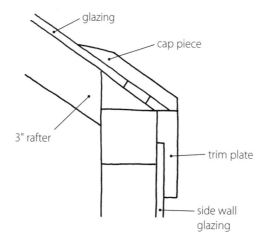

There are also certain construction details related to the ridgepole. While I've chosen to support the ridgepole of my long greenhouse with a double vertical center pole, a single vertical support would work just as well. The glazing (polycarbonate in the illustration above left) is laid on the rafters and held in place by a cap piece on each rafter. At the ridge the glazing is fitted under a covering board mitered to suit the angle of the roof. This covering board is either epoxied or caulked at the mitered, vertical joint so that it remains watertight. In fact, by sloping the upper edge of the covering board and caulking it to the glazing, I have found that it stays watertight in almost all conditions.

The Side Walls

The glazing is also caulked at the bottom of the sidewall to keep out moisture. In addition, the glazing rests on hard rubber pads to help absorb its weight and to give it a little room to expand and contract. If the foundation is insulated, you should make sure that the weight of the structure rests on the concrete portion of the foundation instead of the portion over the insulation. Because the greenhouse is set back from the edge of the foundation, it's important to add some flashing to direct water away from the wood.

Window Construction

A single window is not too difficult to build; however, even the simplest window can be cumbersome to operate if appropriate materials are not used. For example, in my heated greenhouse, I used $1 \times 1\frac{1}{2}$ stock to frame the 24-inch by 18-inch windows in the structure. After a season of use, however, I found that the lightweight wood frame was distorted where the weight of the glass pulled down on the corners and where the hinges, located nearer the middle of the frame, held it to the framing member. The cure was to increase the size of the horizontal frame members to better support the weight of the glazing.

One difficulty in making windows is accommodating the size of the glazing. If you use double-pane glass, it will probably be at least $\frac{3}{8}$ inch thick. This requires that the wooden part of the

Insulation added to a foundation (**A**) significantly improves heat retention in the greenhouse. In warmer climates, you may not need insulation (**B**).

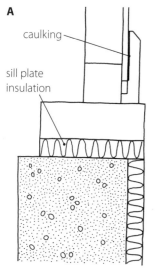

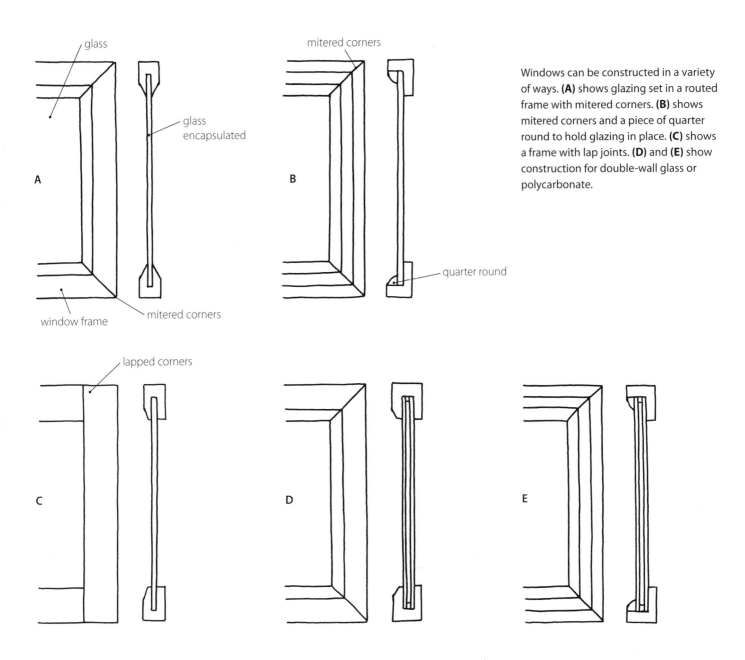

glass

glass
encapsulated

A

window frame

mitered corners

mitered corners

B

quarter round

Windows can be constructed in a variety of ways. **(A)** shows glazing set in a routed frame with mitered corners. **(B)** shows mitered corners and a piece of quarter round to hold glazing in place. **(C)** shows a frame with lap joints. **(D)** and **(E)** show construction for double-wall glass or polycarbonate.

lapped corners

C

D

E

structure is at least 1 inch thick in order for there to be sufficient material on either side of the glazing. In addition, because the glass weighs a fair amount, your structure must be quite strong.

Fastening the glazing in place can also be problematical. For the single-pane window shown in (A) in the illustration above, the wooden frame is routed or sawed to suit the thickness of the glass. The corners are mitered and attached with biscuits to increase their strength. The glass is inserted before the framing is fully closed and is held tightly in place by the frame. With this method, if the glass in the window breaks, you'll have to take apart the frame to insert a new piece of glass. Yet there is no tricky nailing of trim or quarter round to hold the glass in place.

In (B) in the illustration, you can see how a piece of quarter-round wooden trim is inserted to hold the glass in place. I have found, to my chagrin, that it is very easy to break the glass when nailing quarter round in place.

Making windows for double-pane glass or polycarbonate introduces more difficulties in terms of the frame thickness. Different methods are used to hold double-pane or polycarbonate in place, mostly involving greatly increasing the thickness of the framing material.

To make a window, first determine how much lumber you'll need. Let's say you are going to make a 24-inch by 18-inch window for the side wall of the greenhouse. You'll use 1½×3 stock. (Because double-pane glass is ⅜ inch thick, you'll need a substantial frame thickness.) Calculate the perimeter of the window to make sure you buy the right amount of stock. For a 24-inch by 18-inch window, multiply 24 inches by 2 lengths and 18 inches by 2 widths and add them together:

$$(24 \times 2) + (18 \times 2) = 48 + 36 = 84 \text{ inches or } 7 \text{ feet}$$

If you buy an 8-foot length of stock, you'll have a little extra for the corners, depending on the joints you decide to use. In this case, let's say you'll use simple lap joints.

You'll also have to determine the size of the opening for the glass. If the stock is 3 inches wide (actually 2½) and you want the glass to overlap the frame by 1 inch, the opening will be:

$$24 - (2 \times 2.5) = 19 \text{ inches tall and}$$
$$18 - (2 \times 2.5) = 13 \text{ inches wide}$$

But you'll need some overlap to hold the glass in place. If you allow 1 inch of overlap, the final size of the opening for the glass is 21 inches by 15 inches. This size requires that you specially order the glass, which you should do before beginning the window construction. If you use single-pane glass, it will be ⅛ inch thick, but for better insulation value, go with double-pane glass at ⅜ inch thick. If you were to use true 1-inch stock for the window frame, you could easily take out ⅜ inch of material and have some meat left over, but if you use standard 1-inch lumber, which is actually ¾ inch, and cut ⅜ inch of material from it, you'll end up with ⅜ inch of material left to support the glass. This means you'll have to screw a cap to the window frame to hold the glass in place.

Once you cut from the wood the 1-inch by ⅜-inch piece for the glass by running it through the table saw or routing it, you'll end up with an L-shaped piece of wood.

Cut the wood to length to get two 24-inch pieces and two 18-inch pieces, then cut lap joints in each corner. Remember that the laps on the shorter sides will be opposite the laps on the longer sides. With everything cut, you can glue up the frame. I prefer epoxy, but any waterproof glue will do the job. You may want to add a couple of ⅝-inch wood screws in each corner, but it's not necessary. Check that the frame is square by measuring the diagonals and using a framing square. The glass is square, and if your frame is slightly off, you'll have to do some chiseling. If you plan on painting the frame, now is the time to do it, before you install the glass. If you plan to use caulking, set it in place on the painted wood, then install the glass.

A typical window frame with recessed glazing. Cutting a 1-inch by ⅜-inch piece of wood from the frame leaves an L-shaped frame to accept the glass (A). (B) shows the measurements and construction of the frame.

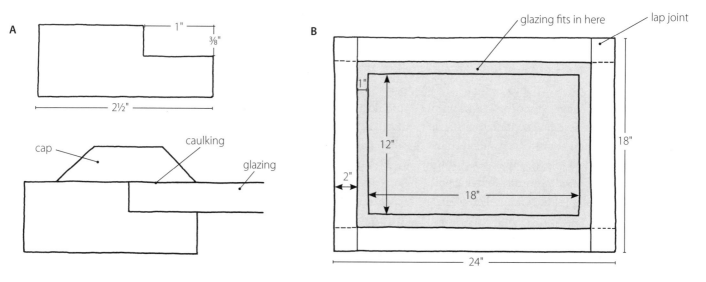

Next, you'll need to make a cap piece. This can be made from ½-inch by 2-inch wood tapered on each side and screwed to the frame to hold the glazing in place. Remember to paint the cap piece before attaching it.

The last job is to install the hinges and any closing hardware. I prefer to do this after the glass is in place, but you may want to cut the hinge recess before you install the glass. The completed window is now ready to be installed in the framed opening.

Making Overhead Windows

Because I have a great deal of experience designing boats, I look upon overhead windows and vents as similar to hatches on a boat. Both are intended to keep water from entering the structure. The following illustrations show my design for an opening window in the roof of my greenhouse. The method for constructing a window like this is similar to that for regular windows, but in this case, the window frame is larger than the opening and fits over a lip that stands about 1 inch high. When water runs under the hatch, it is this lip that keeps the water from running down inside the greenhouse.

The lip is made of ¾-inch by 3-inch stock and runs around the inside perimeter of the opening. To make the hatch lighter, the glazing for the window can be made of single- or double-wall polycarbonate screwed directly to a wooden frame. Although this type of window is relatively light and simple to lift, it racks easily, the corner joints can break, and it does not retain heat as well as a hatch cover with double-pane glass. For a more substantial hatch cover, make a window as you would for a side wall (see the previous instructions) and screw it to the hatch frame that fits around the lip.

The lip is high enough to come within ⅛ inch of the underside of the window frame. On top of the lip, a strip of soft foam butts against the frame and keeps the entire structure airtight. This style of window can be made to suit any size opening and keeps it airtight as well as waterproof. The major problem that I have encountered is window weight (especially with double-pane glass windows; mine weigh about

9 pounds each). This heavier weight makes it difficult to use automatic window openers, even though some are advertised as being able to lift heavy windows. The heavy-duty window opener shown in chapter 4 would probably work well with this hatch, however.

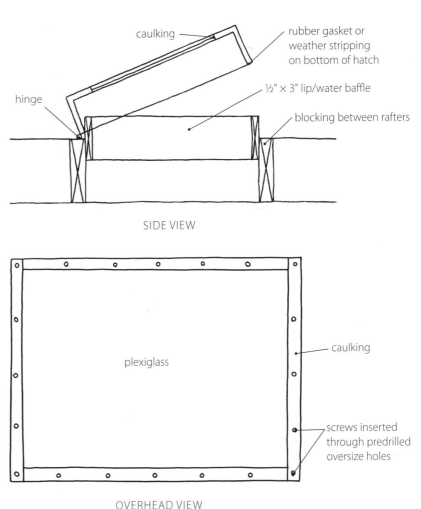

This style of overhead window keeps rain out of your greenhouse.

caulking

rubber gasket or weather stripping on bottom of hatch

½" × 3" lip/water baffle

hinge

blocking between rafters

SIDE VIEW

plexiglass

caulking

screws inserted through predrilled oversize holes

OVERHEAD VIEW

Making Doors

In most cases, you'll buy a door for your greenhouse. Commercially made doors often come with premade trim and a casing requiring a rough opening (37½ inches for a 36-inch-wide door). You can make your own door, however, referring to plans in a number of books on carpentry.

For outdoor protection, it's best to paint a door. With a glass insert, the door adds light to the interior of the greenhouse and a screen insert aids in air circulation, but if you plan to set a door into an unglazed end wall or a north wall, you might want to make it of solid wood. If the door is to be the outer entry to an air lock, you can add rigid foam insulation to the frame to increase its insulation value and then cover this with ⅛-inch or ¼-inch waterproof plywood to help prevent rot.

Installing Glazing

When I was building my freestanding greenhouse, one evening I set the large pieces of 34-inch by 76-inch glass glazing on top of the framework and stopped work for the day. In the morning, I found that one of the sheets of glass had been blown out of its frame and had slid off the greenhouse. Fortunately, it landed on a pile of leaves and didn't break. Since that experience, I have come to the conclusion that the glazing of any greenhouse should always be firmly fastened to the greenhouse frame!

Spacing the Rafters

There are several ways to fasten glass, polycarbonate, or fiberglass glazing to the rafters. The first, most important step is to make sure that your rafters are suitably spaced for the kind of glazing you'll be installing. For example, for glass panes that are 34 inches wide, while you might assume that the rafters should be spaced 34 inches on center, there should actually be ⅜ inch of space between each pane to allow for expansion and to fasten the cap piece in place. This means the rafters should be spaced 34⅜ inches apart.

If your glazing is 48-inch-wide polycarbonate panels and you intend to fasten these directly to the rafters, you'll need to space the rafters 48 inches apart. If you plan to use a commercially made cap piece, locate the rafters at a distance determined by the manufacturer of the cap so that the glazing will fit into or under each

Glazing on the roof can be installed in three ways, depending on the kind of glazing used: In **(A)** and **(B)**, glazing is installed on top of rafters. In **(C)** — best for double-pane glass — glazing is flush to rafters and supported with blocking set below rafters.

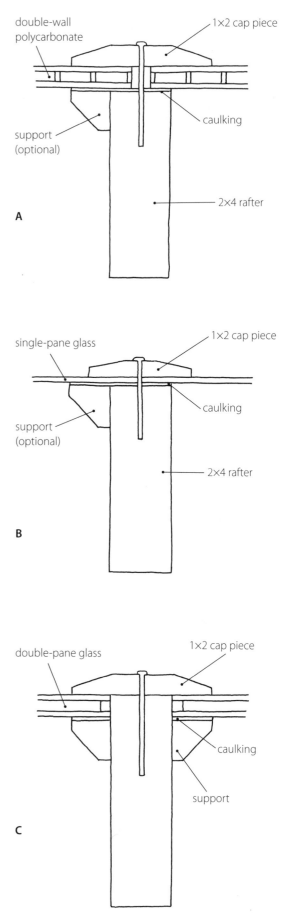

cap piece. Make sure that you check this distance before you start building.

Fiberglass glazing is often overlapped when installed. Thus, if your fiberglass panel is 48 inches wide, space your rafters 46½ inches on center to ensure that each panel fully overlaps the rafter.

Installing Roof Glazing

The illustration on page 148 shows how several types of glazing are fastened to rafters (**A** shows polycarbonate panels, **B** shows single-pane glass, and **C** shows double-pane glass). If you find that a ¾-inch-wide rafter is not sufficient to support a large sheet of polycarbonate or glass, you can add an extra support along the edge of the rafter. The first and second drawings (**A** and **B**) show this support mounted at the top of the rafter, while the third (**C**) shows it set slightly below the top edge, with the glazing set flush to the top of the rafter. While method **C** requires more precision when you're building the greenhouse, it does allow you a full 1½ inches on which to screw or nail down the cap, whereas methods **A** and **B** allow only ⅛ to ¼ inch between the glazing panels to insert a nail or screw. I prefer to use methods **A** and **B** for polycarbonate glazing and method **C** for glass.

Installing Glass If you use method **C** to install glass glazing, spacing rafters and supports to match exactly the width of the glass panes and mounting blocking on each rafter to support the panes, it's important that the entire greenhouse frame is very rigid. If it flexes at all, the glass will crack. In general, the more flexible the greenhouse frame, the less suitable it is for glass glazing. Polycarbonate's "give" better accommodates this flexing and poses less risk of injury if it breaks.

Because glass is a fragile material, it must be installed very carefully. Snagging a sheet of glass on a nail or screw, bending it as you lay it in place, or trying to install it on a windy day can easily lead to picking glass out of your greenhouse frame and beds.

To prevent water from getting under the glass, mount it on waterproof caulking such as isobu-tyl or polybutylene. (See chapter 7, Caulking and Weather Stripping, on page 98, for more information on using caulking with greenhouse glazing.) After the caulking is applied, lower each glass pane into place and wedge it along the bottom and sides with hard rubber blocks. Once the pane is in place, I use a piece of quarter round or a cap piece over the glazing to hold it. You can also use good-quality caulking such as isobutyl or polybutylene or even silicone in place of a cap piece, if you prefer. If you use caulking, however, be aware that it may be difficult to remove the glass should it be necessary to replace a pane.

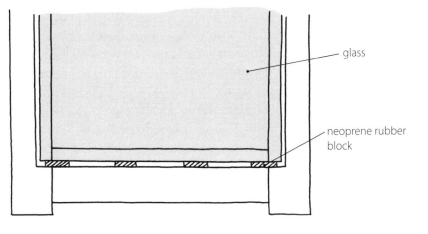

glass

neoprene rubber block

Glass is installed on neoprene rubber blocks to allow it to expand and move slightly when the greenhouse structure flexes.

When installing the quarter round to hold the glass in place, take care that nails holding the quarter round to the greenhouse frame do not touch the glass. It's preferable to use a pneumatic finish nail gun for this job rather than a hammer to prevent glass and nail contact, or, best of all, you could screw into predrilled holes. When attaching beading around the glass pane, insert the nails parallel to the glass surface to keep them clear of the glass. Of course, if you're uncomfortable nailing the quarter round in place, you can use glazier's points and putty, but a new greenhouse has a lot of glass and applying that much putty is not my idea of fun.

Installing Polycarbonate Panels According to the manufacturers, you should adopt some general practices when working with polycarbonate panels. Store the panels in a cool, dry spot, preferably indoors, and leave their protective coverings in place to prevent scratches and damage; you can remove them after the installation is complete. Seal the ends of the sheets with the special tape or U-shaped channels supplied by the manufacturer to prevent insects and moisture from getting inside the greenhouse once the panels are installed. When cutting panels, do it carefully and slowly, using a circular saw with a hollow ground blade and 10 to 12 teeth per inch, a jigsaw with a fine-toothed blade, or a lino cutting knife. (See the box Cutting Polycarbonate, below.)

In order to allow the polycarbonate sheets to move when they expand, any holes you drill for fasteners should be slightly oversized. According to the International Greenhouse Company Web site (see Resources, page 247), you should drill a ³⁄₁₆-inch hole for a ¼-inch screw, and any holes near the edge of the sheet should be at least twice the fastener diameter or ½ inch, whichever is greater.

Also to allow for expansion, leave a space between panels when you install them. Some manufacturers suggest a space of up to ⅛ inch per 3 feet of width or length where temperatures may vary by up to 100 degrees. Bronze-tinted panels require 30 percent more expansion space. After installation, use a clean sponge or cloth to wash the panels with mild soap and water (do not use ammonia-based cleaners, which will deteriorate the glazing), and rinse them thoroughly.

There are several ways to fasten polycarbonate glazing to the greenhouse roof and walls. The easiest is to use a polycarbonate extrusion that looks like a sideways letter *H*. This piece is fastened to the frame and the polycarbonate panels fit into it. There are a number of variations on this extrusion, all made of polycarbonate.

Another method involves laying a rubber or butyl gasket on the greenhouse frame. The poly-

Cutting Polycarbonate

The following installation information comes with permission from Suntuf, Inc., manufacturer of square, corrugated polycarbonate panels. While the instructions are specific to its sheets, the information is applicable to all other polycarbonates.

To cut polycarbonate panels, use a circular saw, a utility knife, and a straightedge. Reverse a plywood blade in the circular saw, then run the saw through the sheet at a slow speed. Support the polycarbonate sheets as you cut them to prevent vibration. Using this method, up to five panels can be stacked and cut at one time.

Install panels with the label side facing up toward the sky (sheet corrugations at each side will then face down). Closure strips or caps for the joints between the glass are made of either wood or foam. Foam closures are recommended because they can be stretched slightly to align with the panels and form a compression fit. Suntuf fasteners with neoprene washers are formulated to be compatible with Suntuf polycarbonate panels. Whatever the brand of polycarbonate panels you choose, be sure to use only the manufacturer's recommended fasteners to install them. Predrill all fastener holes oversized — with a ³⁄₁₆-inch drill bit — to accommodate the thermal movement of the panel. Failure to accommodate for thermal movement will cause the sheet to buckle after it's installed.

Attach fasteners on the crown of every other rib in the horizontal direction. In high wind areas, fasten on the crown of every rib. Use 2-inch fasteners (special long screws with load-distributing heads) for all roof applications. Do NOT overtighten fasteners, which will cause the rubber washers to compress. *Tip:* Back out the fastener one-half turn after the neoprene washer touches the panel. When installed properly, the neoprene washer should just touch the panel.

Avoid contact between the panels and any chemicals, paints, adhesives, or other synthetic materials that are incompatible with polycarbonate. Never use glass cleaners with ammonia or ammonia-based products to clean the panels. Instead, clean them with a lukewarm, soapy solution using a soft cloth or sponge. Do not use abrasive brushes; these will mark the surface.

carbonate panel is laid on top of the gasket and a rubber gasket and metal bar cap are screwed in place over the joint.

Note that polycarbonate panels should always be installed with the ribs running vertically, to help water run off them. Most manufacturers suggest that you drill ¼-inch weep holes in the bottom end cap every 12 inches or so to allow an escape for moisture that has drained to the bottom of the panels.

Panels can be screwed directly to a wooden structure, but where the panels butt together, the joint should be covered with a rafter bar. When screws are inserted through glazing, they impose a point load on the glazing. By installing a rafter bar over the glazing and screwing through it, the point load is spread over a larger area. The rafter bar also eliminates screw holes near the edge of the panel. The International Greenhouse Company recommends very specific locations for screws when you are installing multiwall polycarbonate panels. When polycarbonate is installed on aluminum-framed greenhouses, the multiwall material is slotted directly into the extruded frame, which supplies a built-in expansion gap.

Installing Fiberglass Panels Greenhouse fiberglass comes in rolls usually 50 or 100 feet long and 4 feet wide. Flat fiberglass is flexible and is easily cut to size, although you should wear gloves and a dust mask when working with the material. Some types of greenhouse fiberglass are not particularly smooth and you can get painful fiberglass splinters in your fingers if you don't wear gloves when installing them.

When fitting fiberglass to the greenhouse roof, flat panels should be overlapped and carefully screwed or nailed in place. The rafters for fiberglass should be 23½ inches on center to allow enough space to overlap the glazing at the edges. A bead of caulking at the overlap is usually enough to prevent rainwater from penetrating the covering. Next, install a long batten over the overlap and screw through the batten to make sure that the load is evenly distributed along the edge of the material or use screws or nails that pass through felt washers backed with

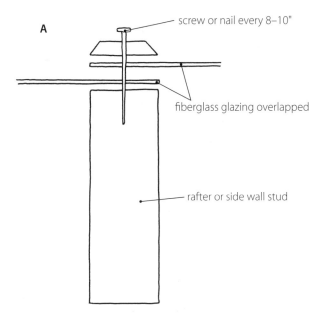

A — screw or nail every 8–10"

fiberglass glazing overlapped

rafter or side wall stud

Overlap fiberglass when screwing the caps in place to ensure that there will be no leaks **(A).** Because fiberglass can flex, it should be screwed down around the edges, with screws about 8 to 10 inches apart. Edges are fastened down using long battens and screws **(B).** If you use corrugated fiberglass, make sure that you position filler pieces at the top and bottom of the panels to ensure that there is no heat loss at these points.

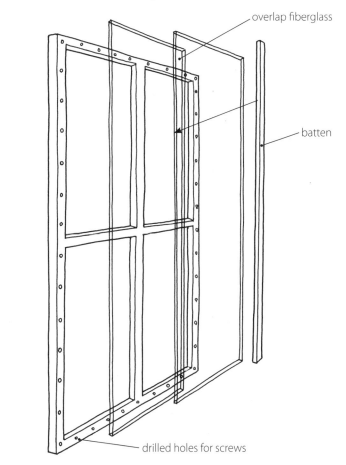

B

overlap fiberglass

batten

drilled holes for screws

steel washers to help distribute the load. This will help prevent the material from tearing away from nail heads in high winds.

Install corrugated fiberglass by screwing it to specially designed spacers that match the corrugations in the panels. Screws should be installed through the ridges, not in the valleys, where they can cause leaking. When screwing down the material, drill oversized holes through the sheet and use large felt washers backed with metal washers to hold the fiberglass without tearing through the sheeting.

Installing Acrylic Panels Because acrylic expands a great deal, you'll need to allow for this expansion when fastening the material to the wooden structure of the greenhouse: All drilled holes should be oversized and large washers should be used to hold the material in place; panels can also be fastened with battens screwed into place. If you are building a kit greenhouse, the acrylic glazing will fit into the extruded aluminum frame and is held in place with either flexible stripping or special clips that are pressed into place.

Also helpful in allowing for the expansion of acrylic sheets is the installation of support bars across them. In most other ways, the installation of acrylic sheets is very similar to the installation of polycarbonate panels; refer to the instructions in Installing Polycarbonate Panels, page 149.

Installing Wall Glazing

Wall glazing is installed in a manner similar to that for roof glazing. As for the roof, confirm the size of glazing and the required support spacing before you build your greenhouse. The illustration at right (representing a view from above) shows how wall glazing is attached. In the first illustration **(A)**, polycarbonate glazing is attached using a cap piece milled from ¾-inch by 1½-inch stock. In the second drawing **(B)**, glass glazing is recessed into the support, which requires cutting or routing out part of the support to allow the glass to fit. Once in place, the glass is held by a trim piece that is either nailed or screwed to the upright stud. The third illustration **(C)** shows an arrangement for either

polycarbonate or double-pane glass. Because the side wall provides only 1½ to 2 inches of attaching surface (depending on the size stud you use), you might want to add additional supports as shown. They can provide more integrity

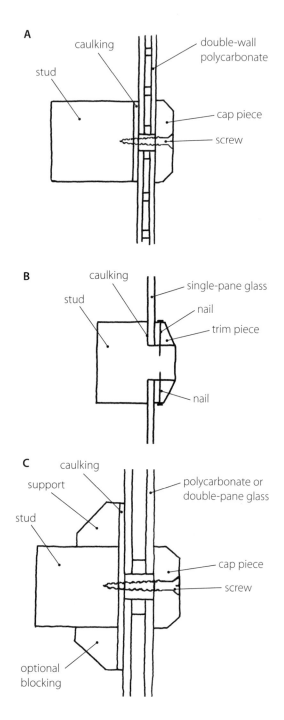

Installing wall glazing. **(A)** shows a method for double-wall polycarbonate, **(B)** shows a method for single-pane glass, and **(C)** shows a method for either polycarbonate or double-pane glass.

if you live in a windy area or one that is hurricane-prone, although they block more incoming light.

Installing Polyethylene Sheeting

Installing polyethylene (plastic) sheeting to a wood-frame greenhouse may require simply laying the sheeting over the top of the greenhouse and fastening it in place. In my experience, however, the best way to attach plastic sheeting to a greenhouse frame is to lay furring strips over the uprights in the frame or any supports and nail or screw the sheeting through the furring strips. This method helps to prevent the plastic from ripping off the nails in strong winds.

Note that using a commercial-grade covering on a PVC hoop house that you have built yourself will invalidate the manufacturer's warranty. You might use construction-grade polyethylene as a covering. The easiest way to cover a hoop house with a PVC pipe frame is to nail or screw the plastic to the baseboard on the perimeter of the greenhouse through wood or furring strips, though with only the bottom fastened to the greenhouse, the top tends to flap around in the wind. I've solved this problem by tying lengths of string from the baseboard on one side of the structure to the corresponding baseboard on the other side. This eliminates the flapping and cuts down on tearing of the material. Construction polyethylene tends to tear along the fold lines, but any rips can easily be repaired with clear polyethylene tape or, in a pinch, with duct tape.

10 Wiring, Plumbing, and Heating: Systems Design and Installation

IN THIS CHAPTER you'll learn how to calculate how much electrical power your greenhouse requires and the basics for designing and installing a suitable electrical system. We'll also discuss how to design and install various types of watering and heating systems. Even if you are hiring someone to build your greenhouse and install these systems, this chapter will help you ensure that the contractor is installing what will work best for you. For general information on electrical, heating, and watering systems and choosing which will work for your needs, refer to chapter 5, Controlling the Greenhouse Environment.

Installing Electricity

Before we begin any discussion of installing electricity in the greenhouse, it's important to stress that a greenhouse is a humid, sometimes wet environment. The combination of electricity and water is a very dangerous one. To make sure your installation is as safe as possible, *all electrical switches and fixtures should be installed in waterproof outdoor-rated housing* to prevent the accidental flooding of any electrical outlet. All outlets should be waterproof as well and should be installed higher in the greenhouse, away from the floor, where they are most likely to get wet. I like to locate them under the bench tops or at roof level. For your safety, all electrical circuits in and around the greenhouse should be pro-

tected by ground fault interrupter breakers (see the specific information on these on page 158). *If you've done electrical work before and choose to do this work in your greenhouse as well, you should still have a professional check the project as you go and before you turn on the electrical system.* Don't rely on the final check of a building inspector to assess whether your system is ready and safe to operate. The job of a building inspector is to determine that everything is done to code, not to see if you have connected everything properly. By contrast, an electrician can perform a continuity test on the circuit to see that your connections are safe and correct.

If you are going to do the work yourself, you'll need more than a passing familiarity with the National Electrical Wiring Code (NEC) and you will be required to obtain wiring permits *before* you start designing and cutting and stapling wires. You can buy your own copy of the NEC for a little more than $100. *If you've never done electrical work before, hire a professional electrician to do the job start to finish.*

Your Electrical Needs in a Greenhouse

Before you (or an electrician) begin wiring the greenhouse, you should determine what kind of lighting you'll need and how many outlets your setup requires for lights, fans, heating apparatus, and so forth. You'll also need to determine the kind of lighting required for different areas of the structure (for example, overhead lights that illuminate the entire greenhouse and task lighting for specific areas where you'll perform certain jobs). Overhead lighting can be a single 100-watt bulb or can consist of two or more waterproof fluorescents. Remember that all lighting should be housed in waterproof fixtures. For information on the kinds of lighting available for use in a greenhouse and how to determine your lighting needs for different areas of the structure, refer to chapter 5.

Drawing a Wiring Layout and a Circuit Diagram

As you make decisions about your electrical system, you should incorporate them into a complete wiring layout (see the one on page 60) and a circuit diagram (see page 157). These will show the location of the breaker box, the thickness and type of each cable required, any switches or fuses that are in the circuit, and a load calculation to indicate how much power is passing through each circuit. Note that the layouts and diagrams here are for demonstration purposes only and are based on my 6½ years of experience as an electrical engineer. *You should not attempt to determine the particulars of an electrical design or install wiring in your greenhouse unless you have some experience with installing electricity.*

Determining Electrical Needs for General Greenhouse Lighting

The lights that illuminate the walkway and the remainder of the greenhouse when the growing lights are not on will be used more often than any others, so they should have their own switch at the door of the structure. For example, in an 8-foot-wide by 12-foot-long greenhouse, your general lighting might consist of two fluorescent fixtures with two 40-watt fluorescent tubes in each. To determine if these can be placed on the same circuit, see Calculating Your Electrical Needs, page 156, and the circuit diagram on page 157.

During the winter months, the overhead lights in the greenhouse may be on quite a bit, but these lights will be little used in summer, when daylight can last for 14 hours. Rather than turn lights on and off daily, you might install a simple timer that can do the job and be adjusted twice a year for daylight saving time.

After you've made your decisions and calculations for general lighting, incorporate all results into your wiring layout and diagram.

Determining Electrical Needs for Task and Plant Lighting

To determine your specific task and plant lighting needs, you'll first have to define the area(s) you want to light. In general, for plant lighting you'll need 30 to 40 watts per square foot of growing bed. When the plants are small, fluorescent lights may be located within 2 inches of the growing bed, but as the plants grow, the lights will have to be raised. Fixtures should be hung to allow for this adjustment. For larger plants in a greenhouse bed, you may want to use high-intensity discharge (HID) lights. But because these lights generate a great deal of heat and the light reflectors shade the plants from natural sunlight, you must be able to raise and lower these lights, too. This means you'll have to consider carefully the location of the outlet boxes for the lights and the length of cable between them and the fixtures.

> If you've never done electrical work before, hire a professional electrician to do the job start to finish.

For larger beds, you might want to install high-pressure sodium or metal halide lights (see page 58) to generate the high levels of light required. In this case as well the lights must be able to be raised and lowered and will need to be protected from water. Purchase fixtures outfitted with screens to help contain the glass should the lightbulb shatter.

Each of your task lights must be wired with an on/off switch. You can string several lights together on the same circuit, but be sure to determine amperage on the wire to avoid putting too many lights on one circuit. (See Calculating Your Electrical Needs, page 156.)

After you have made your decisions and calculations, incorporate all results into your layout and diagram.

Locating Outlets

Although there are no codes for placement of outlets in a greenhouse, at the minimum they should be located 18 inches above the floor, as the National Electric Wiring Code (NEC) requires, to help protect them from getting wet. As the sample wiring layout on page 60 indicates, outlets can also be located directly under the top of a bench to help protect them from water. Because potting soil and pots may also be stored under the benches and block access to outlets, however, a single outlet may not do the job, so you might install several (the greenhouse in our layout has four outlets located at strategic positions under the bench tops). If you intend to set up a bench for propagating or growing seedlings, you'll need an outlet near the bench for heating or germination mats and cables and perhaps additional task lighting. The layout shows an outlet on the left for this purpose. You should also include in your layout outlets for plant lighting and for any electric tools you'll be using.

TIP

According to an electrician I know, a rough rule of thumb is to put no more than eight or nine lights on one 15-amp breaker.

Determining Other Electrical Needs

In addition to lights, fans, electrical heaters, and humidifiers or misters will all need to be plugged in or hard-wired, usually on their own circuits and with their own on/off switches. A fan can be plugged into an outlet at bench level, but if it is to be located high in the greenhouse, you may need an outlet box closer to it. Along with its on/off switch, the fan wiring should include a thermostat in the circuit (see the diagram on page 157). Each of your greenhouse electrical "appliances" and lights should be wired to a distribution panel with a ground fault interrupter breaker in the panel. This will cut the circuit as soon as the slightest amount of power goes to ground so that should you get water on an appliance, the power will be turned off before you can get an electric shock. (See Ground Fault Interrupter Breakers, page 158). The panel will have breakers to suit the amount of amperage flowing through each circuit in addition to a main breaker that turns off power to every greenhouse system at once.

Along with locating your lights, outlets, and panel, you and/or your electrician will have to determine how the circuits are to be laid out and calculate how much power each circuit must provide (see the diagram on page 157).

Calculating Your Electrical Needs

Although an electrician calculates the amperage a circuit can handle, it's useful to understand how he or she arrives at these figures. In calculating the amperage for lights, for instance, first add together the wattage of each light. For example:

ten 100-watt lights on a single circuit = 1,000 watts

Next, divide wattage by voltage to determine amperage:

1,000 watts ÷ 120 volts = 8.333 amps

On this circuit an electrician would use a 15-amp breaker to allow for fluctuations in the power and the possibility that you want to use a 150-watt light in one of the sockets.

Referring to the wiring layout on page 60, at 400 watts each, the four HID lights over the growing beds add up to 1,600 watts of power at 110 volts. Thus, the total amperage needed is:

1,600 ÷ 110 = 14.00 amps

This is quite a load for a 15-amp circuit breaker because AC power fluctuates between 100 and 120 volts. At 100 volts, the load would be 1,600 ÷ 100 = 16 amps, which would trip the breaker. You may also trip the breaker by plugging in a slightly larger lamp. There are two options in this case: (1) Put all the lights on one circuit with a 20-amp breaker to handle any power fluctuations and an automatic switch capable of handling the 20-amp load; or (2) use two circuits, each with a 15-amp breaker, hard-wiring the lights to ensure that no other power load can be plugged into the same circuit (although it might be possible to plug a larger lightbulb into the lamp and increase the power load.)

Referring again to the circuit diagram below, we can identify and calculate the electrical needs for each circuit.

Circuit A (top circuit in the diagram): The frequency with which thc lights go on and off is controlled by an automatic timer. There are two 400-watt HID lights on this circuit:

400 × 2 = 800 watts
800 watts ÷ 110 volts = 7.27 amps

Because the total amperage for this circuit is 7.27, we can use a 10-amp breaker.

Circuit B: This circuit, too, has two 400-watt HID fluorescent lights, so it will also use a 10-amp breaker.

Circuit C: On this circuit are the fluorescent lights that illuminate the germination chamber — one 200-watt fluorescent light and two overhead 40-watt fluorescent lights, for a total of 280 watts. To determine amperage:

280 watts ÷ 110 volts = 2.5 amps

To be consistent, we can use a 10-amp breaker here too, with additional amperage available to put in more lights later.

TIP

Though the AC power might be formally 110 volts, the voltage can fluctuate, measuring as high as 120 volts or as low as 100 volts. This fluctuation should be taken into account when determining the amperage a breaker can handle.

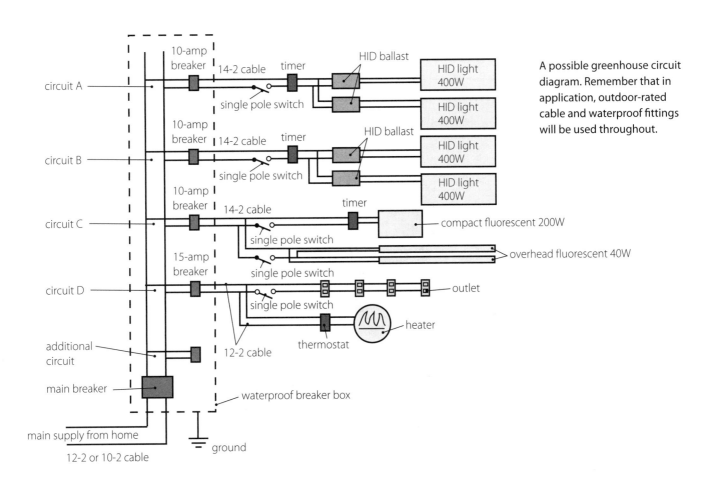

A possible greenhouse circuit diagram. Remember that in application, outdoor-rated cable and waterproof fittings will be used throughout.

Circuit D: This circuit has four outlets, typically rated at 15 amps each, and the heater circuit. Because the heater needs only milliamps to fire off the igniter, we don't need to factor in its requirements. You never know, however, what will be plugged into the sockets, so a 15-amp breaker is installed here.

Additional Circuit: Marked "spare" on our circuit diagram, this circuit can also be installed from the house instead of the greenhouse. It is made up of a 3-wire circuit for the exterior greenhouse approach lights and allows the greenhouse user to turn lights on and off at both the greenhouse and at some point on the approach to the structure so that no one will have to walk to or leave the greenhouse in the dark. The circuit has three 150-watt outdoor path lights with a switch at each end (450 watts total).

$$450 \text{ watts} \div 120 \text{ volts} = 3.75 \text{ amps}$$

Thus, we could use a 10-amp circuit breaker for this circuit, although a 15-amp breaker is more commonly used.

Each of these five circuits will go to its own breaker in the distribution box.

Wiring Tips for Safety

- For a greenhouse application, only outdoor-rated UF cable should be used. Indoor wiring cable is unsafe in the consistently wet, hot, and humid greenhouse environment. In fact, many building codes mandate that outdoor cable be used.

- Electrical cable for this application is rated according to American Wire Gauge (AWG) as 10-2, 12-2, or 14-2. The first number refers to the wire gauge (diameter). The higher the number, the thinner the wire. For example, a 12-2 cable is thicker than a 14-2 cable and is rated to handle a 20-amp circuit (while the 14-2 cable is rated for a 15-amp circuit). The second number refers to how many wires are in the cable. For example, a 12-2 cable has two wires, one white and one black, along with a copper ground wire, which is not included in the count but is part of every electrical wire.

- Copper ground wire should be attached to the casing and socket of every fixture to ensure that any ground faults go directly to the electrical grounding line rather than passing through you.

In calculating the electricity called for in your greenhouse, you should determine the wire you will be using and the amperage it can safely carry. In almost all cases you will use either 12- or 14-gauge wire. If you will be installing a 220-volt heater (as opposed to a 110-volt model), however, you might require a larger wire, in which case you should hire an electrician to do the work. A 220-volt heater cannot be installed on a 110-volt circuit. A higher-voltage heater requires an entirely new circuit. Incidentally, a 220-volt heater can be an expensive form of heating a greenhouse in a climate like New England's: A friend who uses one had a heating bill that topped $600 for the coldest month of the winter!

A 12-gauge wire can carry 2,300 watts but most electricians operate on the assumption that it can carry only 2,000. A 14-gauge wire can carry up to 1,700 watts, but for practical purposes, assume it can carry only 1,500. According to State Farm Insurance, a circuit with a 12-gauge wire should have a 20-amp breaker and a 14-gauge wire should have a 15-amp breaker. A 10-gauge wire can carry 3,400 watts (assume 3,000 watts) and should have a 30-amp breaker.

Ground Fault Interrupter Breakers

For all outdoor and interior greenhouse work, an electrician should install a ground fault interrupter (GFI) breaker, which turns off the electricity the moment ground fault, or contact with moisture, is detected. Conventional breakers may simply send power through the ground line if a fault is detected, whereas a GFI breaker turns off in a fraction of a second. If you are watering your greenhouse and accidentally spill water on a socket, instead of shorting out through you, the GFI breaker turns off the electricity immediately for additional safety.

Rough Wiring

Rough wiring consists of running wiring through the walls and installing outlet boxes. It's done before the insulation and drywall are installed, if your greenhouse is to include these two materials. Rough wiring can be installed in several ways. The least expensive method is simply to staple the wires to the wooden frame of the greenhouse as they run from the breaker panel. Staples should be a maximum of 18 inches apart and no more than 6 inches from each outlet box.

If you have a custom greenhouse with insulated walls, holes can be drilled through wooden studs or supports and wire can then be run through the holes. Each hole must be a maximum of ⅜ inch in diameter. If you choose this option and plan to install drywall or some other interior wall covering, you should nail a metal plate over the stud at the same level as the hole to prevent drywall screws from entering the stud and wiring right where the hole is. (A screw that has contacted or penetrated the wiring is a fire hazard.) You should check your local codes to see what kind of installation is required in your area.

Switches and Breakers

Unlike an exposed water pipe, which reveals any leaks, wires do not indicate whether an electrical circuit is leaking power to the ground. Consequently, every circuit should have a breaker in addition to an on/off switch.

In the house, breakers are located in an electrical panel located in the basement or in a cupboard under the stairs. All electrical power coming into a house passes through this main panel, and it should have its own circuit breaker (some have a separate circuit breaker between the main breaker panel and the incoming line) so that electrical power to the entire house can be cut off if necessary. For safety, before an electrician adds the wiring from your greenhouse panel to the main breaker panel, he or she will turn off the power to your house.

Finish Wiring

Finish wiring is the point at which wires are joined to the actual electrical sockets, light fixtures, hard-wired heaters, fans, and switches.

It is easiest and safest to begin finish wiring by installing the outlets farthest away from the main breaker panel and installing the breaker last. If the breaker panel is wired first, somebody could turn on the power while you or the electrician is still working on the system.

When all the sockets, light fixtures, heaters, fans, and switches have been wired and all circuits have been wired into the breaker panel, power can be brought from the main breaker board. After this, the wiring is ready to be checked. The electrician will use a multimeter to test the continuity or determine whether the circuit is complete. By turning the breaker on and off, the continuity between the black and white terminals in each circuit can be tested. There will be some resistance if there are lights or appliances in the circuit. If there is none — for example, the circuit is entirely outlet boxes — there will be no deflection (movement) of the needle on the meter, meaning that the circuit is open. If a light is plugged into a socket to close the circuit, there will be some deflection of the meter's needle. After testing the circuit continuity, the continuity between the ground line and the black line in each circuit is checked with the circuit turned off and then turned on. In both instances, there should be no deflection of the needle (the meter's needle shows no movement).

Running Cable from the House

Electrical wiring should be run underground or on poles from your home's main breaker panel to your greenhouse (or to the breaker box in the greenhouse). If underground, it should be buried deep enough so that it cannot be damaged by a digging tool. The National Electrical Code (NEC) stipulates that UF cable should be buried more than 24 inches and at the least should be protected with sand. A preferable method consists of protecting regular nonmetallic (NM) cable by installing it in conduit before burying it, which also makes it easier to replace the cable if it fails. Metal conduit is safest because plastic shatters easily, which can contribute to a cable's damage or failure.

The cable should be duplex of a suitable size to carry the power load desired from your house to the greenhouse (either 8-, 10-, 12-, or 14-gauge two-wire cable — 8-2, 10-2, 12-2, or 14-2).

Electrical wire offers some resistance to the voltage that goes through it. If the cable is long enough, this resistance becomes significant enough to cause what is known as *voltage drop*. Because thinner wires offer more resistance than heavier-gauge wires, the solution for a longer run is to increase the wire thickness. Most electricians allow for a maximum 2 percent voltage drop along the wire and for a 14-gauge wire with a 15-amp breaker that should not run more than 75 feet. If you install a 12-gauge wire and a 20-amp breaker or a 10-gauge wire with a 30-amp breaker, the maximum distance the wire should run is 85 feet. If you need to go farther, you can install a 20-amp breaker on 10-gauge wire and travel 130 feet or you can put a 30-amp breaker on 8-gauge wire and cover 150 feet.

In our sample greenhouse circuit diagram, the total amperage is the total of all the breaker sizes or 45 amps. Thus, for this greenhouse, the cable should be able to carry at least that amount of load over a distance of 30 feet from the house to the greenhouse. Remember, though, that it's unlikely that all the lights and heaters and outlets in the greenhouse will be in use at the same time. Also, the greenhouse represented here has a great deal of equipment in it; yours may not.

It's important, too, that the breaker in the main house panel be at least 50 amps, large enough to support the entire load plus any surge loads. (Surge loads often occur when something is turned on from a dead stop. For example, an electrical motor may use 10 amps to run continuously, but when the motor starts from a dead stop, it might absorb 15 or 20 amps until it is up to speed.) Typically, a large greenhouse requires a 30- to 40-amp service, while most smaller, hobby greenhouses may require only a 20-amp service. Once the cable is wired to the breaker panels at both the greenhouse and the house ends and the circuits have been tested, the wiring can be turned on. With the breakers on this time, the electrician will turn on each circuit to make sure it works.

Installing Plumbing

In most greenhouses, the plumbing consists of a water line running to a spigot in the greenhouse,

but if you are a little more ambitious, perhaps you'll want to install a sink and a drain.

If your garden is in an area that's subject to frost and the greenhouse is unheated, the water line will have to be drained each fall or installed well below the frost line. Of course, the drain line will also need to be below the frost line, but where should it drain? Running it into your leach field is usually not a good idea because water that drains may contain a pesticide or herbicide spray. The best option is a dry well (see The Dry Well, page 163).

The first step in installing a water system is determining where the water line will enter the greenhouse, where the outlets will be, where the drain will be located, and where the dry well will be and then mapping these out much like a wiring diagram. As pointed out in chapter 8, The Foundation, if you are designing your greenhouse to sit on a slab, you need to think about these features before you pour the slab. It's much easier to install water and drain lines before the concrete pour.

Determining Locations for Water Outlets

The following illustration shows possible locations for a water line and drain line in a greenhouse. Incorporated in this sample system are a simple sink, spigot, and a line for sprinklers or a drip irrigation system. The sink can be used for cleaning tools and rinsing vegetables before taking them indoors and the spigot can be used for filling watering cans and attaching the garden hose. If we look at this layout in conjunction with the wiring layout on page 60, we can see where potential conflicts between water and electricity outlets may occur. Such a comparison enables you to ensure that electrical lines are located where they cannot come in contact with water. In this case, the electrical outlet that powers the overhead light is situated high above the sink.

In some greenhouses, the spigot, sink, and sprinkler or misting systems all have their own outlets, but in this installation, there is a line by the door and a two- or three-way outlet attached to the spigot to allow a hose, sprinkler, drip irrigation line, or mister to be attached.

A single line attached to the sink drain near the spigot is also included on the diagram. This line empties into a dry well.

Installing the Water Line to the Spigot

The water line comes from the house and is typically a 1-inch copper or plastic pipe (depending on what is required by the local zoning code), but if the distance is reasonably short and local code allows it, you can use 10-foot lengths of schedule 40 PVC pipe of the same diameter. When using short lengths of pipe, glue each joint carefully to ensure that it will not leak: Coat the end of pipe with pipe cement and push it into the connector until it is fully seated. Note that some PVC piping has been linked to the leaching of chemicals into the water line, so buy with care. Once you determine the type of pipe specified by local code, consult a plumber for the best option.

If you garden in a part of the country where the ground freezes and your greenhouse will be unheated, the water line must be located below the frost line. This means that you must dig a trench and bury the line 3 or 4 feet deep. When you backfill the trench, cover the pipe with sand or screened loam to ensure that it won't be damaged by stones in the fill. Some experts recommend that you install PVC pipe inside heavier conduit such as schedule 40 pipe to ensure that it will not be crushed (see chapter 6), but this can nearly double the cost of the installation. The alternative to burying the line deep is to put a drain at the house end of the line and make sure that the line slopes from its uphill greenhouse end to this lower drain end so you can empty it completely each fall.

Whatever installation method you choose, the water line must have a valve at both ends so that, should it burst, you can isolate the line from the house. Because you may be spraying fertilizer or pesticides with a hose-end sprayer, it's also important to install a nonreturn valve at the greenhouse end of the line to prevent these materials from being drawn back into the house plumbing.

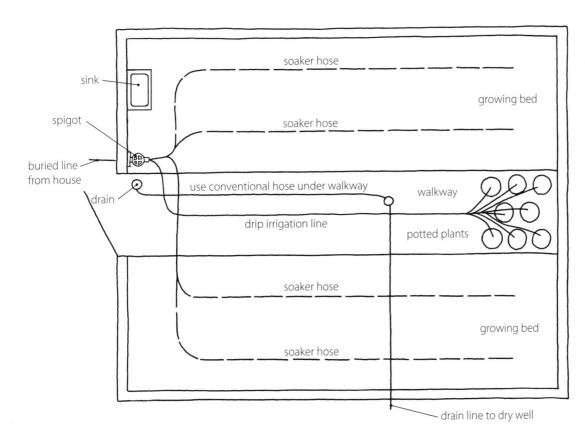

Devising a plumbing layout helps you to see where everything will be located.

Connecting the Lines

As indicated above, a water line to the greenhouse should have a valve at both ends. First, you must cut the line square with a pipe cutter: Clamp the tool onto the pipe, rotate it, tighten the cutting screw, and rotate the cutter again around the pipe. If this doesn't cut the pipe, tighten the cutter blade a little more and rotate it until you cut through the material.

Before you solder or glue (depending on whether you're using copper or PVC pipe), work steadily through the plumbing system and dry-fit everything. Dry fitting first enables you to be sure that the entire system will fit together and that all the pieces are the right size.

How to cut a pipe using a pipe cutter

push together both pipes and heat them with the torch as you apply solder to the joint until the material runs out of it.

This method will produce a solid joint. Be extra careful if you are installing pipe near the wooden frame of your greenhouse. The propane torch can burn the greenhouse frame just as easily as it melts solder. Plumbers who do this work all the time often use metal or asbestos blankets to cover any wood in the immediate working area.

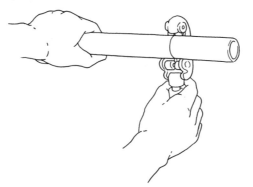

How to connect copper piping: Rub the end of the copper pipe with sandpaper, emery cloth, or a pipe sander **(A)**. After heating the pipe, apply solder so it's drawn between the joined pipes **(B)**.

Connecting Copper Lines

To connect copper lines, you'll need a propane torch and a roll or stick of good-quality, rosin-cored solder. First, rub the end of the copper pipe with 320- or 400-grit sandpaper, emery cloth, or pipe sander about 2 inches in from the cut end until the copper is shiny. Then, heat the end of the copper pipe with the propane torch and apply solder to the outside of the pipe. Don't hold the solder in the flame and let it drip on the pipe. Instead, push the solder directly onto the hot pipe; you'll get a good joint only if the solder adheres to the pipe. Apply it all around the pipe and with an old rag, wipe the solder on the end of the pipe so that the first inch or two of the pipe is fully coated.

Next, take the other side of the connection (which might have a T, L, straight, or flared end) and wipe the inside of the end with sandpaper or emery cloth until it is shiny. Coat this area with solder as you did with the first pipe and then

Connecting PVC Pipe

First, note that there may be code restrictions on using PVC pipe. Check your local code before installing any piping. If you are using PVC water pipe, you'll need to clamp the pipe to its fittings with hose clamps. Some faucets are made for plastic pipes that have smooth ends; other fit-

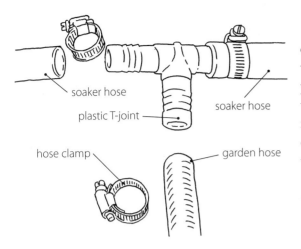

soaker hose
plastic T-joint
soaker hose
hose clamp
garden hose

Connecting PVC pipe using clamps and a T-joint

tings have a screw thread and require clamping a connector to the fitting before it can be inserted into a threaded hose pipe. Its best to use stainless-steel hose clamps and to use two clamps on each joint so that if one comes loose, the line won't leak.

To connect PVC pipe, you'll need PVC pipe cement (a small can costs about $5). The mixture comes with a small brush in the can lid. Simply wipe the end of the hose line with a dry rag, paint the surface with the glue using the brush, and push the pipe into the T-, straight, or elbow joint. Let the connection set before you move the joint.

The Sink

The best type of greenhouse sink is a deep, plastic, tub style that easily allows you to wash tools and gear — the kind of utility sink that many people install in basements. Stationary tubs are reasonably inexpensive and usually come with legs. Most have a single faucet with two on/off handles (one for hot water, one for cold), but you will be using only one of them. Installing a stationary tub is straightforward, involving fitting its legs, plumbing the faucet on the rear of the fixture, and connecting it to the main plumbing system.

To install the sink, first set it in position and connect the U-shaped drainpipe by bolting one end under the drain hole and the other to the outlet pipe.

Next, connect the faucet. While the method differs depending on the style of faucet you have, usually it requires that you coat the cold-water pipe with pipe compound, push the pipe into the existing socket of the faucet, and tighten the nut (which comes attached to the pipe) to hold everything in place. Repeat this procedure for the hot-water side and the job is finished.

Installing Drains

Drain lines are usually made of 2-, 3- or 4-inch schedule 40 PVC pipe that's joined as you would join the pipe for any line (see Connecting PVC Pipe, page 162). If a flush-mounted shower drain is to be set into the floor of the greenhouse, you should install rough plumbing with the drain at the correct height before the concrete greenhouse floor is poured (see page 124). The top of the drainpipe should be cut to the right level for the flush-mounted floor drain, and when the floor is smoothed, the slab should be sloped toward the drain so that any water on the floor will drain easily. You may find it simpler to install the drain grate before the pour and then tape the top of it to prevent concrete from sealing it during the pour. If you choose not to install the grate before pouring concrete, make sure that you push this cover over the pipe while the concrete is still wet to ensure that the drain grate fits flush with the floor.

The Dry Well

Rather than run the greenhouse drain into your septic system, where any pesticides you use may be harmful, run it into a dry well. A properly installed drywell can cost about as much as a greenhouse. It is basically an open-bottomed concrete tube or container filled with gravel and a sediment trap or filter. Water drains into it for dispersal. Before construction, check with the local zoning office to see what is allowed in your area. In some municipalities, you may have to obtain a permit or meet other requirements in order to install a dry well.

These systems are often used as laundry drains to ensure that the soapy water from the laundry does not enter a septic system. The problem with a laundry dry well is that it eventually becomes clogged with lint, and the problem with a greenhouse dry well is that it can eventually become clogged with plant residue or potting soil. To cut down on cleaning the dry well, install a sediment trap in the drain line and clean it regularly. You can also install a cover on top of the trap or on the well.

Installing a dry well requires digging a large pit and burying an open-bottomed tank or container in it. The container is then filled partially with gravel and the greenhouse drain line is run first into the sediment trap and then into the middle of the dry well. It is a very simple and effective system.

A dry well system

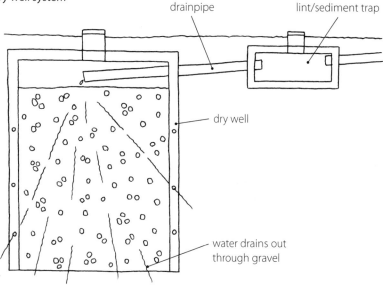

drainpipe

lint/sediment trap

dry well

water drains out through gravel

Installing a Heating System

See chapter 5 for information on types of heating systems that can be used in a greenhouse and how to choose which one is best for your needs. Sources of greenhouse heat are gas, wood, and electric heaters. One location for a heater in the greenhouse is under a bench so that it can heat the cold air that is lower down in the structure, which then rises and circulates.

Installing Gas Heating

Gas heaters are usually stand-alone devices that are fed from a propane or natural gas source outside the greenhouse. A gas heater and

the necessary gas line should be professionally installed and the line should be tested carefully for leaks before it is used.

Before deciding on gas heat, it's important to check with the local building inspector to determine whether you need a permit to install such a heater in your greenhouse. Some municipalities require that all heating systems have a permit and that every system be put in by a licensed installer. Others may have special requirements about storing propane or natural gas. For example, you may not be allowed to stand a propane tank outside the greenhouse near the glazing, but you might be allowed to locate it against a solid house wall.

For a number of years in my warm greenhouse I used a Southern Burner propane heater — an open-flame, under-bench heater with its own pilot light and thermostat. It sends a great deal of hot air up toward the glass, where the air becomes cooler through its contact with the glazing and its movement throughout the greenhouse. When the air has cooled and sinks to the ground again, it gets sucked back toward the heater, setting up a circulation that is beneficial for plants.

Note that if you decide to install a propane heater, you must provide an air intake to the heater to prevent it from consuming all the oxygen inside the greenhouse, which could cause plants to die and jeopardize the health and well-being of you and others who work in the structure. To accomplish this, you (or a professional) can install a 2-inch schedule 40 PVC pipe in the wall to allow external air to be sucked into the greenhouse. The pipe can be cut to size and glued, if necessary (see Connecting PVC Pipe, page 142), and you can fit the exterior with wire mesh to keep rodents or pests out of the greenhouse.

After a professional installs the heater, you can install (or have installed) the thermostat, which is connected to the regulator block.

Before turning on the heating unit, it should be tested for leaks. The installer may accomplish this by brushing soapy water onto every joint in the copper pipe and then turning on the propane tanks. Any bubbles in the soapy water indicate a leak. If you or the installer see any bubbles, shut off the gas and take apart and remake the joint. When all the joints are bubble-free, the installer will light the pilot light and turn up the thermostat full blast to make sure that the heater engages. After the heater lights, you can turn down the thermostat to the desired temperature.

Installing a Wood-Burning Stove

If you have a large greenhouse, a wood-burning stove is a reasonable option, especially if you have access to a woodlot. Such a stove does require a lot of maintenance, however, and you must fill it regularly to ensure that it keeps going. On a cold winter night, this can be a real chore.

Before any woodstove installation in the greenhouse, check with the local building inspector to see what's allowed and how far the stove must be from other combustible materials. If you don't have a building code for combustible surfaces, to prevent fire, assume that there should be no surfaces or plants within 24 to 30 inches of the stove. This distance is even greater for some of the more stringent fire and building codes. You'll also need to determine how the chimney will exit your greenhouse and what the required setbacks are for combustible materials around the chimney.

To install a wood-burning stove, first locate it on the floor of the greenhouse. Ideally the floor should be concrete; if it's not, you'll need to install an insulated slab on which the stove will sit.

Next, install the stovepipe, which will extend through the greenhouse roof. *Attempting to operate a woodstove without a stovepipe inside your greenhouse is extremely dangerous. Smoke will have no way of escaping the structure.* Most pipes are 6- or 7-inch steel, fireproof tubing that radiates heat as the smoke passes through it. To install it, simply push the crimped end of one section inside the smooth end of another and fasten the pieces together with a couple of sheet-metal screws. Secure the pipe with strapping or brackets so that it's at least 24 inches from any wooden surfaces. You can use perforated metal water-pipe strapping to hold the chimney if nothing else is available.

Installing Additional Window Insulation

To cut down on heat loss during the winter, consider covering the glazing of your greenhouse with a layer of heat-shrink film, a transparent film that comes in various sizes in kits that include double-sided installation tape. Kits are available in most hardware stores for a few dollars.

To install the film, first press the double-sided tape around the window. Then cut the film to size and apply it to the tape. Finally, use a hair dryer to shrink the film so that it makes a tight, clear "window" inside the greenhouse glazing.

You can also install polyethylene sheeting over the inside of the windows, holding the plastic in place by nailing battens to the interior framing of the structure; or you can cover the entire outside of the greenhouse with polyethylene sheeting, holding it in place with battens nailed to the exterior framing; or install bubble wrap insulation over the inside greenhouse glazing, holding it in place with battens or tape.

If you own a conservatory or attached greenhouse, you may find that heat loss from your home through the glazing during a winter night is quite high. Rather than have unattractive polyethylene or bubble wrap stuck to the walls, you might prefer to add movable insulated roman shades or cellular shades (see Resources, page 248). Both are installed on tracks that are placed on either side (or at the top) of the window and completely block off the glass. Once quilted insulated window shades are pulled down, the insulation value of the window can approach R-11.

11 Greenhouse Accessories

PUTTING ANY GREENHOUSE into operation requires an investment in making or acquiring a number of accessories. At the very least, you'll need potting soil, pots, trays, tools, and a place to pot plants (possibly a potting bench), but you may also need growing beds or benches, a germination setup or growing chamber, tool racks and other storage for tools and supplies (possibly a secure storage cupboard or locker), a wheelbarrow or cart, window screens and other supplies for insect control, and other accessories. While some of these must be purchased, many of them can be made or improvised by a competent do-it-yourselfer.

Benches

Most people like to set their potted plants on benches in the greenhouse because raising the plants allows air to circulate around them. In addition, plants on benches are raised above the layer of coldest air near the floor of the greenhouse. As part of their greenhouse kits, many manufacturers offer benches that fasten onto the greenhouse structure. When buying a greenhouse kit, check to see if such benches are included and if they are strong enough to hold the weight of a large number of plants. If a bench buckles and it's supported by the structure, it can distort the greenhouse frame and cause leaks or air gaps. The best benches are freestanding. These come in many shapes and forms.

Types of Benches

Types of benches range from a homemade wooden table sitting on concrete blocks to a simple potting bench to a sophisticated hydroponic bench complete with vents and drains, used by retail plant growers.

The most basic greenhouse bench can be made from 2×4 supports with 2×6s or 2×8s used as a top. For many greenhouses, however, a heavy lumber bench like this is too clumsy, in which case a lighter top of 1×4 or 1×6 cedar can be used. You can also make the bench top from 1-inch wire mesh to allow dirt to fall through and light and fresh air to circulate around and under plants. Mesh is also easier to clean and keep free of insect eggs and disease than is a wooden bench surface. Wire mesh is usually galvanized after it has been welded, so it should last for a few years in the humid greenhouse environment. Do not use mesh that has not been galvanized, and beware of damaging the galvanized covering when stapling the mesh to its supports. Bench-top mesh comes in widths from 2 feet to 8 feet and lengths up to 100 feet. To make your own bench tops, it may be economical to buy a roll of the material.

Another bench-top option is expanded metal mesh. This surface has diamond-shaped openings and comes in sizes from 2 feet by 6 feet to 6 feet by 8 feet. It is relatively simple to staple this material to a wooden frame.

It's also easy to make the frame for a mesh-topped bench. Two of the most common bench frame materials are metal galvanized pipe and

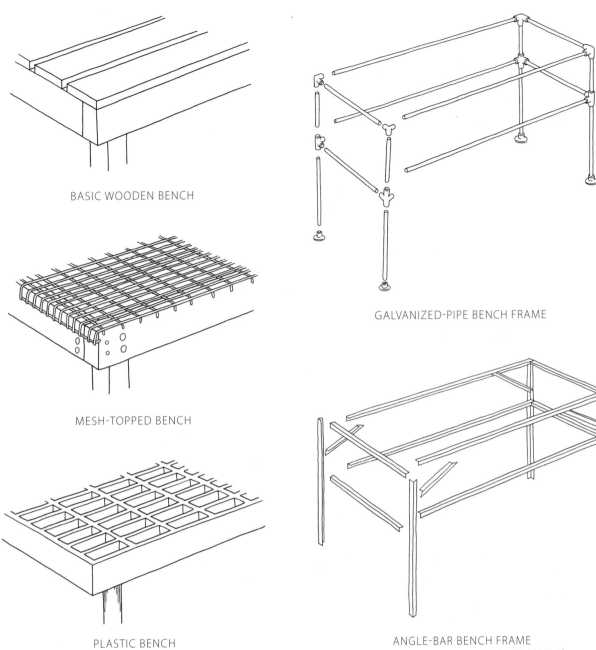

BASIC WOODEN BENCH

MESH-TOPPED BENCH

PLASTIC BENCH

GALVANIZED-PIPE BENCH FRAME

ANGLE-BAR BENCH FRAME
(CORNERS CUT AT A 45-DEGREE ANGLE)

steel-slotted galvanized angle bar. To build a metal pipe bench, buy the necessary parts based on accurate measurements of desired width and height. The structure will probably settle on four or six flanges for the base with screw-in legs. At the top you can use either two- or three-way angles to frame it. To connect the pipes, you can either use slip fittings or add threads to pipe pieces cut to the right length. (A plumber can help you cut threads on the pipe ends.) Once everything is assembled, the mesh frame can be

stapled to a wooden frame fastened to the top of the pipe frame with pipe brackets.

You can make an angle-bar bench by first purchasing 1-inch or 1½-inch slotted galvanized angle bar at your local hardware store, then bolting together all the pieces. Don't weld the pieces because welding galvanized metal causes the emission of toxic fumes and the heat generated by the process destroys the galvanized finish (meaning you'll have to paint the bench later).

Of course, you may not want to go to the time and expense of building either a wooden

WOODEN SHELVING

VINYL-COATED-
WIRE SHELVING

or a metal bench. In this case, there are snap-together heavy-duty plastic benches (some are made by the manufacturer Benchmaster). A typical 3-foot by 8-foot bench can cost less than $100. The recycled UV-stabilized plastic is durable and readily assembled, can be hosed off easily, and will support heavy loads. In addition, should you decide to change your bench configuration, these benches can be disassembled and reassembled in minutes.

Shelving

Shelves are an essential part of most greenhouses. In my lean-to greenhouse with a back wall that's almost 12 feet high, I find that shelves allow me to place a large number of potted plants in areas where they would not normally be located (though I need a ladder to reach the topmost shelves).

Commercially made brackets make the best shelf supports. You can use fixed brackets screwed directly to the wall or frame of the greenhouse, but slotted shelf standards allow you to adjust shelf heights as plants grow.

Shelves can be made of any material, as long as it can support the load of lots of filled pots after plants have been watered. Some options are cedar, painted wood, and expanded metal, but I've also found that vinyl-coated-wire closet shelves work well in the greenhouse. They are lightweight, have a lip along the front edge, lock into place, and can support a fairly heavy load. They come in various lengths from 2 feet to 10 feet. They should be painted, however, before you install them in the greenhouse. The vinyl layer on the shelf might stand up to closet use, but it doesn't seem to last for more than two or three seasons in a greenhouse. Once the layer is broken or chipped, the metal underneath rusts quite quickly.

A conventional kit greenhouse may not have many places to locate shelves; you may have to compromise on where you put them. Possible shelving locations is one of the factors you should check for when you buy a greenhouse. Some extrusions have slots that allow you to install shelf supports from the ceiling or walls in any configuration. On wood-framed greenhouses, the shelf supports or brackets can be screwed directly to the frame, but beware of fastening too many shelves on greenhouse framing. It may not be designed to hold the weight.

Growing Beds

If you decide to grow directly in the ground inside the greenhouse, its best to divide growing areas with lumber or with one of the brands of plastic or composite lumber that are available now and are reputed to be rot-proof. In my greenhouse I use half-width concrete blocks (they're half the width of regular concrete blocks) or bricks to divide the growing beds from the walkways.

When developing a growing bed, the trick is to improve the soil to suit the plants you want to grow. For example, most brassicas, onions, and corn are heavy feeders, so you'll need plenty of manure and soil supplements. In my cold greenhouse, I can dig these amendments into the beds any time during the winter and leave them to break down. Because greenhouse beds are not subjected to snow and rain, the supplements will not leach out of the soil.

If you plan to grow tomatoes in your greenhouse, manure is the wrong thing to put in to the soil. Adding manure yields lush, green healthy plants but no fruit. Instead, add phosphates and potash to ensure that tomatoes will set fruit early and for a long season. Any good gardening book can tell you the precise amounts that you need and what types are best for your soil.

If you've excavated for a greenhouse foundation, much of the soil in the greenhouse may be subsoil left over from the excavation. In my opinion, the best way to improve this soil is to dig it out and replace it with a mixture of manure, compost, screened loam, sand, and any other additives that might be necessary. Once you've improved your greenhouse soil, test it. The local extension service can usually perform the test or walk you through the steps necessary to do it yourself.

Raised Beds

Raised beds in the greenhouse are especially serviceable and accessible by those in wheelchairs or those who cannot bend down easily to work in-ground beds — and they can be built as high as necessary. In a greenhouse, it is relatively simple to make raised beds provided the decision to install them is made early on in the design process.

Raised beds in the greenhouse are especially serviceable and accessible by those in wheelchairs or those who cannot bend down easily to work in-ground beds — and they can be built as high as necessary.

The major choice involved in a raised bed is what material you will use for its support structure. Instead of lumber, I use stone for some bed walls and half-width concrete bricks for others (to allow more space for the growing medium). It's also important to determine how you plan to fill the raised bed area. If you want hot beds (heated growing beds), you will need to refill them every fall (because they are active for only 4 to 6 weeks at a time), which can be a real chore if you haven't planned out how you are going to do it. The process for emptying and refilling raised beds involves being able to get a large wheelbarrow right next to the bed, removing the material that supports one end of the bed, and shoveling the soil out of and into the bed (or you can use a small power vehicle such as a Bobcat if your greenhouse space allows). The best time to make these decisions about activities that require room to navigate is before the greenhouse is built, when you still have the design on paper.

Tools and Equipment

The tools I use in my greenhouse are stored on a rack in a small annex to the structure, which my wife refers to as the potting shed. Along with tools, this small area contains all the fertilizers, plant pots, and insecticides that I use in the greenhouse. Anything that is at all hazardous or potentially harmful (such as fertilizers and insecticides) is kept in cupboards located high on the wall, out of reach of small children.

Following are some tools and equipment that are basic to most greenhouse operations.

Hand Tools

I modified a rake, small shovel, and hoe for use in the greenhouse by cutting down the handles to 3 feet — long enough to work in the raised beds but not so long that I risk poking the handle through a window when I'm working in the cramped space.

I also use several trowels in the greenhouse. Some have short handles (making them easy to use with one hand); others have longer handles to reach the rear of the raised beds. The best

tools I own are made by the English toolmaker Burgon and Ball (see Resources, page 248). They're all stainless steel and are made for use in close spaces. These tools now have pride of place on my greenhouse tool board.

Other essential tools are a dustpan and brush, although I have to admit that I drag the shop vacuum cleaner into the greenhouse for a major spill. I also always carry clippers when working in the greenhouse; you never know when you'll have to trim a plant or clip an errant root. Another very useful tool is a squeegee, for cleaning the glazing. (To get the maximum amount of light into the greenhouse, the windows should be cleaned regularly inside and out; see chapter 12.) I have two: a long-handled one for the roof glass and a short-handled one for the sides.

Twine is essential in a well-maintained greenhouse. I use degradable hemp twine so that it can be discarded at the end of the season along with the plants it ties to stakes or overhead supports. Twine can also be tied to the greenhouse rafters so that vines can grow up it. It can be used to hold open windows or doors temporarily and I've used it to tie down the cover of a hoop house during strong winds.

Eyebolts

These bolts screwed into the rafters of wood-frame greenhouses serve as handy anchors for hanging baskets. I make up twelve to fifteen 18-inch hanging baskets each February (I buy them wholesale from my garden supplier) and hang them from eyebolts in the greenhouse rafters. The eyebolts are placed directly over growing beds so that any water that drains from them falls right to the plants in the beds. In spring, when I move the hanging baskets to the deck,

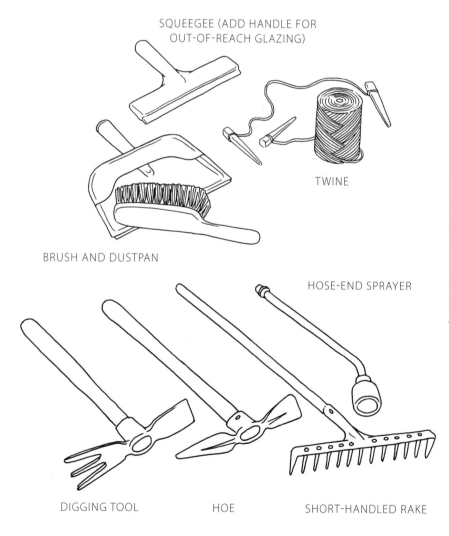

SQUEEGEE (ADD HANDLE FOR OUT-OF-REACH GLAZING)

TWINE

BRUSH AND DUSTPAN

HOSE-END SPRAYER

DIGGING TOOL   HOE   SHORT-HANDLED RAKE

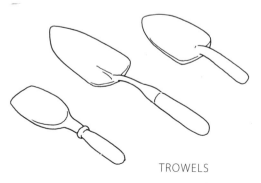

TROWELS

I tie long lengths of twine to the eyebolts and train tomatoes, beans, and peas up them.

A Riddle or Sieve

Another important greenhouse tool is a riddle. Sometimes called a screen or sieve, this tool can be used to screen potting soil for starting fine seeds. It can also be used to separate weeds and roots from good, reusable greenhouse soil and for sifting small stones from fresh loam. In the greenhouse I use a small circular riddle with different-sized meshes, available from Lee Valley Tools (see Resources, page 248).

Sprayers

Sprayers are also useful in the greenhouse. I use three sizes: a small, half-gallon one for locally spraying plants that have special requirements, such as a foliar spray; a larger, 2-gallon sprayer reserved for pesticide or herbicide applications (which is never used for anything else); and a 5-gallon backpack sprayer for spraying fruit trees outdoors. I often spray the greenhouse trees using this after I've moved them to their summer locations and before they go back in the greenhouse in the fall.

Wheelbarrows and Carts

I regularly use several kinds of barrows and carts in the greenhouse — a wheelbarrow, a garden cart, and a specially made flat-decked cart — to tote heavy items into and out of the structure. If your greenhouse has a concrete floor, you might want to invest in a wheeled dolly to help move heavy plants. Available at most hardware stores and home centers, these are made of wood and have swiveling casters. Car stores have similar products called creepers to help you get under a vehicle while lying on your back.

If your greenhouse does not have a concrete floor, you may have to use a large, wheeled garden cart to move things around, which usually means lifting heavy pots into and out of it. Another useful cart is the type of two-wheeled dolly that delivery men use to bring in heavy parcels, but if you're moving a big tree on one of these, you'll need to tie it down to keep it stable and upright while you move it.

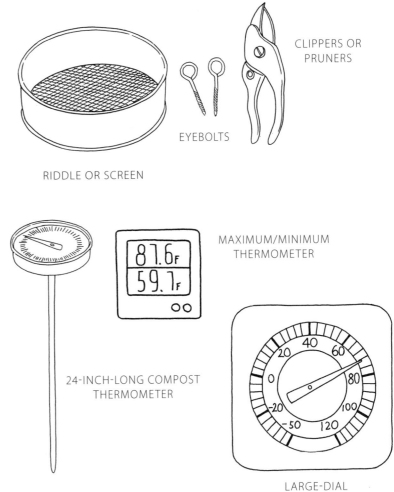

CLIPPERS OR PRUNERS

EYEBOLTS

RIDDLE OR SCREEN

MAXIMUM/MINIMUM THERMOMETER

24-INCH-LONG COMPOST THERMOMETER

LARGE-DIAL THERMOMETER

Thermometers

An essential greenhouse tool is a thermometer. The best kind is a maximum/minimum thermometer that shows and records the daytime high and nighttime low temperatures. I also like to have a pair of large-dial thermometers (one at each end), which allow me to view the temperature at a glance from outside the building. Finally, I have a 24-inch-long thermometer to check the temperature of the compost pile. It looks like a larger version of the thermometer that you stick in a roasting chicken to see if it's

TIP

Replace the pneumatic tire of your wheelbarrow with a solid rubber tire, available from hardware stores for about $30. A solid tire means you won't have to worry about checking air pressure or puncturing it while working.

done. With it I can determine when the compost pile and hot beds have cooked sufficiently and are cooling down. You can also get a number of remote sensing thermometers that allow you to monitor your greenhouse from indoors. These are sold by most greenhouse suppliers, and even Radio Shack has one.

Watering Cans

Last but not least is the tool used most often in the greenhouse: a good watering can. It's easy to dip this tool into the greenhouse water tank or fishpond, add a teaspoon of fertilizer, and water the potted plants. I use a 2-gallon watering can with an adjustable spout, but I also have a 1-gallon can from Lee Valley Tools with a long spout for reaching plants at the rear of the beds.

Hose End Fittings

A variety of fittings for the end of your garden hose can be useful in the greenhouse. A pressure-breaker hose on the end of a long wand (it looks like a walking stick with a large, circular head on the end) is helpful for watering hanging baskets. When you turn on the garden hose, this attachment reduces the pressure of the water coming out of the end so that you don't blast dirt out of the garden beds or hanging baskets.

An attachable fertilizer jar available from most garden centers can be used to fertilize while you water. And you'll need a powerful sprayer to blast dirt off the greenhouse glass and a head with a gentler spray that you can use to water plants in growing beds.

A seed-starting or germination chamber

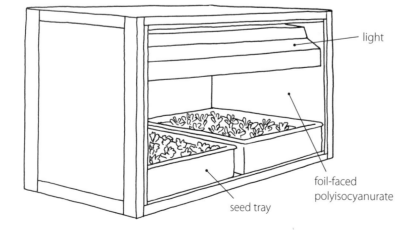

light

foil-faced polyisocyanurate

seed tray

A Germination Chamber or Seed-Starting Box

Do you start your own plants from seeds? If you haven't up to now, owning a greenhouse may prompt you to start all your plants. Seeds start best when they have a favorable temperature, and different types of plants require different temperatures. For example, many flower seeds prefer 70°F to 75°F to germinate, while wild-flowers tend to germinate at temperatures of 65°F to 70°F. Brassicas and other green-leafed vegetables prefer 65°F to 72°F, while tomatoes like 75°F to 80°F. Obviously, if you can satisfy the germination requirements of each of these plants, you'll be able to grow more seedlings.

To make a seed-starting box or germination chamber, you'll first have to make a frame capable of supporting the weight of one or two 4-foot incandescent 15- to 40-watt lightbulbs. The inside of the frame is covered with foil-faced polyisocyanurate, available from a building supplier. This insulation keeps the box warm and the foil facing reflects light back toward the plants. If you make the box wide enough to hold two seed trays and the lights above them, it should be at least 4 feet wide and 22 inches deep on the inside, which allows room to place two 22-inch flats end to end under a single light fixture. It should be tall enough inside only to prevent the lightbulbs' heat from burning the plants; about 24 inches tall is usually sufficient. I added a couple of holes in the top and bottom to allow air to circulate and extra heat to vent from the chamber, though I use 40-watt lights; you may find that you don't need air holes if you use lightbulbs that are only 15 watts.

The lights are operated by a timer and stay on for a set period. The "on" period depends upon the type of seed you want to germinate. For example, the light is left on for up to 20 hours a day for impatiens seeds because they need almost continuous light to germinate. Primulas also require a long period of light to germinate. As soon as seeds have germinated, I move the trays to a growing area, where the lights are turned on for up to 14 hours a day. This frees up the germinating chamber for new plants. I find that I keep the germinating chamber going for 3 to 4 months in the early part of the year. I start using it around December with perennial flowers, followed by annuals, vegetables such as leeks and onions that require a long growing period, and then the faster-growing vegetables so that by mid-April (in Rhode Island) the plants are ready to go out into the cool greenhouse and from there into the garden.

A Growing Chamber

My growing chamber, located in the basement of my house, allows me to grow seedlings when it's snowing outside. Here in Rhode Island, I start pepper and eggplant seedlings in the middle of January, while I start many perennial flower seedlings in late fall and then move them to the greenhouse for the winter.

The growing chamber was easy to build. It uses four 40-watt fluorescent shop fixtures (two tubes per fixture) on each level (each with a cool white tube and a warm white tube for the best growing light). The area of each level is slightly more than 4 feet by 4 feet, which allows eight flats of seedlings per level. The sides are framed with 2×4s with furring strips bridging the gap between both sides. The sides of the growing chamber are lined with foil-faced insulation to reflect heat back to the plants. If the area around your growing frame is open, you might want to line it with polyethylene sheeting to keep in heat and humidity. Beware of completely cutting off the air circulation, however. It's easy for the chamber to build up plenty of heat and moisture and cook your plants. A low-power fan could help circulate the air. In 15 years of using this growing chamber, I have yet to have seeds mildew or damp off, probably because the low heat given off by the lights keeps it warm enough.

I found that placing seed flats directly on the furring strips allows heat from the bottom lights to warm the plants in the flats above. In order to keep flats from falling off the strips, you could install wire mesh over the furring on each level, which still allows rising heat to come through from below to the plants above. I place heat-loving plants such as peppers and tomatoes at the top of the growing chamber and plants that prefer cooler conditions lower down.

On each level, the fixtures are placed a few inches above each seed flat and are controlled by a heavy-duty timer. The idea is to provide the maximum amount of light for the plants, but not to burn them by putting the light fixtures too close. As the plants grow taller, the light fixtures are raised until there is no more space in the chamber to raise them. At this point, the plants are potted up and taken out to the greenhouse.

Be sure to water or mist seedlings as they are growing. You can water them by removing each seed flat or tray one at a time and gently pouring water into each cell. I use a small watering can with lukewarm water. Be very careful when misting trays in place, given that the lights are in close proximity. One drop of water on a light-bulb can be enough to break it. I find that it's easiest to remove the seed trays to mist them, as I do for watering.

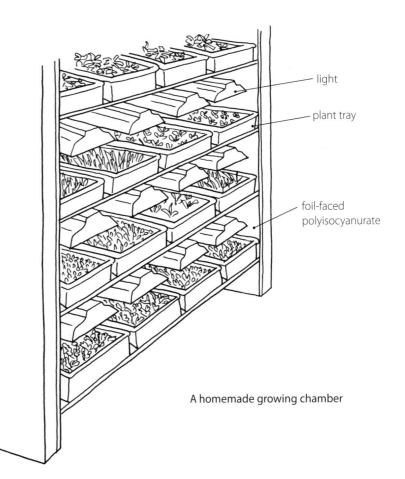

light

plant tray

foil-faced polyisocyanurate

A homemade growing chamber

A Potting Bench

If you do any kind of serious greenhouse gardening, you'll need a potting bench, which helps to contain the soil so that it doesn't go everywhere when you are repotting plants. The best benches have a small sink and running water. A basic bench is not difficult to construct (for a plan, see chapter 13, project 11).

My bench, framed with 2×2 lumber, stands 36 inches high, although you can adjust the bench dimensions to suit your height or the height of those who will use it. The entire work top, except the front, is enclosed to keep the potting soil on the tabletop. On my bench the corners are curved a bit (they are built up with two layers of ⅛-inch plywood — layers of masonite epoxied together will also serve) to form a smooth bend. The curve makes the bench top easy to clean with a single sweep of the brush. Under the bench is storage for potting soil and plant pots, as well as a garbage bin for all those bits and pieces of plants that you snip off when repotting. A covered slot in the bench top directly over the garbage bin allows me to sweep away refuse. A fold-out drawer holds pot

labels, felt-tipped pens, and twist ties. Tools are mounted on the outside of the potting table and on its back, where they are near at hand but not in the way when I'm working.

I made the bench top 36 inches deep and 42 inches wide to give myself plenty of work space, but you can adjust the top dimensions to suit the space available. You can also put the bench on casters so that it can be moved around the greenhouse.

A much simpler, movable bench hooks onto the benches over the walkway. This particular model is handy because you often need to pot plants near their location rather than drag them to a stationary potting bench, repot them, and then drag them back to where they'll grow. It's made with rounded corners, but instead of having legs, it has cleats on the sides designed to attach to the greenhouse benches. Note that this bench will work only if your walkways are parallel. Otherwise, it will be difficult to fit the bench in place.

Storage

Storage space is essential for a greenhouse. If you buy fertilizer or potting soil in large bags, you'll need a place to store them. Sure, they can be kept outside, but in early spring or the middle of winter, when you are about to start seedlings, you'll have to bring a frozen bag of potting soil into the greenhouse to thaw before you can begin your work. Aside from the delay, the thawing potting soil will draw heat from the greenhouse just when you need it most. In addition to making your work easier, it's neater to have a space in the greenhouse for storage than to leave supplies piled outside.

Storage can be as simple as shelves (see Shelving, page 168) or an open space or air lock, where you can store big bags of potting soil or greenhouse clothes, or it can take the form of a tidier cupboard that can be locked for added safety if any potentially dangerous materials (such as pesticides) are to be stored in it. I store many items — insecticides, sprays, fertilizer, and small pots — in two inexpensive shelf-mounted

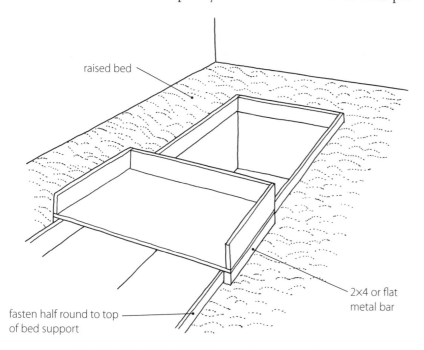

raised bed

fasten half round to top
of bed support

2×4 or flat
metal bar

A potting bench that attaches to perimeter greenhouse benches across a central aisle. The runners for the bench can be made of metal or wood, though metal slides more easily on the edges of the growing beds.

closets that fit against the back wall of my potting shed. My other storage is located under the deck in my heated pit greenhouse. In this area I can fit up to six large bales of potting soil and a few pots.

Under Benches

The knee wall of many greenhouses offers storage possibilities. If the benches next to this wall are raised to about 36 inches, you'll find that there's plenty of space under the bench to store items out of sight or, if the area is glazed, even to grow plants that can live with lower light levels. Plants such as Christmas cacti and amaryllis that are resting, some ground covers, coffee plants, begonias, ferns, and other understory plants can live happily under a bench, provided they are kept warm. If your under-bench plants need more light, you can install waterproof lighting on the underside of the bench. These lights have the added benefit of warming the bench itself, supplying a home for heat-loving plants on top of the bench.

If you are going to store only equipment under the benches, it's best to block the lower part of a glazed greenhouse to hide the unsightly pile of dozens of pots and bags of potting soil. Of course, a low knee wall of poured concrete will hide stored materials from outside view. On the inside you can install wood-framed mesh doors on the bench in front of the wall to hide the mess but still allow air to circulate.

Remember that any under-bench storage area must be cleaned periodically to keep it free of insects and unnecessary clutter.

Making a Secure Storage Locker

Leaving tools in your greenhouse is a sure way to broadcast what you own, increasing the chances that they'll be stolen. After all, anyone can break a pane of glass to get to your belongings, leaving your plants exposed to cold in the process. Making a storage locker or cupboard for tools, materials, and potentially dangerous garden substances is a good idea. A padlock makes its contents even more secure.

A simple locker can be framed with 2×2 lumber and covered with plywood. Be sure to measure your tools before beginning construction; the locker should be wide enough to hold your widest tool, tall enough to fit your longest rake or spade handle, and deep enough to allow space for all your tools and bigger items.

Making a storage locker for tools, materials, and potentially dangerous garden substances is a good idea. A padlock makes its contents even more secure.

If you have a small hobby greenhouse or a kit greenhouse that has no room at all for a storage locker, consider another structure, such as a garden shed, for storage. A separate shed can also store larger lawn and garden equipment and can be easily locked. It might also have a wider door (3 feet or more) to allow easy access for wheelbarrows and other equipment.

Greenhouse Clothing

I wear old clothes when I go into the greenhouse. Usually, I have no idea what needs to be done when I enter, but a plant might need repotting or trimming or moving, and often I end up getting dirty. If you don't want to change your clothes entirely before beginning work, hang an apron or coveralls in the greenhouse where you can put them on easily (perhaps on a peg or hook just inside the door). A rubber apron allows you to spill water and wet potting soil without worry or discomfort. You may also want to wear light summer clothes while you work in your greenhouse. These structures can become hot in the sunlight, reaching temperatures of more than 80°F even in mid-winter. Besides being comfortable in this warm environment, summer clothing can give a real boost to the spirit on icy winter days. Avoid loose-fitting clothing, however. It can catch on branches, which can bring even great potted plants crashing to the ground.

If you are going to pot up plants or fill seed flats, you may want to wear a pair of rubber gloves. The best for working with water or damp soil are the rubber gloves used for dishwashing. With their longer cuffs, they keep your wrists and arms clean, too. Finally, a pair of watertight or rubber boots can be useful if you plan to spray water in your greenhouse; if your greenhouse work is reasonably dry, however, normal gardening shoes will do.

Gear for Spraying Chemicals or Pesticides

Even the most "benign" pesticides such as dormant oil can irritate the skin and pose a threat, especially if sprayed in an enclosed area. If you plan to spray greenhouse plants with chemicals or any form of pesticide, you'll need a respirator, a face mask or goggles, and rubber gloves. Consider investing in a suit with a hood to protect you all over. (I prefer to wear a Tyvek suit.) The respirator should have a filter suitable for the chemical that you're spraying. (Read all manufacturer's instructions on content and safety before you begin applying any material.) You can buy a respirator for $50 to $75 and filters for a few dollars more. The investment is well worth it.

Once you have sprayed any pesticides, it's important to stay out of the greenhouse for a few hours to give the spray time to dissipate.

Accessories to Control Insects

Most hobby greenhouses will have insects at various times during the year. Whiteflies and aphids are common pests that can be eliminated by spraying with any insecticide, although I prefer to use biological or organic controls such as ladybugs and praying mantis unless the infestation gets out of hand. Remember that the first line of defense in any greenhouse is to screen open windows. This helps to keep insects out, although some insects will get through larger mesh. Dense mesh, however, blocks substantial light and air, so you'll have to find a balance that controls insects without compromising the light and air environment for your plants.

If you do have a plant that becomes infested with insects, it's best to move it outdoors for spraying, even in the dead of winter. After all, if the plant is going to die because of insect infestation, it's better to kill it (by exposure to cold weather) or cure it before it infects everything else inside the greenhouse. You can also use a 20- or 30-gallon aquarium as an isolation chamber and spray area for insect-ridden plants. The best plan, however, is to control strictly which plants are taken into the greenhouse and quarantine those that are suspect before they can infect other plants.

If screens fail to keep out a number of insects, you may have to resort to other controls. I use sticky yellow pads to catch and control whiteflies, but occasionally I do have to spray when the bugs proliferate. I use Safer's insecticidal soap and pyrethrin sprays with great success, though heavy application of pyrethrin can leave a gray deposit on all surfaces in the greenhouse and the odor may linger for days or weeks, depending on how much is applied. This can be especially worrisome in an attached greenhouse, where the odors and spray can find their way into your home.

12 Greenhouse Maintenance

GREENHOUSES, LIKE REGULAR HOUSES, require some maintenance from time to time. If you don't maintain your greenhouse, eventually paint will peel, glazing will be covered with dirt or algae, and glass glazing will crack or drop out of its frame. If all of this happens, your greenhouse could end up holding a lot of dead or dying plants and enough leaves to mulch a forest, and it may smell pretty bad, too.

The trick to keeping a greenhouse in top condition is to do a little maintenance whenever you enter it. Most maintenance chores are fairly simple: removing leaves that fall on the floor, cleaning up spills, cleaning the glazing, and making sure that everything is working properly. Along with more frequent maintenance, at least once a year you should conduct a maintenance blitz that brings back every part of the greenhouse to tip-top condition.

Greenhouse maintenance is ongoing. Neglecting it one year means that you'll need to catch up with it the next. Performing a little maintenance every time you enter it reduces the onerous chore of spring or fall cleaning to a day or two rather than a week. If any greenhouse parts need replacing, try to perform this maintenance in the winter (for a cool greenhouse) or in summer (for an empty heated greenhouse), when the garden does not demand so much time (unless the repair involves the function of heating or lighting). For example, I planned on replacing acrylic-covered windows with double-pane glass ones, so I built the new windows in the basement over the winter and fitted them into the greenhouse in summer, during a regularly scheduled maintenance session.

Regular Chores

Some chores and monitoring in the greenhouse must occur on a regular basis to keep your plants healthy and the greenhouse in fine working order.

■ **Look for signs of systems/structural problems.** Whenever you're working in the greenhouse, check plants for signs of disease or damage and ascertain the cause. It may be that systems and conditions need maintenance attention or repair. For instance, the heater may be malfunctioning and poisoning plants with fumes. Learn the plant signs of greenhouse structural or systems problems. For example, open-flame propane burners may emit a small amount of sulfuric acid, which shows up as white spots on plant leaves. During the winter, check your heating system daily to avoid finding all your plants frozen. Simply make sure that it is running properly and that the greenhouse temperatures are where they should be.

■ **Perform general cleanup.** Remove dead leaves before they accumulate and start to rot. A dead leaf resting on a plant can invite a potentially fatal bacterial infection that might spread throughout the greenhouse. When you pot up plants, clean up spills and detritus right away. Wipe surfaces with a solution of 1 tablespoon of bleach mixed with 1 gallon of water to eliminate germs.

■ **Keep mold and algae at bay.** In the moist, warm atmosphere of a greenhouse, mold and algae grow readily. The only way to keep them at bay is to clean everything religiously whenever you finish a job. Pelargoniums that are moved into the greenhouse in fall seem especially susceptible to leaf mold as temperatures fall.

■ **Clean glazing.** Although the glazing on your greenhouse always needs to be monitored for cleanliness, it's especially important to do so during winter, when light levels are low and you want the maximum amount of light to reach your plants. Use a commercial window cleaner on the inside windows, but test it first on plant leaves. Some window cleaners will adversely affect plants.

The best way to clean outside glazing is to start with a mop on the end of a long broomstick to wet the glass or polycarbonate or other material and swab away the worst of the dirt, and then to wash the exterior with a hose. Finally, squeegee the surface to get off the moisture before it dries. I use ordinary dishwashing soap and water for my cleaning, but a proprietary window cleaner does an equally good job; it just costs more. Of course, if you live in an area that experiences cold and icy conditions in winter, you'll have to wait for warmer, fair weather to clean glazing on the outside.

You'll find that most of the dirt builds up on the inside of the glazing, where the humid atmosphere of the greenhouse makes it easy for grime, green algae, and insects to colonize window spaces. For this inside dirt, household window cleaners may do a better job than soapy water alone. If your glazing is glass, take extra care when wiping cracked panes, which can easily cut both rags and fingers. If the green algae buildup is severe, the only way to remove it may be to pressure-wash the windows.

Monthly or Quarterly Maintenance

A number of maintenance checks and chores should occur on a monthly basis or at least every 3 months.

■ **Check the condition of the glazing.** You could also do this more frequently, when you clean the glazing. It's especially important to monitor its condition if it's been installed with putty or is the old-fashioned overlapping variety. Look for cracks, chips, and scratches. Cracks and chips especially could be indicative of fractures about to form or could point to a potentially more serious problem: The greenhouse is twisting, or racking, in the wind and the glazing is not moving with it. A small crack will eventually become a big one, so catching it when it's small may prevent a more costly repair or help to diagnose a larger problem early on.

■ **Check caulking throughout the greenhouse.** Some types of caulking turn brittle as they age. The first sign of this is often loose or damaged caulking pulling away from the glazing. If you have to replace caulking, silicone sealants perform well, but they cannot be painted. If you want to paint it, use polysulfide caulking (see chapter 7, Caulking and Weather Stripping, page 98).

■ **Check your greenhouse frame for signs of rot, decay, and rust.** If you have a wood-framed greenhouse, examine the wood inside and outside the structure. Look for flaking paint, soft spots, and areas that stay wet after a rain. These could all be indicators of the onset of rot. If you find any areas that are soft, check to see what's causing the softness. If the wood is rotting, it should be replaced as soon as possible. If paint is flaking from exposure to sunlight and the elements, scrape and sand away the flaking paint, let the area dry, and repaint it with an outdoor primer before top-coating it. As I've mentioned, I used a marine paint for one of my greenhouses and it's held up very well. (See chapter 6 in general and specifically Painting Your Greenhouse, page 88, for more information on kinds of paint and painting procedures for this application.) If you have wooden benches, check them as well and repair and repaint them as needed.

If you have a metal greenhouse and find an area of rust, either sandblast or sand and scrape it until it's shiny and new-looking again, then paint it with an outdoor enamel metal primer or other outdoor primer before covering it with a top coat. Do the same for any metal benches and shelving in the greenhouse.

■ **Check the frame and surfaces for mildew.** Even if the paint coating on your greenhouse is in good shape, it may be discolored with mildew. You can remove mildew with soapy water or with a proprietary mildew cleaner. If you plan to paint the greenhouse, remove all mildew before applying paint. In this case, it's best to wipe the woodwork with a solvent to keep mildew from ruining your paint job.

■ **On a monthly basis, check the heating elements or pipes.** Wipe them down to remove dust. Vacuum fin tubing, if it's part of your heating system, to keep it at its maximum efficiency. If you have a burner in your heater, check to see that it's not clogged with soot or other debris.

■ **On a monthly basis, check the temperature-alarm system and greenhouse insulation.** I once discovered that a mouse had tunneled into the insulation and set up housekeeping behind the drywall! Needless to say, I had to catch it before it made a snack of my newly planted seeds.

Biannual or Annual Maintenance

It's best to make biannual checks on your greenhouse in spring and fall. If you have a cold greenhouse, you can check its condition any time during the winter to ready it for the coming growing season. A warm greenhouse should be checked in late summer or early fall, before plants that have summered outdoors go back inside for the winter. All greenhouses should be cleaned thoroughly at least once a year to keep ahead of mold and algae. I have settled into a routine of cleaning the warm greenhouse every summer and the cold greenhouse every winter, when both are empty. This entails washing all the woodwork with a solution of bleach and water to get rid of mold and mildew before it has the opportunity to grow. A shiny paint on the surface of wood or metal is easier to wipe clean than is a flat paint.

Spring Chores for the Cool Greenhouse

Certain chores in a cool greenhouse should be tended to in the spring to ready the greenhouse for the growing season.

■ **If you don't do so more frequently, completely clean all the glazing inside and outside.** This ensures that plenty of light can get to newly started plants. For this kind of thorough cleaning, a sponge soaked in a solution of water and bleach to kill plant disease pathogens works well.

■ **Lubricate door and window hinges and locks.**

■ **Touch up paint as necessary.**

■ **Check all lights.** If you have supplementary grow lights to increase the spring day length, you should check them and make sure that all the bulbs are working properly. (See chapter 5 for more on light choices for the greenhouse.)

■ **Prepare growing beds.** I find that I need to water the growing beds copiously for about a week if they've been left empty during the winter. Before doing this, make sure to thoroughly incorporate all soil amendments, fertilizers, and manure.

■ **Check fans, window openers, screens, and vents, doors, and windows.** Make sure everything is clean, oiled, and ready to go. If you have a cooling system, clean the filters and check it for leaks.

Late-Summer Chores for the Heated Greenhouse

Certain chores must be accomplished in a heated greenhouse to prepare for the shorter, colder days of winter.

■ **Remove shading material.** Before storing it where mice and other rodents can't burrow into it, check that the material has not caused any damage to the roof or to the roof glazing and caulking and check for damage to the material itself. Usually, removing the shading material goes hand in hand with cleaning the glazing beneath it.

■ **Check your lighting system.** Make sure that it's ready to face the winter. Remember that fluorescent bulbs gradually weaken and may need to be replaced long before they actually fail. The ends of the tubes of older fluorescent bulbs will turn black. When you see this telltale blackening, change them. Clean all reflectors, and the tops and bottoms of lights, and check terminals for corrosion. A quick spray with CRC or a similar anticorrosion and lubricant material can prolong terminal life indefinitely.

■ **Check the heating system.** I find it's best to do this check in August so that I have time to order parts to correct any problems. If you wait until late September or October, when the greenhouse is full of plants, it could be difficult to get parts and repairs done in time to heat the structure before the first frosty nights.

Start by cleaning the thermostat with compressed air to get rid of spiderwebs and insect debris. You may also have to wipe the contacts if they are exposed to ensure that they make and break properly. A quick swipe with an emery board cleans any exposed contacts. Look over all the wire connections to make sure that none is loose or about to break. Check the cable from the thermostat to the burner to make sure no portions are frayed.

Check the on/off valves of propane or natural gas burners. Make sure that they move freely.

Look over the wiring and the burners. Clean all the debris and soot from heating units. Light the pilot light and confirm that the burner goes on when the pilot is lit.

If you have a hot water baseboard heating system and haven't been doing so on a monthly basis, vacuum all the fins on the heating pipes and make sure that air can flow freely to the burner or furnace.

Check furnace filters, burners, flue pipes, motors, and igniters. Make sure that the burner chamber is free of soot, which can increase energy usage by up to 10 percent. Check that the furnace runs smoothly and operates within a few degrees of the thermostat reading. Make sure that the flue has no leaks or holes created by rust, and repair all problems.

Note: A wood-burning stove and chimney should be cleaned and checked for damage and leaks in *spring*, after the winter's heavy use. At the same time, cover the log pile (you may want to purchase wood early on, when prices should be lower, and allow it to dry for a few months) so that it's ready for winter. Sprinkle stove ashes on your garden or add them to the compost heap to be mixed with composting materials.

■ **Perform a greenhouse heat-retention check.** Look to see if you need to apply additional glazing or an inner liner to the greenhouse to increase heat-retention capacity. You may want to install weather stripping or other materials to increase the R-value of the glazing. Check doors and windows to make sure that weather stripping and seals are in place and functioning properly.

If You're Not Using Your Greenhouse in Winter

There are a number of chores to be taken care of if you plan on shutting down your greenhouse for the cold winter months.

■ **Choose and install a rodent-deterrent method.** A greenhouse is a great place for these small animals to set up house in the winter.

■ **Drain water lines, turn off electrical power, and close all the windows and vents.**

■ **Disable automatic window openers.**

■ **Store items safely.** Wheelbarrows, lawn chairs, outdoor furniture, and garden carts should be stored in the greenhouse away from where any leaks might occur. Take your lawn or deck chair cushions into the house, where they will remain clean and dry.

A greenhouse should be protected and maintained just as you maintain your other assets. It adds value to your property and provides you with the means to unwind and enjoy your hobby. Keeping it in tip-top shape preserves and perhaps increases your enjoyment of it as well as its overall value.

13 Greenhouse Plans

THE PLANS IN THIS CHAPTER are geared for handy, do-it-yourself gardeners who have decided to build their own greenhouse. These designs can also serve as models if you choose to have your greenhouse constructed by a builder. There are plans here to suit a variety of needs, and many can be modified according to the materials you have on hand, your terrain or your home's location, the space you have available, and how you will be using the structure.

Each greenhouse has a different style of foundation, and all, accordingly, require varying levels of skills to build — from the simplest structures such as a season extender and a PVC-framed hoop house to more complex greenhouses such as a lean-to structure and a slant-front insulated building. A number of the structures can be glazed in a variety of ways as well. Many of the projects incorporate polycarbonate glazing because it's easy to acquire and install, but you may prefer glass or have access to acrylic or other material. You can also add lighting or plumbing — or modify systems — for a number of these greenhouses, or, in several instances, leave them out altogether for the simplest construction. The following plans are, in many instances, starting points. Combine them with your imagination and skills so that you can make your greenhouse the best for your garden.

For more information on foundations, building techniques, and glazing than is provided in the individual steps for each project, refer to chapters 7, 8, and 9.

1. Basic Conventional Greenhouse

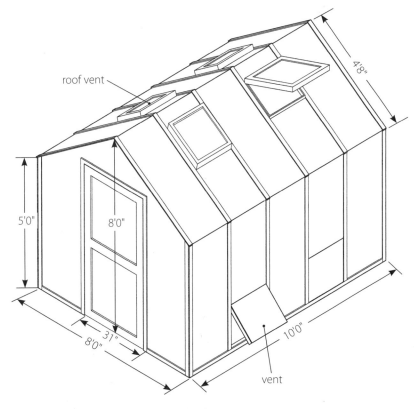

roof vent

5'0"

8'0"

31"

8'0"

10'0"

vent

Structural schematic of greenhouse

This 8-foot by 10-foot greenhouse is conventionally framed and intended to be glazed with 6 mm polycarbonate. The wood used for the frame comprises cedar or oak 2×2s with a 2×4 eave support and a 2×6 ridgepole. Glazing in the roof opens like windows to add ventilation.

The polycarbonate is simply screwed onto the surface of the frame and the seams between sheets are covered by cap pieces. In this greenhouse, all the joints are lapped for ease of construction (see information on lap joints in chapter 8).

CONSTRUCTING THE FOUNDATION

Materials

- Four 10' 2×10s
- Eighteen 3' 2×4s
- String
- Spare pieces of wood for batter boards
- A few bricks
- One 10' length of 2-inch schedule 40 PVC pipe
- One 2" 90-degree elbow
- One drain grate to fit 2" PVC pipe (to be flush-mounted)
- 1½ cubic yards of concrete
- Scaffold nails
- Up to 3 yards of gravel or pea stone

The foundation is a simple concrete slab with a drain hole running to a dry well. The water line enters through the side of the greenhouse, as does any wiring, so there is no need to set conduit or plumbing in the foundation.

STEP 1: Lay Out the Foundation.

Please refer to chapter 8, Constructing a Concrete Foundation and Slab, page 116, for further infor-mation about building forms for a slab, obtaining concrete, and pouring a slab. Lay out the foundation using the method explained in chapter 8: Mark out an 8-foot by 10-foot rectangle with string and check the diagonals. Each diagonal should measure 12 feet 9⅝ inches. Set batter boards at each corner and check the strings a second time to make sure everything is square.

STEP 2: Excavate for the Foundation

Excavate the area to a depth of 10 to 12 inches. Save the topsoil for another project.

STEP 3: Build Foundation Forms

Because the concrete will be only 6 inches thick, the forms can be made from 2×10s. Using batter boards and string, on the 10-foot side mark 1½ inches out from the string in two spots about 6 inches from each end. At each spot hammer a stake into the ground. Then place another stake in the middle of the 10-foot side and then two more stakes between these three.

Using bricks to support the wood, position one of the 10-foot 2×10s so that its top edge is at grade level—that is, exactly where the top of the

Base structure of greenhouse

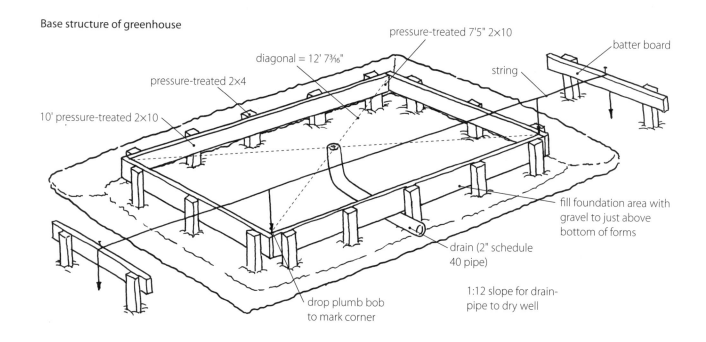

pressure-treated 7'5" 2×10

batter board

diagonal = 12' 7³⁄₁₆"

string

pressure-treated 2×4

10' pressure-treated 2×10

fill foundation area with gravel to just above bottom of forms

drain (2" schedule 40 pipe)

drop plumb bob to mark corner

1:12 slope for drain-pipe to dry well

concrete slab will be. Nail the plank to the stakes and check that it's perfectly level. Repeat this entire procedure on the opposite 10-foot side of the area. When you have the second plank in place, stretch a third 2×10 across the top of these two forms to ensure that both sides of the foundation are at the same height.

Cut the last two 2×10s to 8 feet 3 inches long. Nail these to the ends of the two long forms already in place to make the forms for the width of the greenhouse. Three scaffold nails in each will be easy to remove later. Brace the 8-foot 3-inch lengths with three or four stakes along each side.

Once the formwork is in place, check that everything is square and that the diagonals match.

STEP 4: Install the Drainpipe

Now, working carefully so that you do not disturb the formwork, set your drainpipe in the middle of the area. To find the middle, simply use strings from each corner across the diagonals and drop a plumb bob from their meeting place. Once you've determined the middle, use a long plank to find the grade level (the height of the concrete floor). Measure down about ¾ inch from this point to determine the grade level in the middle of the greenhouse (the slab will slope down toward the center).

Set the elbow directly in the middle of the greenhouse. Note that when you attach the pipe, you'll need to allow at least a 1:12 slope (for each foot of pipe, the pipe slopes 1 inch) so that the water will drain through it away from the structure. Next, determine the length of the pipe between the elbow and the drain: Measure the amount of pipe that goes inside the elbow, the amount of pipe that goes inside the flush-mounted drain, and the distance from the top of the elbow to the drain and add together these measurements. Cut a piece of pipe to suit and dry-fit it between both the elbow and the drain. Dry-fit the remaining length of pipe (it will be about 9 feet) on the other side of the elbow, heading out of the greenhouse. After dry fitting all pipes, use pipe cement to glue together all pieces of the entire unit.

Because you'll be pouring concrete around the drain, cover the drain top with duct tape to keep it from clogging. Use blocks or bricks to set the drain at the correct height and run the long side of the pipe out under the formwork.

STEP 5: Pour the Concrete

With the drain and formwork in place, fill the excavated 10-inch or 12-inch hole with gravel or pea stone to about 6 inches below the grade level. This will give the concrete slab a surface to "float" on and allows it to shrink and expand as needed without cracking. Rake the gravel until it's level, then lay over it 6-inch wire mesh cut to within 4 inches of the forms and support it about 1½ inches above the gravel by placing small stones beneath it. Make certain the mesh does not touch the formwork anywhere. Any area of contact will provide an opening for moisture to get to the steel and corrode it. Check the diagonals and the levels of all the forms one last time. The slab is now ready for the pour.

You'll need 1½ yards of concrete for the slab if the gravel is 6 inches below grade level. Follow the instructions in chapter 8 on leveling, screeding, floating, and edging poured concrete. (You'll probably find that your drain has disappeared and needs to be located.) During this process, determine if you want the surface rough or smooth (remember, a smooth greenhouse floor tends to be slippery when wet).

Allow the slab to dry for an hour or so, then insert bolts into the wet concrete 1 inch in from the edge with 2 inches of the bolt protruding from the top of the slab. This will allow the bolt heads to be level with the top of the base plate of the greenhouse when the two are attached. If the day is warm and sunny, you might want to cover the slab with moist cloths so that it will dry more slowly.

BUILDING THE GREENHOUSE

Materials

FOR THE SIDE WALLS
- Four 10' 2×2s
- Twelve 5' 2×2s
- Two 1' 10" 2×2s for the opening windows

FOR THE END WALLS
- One 8' 2×2
- Four 6' 4" 2×2s
- Four 4' 8" 2×2 rafters
- One 3' 7" 2×6 header
- One 1' 2×2 ridge support
- One 10' 2×6 ridgepole

FOR THE FOUR SIDE-WALL VENTS
- Sixteen 1' 10" 2×2s
- Eight 3" hinges
- Screws for hinges and four barrel bolts, hooks and eyes, or any other hardware you want to use to latch vents
- Polycarbonate to cover the vents

FOR THE ROOF VENTS
- Sixteen 2' 1×2s
- Eight 3" hinges

- Screws for hinges and barrel bolts, hooks and eyes, or any other hardware you want to use to latch vents
- Polycarbonate to cover the vents
- Four 1' 10" 2×2 crosspieces
- Four 2' pieces of ½" by 3" stock for the lip of each roof vent

FOR THE DOOR
- Three 3' 1×4s
- Two 6' 8" 1×4s
- Three 3" hinges, a handle, and a barrel bolt

- Screws and 6 mm polycarbonate to cover the door

FOR THE GLAZING
- 300 square feet of 6 mm polycarbonate glazing (75 longitudinal feet of 4' polycarbonate panels) *Note:* This type of polycarbonate is available in 48" and 72" widths, but 48" panels are easier to handle.
- One piece of 10' 1×4 trim to fit over the ridgepole
- U-shaped caps to fit over ends of polycarbonate panels

You can build the sill plate and walls in a space off-site and bring them to the slab when it's time to erect them. Once they're erected, the ridgepole is set in place and the rafters are added.

As shown in the following illustrations, the side walls will be 5 feet 2 inches tall (5 feet plus a cap plate) and the ridge of the roof will be 8 feet tall. Because the polycarbonate panels are 4 feet wide, the spacing of the support posts and rafters will be every 2 feet.

STEP 1: Build the Side Walls

To build each 10-foot side wall, use one 10-foot cap plate and one 10-foot base plate with six 5-foot 2×2 studs between them. Put together all four 10-foot 2×2s and carefully mark out 2-foot intervals for the support pieces (which will be placed as shown in the following illustration). Depending on your skill level, you can cut lap joints where the supports will attach to the cap and base plates or you can drill a hole at the center of the longitudinal and at the bottom

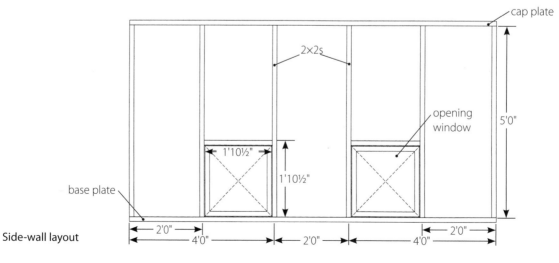

Side-wall layout

of the support post and insert a dowel to hold the pieces together. If you do use lap joints, you should use epoxy to join the parts. (See chapter 9, page 141, Using Epoxy, for more information on working with this material.) After construction, check the diagonals of each wall to ensure that everything is perfectly square.

STEP 2: Build the End Walls

The end walls require some careful laying out and measuring to ensure that they'll fit. Each will be slightly narrower than 8 feet (7 feet 8 inches, to be exact) to fit inside the side walls (which are a full 10 feet long). When all four sides of the structure are erected, the entire greenhouse will fit perfectly on the 8-foot by 10-foot slab.

For the end wall without a door, cut two of the 8-foot 2×2s to measure 7 feet 8 inches each. These will be the base plates for your greenhouse. For the nonopening end, mark the position for the 6-foot 4-inch support post 1 foot 11 inches in from each side. In the middle of the base plate, mark the location of the 8-foot 2×2 support. Because the polycarbonate is 4 feet wide, one piece will cover the distance from the side to the center line and two pieces will cover the entire end wall. (See the illustration at top right for this layout.)

In the opposite end wall, the door will be 3 feet wide to ensure that you can get a wheelbarrow into the greenhouse (though you could make it 30 inches wide if you don't plan on working with a wheelbarrow inside the structure). The two 6-foot 4-inch supports will hold up a 2×6 header. The 1-foot 2×2 should be cut to 6 inches to support the ridgepole.

Next, you'll need to install the two roof rafters on each of the end walls. Each 4-foot 8-inch rafter must be cut to suit the angle of the roof—55 degrees—and will butt up against the ridgepole. Measure this angle carefully. I find that the easiest way to do this is to lay the rafter on the wall when the wall is lying on the ground and mark the location of the center pole and the side wall. The other end of each rafter is cut to fit the side wall by making a 35-degree cut exactly 2 inches

deep and then making a cut at 90 degrees to the 35-degree cut. Because the ridgepole won't be placed until you get all pieces to the greenhouse site, on the nonopening end wall you might want to tack a piece of scrap wood over the ends of the rafters to hold them and the support posts in place until you erect them. On the door-end wall, you won't need this scrap brace because the door header supports the two rafters.

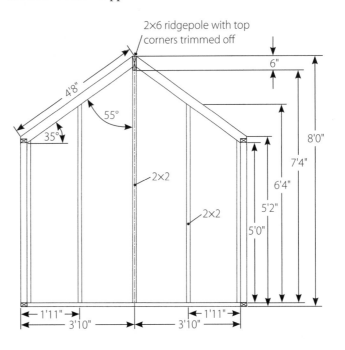

End-wall layout

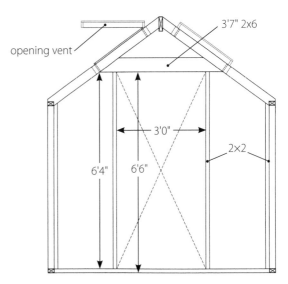

End-wall layout with door

STEP 3: Assemble the Walls

Bring all four walls to the site and stand them up on the slab. You may need an extra pair of hands to help with this or bracing for the walls as you erect them. When you've set up the walls and made sure they are perfectly vertical and that the diagonals are equal (the walls are square), drill and bolt them together, first bolting the base plates to the sill plate. Recess the bolt heads so that they will not rub against the polycarbonate when it is installed.

STEP 4: Add the Ridgepole

After the walls are assembled, the ridgepole can be slotted into place. Before installing it, saw off the top corners. This will allow the polycarbonate to lie flat at the ridge when the glazing is installed over the pole.

STEP 5: Install the Rafters and Add the Roof-Vent Framing

The rafters are installed as shown in the following illustration. Each 4-foot 8-inch piece is both glued and screwed into place. With the rafters in place, the greenhouse should now be quite rigid.

Next, build the frame around each window opening on the roof. To do this, secure two 1-foot 10-inch 2×2s to frame each window. The lap joints in the rafters that will accept these 2×2 crosspieces should be cut prior to installing the rafters. The crosspieces can then simply be dropped into place. Next, glue and tack into place the ½-inch by 3-inch pieces that have been cut to fit around the openings. Make sure the corners have plenty of glue to prevent leaks.

STEP 6: Make Vents and Doors

This greenhouse has four lower vents, four opening vents in the roof, and a single door. All are covered with polycarbonate, as are the walls. Construct the frame of each of the vertical vents in the side walls with 2×2s lap-jointed at each corner.

The roof vents are made with 1×2s glued together at the corners. The entire top surface of each vent is then covered with polycarbonate. Once built, each vent is attached to the roof framing. By making the roof vents light, you will be able to open them with solar-powered window openers. Set the 3-inch hinges into the frame 4 inches from the outer edge of the top of each vent and install the barrel bolt on the side opposite the hinges.

The door for this greenhouse has a simple design. Each joint is a lap joint glued and screwed together. When all the pieces are assembled, mount the door using three hinges and add a handle and a barrel bolt to keep it closed.

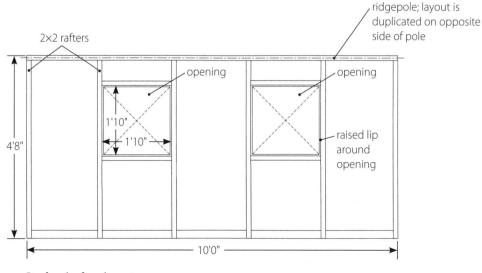

Roof and rafters layout

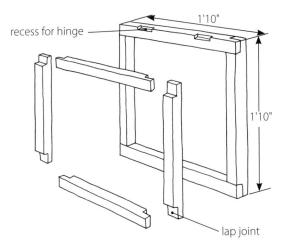

recess for hinge

1'10"

1'10"

lap joint

Window-vent layout on side walls

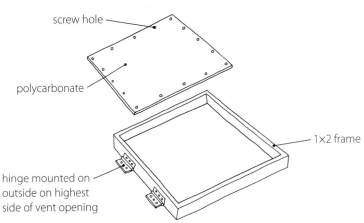

screw hole

polycarbonate

hinge mounted on
outside on highest
side of vent opening

1×2 frame

Roof-vent layout

STEP 7: Install the Glazing

When the framing is finished, the greenhouse is
ready for glazing. Install all glazing on caulking
to minimize any leaks. Simply screw the 6 mm
polycarbonate to the outside of the framing and
cover the joint between panels with a cap piece.
If you want to make the entire greenhouse more
attractive, install cap pieces over the glazing at
every support post.

First glaze the vertical walls. For each side
you'll need two 4-foot by 5-foot 4-inch pieces
and one 2-foot by 5-foot 4-inch piece. Cut out
openings for the vents in the two larger pieces
before you install the panels on the greenhouse.
Each joint should be covered with a ¼-inch by
2-inch by 5-foot 4-inch cap piece except around
the window. For the end walls you'll need two
4-foot by 8-foot pieces of polycarbonate. (To
save on waste, you can make the rafter cut and
then turn the polycarbonate so that the triangular shape becomes the rafter cut on the other
side.)

The tops of all the side walls will be covered
with the roof glazing, which is carried outward
at the ends slightly to cover the side wall glazing.
Note that with polycarbonate, the screws holding the cap strips in place can be drilled right
through the glazing. Once you've set the cap
piece in place and determined where the screw

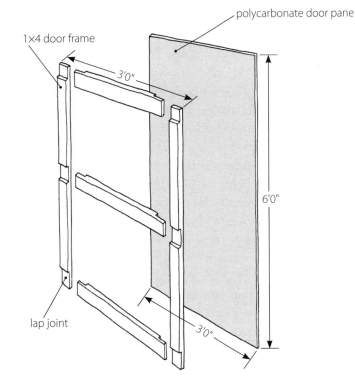

1×4 door frame

polycarbonate door pane

3'0"

6'0"

lap joint

3'0"

Greenhouse door layout

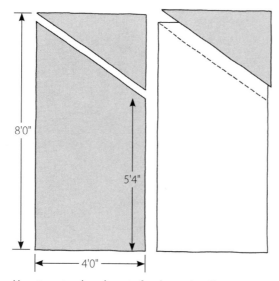

How to cut polycarbonate for the end wall

will be located, remove the strip and drill the hole in the glazing ⅛ inch larger than the hole in the strip to allow for expansion, then screw down the cap strip.

After you've covered the sides and end walls, you can install the glazing on the roof. Again, this is simply a matter of cutting the polycarbonate to size and screwing it in place. As with the sides, each joint should be covered with a cap strip. Cover the entire ridge on both sides with a piece of 1×4 trim cut to suit the angle of the roof and caulk along the middle.

VARIATIONS AND UPGRADES

You can vary or upgrade this greenhouse quite easily. Simply switching to glass glazing makes it fancier and more substantial. If you decide to use glass, you should recess each pane into the greenhouse frame and use a trim piece to hold it in place. If you use glass, the largest piece should be 1 foot 11 inches by 5 feet 1 inch. The end wall will require some modification to ensure that the size of the panes to glaze it is reasonable. I would install a crosspiece to cut down on large pieces of glass. The illustrations at right and on page 191 show how the 2×2 support posts should be cut to recess glass into the frame. Because the roof glazing will also need to be recessed into the greenhouse frame, you'll have to modify the structure somewhat. See the illustration at right on page 191 for details on modifying roof vents. This style is much stronger than the style used for polycarbonate, which tends to rack and twist in the wind.

Other variations and upgrades are shifting to thicker polycarbonate, which adds greater insulation value; and installing stronger window and door frames or even a sliding door instead of a traditional swing door. You can also adjust the size of the greenhouse, increasing the length in 2- or 4-foot increments or making it wider and taller.

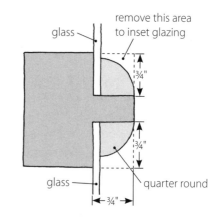

Installing glass glazing

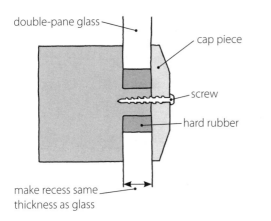

Installing double-pane glass
recessed in window

double-pane glass

cap piece

screw

hard rubber

make recess same
thickness as glass

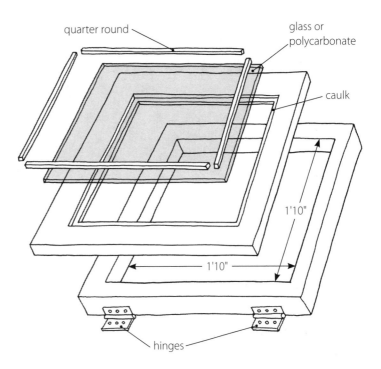

quarter round

glass or
polycarbonate

caulk

1'10"

1'10"

hinges

Constructing the roof vent for glass glazing

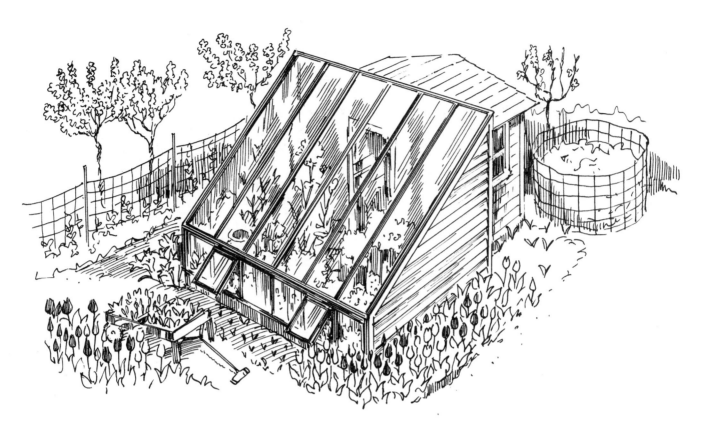

2. Slant-Front, Insulated Greenhouse

with Attached Potting Shed

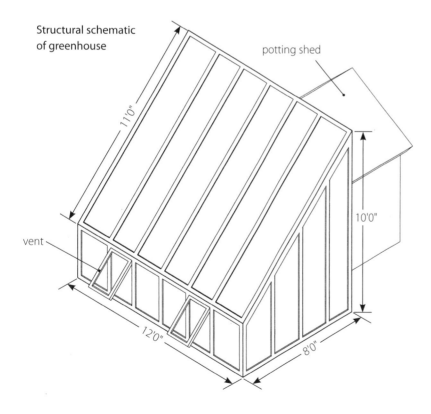

Structural schematic
of greenhouse

potting shed

11'0"

vent

10'0"

12'0"

8'0"

This greenhouse is a 12-foot by 8-foot free-standing building with a door in one end, a vertical rear wall with attached shed, and a sloped front. The vertical rear wall and both ends are insulated, and can be finished to match your home. In this project they are sheathed in CDX plywood (see chapter 6, page 81) and are then sided with wood clapboards. The greenhouse has a low knee wall on all sides (glazed in the front) with opening windows or vents set into the front glazing. The rear windows and vents are set high in the back wall. It is designed for polycarbonate sheet glazing that runs from top to bottom on the slant roof.

The structure is built on a foundation set below the frost line, although it could just as easily be sited on a walled foundation or a simple lumber or pea stone base. It calls for a water supply, raised beds, and lighting in both the attached potting shed and the main greenhouse; thus, you'll need to bring in a water line and an electrical line before pouring the foundation.

CONSTRUCTING THE FOUNDATION

Materials

- 2×4s and ⅜" or ½" plywood for forms totaling for the outer wall 40' in length by 4' in height and for the inner wall 36' in length by 4' in height
- 20 cubic feet (¾ cubic yard) of concrete for the footing (if trench is 1' wide)
- 3 cubic yards of concrete for the foundation
- Scaffold nails
- Bolts, nuts, and washers for assembling formwork
- One 1' length of 1" hose for a water-line conduit
- One 1' length of metal electrical conduit
  Note: This conduit typically comes in 10' lengths. Use the entire length if you have space in your electrical trench.
- One 10' length of 2" PVC drainpipe
- Twenty 2' by 8' panels of 2" rigid foam insulation
- 2 gallons of exterior cementlike covering such as Structural Skin from Conproco
- 1½ cubic yards of pea stone
- Twelve ⅜" or ½" diameter bolts, each 6" long or 8" long
- 2" rigid foam insulation panels, 8' by 4' each

The foundation is set below the frost line and has a low wall 12 inches above grade and 4 inches thick. This wall should be insulated with 2 inches of polystyrene before the foundation is backfilled. To avoid the pink of the insulation showing above grade and to protect it from damage from animals and machines such as string trimmers, coat the installed polystyrene with a cementlike material such as Structural Skin from Conproco.

STEP 1: Lay Out the Foundation

The first step is to lay out the foundation, using string and batter boards, as shown in the illustrations on page 117 and as discussed in chapter 8 and project 1 (page 184).

STEP 2: Excavate the Foundation

This foundation is excavated deeper than for a simple slab and has around its perimeter a trench about 3½ feet deep and at least 1 foot wide. The middle of the greenhouse foundation should be excavated to only 1 foot or so below grade.

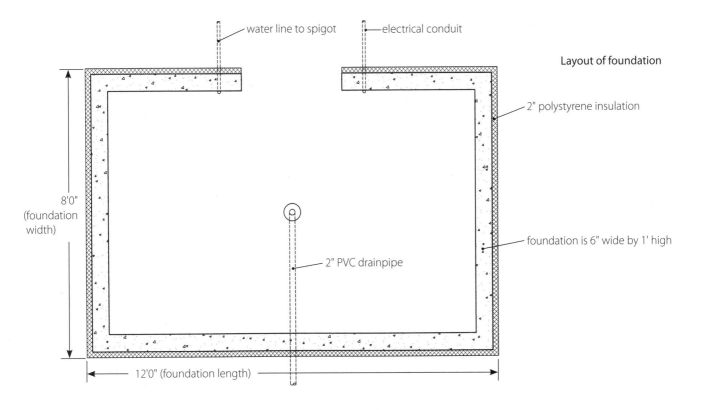

water line to spigot — electrical conduit

Layout of foundation

2" polystyrene insulation

foundation is 6" wide by 1' high

8'0" (foundation width)

2" PVC drainpipe

12'0" (foundation length)

STEP 3: Pour the Foundation Footings

First pour the footings at the bottom of the perimeter trench. These should be twice as wide as the walls will be. Carefully level the surface of the footings after they've been poured.

STEP 4: Build Foundation Forms

When the footings are completely dry (about a week after the concrete has been poured), you can set up the forms for the foundation itself. During this process, check the diagonals several times to make sure that the footings and the foundation of the greenhouse are exactly square. Any errors at this stage will be difficult to correct later and will affect the installation of glazing.

In building and erecting the forms, note that there will be a 37½-inch-wide gap for a door in the knee wall. To allow for this, cut two 2×8s to the height of the knee wall and set them between the forms at the doorway. Use scaffold nails to hold them in place, and during the pour, remember not to pour any concrete in this area.

You will also need to set a 2-inch PVC pipe into the foundation wall for the water drain in the greenhouse. The illustration on page 193 shows the location of the drain and drainpipe in the foundation so that you can place the PVC pipe before the pour. Also note that on either side of the space for the door, there is a conduit for the electrical cable and for a 1-inch water pipe for a spigot. Both will come from the main house. Because you don't yet know how long the pipe work will be inside or outside the greenhouse, for now simply install this conduit and add necessary extensions later.

STEP 5: Pour the Concrete for the Foundation

The entire foundation pour (taking into account that no concrete is needed for the door area) will require about 2 cubic yards of concrete. See chapter 8, page 123, for information on pouring concrete and working it after the pour to ensure

that it's level and free of air bubbles. After it has been worked to completion, allow the foundation to dry for about an hour and then push 6- or 8-inch-long ⅜-inch or ½-inch bolts into the concrete 3 inches from each side until only 2 inches of each bolt protrudes from the surface. (Use a minimum of three bolts per side.) After the sill plate is installed, this will give you ½ inch of bolt showing for each ½-inch washer and nut.

A week or two after the pour, you can remove the formwork.

STEP 6: Add Insulation

Next, add 2-inch rigid foam insulation to the foundation wall. This type of insulation is available in 8-foot by 4-foot panels that have tongue-and-groove edges for a tight fit. Set each piece against the foundation wall and glue it in place with caulking. (Be sure you use a caulking that does not react with polystyrene.)

Once the insulation is in place, coat it to about a foot below grade level with a cementlike finishing material. Finally, backfill the foundation trench to grade level.

STEP 7: Prepare the Slab Area

Inside the greenhouse, tamp down the soil to 10 inches to 12 inches below grade and pour about 1½ cubic yards of pea stone or gravel into the area. This will form the base for the concrete slab and enable it to drain easily. At this point the water, electrical, and drainpipes should stand about 6 inches above the final grade level. Remember to angle the drainpipe so that the slab can be sloped toward the drain, which will allow water to drain more easily from the greenhouse floor (see project 1, page 185). Set a flush-mounted drain on the top of the drainpipe (see chapter 8, page 124, and project 1, page 185) and cover it with duct tape to prevent concrete from blocking the drain during the pour. If you've sloped the drainpipe, the drain will be ¾ inch to 1 inch below the final grade level.

STEP 8: Pour the Slab

The final step for the foundation is to pour about 1½ cubic yards of concrete for the greenhouse floor. As described in chapter 8 (page 124), screed, level, and trowel the concrete. Make sure that it's even with the door sill and that the central drain is flush with the surface of the concrete, which is sloped slightly toward it.

BUILDING THE GREENHOUSE

Materials

FOR THE SILL PLATE

- Two 12' 2×8s and two 8' 2×8s
  Note: A sill plate of pressure-treated lumber helps to keep insects away from the other wood in the greenhouse frame.
- Sill insulation (a thin layer of insulation that's installed under the sill plate)
- 12 washers and 12 nuts (minimum) for the bolts in the sill plate

FOR THE REAR WALL

- Eighteen 10' 2×4 vertical supports
- One 10' 2×4 base plate
- Two 10' 2×4 top plates
- Three 8' by 4' sheets of ⅜" or ½" CDX plywood
- 8d and 16d galvanized nails

FOR THE END WALLS

- Fourteen 2×4 vertical supports cut from 3'6" to 10', as needed
- Two sheets of ⅜" or ½" CDX plywood

FOR THE FRONT WALL

- Eleven 3' 2×4 vertical supports
- One 12' 2×4 base plate
- Two 12' 2×4 top plates

FOR THE GLAZING

- Approximately 180 square feet of 8 mm twin-wall polycarbonate (three 11' by 4' panels plus three 3' by 4' pieces)
- Trim to hold the glazing in place

OTHER MATERIALS

- Caulking, screws or nails, hinges, locks

With the foundation in place, you are ready to begin building the structure.

STEP 1: Install the Sill Plate

A 4-inch-wide foundation wall and 2 inches of insulation add up to a wall that's 6 inches thick. To make the sill plate, use a 2×8 with the outer 1½ inches of the plank routed at the bottom of its outer edge to form a drip edge.

Ideally, the sill plate is made from two 12-foot 2×8s with lap joints at the corners, but you can use shorter pieces if you join them with lap joints. Place the sill plate on top of the bolts and tap it with a mallet to mark the location of bolts you've set in the foundation. Before installing the sill plate, lay down a length of fiberglass sill insulation cut to 4 inches wide and install the sill plate on top of it after you've drilled holes for the bolts. Fasten the sill firmly using washers and nuts.

STEP 2: Build the Rear Wall

Refer to the illustration on page 196 for the rear-wall layout. To construct the wall, place the top and base plates on a flat surface and mark the location of the vertical posts 16 inches on center. The door will be 30 inches wide, which means that the rough opening will be 37½ inches. Once the vertical supports are in place, use three 16d galvanized nails to fasten each support to the top and base plates. The wall has a second cap plate at the top and a second 2×4 mounted vertically to allow the rafters to be set up properly. (See top left of the illustration on page 196.)

The illustration also shows where to install cross bracing to help prevent the vertical supports from bending. Frame out the vent openings as shown and nail the door header and framing in place to finish the wall. Before erecting it, you can sheath the wall with either ⅜-inch or ½-inch CDX water-resistant plywood to

Rear-wall layout

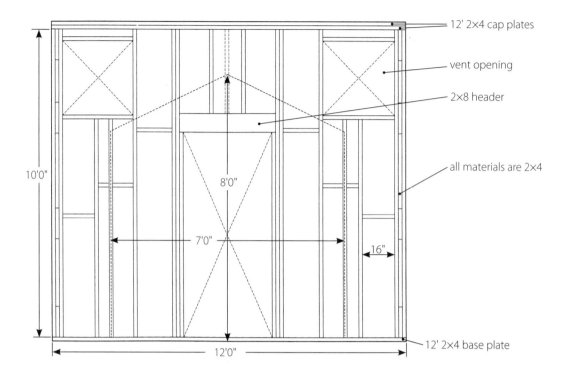

12' 2×4 cap plates

vent opening

2×8 header

all materials are 2×4

12' 2×4 base plate

10'0"

8'0"

7'0"

16"

12'0"

help stiffen the structure. Installing the plywood will make the wall fairly heavy, however, so if you don' have a crane or several strong friends, you can erect the framework and then install the sheathing. You'll address the window openings later.

STEP 3: Build the End Walls

The end walls of this greenhouse will also be insulated and with the rear wall will form a snug box for your plants.

First cut two 8-foot base plates to 7 feet 4 inches each. These will fit inside the 10-foot front and back walls. On the base plates mark out the placement of the vertical studs 16 inches on center. Next, set one 10-foot 2×4 vertical at the end that will be at the back of the greenhouse and one 3-foot 2×4 vertical at the low front end of the sloped side, abutting the front knee wall. The end walls have double cap or top plates to tie the structure together and to set the top of the wall exactly level with the rafters.

Nail one of the top plates in place and then cut, place, and fasten in place each vertical stud. Finally, add the second cap plate cut at an angle on both ends to form a smooth top to the wall

from front to back. See the illustrations on page 197 for the layout of both end walls and the detail of the top of the ridge plate with two horizontal 2×4 cap plates and a vertical 2×4 cut to suit the angle of the roof. This 2×4 sits on top of the horizontal cap plates and fills the gap between the glazing and the vertical sheathing.

STEP 4: Build the Front Wall

The front knee wall (only 3 feet tall) is fully glazed. Because the polycarbonate comes in 4-foot sheets, the front wall must have supports at 2-foot intervals. It will incorporate two windows. See the illustration on page 197 (bottom right) for the layout of the front wall and rafters.

The only difference in this wall's construction is that the vertical supports are placed 2 feet on center rather than the 16 inches on center used on the nonglazed walls. The glazing will be screwed on the outside of the frame and overlap the end walls slightly. At this stage, before erecting the frame, all the walls should be painted with an oil-based paint and top-coated to help prevent the wood from rotting. Remember that white paint has higher reflectivity, making the interior of the greenhouse much lighter. In

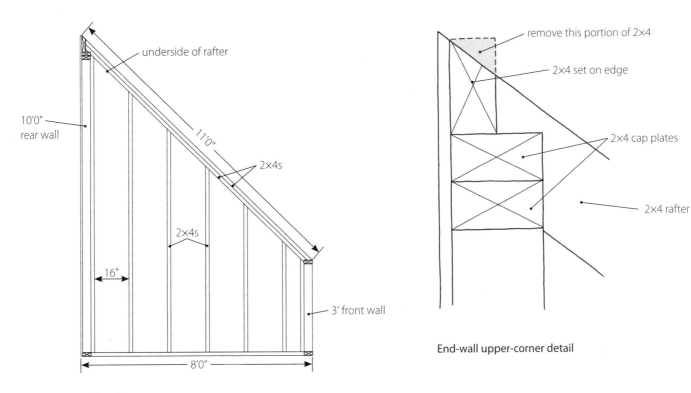

underside of rafter

10'0" rear wall

11'0"

2×4s

2×4s

16"

3' front wall

8'0"

End-wall layout

remove this portion of 2×4

2×4 set on edge

2×4 cap plates

2×4 rafter

End-wall upper-corner detail

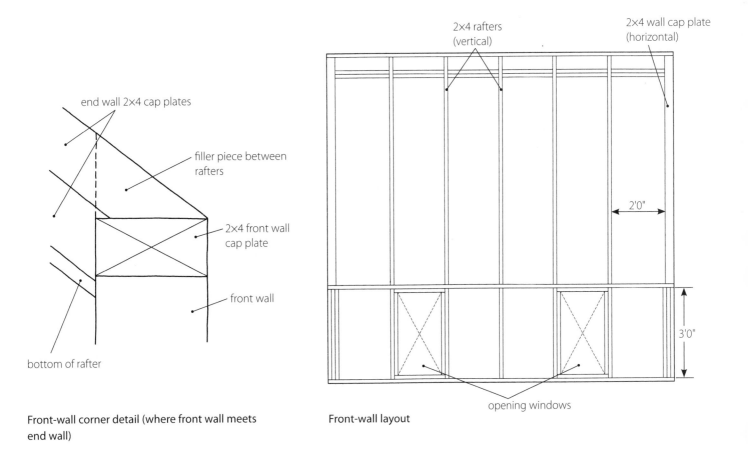

end wall 2×4 cap plates

filler piece between rafters

2×4 front wall cap plate

front wall

bottom of rafter

Front-wall corner detail (where front wall meets end wall)

2×4 rafters (vertical)

2×4 wall cap plate (horizontal)

2'0"

3'0"

opening windows

Front-wall layout

addition, you can sheath the nonglazed walls at this time.

STEP 5: Assemble the Walls

With the sill plate bolted in place, the walls can be nailed or screwed to the sill plate. You will probably need another pair of hands to erect the walls, or you can brace each as you erect it before erecting the next. Make sure that all the walls are perfectly vertical and the diagonals are equal (the walls are square) before you start sheathing (if you haven't sheathed the nonglazed walls before now).

STEP 6: Install the Rafters

The rafters are added after the building is sheathed. Cut each rafter and nail or screw it in place. Be sure to paint all surfaces of the rafters before installation.

STEP 7: Install Glazing

Installing glazing often requires two people, one inside the greenhouse and one outside. First, lay a bead of caulking on the first and third rafters and across the top and bottom of the rafters. With one person in the greenhouse and another outside, each polycarbonate sheet should be carefully lifted over the opening and lowered into place. Set it down carefully to ensure that it's precisely positioned and the caulking forms a tight seal all around the polycarbonate. Set all three sheets in place and then screw trim or capping in place over the seams between the sheets. Remember to space screws about 12 inches apart and drill oversized holes in the caulking to allow for expansion. (See the illustration below and chapter 7 for more information on installing glazing.)

At the side walls and at the ridge, cover the edge of the caulking with 1×6 trim pieces cut to fit over the polycarbonate (see illustration below left). Remember to caulk any joints between the trim pieces and between the polycarbonate and trim to eliminate the chance of leakage.

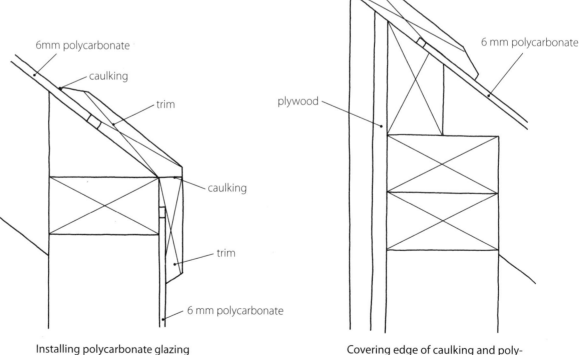

Installing polycarbonate glazing at side walls and ridge

Covering edge of caulking and polycarbonate with trim on top corner

STEP 8: Add Insulation

If you plan on heating this greenhouse, you can use thicker polycarbonate for the glazing and install insulation on the inside walls. Because a greenhouse is warm and moist, it is an ideal breeding ground for molds and fungi, so I don't recommend that you use fiberglass batting for insulation. Instead use polystyrene or expanded foam insulation to keep the north wall warm. You can either fit it between the frame structure or cover the entire rear-wall framing with 4½ sheets of foil-faced foam board. You will need another 4 sheets for the end walls. Tape the seams with either duct tape or foil-faced tape that's made especially to cover seams for this kind of insulation.

STEP 9: Finish the Greenhouse Exterior

Probably because I live on the New England coast, I do like a shingled exterior. First cover the sheathing with a house wrap such as Tyvek and install shingles according to the instructions provided in chapter 9. You can paint the corner trim white and stain the shingles if you like.

BUILDING THE POTTING SHED

A substantial upgrade to this greenhouse is the addition of a potting shed/air lock at the back of the structure, with a door in one side and a lean-to-style roof. The drawback to this location, however, is that a wheelbarrow must be turned 90 degrees to maneuver it from the entry door into the greenhouse itself. For this reason, I've installed the door to the potting shed/air lock in the wall directly facing the greenhouse door. With both doors open, it's easy to run a wheelbarrow in and out.

The addition of the potting shed requires that you pour a concrete slab for its base when you pour the greenhouse slab. As for the structure itself, you'll have to install base plate bolts in the concrete while it's still wet. If the shed is to have running water and electric lighting, you must run conduit for these before the concrete slab is poured, just as for the greenhouse slab.

The details of the potting shed are shown in the illustrations on pages 200–202. With no window, it will remain warm, assuming that the greenhouse door will be left open while you work in the shed. You can, however, put a window behind each workbench on the side walls of the shed, as shown. The shed/air lock has two fluorescent lights over the work area, and if you plan on starting seeds there, you can install an outlet on the shed wall that's shared with the rear wall of the greenhouse.

Materials

- Twenty-two 8' 2×4s for vertical supports
- Eight 6' 2×4 base and top plates
- Twelve 6' 2×6 rafters
- One 7' 2×6 ridgepole
- Miscellaneous 2×4 and 2×6 blocking
- Two 3" 2×6 header plates
- 5 sheets ⅜" or ½" CDX plywood for sheathing

STEP 1: Build the Side Walls

Lay all four 6-foot base plates on a flat surface and mark out the placement of vertical supports for the walls. Each side will have six studs spaced 16 inches on center. Because the front wall will be made with extra blocking at the corners, the side-wall base plates should be cut to 5 feet 8½ inches long. Each stud is cut to 5 feet 3 inches, making the side walls 5 feet 6 inches high. Nail each stud to the base plate with three 16d galvanized nails.

STEP 2: Build the Wall with Door

First lay out the top and base plates on a flat surface. Mark off the stud locations 16 inches on center. Next, nail the studs to the top and base plates using three 16p nails in each support. At the corners, you'll have to add blocking and additional supports to which the interior sheathing can be attached.

The 3-foot-wide door requires two 6-foot 8-inch jacks to which the header is attached. The space between the header and the top plate can be filled with short 2×4s.

STEP 3: Assemble the Walls

Once the greenhouse is assembled and the rear wall sheathed, you can add the potting shed walls. Stand the side walls on the base and temporarily nail them to the back wall of the greenhouse while you check that they are vertical and square to the greenhouse, then nail or screw them in place.

Next, erect the door wall of the shed and screw or nail it in place. Check again that all walls are vertical and square.

Finally, sheathe the potting shed with ⅜-inch CDX plywood to match the back of the greenhouse.

STEP 4: Add Plumbing and Wiring (Optional)

Refer to chapter 10 for information on wiring and plumbing. If the shed is to be plumbed, you'll have to install water lines and a drain prior to pouring the slab.

STEP 5: Install the Rafters

Locate the ridgepole between the back of the greenhouse and the opposite entry door wall of the shed.

The rafters are 2×6s cut to length and placed 16 inches on center. One end of each rafter is cut to fit flush against the ridgepole and the outer end of each has a bird's-mouth cut. Nail or screw them in place. When the rafters are in place, add the rafter plate on the outside end of each rafter and the trim pieces (fascia boards), which cover the rafter plate and the ends of the eaves. If you add trim at this stage, remember to leave ½ inch above the rafter ends to cover the end of

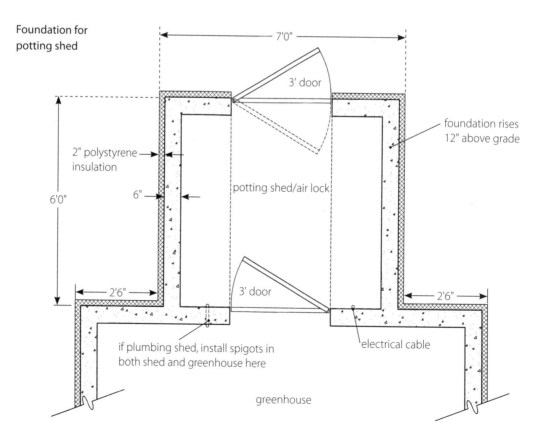

Foundation for potting shed

7'0"

3' door

foundation rises 12" above grade

2" polystyrene insulation

6'0"

6"

potting shed/air lock

2'6"

3' door

2'6"

if plumbing shed, install spigots in both shed and greenhouse here

electrical cable

greenhouse

the plywood sheathing. Cut plywood to suit the eave overhang around the potting shed and nail it in place from underneath. Prime the trim and eave surfaces so they can be painted later.

STEP 6: Add Roofing

Now the roof can be sheathed with ⅜-inch or ½-inch CDX plywood cut to suit its shape. The ends of the plywood will be covered by the trim pieces that are screwed or nailed to the rafter plates. After the plywood is in place, tack roofing felt to the roof and tack flashing to the join between the potting shed roof and the greenhouse wall. Cover the flashing with roofing felt. (The vertical portion of the greenhouse wall will be covered with shingles or shakes, which will also cover the flashing.)

At the bottom of the roof, nail into place aluminum drip edge (this will protect the fascia board from dripping), then begin applying roofing shingles: Set the first row upside down along with the bottom edge of the roof, about ¼ inch beyond the drip edge. Lay the second row of shingles right-side up with the slots falling in the middle of solid strips of the bottom upside-down row (the slots fall exactly halfway between the slots on the bottom row). Work up the roof until you come to the ridge. Cut shingles into thirds, bend them over the ridge, and nail them across the ridge, starting from the outside of the shed and ending at the greenhouse wall and flashing. If you really want to be sure that no water will enter the joint between the greenhouse wall and the potting shed roof, you can tack a second piece of flashing so that about an inch of the metal covers the shingle ends where they butt against the wall.

STEP 7: Sheathe the Structure

Sheathe the body of the shed with ⅜-inch or ½-inch plywood, then wrap it with Tyvek or a similar house wrap and nail in place the 1×4 corner trim. You can paint this trim with a white base coat or primer.

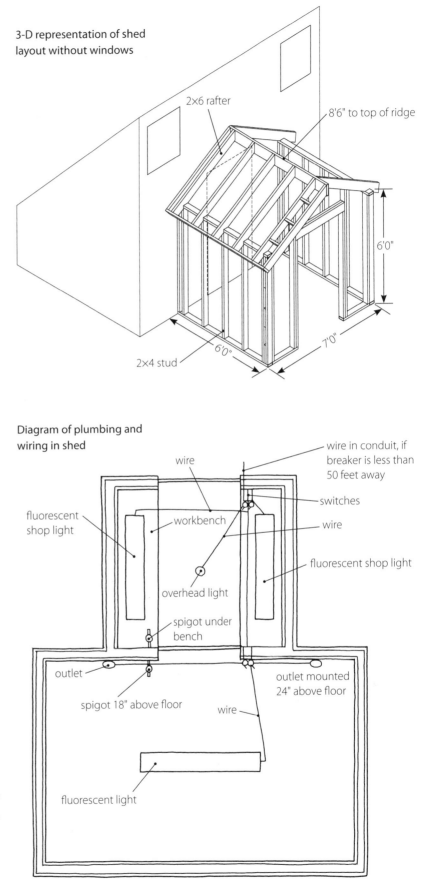

3-D representation of shed layout without windows

2×6 rafter

8'6" to top of ridge

6'0"

7'0"

6'0"

2×4 stud

Diagram of plumbing and wiring in shed

wire

wire in conduit, if breaker is less than 50 feet away

switches

fluorescent shop light

workbench

wire

overhead light

fluorescent shop light

spigot under bench

outlet

outlet mounted 24" above floor

spigot 18" above floor

wire

fluorescent light

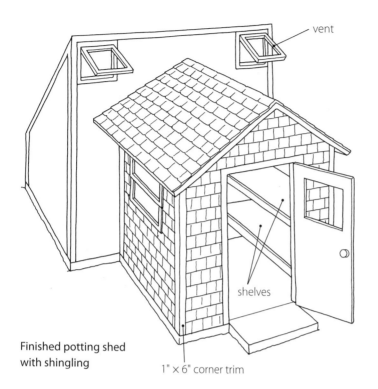

vent

shelves

Finished potting shed
with shingling

1" × 6" corner trim

STEP 8: Finish the Exterior

Once the corner trim is in place, the structure
should be shingled or sided to match the greenhouse. Cover the trim with a final coat of paint
and the job is done.

OTHER VARIATIONS AND UPGRADES

You can upgrade this greenhouse by using
34-inch patio glass for glazing instead of
polycarbonate. You can also heat the greenhouse
and use double-pane windows to increase the
insulation value of the glazing. To increase light,
glaze the end walls with polycarbonate.

This style of greenhouse could also be built
directly against a house wall, making it one of
the few types that can be either freestanding or
attached. If you build it against a home, you'll
need to put vents in the roof glazing near the
highest part of the greenhouse to enable hot air
to escape.

The length of the greenhouse can easily be
expanded in 4-foot increments and the width
can be expanded up to 14 feet. Although the
upgrade here calls for putting the potting shed
at the back of the structure, there's no reason
why you couldn't put it at one end.

3. Slope-Sided Greenhouse

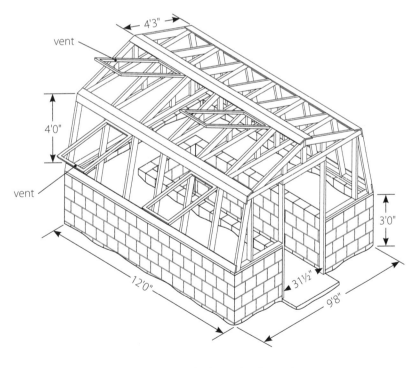

Structural schematic of greenhouse

This slope-sided structure offers a large concrete-block base area but slightly less space at bench level than does a vertical-sided greenhouse. It also requires slightly more structural support because the roof loads are not vertically over the walls. To add this extra measure of support, the roof load is supported by roof trusses, which are attached to the walls and tied together with 1×4 or 1×6 longitudinals. In all, this is probably a less expensive form of construction than that of the vertical-sided greenhouse, and when it's combined with fiberglass or polycarbonate glazing, costs are reduced even further.

If you decide to use glass for glazing, you should set the material into the supports and rafters, but fiberglass, like polycarbonate, can be screwed to the outside of the support structure.

CONSTRUCTING THE FOOTING, FOUNDATION, AND FOUNDATION WALLS

Materials

FOR THE FOUNDATION FOOTINGS FOR CONCRETE BLOCK WALLS (40' AT 18" WIDE BY 12" DEEP)

- 2.5 cubic yards of concrete

FOR THE FOUNDATION WALLS/RAISED BEDS

- 425 concrete blocks for a foundation set 12" below grade (for each row of block deeper than this, add 77 blocks; for example, if footings will extend deeper than the 3' frost line, you'll need three more rows or 231 additional blocks)
- Mortar
- Fourteen ½" bolts, each 6" long

The walls and foundation are 36 inches above the concrete slab and are filled with good-quality loam, compost, sand, and manure.

STEP 1: Lay Out the Foundation

Use batter boards and string as explained in chapter 8 (page 117) and project 1 (page 184) and ensure that each wall is square.

STEP 2: Excavate the Foundation

Dig a perimeter trench for the footings. If you live in an area that doesn't freeze, this can be 12 inches to 18 inches below grade. If the ground in your area freezes in winter, the trench should be 3½ feet deep and at least 18 inches wide.

STEP 3: Pour the Foundation Footings

Pour the footings at the bottom of the perimeter trench. These should be twice as wide as the walls will be. Carefully level the surface of the footings after they have been poured.

STEP 4: Build the Foundation Walls/ Raised Beds

The plans call for building foundation walls/ raised beds on either side of the central walkway using concrete blocks and making the greenhouse full height. This design will cut down on the glazing required and will make the wooden frame of the greenhouse slightly lower than if the greenhouse was built on a conventional slab.

The greenhouse is 12 feet long and 9 feet 8 inches wide, allowing room for two 3-foot 4-inch-wide beds and a walkway that's 3 feet wide. By making the doorway exactly 3 feet wide as well, you can build the walls without having to cut any blocks. This does require you to build the door as opposed to using a stock item. (See Building the Greenhouse, page 205, and specifically Install the Door, page 207.)

The raised beds are constructed using concrete blocks, as shown in the illustration at left. You can make the walls of this greenhouse from brick for a more attractive look, or stucco the blocks or use parging (see chapter 8) after the wall is built.

Build the walls with mortar as described in chapter 8 (page 126), making sure to point both sides carefully. When the walls are built, fill the center holes of the concrete blocks with mortar about 14 inches from the top of the wall. After it has set for a half hour, place bolts in the wet mortar (one bolt approximately every 3 feet) to hold the sill plate in place. Be sure to leave 1½ inches of bolt protruding from the concrete.

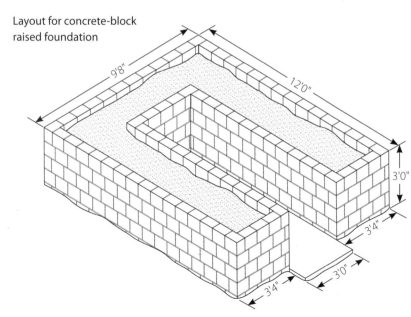

Layout for concrete-block raised foundation

9'8" 12'0" 3'0" 3'4" 3'0" 3'4"

BUILDING THE GREENHOUSE

Materials

FOR THE SILL PLATE
- 34' of 2×4s
- 10 to 12 bolts, nuts, and washers to fasten greenhouse base plates to sill plate

FOR THE END WALLS
- 34' of 2×2s for the base plate (preferably oak, cedar, or teak)
- Two 6' 6" 2×2s for the door supports
- Two 6' 6" 1×2s plus one 33" by 1" by 2" piece for the door jamb
- One 36" 2×4 for the header

- Seven 4' 2×2s for the rafter truss supports

FOR THE SIDE WALLS
- Fourteen 4' 2×2 supports
- Four 12' 1×6 top and bottom plates
- Two 12' 2×2s cut to fit between the supports and with outer edges angled to match the slope of the side wall

FOR THE RAFTERS
- Seven 8' 2×2s
- Fourteen 4' 3" 2×2s

- Seven 16" 2×3s
- Fourteen 10" 2×2s

FOR THE GLAZING
- Four 12' by 4' polycarbonate panels for the roof
- Four 12' by 4' polycarbonate panels for the side walls
- Four 6' by 4' pieces of polycarbonate for the end walls
- Four 4' by 13" triangle-shaped pieces for the corners of the end walls

FOR THE DOOR
- Two 6' 8" 1×4s
- Three 3' 1×4s
- One 6' 6" by 3" piece of polycarbonate for the door

ADDITIONAL MATERIALS
- Caulking, epoxy, stainless screws, cap pieces for glazing joints, hinges, window clasps

With a door at one end, almost 75 percent of the space in this greenhouse can be used for growing.

STEP 1: Install the Sill Plate

Lay the base plate on top of the bolts in the concrete blocks and gently tap the wood with a mallet to mark the bolt holes. Install fiberglass sill insulation on top of the concrete blocks. Drill the holes in the sill plate, lap all corner joints, set the plate in place, and secure it to the bolts in the blocks with nuts and washers.

STEP 2: Build the End Walls

Refer to the illustration at right for end-wall construction details. For this greenhouse, it may be easier to build the end walls on the job because the roof truss must be installed to hold the wall together. Installing the roof truss requires that the door supports in the end wall with the door be installed accurately. Be sure to measure twice!

First, accurately position the door supports and set them on the ground or shop floor (if you're building the walls off-site). Measure the sill plates bolted to the concrete blocks to

determine the exact location of the base plates on either side of the door and glue and screw them in place onto the sill plate. (If you are building the walls off-site, you can screw the pieces together on the sill plate and glue them only when you've ensured that it all fits together properly on-site.)

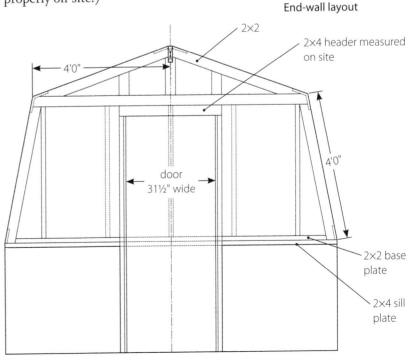

End-wall layout

Next, frame the door in the end wall that has one: The door frame uses 2×2 header supports and a 2×4 header. *Note:* Because the mortar thickness between the blocks may vary slightly, you should measure the thickness of the header at the job site and cut it to suit. Inside the door frame there is a ¾-inch by 2-inch jamb, so the entire door width will be 31½ inches (an odd size; plan on building your own door).

Build a roof truss and attach it to the top of the truss supports and door supports (or the three truss supports on the nondoor wall). If everything fits perfectly, apply caulking to the mortared wall on each side of the door frame and on top of the sill plate before gluing and screwing together the end wall.

STEP 3: Build the Side Walls

Build the side walls with supports spaced 24 inches on center. The top and base plates are 1×4s or 1×6s, as shown below. Join these plates to the supports with lap joints on either end of the supports. Before erecting the wall, cut the base plate to match the slope of the greenhouse walls and set it in between the wall supports before gluing and screwing it to the sill plate.

STEP 4: Install the Rafters

Unlike the greenhouses in the first projects in this chapter, this structure uses rafters (trusses) to actually support the roof. These can be made in the shop and brought to the job site. Each truss

fits over the corresponding side-wall support. You'll need to tack the rafters in place before adding the recessed 1×6s at the top of the side walls and at the center of the roof. By recessing these pieces into the rafters, the entire exterior of the greenhouse is even and ready for glazing.

STEP 5: Install the Glazing

Install the glazing on the 2-inch side-wall supports according to instructions in projects 1 and 2 and chapter 7, holding the panels in place and covering their seams with long ½-inch by 2-inch battens. Remember to drill oversize holes for the glazing and to caulk each joint as described in chapter 7. The center ridge of the roof and roof corners should also be covered with battens — ½ inch by 4 inches or ½ inch by 6 inches — which should be caulked and screwed in place to cover any seams in the glazing.

STEP 6: Build the Vents

All the vents on this greenhouse are made of 2×2 lumber. Each vent is framed with lap joints at each corner and is joined with epoxy. When the roof and side walls are in place, carefully measure for the vents. In theory, all vents should be the same size, but in practice the trusses may be off by about ¼ inch, causing vent sizes to vary a bit.

To prevent water from coming into the greenhouse, you can build the roof vents so that they have a slight overlap on the trusses. If you decide to do this, you'll need to cut a ½-inch

Side-wall layout

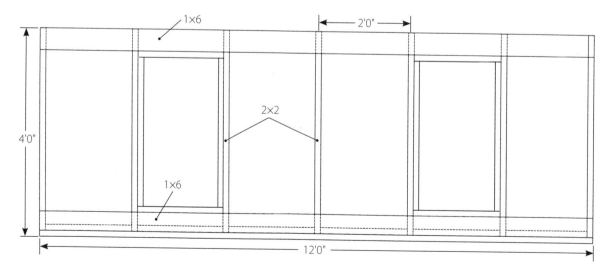

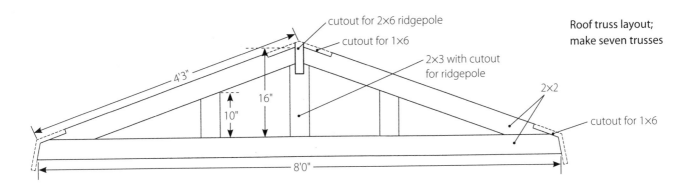

cutout for 2×6 ridgepole

cutout for 1×6

2×3 with cutout for ridgepole

2×2

cutout for 1×6

4'3"

16"

10"

8'0"

Roof truss layout; make seven trusses

rabbet in the trusses on each side of the vent and make the vent ½ inch wider all around. Insert caulking or rubber sealant strips in this rabbet to prevent water from flowing into the greenhouse.

Another way to prevent water from coming through the roof vents is to overlap the glazing onto the trusses on either side of the vent. Caulking or rubber stripping can be laid under the glazing.

Glue together each vent and check that all are square before dry fitting each to make sure it fits properly. Once the vents are installed, attach hinges to the top of each and make sure they open as they should. Only when you are satisfied with the fit should you install the polycarbonate glazing.

STEP 7: Install the Door

The finished door is 6 feet 6 inches tall by 31½ inches wide. The pieces of the door are joined with simple lap joints and are then glued and screwed. The entire door is covered with one piece of polycarbonate glazing cut for the door opening.

STEP 8: Finish the Walkway Floor

You can make the greenhouse floor any material that is comfortable to walk on. I use pea stone in one greenhouse and wood chips in another, but concrete and brick pavers are options too.

STEP 9: Prepare the Growing Beds

Fill the raised beds with good-quality loam, compost, manure, or a mix to suit the plants you want to grow. I made the raised bed in my heated greenhouse a hot bed for the first winter. As the compost continued decomposing, the bed sank. In the spring, I topped it with more screened loam and sand, which allows me to dig in it bare-handed knowing that I will never encounter a rock. Be sure to avoid walking on the growing beds so that the soil remains light and fluffy rather than compacted.

VARIATIONS AND UPGRADES

The entire greenhouse can be glazed with glass or fiberglass if desired. If you want to grow in winter, you can install double- or triple-wall polycarbonate for greater insulation.

The raised beds can easily be converted to hot beds for winter growing: Simply dig out a bed and install a 24-inch-high pile of horse manure and compost mixed with straw or wood chips. Cover this with a 12-inch layer of screened loam and plant your seeds. The heat from the com-posting manure will keep plants growing all winter long. In the coldest months, cover the growing beds with spun fleece to keep the heat close to the plants.

Another upgrade is to apply insulation on the exterior of the blocks and coat the insulation with a cementlike finishing material, but if you do this, be sure to install flashing between the base and sill plates, and remember to extend it out over the insulation.

4. Gothic Arch Greenhouse

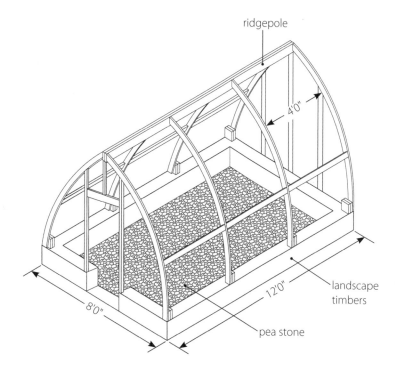

ridgepole

4'0"

8'0"

12'0"

landscape
timbers

pea stone

Structural schematic of greenhouse

There are two points about this greenhouse that should be said right up front: The framework is slightly more complex than a conventional greenhouse because the arches are curved and, because of this arch shape, the glazing must be either thin polycarbonate or fiberglass, which makes the greenhouse slightly more expensive to heat. On balance, the foundation made of pea stone and landscape timbers is easy to construct.

CONSTRUCTING THE FOUNDATION

Materials

- Five 8' 8×8 landscape timbers
- Twelve to sixteen 18" pieces of rebar (enough to space them 2' apart on the landscape timbers
- 2 cubic yards of pea stone to fill enclosed greenhouse area

This greenhouse is set on landscaping ties lap-joined together. The area inside the ties is filled with pea stone or gravel. Don't use sand or crushed stone; both materials produce a great deal of dust when the area inside the greenhouse dries out.

Because landscaping ties can be installed quickly and removed easily, this type of foundation is ideal for a greenhouse structure that may eventually have to be moved. You can also use this greenhouse to cover a crop temporar-ily, moving it to another area once the crop is established.

STEP 1: Lay Out the Foundation

Mark out where you are going to locate your greenhouse, measure the diagonals to ensure that the lines are square, and set the landscape timbers around the area.

STEP 2: Join the Timbers

Make lap joints at each end of the timbers and pin together the timbers with either 8-inch spikes or pieces of rebar spaced 2 feet apart (see chapter 8, page 132). The long rebar can be driven through holes in the timbers and into the ground so the wood will not move.

Once the timbers are in place, measure the diagonals again to confirm that the rectangle you've just laid out is square.

BUILDING THE GREENHOUSE

Materials

FOR ARCHES METHOD 1
- 6 sheets of ½" CDX plywood
- One 12' 3×2 for the ridgepole
- 2×2 blocking to fasten the arches to the ridge and to the base plate (you can also use metal angle brackets)

FOR ARCHES METHOD 2
- Twenty 1×1 pine strips at least as long as half the exterior length of one of the greenhouse arches (about 9'4"). You'll use two strips per arch — it's helpful to have a few extra in case one or two snap.
- At least eighty 6" 1×3 pine blocks (six or seven per arch)

FOR ARCHES METHOD 3
- Laminate wood strips ⅛" or ¹⁄₁₀" by 2" (ten ⅛" strips or fifteen ¹⁄₁₀" strips per arch)
- Thirty-two pieces of 1½" to 2" blocking

FOR THE END WALL WITH NO DOOR
- Polyethylene sheeting or poly-carbonate or 2 sheets of ½" CDX plywood

FOR THE RIDGEPOLE
- Two 12' 1×4 plywood strips glued together

FOR THE END WALL WITH DOOR
- Two 2×2 supports (measure from the arch to the base plate 2'3" from each side)
- Two 6'6" 1×4s (for jacks)
- One 3' 1×4 (for the header)
- One 6'6" by 3' piece of 4 mm polycarbonate

FOR THE GLAZING
- 4 mm polycarbonate sheets or fiberglass or polyethylene sheeting
- ¼" by 1" wood strips or ¼" by ¾" wood strips, depending on arch construction (to cover glazing seams)

OTHER MATERIALS
- A storm door
- Screws
- Epoxy
- Paint
- Door catches and hinges
- For method 3 of arch construction, polyethylene sheeting to prevent gluing arches to the building surface, clamps, and 10 to 20 blocks screwed to a laminating table

This greenhouse measures 8 feet wide and 12 feet long and has an arch every 4 feet. In all, the greenhouse requires four arches. Once erected, these arches are fastened together with two 1×4 longitudinals on each side and a 2×4 center ridge. The arches are covered with thin sheets of polycarbonate caulked and screwed to each member. Alternatively, you can cover the arches with fiberglass or polyethylene sheeting.

There are three methods for building the arches; each one is outlined in the directions below.

STEP 1: Build the Arches

Method 1: Probably the simplest method is to lay two pieces of plywood on top of each other and cut out curves using a template (see the illustration below). In the figure, parts are numbered or lettered. Because you can get only one full arch from one sheet of plywood, the other arches are each made with two shorter lengths of wood. A single arch is strongest if made from two arch forms glued together with their joints widely separated. Note that the longest pieces, such as

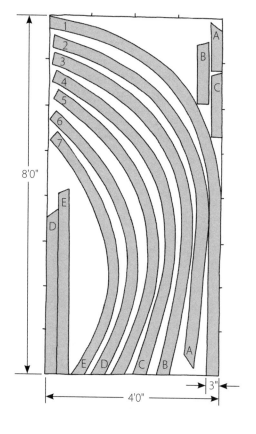

Grid for cutting out arches from plywood

8'0"

4'0"

3"

piece 1 in the illustration, should be glued to the shorter pieces, such as piece 7, so that the joints will be far apart.

To transfer the template, layer two sheets of plywood and mark on the top sheet a grid corresponding to the dimensions and example in the illustration. By measuring the distance and marking points using the illustration as a guideline, and connecting these points with the aid of a thin wooden batten, you can lay out the arches. Once they are drawn, simply cut the layers of plywood and glue together the pieces to produce a series of arches that are each 1 inch thick and 3 inches wide, as shown in the left illustration on page 211. (Smooth the edges of the glued plywood with a sander.)

Method 2: Lightweight polycarbonate or fiberglass glazing enables the arches to be made from flexible lengths of 1×1 pine that are bent into shape and joined at the ridge of the greenhouse. (See the center illustration on page 211.) To make the arch substantial, glue 6-inch 1×3 spacers to each bent arch and then glue another bent piece of 1×1 pine to the inside of the spacers. In addition to attaching the pine with glue, you can screw through the inner piece into the spacers to ensure that the arch is fastened and add more screws from the outside piece of bent pine into the spacers once the glue is dry.

Method 3: If you are making a more upscale greenhouse to complement your home, the wooden arches can be made of ⅛-inch-thick laminate of mahogany (or another dark-colored wood) alternated with laminate of cedar (a light-colored wood), as shown in right illustration on page 211. The laminates are glued together with epoxy. (See chapter 6 for more about epoxy.)

First, lay two sheets of plywood on the shop floor. Draw a single arch on the plywood and place wooden blocks around its outer edge. Screw these wooden blocks to the plywood; these blocks will hold the laminating veneers in place. Before you begin gluing, lay down a piece of polyethylene sheeting to catch the drips and to keep the arches from bonding to the floor and to the blocks. Press the first 2-inch-wide by

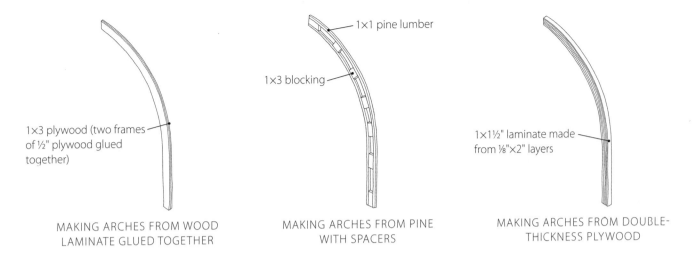

1×1 pine lumber

1×3 blocking

1×3 plywood (two frames of ½" plywood glued together)

1×1½" laminate made from ⅛"×2" layers

MAKING ARCHES FROM WOOD LAMINATE GLUED TOGETHER

MAKING ARCHES FROM PINE WITH SPACERS

MAKING ARCHES FROM DOUBLE-THICKNESS PLYWOOD

⅛-inch-thick piece of veneer against the wood blocks and clamp it in place without any epoxy. Paint the second piece of laminate with epoxy on one side and press it against the first piece, unclamping the first piece to add the second. If you have a professional staple gun, you can also staple the second layer to the first, but take care not to staple the laminate to the blocks.

Build up the layers of each arch, stapling and/or gluing the top layer to the ones already in place. On the final layer, staple through a doubled piece of polyethylene so that you can easily remove the staples after the glue has set up. You will need to build up the laminate to 1½ to 2 inches thick, as shown in the figures above.

Once the glue has set, remove the arch from the blocks and clamps and sand it on both sides to get a smooth finish. Coat the finished wood with two layers of epoxy. When the epoxy has dried, sand it back lightly and apply two coats of UV-resistant varnish.

STEP 2: Erect the Arches

Note that you'll have to choose your glazing material early to determine how far apart to space the arches. Polycarbonate and fiberglass come in 4-foot-wide sheets. For polycarbonate, you should space the arches 4 feet ¼ inches apart to allow for a slight gap between the glazing at the seam. For fiberglass, space the arches 3 feet 11½ inches apart to allow for an overlap of the material. For plastic sheeting, the arches can be spaced 4 feet on center.

This method of setting up the arches works best for those made using method 1: First, lay each arch on the ground to one side of the foundation and screw an L-shaped angle bracket to each half arch at the top where it meets its "partner" arch. These brackets will later be screwed to the ridgepole. With the bracing of both these and the long pieces that run the length of the greenhouse, the arches will be fixed firmly in place. Screw another bracket to the base of each arch to anchor each to the landscape timbers.

Next, prop the ridgepole in place with braces at either end and attach to it with screws first the arches for one side of the greenhouse, then those on the opposite side. An extra pair of hands is a great help with this. You may have to adjust the position of the greenhouse slightly to situate it squarely on the foundation before screwing the angle brackets at the base of the arches to the landscape timbers.

STEP 3: Build the End Walls

The end wall without the door can be solid plywood, polyethylene-covered, or polycarbonate-covered. If you do not want it to be a solid wall, support the ridgepole with a vertical 2×3 support or a 3-inch-wide post made from plywood strips laminated together. Make sure that the outer side of the support is flush with the end-arch plywood so that you can easily fasten polycarbonate or polyethylene sheeting over the entire end wall.

In the end wall with the door, the door opening should be 3 feet wide. The wall will require two supports running from the arch to the base or sill plate and centered 2 feet 3 inches from each side. Inside these supports, install two 6-foot 6-inch 1×4 jacks and fasten the 1×4 header on top of these.

The door itself can be made as shown in project 3: Use 1×4 lumber with lapped corner joints for the frame and cover it with polycarbonate. If you take the time to make two doors, you can cover one with screening for summer use. Instead of building a door, you can use a storm door purchased at a home center.

STEP 4: Install the Door

The door is installed using three 3-inch hinges fastened to the jacks. Set one hinge in the middle of the vertical door support and the other two hinges 12 inches in from either end. On the side opposite the hinges, you might want to install a barrel bolt or a padlock hasp to make sure the door stays shut.

STEP 5: Install the Glazing

Thin polycarbonate panels can be bent over the arches and screwed in place. Have a helper hold the panel vertically and check to see that the edges fall exactly on the arches. Secure the bottom of the first two panels to the base of the greenhouse using a ¼-inch by 2-inch or ¼-inch by 3-inch strip of wood. A vertical 1×2 strip can be screwed through this base strip into the center of the arch about 6 inches up from the bottom. The first 4 feet or so of the wall (from the bottom) is vertical, so it should be easy to install the polycarbonate and the flexible strip.

As the arch curves, you'll need to bend the polycarbonate gently and screw the covering strip into place. This will take patience and care to ensure that the covering strip does not break. Work toward the center of the greenhouse, inserting screws every 9 to 12 inches.

If you want, you can caulk between the glazing layers, but you'll find that this results in getting caulking on everything—your hands, gloves, tools, and screws. If you don't caulk between the glazing sheets, consider installing the covering strips with a bead of flexible caulking between the glazing and the covering strip. If you don't use either of these methods, you'll need to caulk the joint between the glazing and the covering strip to keep out water. Alternatively, you can cover the arches with polyethylene sheeting, as you might cover a hoop house, holding the polyethylene sheeting in place either with flexible battens (as described above) or by tying string over the plastic to contain it when the wind blows.

STEP 6: Build a Vent

Because the roof of this greenhouse is curved, for this structure it would be easiest to make an opening vent for the back wall and a screened door for the front wall or to install a fan in the north wall to blow hot air out of the structure. If you choose to make a vent in the north wall, use two supports spaced 3 feet apart and a crosspiece to create a 3-foot by 3-foot opening. Make a vent cover using the same method employed to make the door and cover it with screening to keep out insects. With a screen door in place and the vent open, you should get plenty of cross ventilation.

VARIATIONS AND UPGRADES

If you take the time and expend the money to build the arches using mahogany and cedar laminates (method 3), consider mounting the greenhouse on a concrete foundation rather than on landscape timbers. (For construction how-to and foundation options, see chapter 8 and projects 1 and 2.) By adding more arches, you can lengthen the greenhouse. Another option is to add lighting and outlets and a water line as described in chapter 10.

5. Lean-to Greenhouse

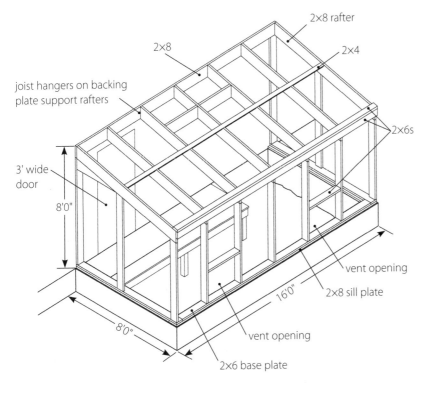

2×8 rafter

2×8

2×4

joist hangers on backing
plate support rafters

2×6s

3' wide
door

8'0"

vent opening

2×8 sill plate

16'0"

vent opening

8'0"

2×6 base plate

Structural schematic of greenhouse

This 8-foot by 16-foot greenhouse is the simplest attached lean-to-style structure. The
roofline can be adjusted to suit the building to
which the greenhouse is attached. One word of
warning: Do not attach the structure to a building where snow is likely to slide from a second-
or third-floor roof onto the greenhouse, potentially damaging the glazing.

Like the other greenhouse projects in this
chapter, this one can be glazed with polycarbonate panels, but because it's a structure attached
to your home, these plans call for using glass.

Because the foundation of the house to
which this greenhouse is attached rises about 2
feet above grade, the structure will be excavated
to become a partial pit greenhouse, which will
enable you to keep taller trees in the greenhouse
and allow for two growing levels, increasing the
overall number of plants that will fit inside the
structure.

Because it's attached to a home, it's relatively
easy to bring electrical power to the structure,

allowing a full range of electrical equipment, including an electric heater, area lights, and plant lights. The greenhouse also has raised beds in one portion of the floor with grow lights over them. In another part of the greenhouse there is a small pond with its own filter and lighting, and near the deck that runs along the back of the greenhouse there is a potting table with lighting, a propagation mat, and a germination area. Stairs from the deck lead down to the greenhouse floor.

CONSTRUCTING THE FOUNDATION

Materials

- Concrete forms for a 16' by 8' foundation
- Snap ties to hold formwork together (one every 3–4 feet)
- 2×4 braces nailed to the forms and wedged into the ground at a 45-degree angle; one brace every 3-4 feet
- 1½ cubic yards of concrete for footings
- 4 cubic yards of concrete for foundation walls
- 2½ cubic yards of concrete for greenhouse floor
- Eight 2' by 8' lengths of 2" polystyrene insulation, each cut in half to accommodate a 4' foundation
- 32' of flashing
- Water and electrical conduit (if installing plumbing and electricity)
- Eleven ½-inch bolts, each 8" long
- 1.8 cubic yards of concrete for the slab (if the 14' by 7' by 6" greenhouse floor will be a slab)
- 2 yards of pea stone (if the floor will not be a slab; no drain is necessary if the floor is pea stone)

Before you excavate a foundation close to your home, determine that you will not be running into any water or power lines (you can contact an organization called Dig Safe for help with this if you are excavating yourself; see Resources, page 248).

The foundation wall for this structure will be set below the frost line and will rise about 12 inches above grade. It should be insulated with 2 inches of rigid foam insulation, with flashing on the sill to protect the insulation. (See the project illustration and page 215 for views of the foundation.

STEP 1: Lay out the Foundation

Using batter boards and string, mark out the greenhouse perimeter using the methods described in chapter 8 (page 116) and project 1 (page 184), making sure the greenhouse is square and aligned with the walls of the house onto which you'll be building the structure.

You might also want to use furring strips to rough out the shape of the greenhouse to ensure that the ridgeline or side walls do not impinge upon any windows or doors in your home and that details such as trim and flashing can be easily added to the structure.

STEP 2: Excavate the Foundation

The foundation should be excavated to a depth of about 4 feet (to reach below the frost line), which will make the completed foundation wall a total of about 5 feet high (4 feet below grade plus 12 inches above grade) As for projects 2 and 3, along with digging the foundation, you should dig a trench 4 to 5 feet deep for the footings. The footings will take up between 6 and 12 inches in the bottom of the trench, depending on the type of soil beneath the foundation (it may be slightly deeper on sandy soils than on hard clay or rock).

STEP 3: Build the Foundation Forms

The foundation will be 8 inches thick, so the forms will be set 8 inches apart. Make sure they are well braced before pouring concrete (one brace every 2 to 4 feet). Locate snap ties every 2 to 3 feet around the walls.

STEP 4: Install the Drainpipe

Because wiring and plumbing will come from the adjacent house, there is no need to allow for a wire conduit or water pipe through the foundation walls. A drain, however, should be installed in the greenhouse floor and roughly plumbed before the concrete is poured. (See chapter 8, page 124, and project 1, page 185, for more information on installing a drainpipe and flush-mounted drain in a foundation before the pour.)

Before pouring the footings, install a 2-inch schedule 40 PVC drainpipe in the middle of the greenhouse. The pipe should slope 1 inch for every 12 inches of length and have an elbow at the inner end on which is mounted a drain, flush with the floor of the greenhouse. When you finish the slab for the concrete floor, make sure the floor slopes toward this central drain. Cover the drain grate with duct tape before pouring the concrete slab to prevent it from clogging.

STEP 5: Pour the Concrete Footings

First, pour the footings and, while they're wet, insert in them 2-foot lengths of rebar to help secure the foundation walls to the footings. (This is important because there will be 4 feet of earth exerting pressure on the outer walls of the foundation.)

STEP 6: Pour and Insulate the Foundation

When the footings are completely dry (a week or two after they've been poured), pour the foundation. After you've carefully leveled the top of the foundation and it has set for an hour or so, insert the ½-inch bolts 3 to 4 feet apart — three in each end and five or six along the front of the greenhouse — to hold the sill plate in place, being sure to leave 2 inches of bolt showing to allow 1½ inches for the sill plate and ½ inch for washers and nuts to secure the plate. Try not to put the bolts where the support posts will be located so that you'll have easy access to them.

STEP 7: Remove the Forms and Insulate the Foundation

When the concrete has set, remove the forms and coat the foundation with foundation sealer before installing polystyrene insulation around it (the insulation should be level with the top of the concrete). You can apply an exterior, concretelike finishing material to the insulation, if desired. Coat the insulation to about 12 inches below grade before backfilling the area.

Foundation plan

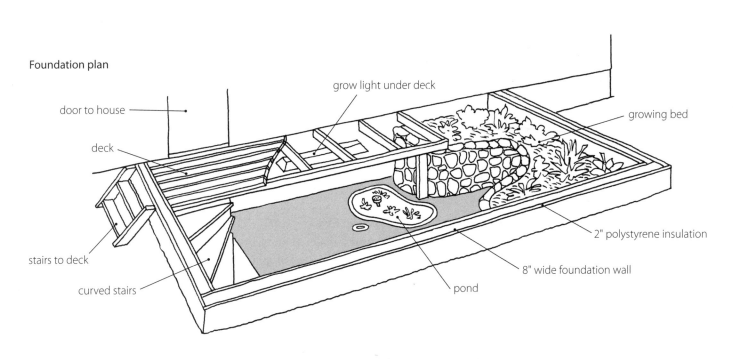

door to house

deck

stairs to deck

curved stairs

grow light under deck

growing bed

2" polystyrene insulation

8" wide foundation wall

pond

STEP 8: Prepare the Pond Area

Before you can install the greenhouse floor, you must set up the pond where you want it and mark out the areas where the raised beds will be. Be sure to block off the raised bed areas so they won't be filled with concrete when you pour the floor. The pond is a simple plastic model available at most home supply stores. Excavate the pond area 18 to 24 inches below the floor of the greenhouse, make a bed of sand in the hole, and set the pond on the sand. Before spreading pea stone or gravel to prepare the greenhouse floor for the concrete slab, make sure that you backfill completely to the pond sides.

STEP 9: Prepare and Pour the Greenhouse Floor

Spread 4 to 6 inches of gravel or pea stone on the greenhouse floor before pouring the 4-inch slab to the level of the flush-mounted drain and underside of the pond (see chapter 8 and project 1). In leveling, screeding, and troweling the floor after the pour, be sure it slopes toward the drain ⅛ inch to ¼ inch every 12 inches. When pouring the floor, make sure that no concrete gets in the pond. To be sure the pond is absolutely clean before you introduce fish, remove it when the concrete is set up or when the greenhouse is finished and clean it thoroughly.

BUILDING THE GREENHOUSE

Materials

FOR THE SILL PLATE
- 32' of pressure-treated 2×8s, painted with an oil-based primer and a layer or two of latex paint
- Sill insulation
- ½-inch nuts and washers to attach the sill to the bolts in the concrete
- 32' of 6" copper or aluminum flashing

FOR THE END WALLS
- Six 2×6 wall supports (three at each end)

- Two 10' 2×8 rafters cut to accommodate the slope of the greenhouse
- Two 8' 2×8 base plates
- Two 6' 2×4s for door framing
- One 3' 2×8 for the door header

FOR THE FRONT WALL
- Five 2×6 wall supports
- Two 4' 2×8 upper window frame pieces
- Two 4' 2×6 lower window frame pieces
- 32' of 2×6s
- 8d galvanized nails or 3" screws

- Eight 2×4 flat deck plates
- One glass door, 3' wide

FOR THE BACK WALL
- One 16' 2×8 bolted to house wall

FOR THE RAFTERS
- Three 2×8s for rafters
- One 16' 2×4 or two 8' 2×4s (glazing supports to be installed in the rafters)
- Five joist hangers (U-shaped metal pieces that, once nailed in place, support a joist or rafter)
- Two 16' 2×6s

FOR THE GLAZING
- 4' panels of polycarbonate (double- or triple-insulated with U-shaped caps and bottom plates; measure lengths at the job site and order to suit)
- Cap pieces for glazing

FOR THE VENTS OR WINDOWS
- Lumber for two 4' by 2' vents (dimensions may change slightly as you build; measure for lumber at the job site). *Note:* If you build the greenhouse against an existing wall, you may have to add blocking next to the wall to set the vent away from the wall so that it can open easily.

Just as you made sure there was no house wiring or plumbing in the area where you planned to excavate the foundation, before building the greenhouse, make certain that there is no wiring or plumbing in the house wall to which you'll be attaching the structure.

STEP 1: Install the Sill Plate

Refer to the illustration on page 217: Place the sill plate on top of the bolts in the foundation and tap with a mallet to mark the locations of the bolts on the plate. Because the sill is 7½ inches wide and the foundation is 8 inches wide, there will be ½ inch of foundation showing on the outside of the building. Cut a lap joint at each corner of the sill plate, drill a ½-inch hole for each bolt, cover the area with fiberglass sill insulation, then set the sill plate back on the foundation, glue the lap joints, and secure the sill plate with nuts and washers.

Next, install 6-inch-wide copper or aluminum flashing, bending it to overlap the sill plate by an inch and the polystyrene foundation insulation by about 2 inches. The greenhouse base plate will cover the inner side of the flashing. When the base plate is installed, run a bead of caulking along the top of the flashing to prevent water from seeping through it.

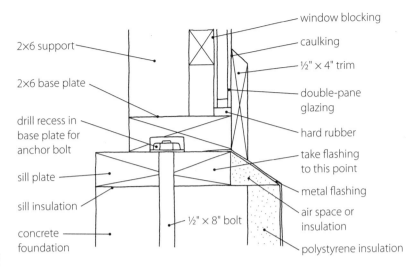

Wall as it meets foundation

STEP 2: Set the Backing Plate

This 2×8 sixteen-foot-long plate is installed on the house wall to hold the highest ends of the greenhouse rafters. You may need help to set it in place properly. Do not bolt it to the plywood wall and sheathing of the house wall. Instead, be sure you are bolting it to the studs in the wall or to the framing at the outer side of the floor joists.

First nail the plate in place with 8d nails, then drill holes for ⅜-inch or ½-inch lag bolts and screw bolts through the backing plate and into the wall joists or studs. Joists or studs are usually placed 16 inches on center, so if you can locate one, you should be able to measure and locate the others. Note that when the house is resheathed above the greenhouse, you will need to install flashing above this plate to ensure that water cannot get behind it.

At 4-foot intervals along this plate, nail joist hangers in place to support the rafters. If you are building the greenhouse against an exterior wall, install 3-foot 10½-inch lengths of 2×8s between the joist hangers where the opening vents will be. This will give you 3 inches to allow the 2-inch-high vent to open against the wall.

STEP 3: Build the End Walls

The end walls are framed as shown in the project schematic on page 213. The supports are spaced at either end and in the middle of the 8-foot base plate. Hammer three 16p nails into each support. Measure from the backing plate to the top of the base plate (approximately 7 feet 5 inches) and nail that vertical to the wall. Repeat for the other end of the greenhouse.

STEP 4: Cut and Install the Rafters

Next, determine the slope of the roof. You might want to make it similar to the slope of the roof of your home, or you could make it drop 3 inches for each foot (so that over the 8-foot width, the roof will slope 2 feet). This means that the outer support will be approximately 5 feet 5 inches long. Toenail it to the base plate (to *toenail* is to fasten a piece of lumber to another by driving in a nail at an angle at the end of it) and brace it so that it's vertical.

Now lay the house end of one rafter in the joist hanger. Slope it so that it rests on the outer support and mark this slope. (I like to nail the rafter to the support post temporarily so that it won't move while I'm measuring.) You'll need to cut the support post along this line to get the correct rafter slope. Before you cut anything, however, have a friend hold it in place and from the joist hanger, draw a line vertically about 2 inches from the wall. Cut the rafters on this line to ensure that their ends abut the wall, and cut the top of the support post to suit the sloped line that you drew.

Next, you'll need to cut a recess in the end of all rafters for the 2×6 vertical face plate and the 2×6 roof plate. At the same time, cut the 2×4 glazing support in the middle of each rafter. Simply clamp all the rafters together and cut them at the same time.

Place a rafter in the joist hanger and attach it to the end-wall support. Use flat 2-inch by 4-inch or 2-inch by 6-inch deck plates on either side of the support to hold the rafter in place.

Measure the midpoint between the end-wall supports and install a vertical 2×8 support at this point. In the end wall with the door, install two 6-foot 7½-inch 2×4s as jacks to hold the header in place. Nail or screw them to the supports. You may have to cut the header on a slope to suit the slant of the rafters. If so, mark it off and cut it. Then nail or screw it into place above the door jacks.

to check your measurements carefully; even a slight misalignment can make it difficult to install glazing. The 2×6 that will serve as the roof plate running above the vertical front plate will have to be cut so that the outer end slopes to butt against the face plate.

With the face, roof plates, and rafters in place, the greenhouse frame is stable and rigid. Install the 2×4 glazing support and the window supports on their own 2×4 jacks. Insert the roof vent blocks between the rafters and add another block against the backing plate.

STEP 6: Install the Glazing

Installing either single-pane or double-pane glass requires certain construction modifications. To keep the double-pane glass flush with the top of the wooden rafters, you can install triangular strips of wood blocking to support the glass, as shown in the illustration below. These are 1½ inches by 1½ inches and are screwed to the 2×6 rafters to form a strong yet moderately light structure.

After placing strip caulking on each glass support, carefully lower the panes of glass into place. Two or three people may be needed for this step. Try not to bend the glass. Caulk the space between the glass and the wood using silicone caulking to ensure that no water can enter there and cover each rafter joint with a cap that's screwed down to secure the wood in place.

For installation of side glazing, see the illustration on page 152.

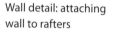
Wall detail: attaching wall to rafters

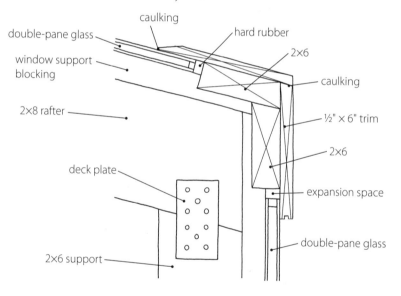

STEP 5: Build the Front Wall

First, measure and cut the front-wall support posts to match the two end-wall support posts. Toenail these in place and brace them to ensure that they remain perfectly vertical. Each support post is assembled with a rafter and two deck plates, just as for the posts on the end walls.

Next, nail or screw in place the 16-foot 2×6 (it will fit into the recess you cut in the ends of each rafter; see the illustration above). Be sure

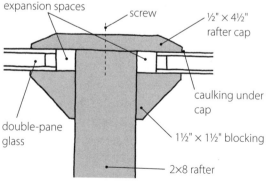
If installing glass instead of polycarbonate, add wood blocking to rafters for support.

STEP 7: Build the Vents

All the vents on this greenhouse are made of 2×2 lumber. Each vent is framed with lap joints at each corner and joined with epoxy. If you plan on using glass for the vents, rabbet the 2×2 and set the window in it. Use caulking around the window and quarter round to hold the glass in place.

When the roof and end walls are in place, carefully measure the greenhouse before cutting vent lumber. To prevent water from coming into the greenhouse, construct the roof vents as shown on page 147 (with an inside lip). Assemble each vent with glue and check that each is square after assembly.

Next, dry-fit the vents in the greenhouse roof, attach hinges, and make sure the vents open properly. So that each vent can be held open, attach a 1-inch by ⅛-inch perforated steel strip to the inside of the vent frame and set a headless screw in the frame. To hold the vent open, simply move one of the holes in the strip over the headless screw. You might want to bend the lower edge of the metal strip upward so that nobody can hit his or her head on it.

STEP 8: Build the Raised Beds

The raised beds in this greenhouse have stone walls that are 6 to 8 inches thick, though they could also be made of brick or concrete blocks. Each raised bed is filled with loam, manure, sand, and compost. The curved wall (see the illustration on page 220) allows you to reach into the beds without walking on them. If you build the wall straight across your greenhouse, you'll have difficulty reaching the back of the growing bed. With a high-intensity light over the top of the beds, plants can grow there year-round.

STEP 9: Install the Pond

The pond is set up with its own filter and fountain and requires only a water outlet somewhere nearby to top off the water lost through evaporation (which can happen quickly in the summer). I prefer to fill my pond from rainwater runoff, which the fish seem to like. Water from your municipal supply may be highly chlorinated and can affect the health of your fish. Once the pond is in place and set up, you can fill it with water and plants. A thorough aquarium book or your local pet store or garden center can provide information on keeping fish.

STEP 10: Install the Wiring

The greenhouse wiring is laid out according to the diagram on page 220. Refer to chapter 10 for more information on installing an electrical system. The main lights are two waterproof fluorescent fixtures. (You can purchase these through FarmTek.) The greenhouse has three high-intensity discharge lights — two over the raised bed and one under the deck. All of these lights are operated on timers, can be raised and lowered as desired, and plug into nearby water-resistant outlets. In addition, two outlets at the front of the greenhouse allow lights, heaters, and fans to be plugged is as needed in winter or summer. Above the potted plants, at the lower left of the diagram, a full-spectrum compact fluorescent light fixture is plugged into the outlet next to the stairs. There's also a 12-watt light in a waterproof box over the stairs. This is dedicated to illuminating the steps any time light is needed there. Finally, there are two accent lights on the stone wall. All the outlets are serviced by a 30-amp GFI breaker in the main fuse panel of the house.

STEP 11: Install Plumbing

There is a single spigot under the deck to the left of the pond. Refer to chapter 10 for more information on installing plumbing in the greenhouse.

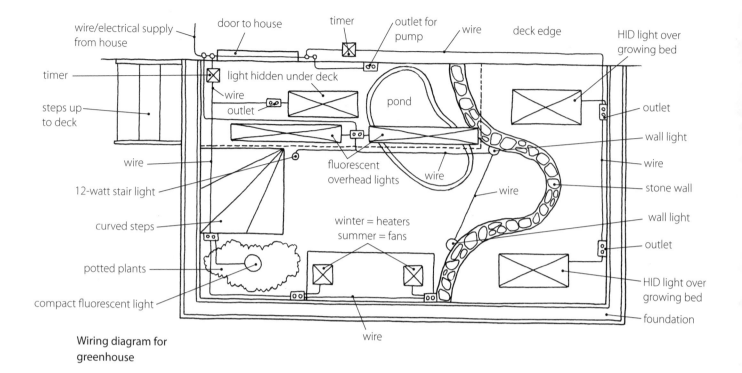

wire/electrical supply from house

door to house

timer

outlet for pump

wire

deck edge

HID light over growing bed

timer

light hidden under deck

steps up to deck

wire

outlet

pond

outlet

wire

wall light

12-watt stair light

fluorescent overhead lights

wire

wire

stone wall

curved steps

winter = heaters summer = fans

wall light

potted plants

outlet

compact fluorescent light

HID light over growing bed

foundation

wire

Wiring diagram for greenhouse

STORAGE SPACE

The area under the stairs can be used as storage space for small tools and other smaller materials. If required, it can be enclosed and secured to allow for safe storage of chemicals and pesticides. With such a crowded greenhouse layout, there is little room for storing potting soil, large tools, and extra pots. Consider adding a storage locker or small shed to the end wall to which the greenhouse stairs are built.

VARIATIONS AND UPGRADES

As for the Gothic arch greenhouse (project 4, page 208), the frame for this lean-to structure can be made using laminated beams to complement your home's decor: If you have exposed beams in your home, you can build the lean-to greenhouse with laminated exposed beams coated with varnish or epoxy to protect them from moisture.

6. Greenhouse Built on Piers or a Deck

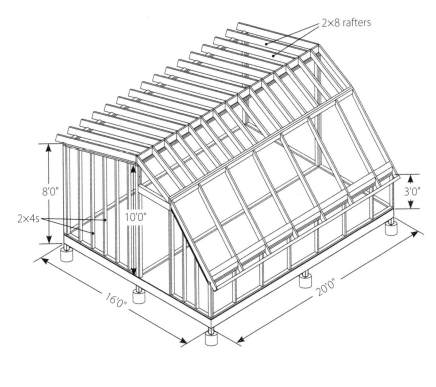

2×8 rafters

8'0"

2×4s

10'0"

3'0"

16'0"

20'0"

Structural schematic of greenhouse

If the ground slopes sharply away from your home or if you live very close to the water and still want a greenhouse, you may have to build it on a deck or piers. This application is also useful if you want to have a greenhouse on a second or third floor. If you decide to use concrete for pilings, you'll need to use fiber form tubes as forms.

This greenhouse was inspired by the southwest Ohio greenhouse of Yvonne Procuniar and her husband, Tim, built on a deck to help keep it warm when the ground freezes and to eliminate the need for a foundation. Their structure was featured in the Hobby Greenhouse Association's magazine, *HGA's News,* in spring 1999. In this greenhouse, the structure is divided into two parts. One part can store the family's lawn tractor and tools, while the other half serves as a traditional greenhouse. Though the Procuniars included doors in each side of the structure, the design in this project incorporates a single door into the "garage" portion of the structure (suitable for only light garden vehicles) and a door through the central wall into the greenhouse. The garage also serves as an air lock to keep the greenhouse warmer in cold winters. In addition, while the Procuniars used metal siding on their structure, the design here incorporates plywood sheathing and siding.

SETTING THE PILINGS

Materials

- Nine fiber form tubes (such as Sonotubes), each 12' in diameter
- Nine post anchors
- Enough concrete to fill each tube (refer to the table on page 112)

STEP 1: Excavate the Holes for the Tubes

Make sure to excavate the nine holes below the frost line if you live in an area that experiences cold winters.

STEP 2: Place the Tubes and Pour the Concrete

Set the tubes in the holes, check that they are perfectly vertical, and fill them with concrete. When the mix has set, the tubes can be either left in place or stripped away. Backfill the holes around the tubes. Once the concrete has been poured, allow it to partially set and then insert a post support, post anchor, or post anchor block into the top of each pier. This is important if your area is exposed to high winds; the supports will allow the greenhouse to be firmly attached to the piers. It's also important if you intend to build the deck from pressure-treated lumber, which can react with concrete; the post support limits contact between the concrete and the wood.

BUILDING THE GREENHOUSE

STEP 1: Build the Base Frame

The greenhouse is built on a 2-foot by 8-foot base frame anchored to nine pilings set deep into the ground. The illustration on page 223 shows how the floor platform is constructed using 2×8 joists set 16 inches on center. You could build the floor in sections and nail ¼-inch plywood on the underside of the floor joists so that 8-inch-thick fiberglass insulation can be dropped between them. After you've added the insulation, nail ⅜-inch subflooring over the joists to seal in the insulation.

To make the structure frame, lay out the 20-foot front and back plates. If you can't find 20-foot lengths of lumber, you'll have to use a 12-foot and an 8-foot length or two 10-foot lengths. Mark out the joist locations 16 inches on center. Nail a joist hanger in the middle of each marked location. Set the planks vertically and place the 8-foot joists in the hangers. Nail each plank with three 16p nails and toenail the joist in place.

In each corner of the base, nail a 4×4 post with its top flush with the joist top. You'll need a few friends to lift the frame on to the concrete posts and fasten the 4×4s to the post anchors.

Materials

FOR THE BASE FRAME

- Nine 4×4 corner posts to support the frame (each post will sit on a post anchor secured to the concrete piling)
- Sixteen 2×8s spaced 16" on center for joists
- 20' of 2×8s for the front
- 20' of 2×8s to be attached to the center joist
- 20' of 2×8s for the back
- 56 joist hangers for 2×8s
- 16p nails
- 10 sheets of ½" CDX plywood for flooring

FOR THE FRONT WALL

- Three 20' 2×4s
- Eighteen 3' 2×4s
- Four 8" pieces of 2×4 blocking
- 2½ sheets of ⅜" or ½" CDX plywood for sheathing

FOR THE REAR WALL

- Thirteen 2×4 studs spaced 16" on center

- Assorted lengths of blocking for spacing end walls
- Two 7' ½" 2×10 headers
- Two 2×4 jacks
- Three 20' 2×4s for top and bottom plates
- 16p nails
- Garage door to fit a rough opening 8' 1½" by 6' 9½"
- 4 sheets of ⅜" or ½" CDX plywood for sheathing

FOR THE MIDDLE WALL

- Fifteen 10' 2×4s
- Three 20' 2×4s for top and bottom framing plates
- Twelve 14¼" pieces of blocking
- Two 2×4 jacks
- Two 2×10s for door header, blocked out to a thickness of 3½"
- Three 3' 2×4s spaced 16" on center (for wall above header)
- Assorted 2×4 blocking
- 16p nails

- Seven sheets per side of waterproof sheetrock or ½" CDX plywood for sheathing

FOR THE END WALLS

- Fourteen 2×4s (cut from 10' 2×4s)
- Two 2×4 jacks
- Two 2×8 headers blocked out to 3½" wide
- One 16' 2×4 base plate
- Two 10' 2×4 headers cut to length for the garage side of the structure
- Two 2×4 headers cut to length for the greenhouse side of the structure
- Four sheets of ⅜" or ½" CDX plywood for sheathing
- One door, 3' wide

FOR THE ROOF

- Five pieces of 4' by 11' polycarbonate for greenhouse windows (take measurements at the job site)

- Eight 11' 4" 2×8 rafters
- Eighteen 10' 8" 2×8 rafters for the garage roof (spaced 16" on center)
- 20' of 2×8s for the front soffit
- 20' of 2×8s for the rear soffit
- 20' of 2×8s for the top ridge
- 40' of 2×8s for the lower ridge
- Seven sheets of ⅜" or ½" CDX plywood for roof sheathing
- Roofing felt
- Eight bundles of roof shingles

FOR THE RAMP

- Two 10' 2×8s cut to suit the ramp slope
- Two joist hangers
- Twenty-one lengths of pressure-treated decking, 3' each

OTHER MATERIALS

- Faced 3½" fiberglass insulation to install between studs

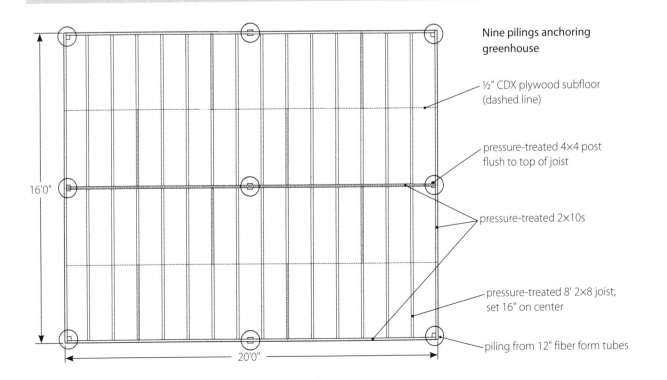

Nine pilings anchoring greenhouse

½" CDX plywood subfloor (dashed line)

pressure-treated 4×4 post flush to top of joist

pressure-treated 2×10s

pressure-treated 8' 2×8 joist, set 16" on center

piling from 12" fiber form tubes

16'0"

20'0"

STEP 2: Build the Front, Middle, and Rear Walls

The illustrations below and on page 225 show the front-, middle-, and rear-wall layouts. The front wall is 3 feet tall, the middle wall is 10 feet tall, and the rear wall is 8 feet tall. The rear wall has a single garage-style door and the middle wall has a regular door between the greenhouse and the storage portion of the structure. In this construction, the storage portion serves as an air lock to keep the greenhouse warmer during cold winter months and provides a place for potting soil that can easily be moved into the greenhouse part of the structure when needed. For summer use, there are windows in the lower front wall that can be opened for ventilation.

The front, middle, and rear walls are constructed of 2×4 pine or pressure-treated lumber spaced 16 inches on center. Lay the top and bottom plates on the greenhouse floor and mark off

the support locations at 16-inch intervals. Nail the supports to the base and top plates as shown.

To frame out the garage door, cut the two jacks to size and nail them to the supports on either side of the door. Each header, made from 2×10s, is only 1½ inches wide and the studs are 3½ inches wide; you'll have to add a ½-inch-wide piece of plywood between the headers to make them total 3½ inches in width. When each wall is finished, lift the walls into place (with the help of an extra pair or two of hands). Brace them and check to see that they are perfectly vertical.

STEP 3: Build the End Walls

The end walls are also made of 2×4 pine or pressure-treated lumber spaced 16 inches on center. There is a door directly into the greenhouse. Although there are no windows in the greenhouse end walls or garage, you can install

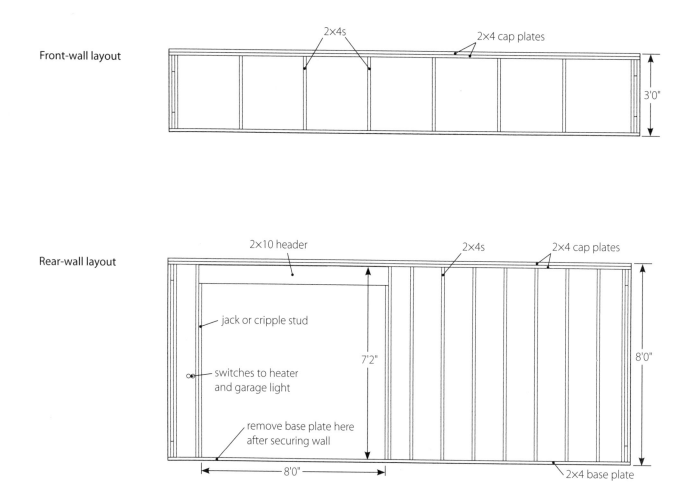

Front-wall layout

Rear-wall layout

them if you so desire. The end walls are built in a manner similar to the front and rear walls: Lay out the walls on the floor and mark the height of the middle wall (measured at the job site) and the height of the front and rear walls (measured at the job site.) Also mark the heights of the supports, cut the supports, and nail them in place.

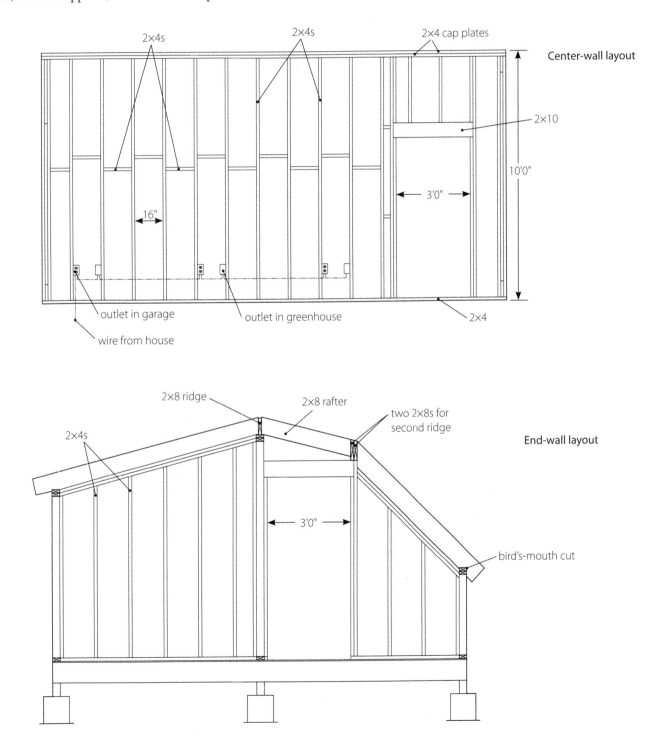

STEP 4: Install the Rafters and Sheathe the Roof

The illustration below shows the rafter layout. The rafters over the storage area are 2×8s spaced 16 inches on center. The rafters over the greenhouse are spaced 48¼ inches on center to allow for 4-foot-wide polycarbonate panels and mounting screws. Overhangs are 9 inches all around the greenhouse.

To install the rafters, measure the length of the structure at the ridgepole and mark each rafter to show where it will butt against the ridgepole. Then, as described on page 140, measure down each rafter using your framing square and mark and make a bird's-mouth cut. Check again that the structure's walls are still square and vertical. Cut the rafters on both sides of the greenhouse garage before you nail them in place and then nail all rafters to the ridge and at the bird's-mouth end. With the rafters in place, you can add the soffit to their ends.

The structure has a 9-inch overhang on each side. To achieve this, cut several 7½-inch blocks, space them 16 inches apart on the outer rafters, and nail them to the rafter and to the wall.

Before nailing the sheathing to the roof, cover this eave with ¼-inch plywood. Leaving out this step (as I have done) could result in squirrels getting inside the greenhouse and chewing away at the structure. Install roof sheathing by staggering the plywood panels. Add roofing felt over the sheathing and then shingle the roof with asphalt shingles.

STEP 5: Sheathe the Structure and Install Insulation

Sheath the structure with ½-inch or ⅜-inch plywood or even ½-inch oriented strand board. Then, so that you can work in the greenhouse in cold weather, install fiberglass batting insulation between the studs and waterproof sheetrock over the studs on the inside walls.

Rafter layout

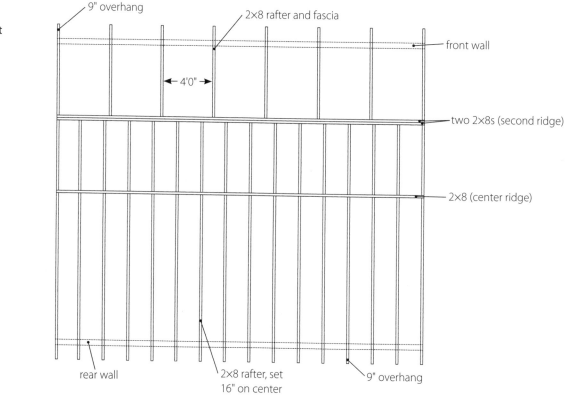

9" overhang

2×8 rafter and fascia

front wall

4'0"

two 2×8s (second ridge)

2×8 (center ridge)

rear wall

2×8 rafter, set 16" on center

9" overhang

STEP 6: Install Glazing

To install the 4-foot-wide polycarbonate glazing, lay it on the rafters, tape it into place, and caulk between the sheets before screwing the cap plate in place over the glazing edges and the seam between the sheets. Cover the top and bottom of the glazing with U-shaped brackets to keep out moisture and dirt.

For a consistent look, instead of sheathing the eaves as described above, you might want to cut two pieces of 9-inch polycarbonate to trim them.

STEP 7: Install the Garage Door

The garage door should be installed by a professional. This service is usually included by the company through which you purchase the door. Install the end-wall door following the instructions included with it.

STEP 8: Install Electricity

Refer to chapter 10, Wiring, Plumbing, and Heating, for more specific information on installing electricity in the greenhouse. There are a number of outlets along the middle wall of the structure that serve both the greenhouse and the storage area. You can also add three or four shop lights in both the storage area and the greenhouse area for general lighting. Outlets can also be used for a fan or small heater.

STEP 9: Build Ramps

Of course, you'll need to build a ramp or steps up to the door of the greenhouse. A ramp is preferable to allow a wheelbarrow into the structure should you not want to go through the garage door. You'll need a ramp into the storage area as well so that larger equipment and materials can be moved into and out of it.

A 36-inch-wide ramp requires spacing the 2×8s upright about 30 inches apart. The ramp end at the garage should be cut vertically and dropped into two joist hangers nailed to the side of the base plate. If possible, also nail through the base plate into the ramp supports. Cut the other end of the 2×8s so that they lie flat on the ground.

Nail the 3-foot lengths of pressure-treated decking to the upright 2×8s. Consider building two smaller ramps to the garage door to suit the wheel span of your tractor instead of creating one wide ramp. If you decide to build a ramp the width of the garage door, you'll need to space vertical 2×8s 20 to 24 inches apart and then nail decking to the uprights.

STEP 10: Finish the Exterior

You can cover the exterior sheathing with shingles or wood clapboards and trim, painted with several coats to protect against the elements.

VARIATIONS AND UPGRADES

In the Procuniar greenhouse, the subfloor is insulated with rigid foam insulation overlaid with plywood. The couple also insulated the middle wall between the storage area and the greenhouse as well as all the exterior walls with fiberglass batting and covered the frame walls with waterproof sheetrock. If you need more doors into the greenhouse than are provided in the plans here, you can follow the Procuniars' lead: They installed three doors — a sliding door in the rear wall, a garage-style door on the right-hand wall, and a smaller door in the middle wall. For sheathing, instead of plywood and shingles or wood siding, you can use metal sheathing, as the Procuniars did.

7. Hoop House or High-Tunnel Greenhouse

Hoop houses are inexpensive and easy to build; the least-expensive high tunnel can be built from PVC water pipe. Each 10-foot section of pipe costs around $2, while pipe joints are usually around a dollar or two, so for less than $100 you can make your own plastic hoop-house frame.

My plastic hoop house runs the entire length of the garden because here in Rhode Island we get very cold winds off the Atlantic Ocean in springtime. By protecting plants in the plastic hoop house, I can ensure that their growth isn't slowed by these winds.

The ends of my high tunnel are made of plywood on the north end and polycarbonate on the south end. A plywood end wall helps to give the structure some rigidity and provides a surface to which you can attach the polyethylene cover.

CONSTRUCTING THE FOUNDATION

Materials

- Twenty 30" lengths of rebar

This type of greenhouse is anchored directly to the ground with rebar that's inserted into the pipe frame at one end and into the ground at the other.

STEP 1: Install the Rebar

For a 14-foot-wide plastic hoop house, hammer the lengths of rebar into the ground 3 or 4 feet apart around the perimeter of the greenhouse space, leaving about 10 inches of rebar showing aboveground.

BUILDING THE GREENHOUSE

Materials

FOR THE FRAME

- Twenty 10' lengths of ¾" scedule 40 PVC pipe, each piece cut in half
- Seven 10' lengths of ¾" PVC pipe cut into 3' lengths
- Thirty 4-way pipe joints
- Plastic pipe glue
- 60' of 2×8s or 2×10s plus pipe clamps (a wooden frame is built around the base of the pipe frame and the pipe clamps are used to fasten the pipe to the wood)

FOR THE END WALLS

- Four pieces of ⅜" 4×8 CDX plywood for the north end of the greenhouse
- Four 48" by 96" 6 mm polycarbonate panels for the south end

FOR THE GLAZING

- 100' roll of construction polyethylene plastic. *Note:* The plastic has a tendency to split along the folds over time.
- Furring strips for nailing polyethylene to side base pieces

FOR THE DOORS

- One old (or new) screen door with hinges and hasps

This hoop house will be 30 feet long.

STEP 1: Build the Frame

Attach a 5-foot length of ¾-inch schedule 40 PVC water pipe on each piece of rebar and glue one four-way joint to the top of each pipe. Add a second 5-foot length of pipe to the four-way joint (for 10 feet of pipe on each piece of rebar). With help, bend opposite pieces of pipe into the middle and attach them in arcs by gluing them to another four-way joint. Each piece of pipe will now form a 20-foot arc with three four-way joints.

Next, insert a 3-foot section into each arc to make a rigid grid of pipe. Last, along the base of each side of the structure, set a 10-foot 2×9 or 2×10 into a trench (about 4 inches deep) and

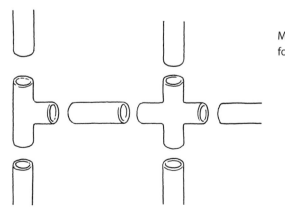

Make a grid of pipes for frame.

Grid assembled and
ready to be covered
with PE sheeting

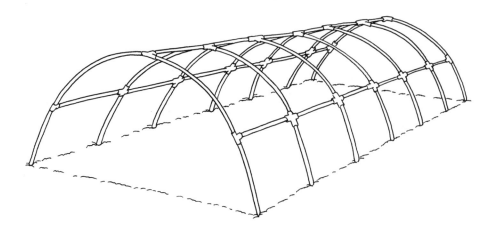

clamp this to the pipes with pipe clamps and screws.

STEP 2: Build the End Walls

To make the end walls, first hold the plywood up to the pipe frame at the north end of the structure and mark on it the arc formed by the pipes. (To do this, stand the sheets of plywood against the end of the frame.)

You can also mark a half circle on four sheets of plywood placed on the ground: Hammer a nail into the plywood at the center. The greenhouse is 14 feet wide, so the radius will be 7 feet. Mark an arc and cut out the arc with a jigsaw. If you decide to make one of the end walls out of polycarbonate, you can use this arc as a template. If the winds are gusty where you live, you may have to reinforce the end walls by screwing them to four or five 2×4s of varying lengths. Using this method, however, may produce arches that are not exactly 14 feet wide and thus will not match the wall exactly.

STEP 3: Install the Polyethylene Sheeting

With the framework in place, the final job is to cover the entire frame with polyethylene. Simply unroll the polyethylene over the frame and staple it lightly to the baseboard. Next, cover the staples with long battens (furring strips) nailed into place. In warmer weather, the furring strips can be detached and lifted to allow air to enter the lower part of the greenhouse.

My experience has been that this structure will not stand up to 50-mile-per-hour winds but withstands any below this mark. Note that a heavy snowfall will weigh on the frame and cover, but it's easy enough to walk inside the hoop house and push the snow from the sheet-

VARIATIONS AND UPGRADES

As mentioned above, you can cover the southern end wall of the greenhouse with polycarbonate instead of plywood to allow even more light in to the structure. Simply use the system described in step 2 to draw an arc on the polycarbonate that matches the arc of the greenhouse frame.

8. Window Greenhouse

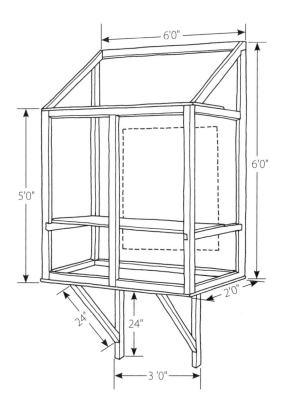

Because window greenhouses are small, they heat up and cool down quickly, meaning the environment in them isn't very stable. With this caveat in mind, however, if this is the only type of greenhouse that will work for your situation, it can add a great deal of pleasure to your gardening experience. In constructing the greenhouse, it's best to build it so that the original window it covers cannot be closed. This will prevent the window greenhouse from overheating when it's warm out or getting too cool on cold days. As with any attached greenhouse, a window greenhouse can supply additional heat and humidity to the room.

BUILDING THE GREENHOUSE

Materials

- Six 30" 2×2s for greenhouse mounting brackets
- One 2' 6" sheet of ½" plywood
- Nine 6' 2×2s for the frame
- Two 8' 2×2s for wall cleats
- Eight 24" 2×2s for shelf landings
- Two 48" 2×2s for top angle pieces
- Polycarbonate scraps (about 6' by 12" each) for shelving (to allow light to reach plants placed beneath shelves)
- 6 mm polycarbonate for the window: one 4' by 4' panel for the front, two 2' by 4' panels for the sides, and two 2' by 2' triangular panels and one 3' by 4' panel for the top

STEP 1: Determine the Size of the Greenhouse

The first job is to measure the window to see how large your greenhouse can be. You can make the greenhouse either the same size as the window or bigger than the window. If the walls of your home are brick, concrete, or stone, make it the same size as the window; these surfaces are difficult to drill into if you make it larger. If you plan on installing a window greenhouse in an apartment building or rental home, you should first get the landlord's permission. If the walls of your home are wood (clapboards, shingles), the greenhouse can easily be fastened to wood and can be larger than the window.

It's best to make the structure no more than 18 inches wider than the window on either side to allow you to reach all shelves easily. As for depth, most people leaning through a window can reach out only 24 to 28 inches, so 28 inches should be your maximum depth. Because of security issues (it's easy to break in to a greenhouse window), it's best not to remove the house window it's built upon.

STEP 2: Build the Frame

The construction of the greenhouse is shown in the illustrations on page 233. In this case, the house window is 4 feet by 4 feet and the greenhouse is 2 feet deep, 6 feet wide, and 5 feet tall, with additional space in the sloped area at the top of the window.

First, make the base of the greenhouse: Fashion a support bracket from 2×2s — two cleats (to be fitted against the house), each made of two 24-inch-long pieces set at right angles. Next, make a 24-inch cross brace and fit it into the cleats. Glue and screw the cleats to the wall of the house, then cut a 2-inch by 4-inch piece of waterproof plywood and attach it top of the cleats. Varnish or paint the base at this stage.

Next, make the frame for the greenhouse: Cut two 24-inch 2×2s and two 72-inch 2×2s and glue together or epoxy these pieces. Check that this construction is square. Repeat the process for a second frame. These two frames, base and top, will be attached with uprights. The two uprights nearest the house are 72 inches and the two on the outside of the greenhouse are 60 inches. Notch these into the base and top frames and glued or epoxy them in place. Build all corners of the greenhouse frame with lap joints. At this point, you can also add cleats to support shelves. The positioning of the cleats (and thus the shelves) will depend on the height of your plants. In the illustration the pairs of cleats are set 1 and 2 feet above the greenhouse base.

To finish the basic structure, add the top 45-degree angle pieces; then, paint, stain, or varnish the greenhouse to suit your home's decor.

STEP 3: Add the Shelves

Install glass, polycarbonate, or plywood shelves, cut to size, on the shelf-support cleats. Remember to keep taller plants at the back (house side) of the window greenhouse so that smaller plants in front can get adequate sunlight, even though this means you'll have to remove the taller plants to reach the smaller ones.

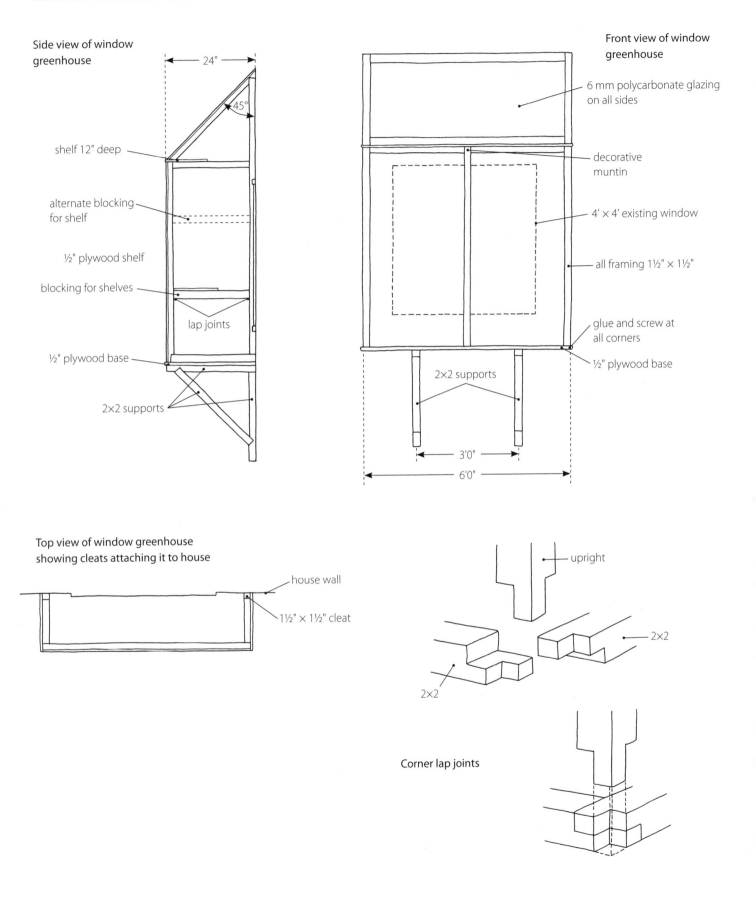

Side view of window greenhouse

24"

45°

shelf 12" deep

alternate blocking
for shelf

½" plywood shelf

blocking for shelves

lap joints

½" plywood base

2×2 supports

Front view of window
greenhouse

6 mm polycarbonate glazing
on all sides

decorative
muntin

4' × 4' existing window

all framing 1½" × 1½"

glue and screw at
all corners

½" plywood base

2×2 supports

3'0"

6'0"

Top view of window greenhouse
showing cleats attaching it to house

house wall

1½" × 1½" cleat

upright

2×2

2×2

Corner lap joints

STEP 4: Install the Glazing

Because a window greenhouse glazed with glass is very heavy, polycarbonate is the preferable glazing material for this type of structure. Cover the entire greenhouse with this glazing, overlapping the lower pieces with the upper ones to keep water from getting inside the structure. If you want, you can cover the corners of the polycarbonate with ⅛-inch by 1- or 1½-inch strips of wood to hide the edges.

STEP 5: Mount the Greenhouse

Set the entire greenhouse on the wall brackets mounted in step 1. Screw the sides to the walls and the base to the bracket so that the greenhouse is rigid and fully supported.

VARIATIONS AND UPGRADES

Instead of using waterproof plywood for the bottom of the greenhouse, you can use marine-grade teak or oak-faced plywood that's varnished or painted so that the surface is easy to keep clean. If you decide to use glass for glazing, insetting it into the wood imparts a cleaner look.

9. Garden Shed/Greenhouse

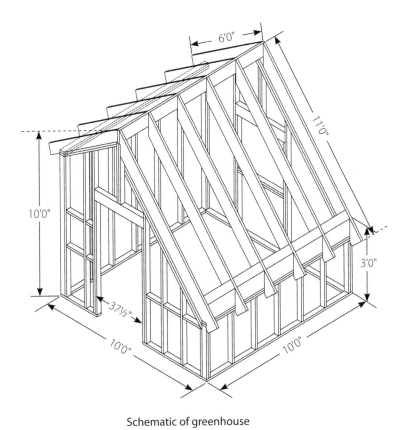

Schematic of greenhouse

This 10-foot by 10-foot shed/greenhouse is a project my son David and I designed and completed together. The structure has an off-center ridge and glazing along the south side. Inside, high shelves hold plants at a suitable height for them to get plenty of sunlight, while under the shelving there's plenty of space for storing greenhouse gear. At the back of the shed there's a potting table along with more shelves for plants and gear. The air-intake vents for this greenhouse are in the front knee wall, while exhaust vents can be built high up in the back wall or on the end walls just under the ridge. The structure is glazed with polycarbonate. The door in the end wall is wide enough for a wheelbarrow or cart.

CONSTRUCTING THE FOUNDATION

Materials for a Slab Foundation	Materials for Four Piers
• Four 2×10s (for forms) • Sixteen 24" 2×2 posts (to serve as verticals for the 2×10s) • Two yards of gravel or pea stone • Two yards of concrete • Bolts for the sill plate	• Four fiber form tubes, each 8" in diameter • Four deck post supports • About ½ yard of concrete (for this small amount, you can use bags of concrete mix)

The greenhouse can be built on a concrete slab or on four piers (one at each corner). Refer to chapter 8 for specific information on constructing a slab and chapter 8 and project 6 (page 222) for information on constructing piers or pilings.

STEP 1: Lay out the Foundation

With batter boards and string, mark out the greenhouse using the methods described in chapter 8 (page 116) and project 1 (page 184). In the process, make sure that the greenhouse is square.

STEP 2: Excavate for Piers or a Slab

For all four piers, excavate the holes below the frost line if you live in an area that has cold winters. For the slab, plan on making the slab about 6 inches thick and excavate 10 to 12 inches.

STEP 3: Build the Foundation Forms (for a Slab Foundation) or Place the Tubes

If building on a slab foundation, you'll need only four 2×10s for the forms. To construct forms, hammer 2×2 posts into the ground at the corners and nail the 2×10s to them. Next, hammer 2×2 supports into the ground about every 2 feet around the outside of the forms. If your area freezes, fill the excavated site with 2 or 3 inches of gravel before pouring the concrete so that the slab can "float" on the stone (see chapter 8, page 123, and project 1, page 185). If you're installing piers, place the fiber form tubes in the excavated holes.

STEP 4: Pour Concrete

If you're using fiber form tubes, refer to the box and chart on page 112 for information on the amounts of concrete needed to fill them. After the concrete has been poured, when the mix has set, the tubes can be either left in place or stripped away. Backfill the holes around the tubes. When the concrete is partially set, insert into the top of each tube either J-bolts or deck post supports to keep the wood from contacting the concrete.

If you're pouring a slab, refer to chapter 8 and projects 1 and 2 for information on smoothing, screeding, and troweling. After pouring the concrete and before it sets, install bolts in the slab near the edge to anchor the base plate of the walls. As described in chapter 7, sink the bolts so that 1½ to 2½ inches of each is visible.

There are no water pipes, drainpipes, or electricity in this shed so there is no need to place conduit before pouring the slab.

BUILDING THE SHED

Materials

FOR THE 10' BY 10' BASE STRUCTURE, FLOOR, OR DECK

- Eleven 10' 2×6s or pressure-treated 2×10s (depending on whether you will be building on a slab or piers)
- 2 sheets of ½" plywood or twenty 10' lengths of 1×6 decking (if building on piers, enough to cover a 10' by 10' base)

FOR THE REAR WALL

- Ten 8' 2×4s
- Three 10' 2×4s (one for the base plate and two for the cap plates)

FOR THE FRONT WALL

- Ten 3' 2×4s
- Three 10' 2×4s for base and cap plates (one for the base plate and two for the cap plate)

- Four 14½" lengths of blocking for vent openings
- Spare blocking for two end studs (so that the side walls can be fastened to it)

FOR THE END WALLS

- Two 10' 2×4s for base plates (one for each wall)
- Four 10' 2×4s for top plates
- Four 6' 2×4s for top plates
- Eight 8' 2×4s for studs
- Six 10' 2×4s for supports
- Two 40½" 2×8s for the door header
- Four 25½" 2×6s for the windowsill and window header

FOR THE RAFTERS AND RIDGEPOLE:

- Four 11' 2×8s
- One 10' 2×8
- One 10' 1×4 face trim piece for end of rafters

FOR THE SHEATHING

- 8 sheets ⅜" or ½" CDX plywood
- Shingles

FOR THE GLAZING

- 10' by 40" sheets of poly-carbonate or glass to cover 100 square feet

FOR EACH VENT (KNEE WALL AND BACK WALL)

- Four 14 ½" 2×2s
- Two pieces of plywood or polycarbonate to cover vents, 14½" by 14½" each

OTHER MATERIALS

- One standard-height exterior door, 3' wide
- One 2' by 3' window (double-pane if the shed will be insulated)
- Roofing felt and shingles for the rear of the roof
- 7 or 8 sheets of waterproof sheetrock (optional)
- Caulking, hinges, clasps, screws and nails, shelf brackets, and shingles or some other material to cover the exterior sheathing, if desired

STEP 1: Build the Base

If you are building on a slab and will not be insulating the floor, there's no need to build a base or deck. Simply build the walls directly onto the concrete slab, securing them in place with the bolts set in the concrete. For some insulating value on the floor of the shed, you can frame the 10-foot by 10-foot slab with 2×8s, then bolt 2×4 or 2×6 lumber blocks to the concrete and nail or screw the base frame to the blocks. (To increase the insulation value, fill the spaces between the 2×8s with rigid polystyrene or fiberglass batts.

If you are building the greenhouse on piers, use pressure-treated 2×10s and nail ¼-inch plywood under the base to secure the insulation in place.

STEP 2: Cover the Base

Cover the base (and insulation) with ½-inch-thick plywood or 1×6 decking fastened with 8d nails. Be aware that if you use decking, there will be a small space between planks — you can lose small items in them and they'll create an air gap that may well prevent using the shed to grow plants in winter.

STEP 3: Build the Rear Wall

The rear wall is built as shown in the illustration below. Clamp together top and base plates and mark out placement of studs 16 inches on center. Using 16p nails, fasten the studs to the top and base plates, then nail ⅜-inch CDX plywood on the outside of the wall.

Rear-wall layout (top) and front-wall layout

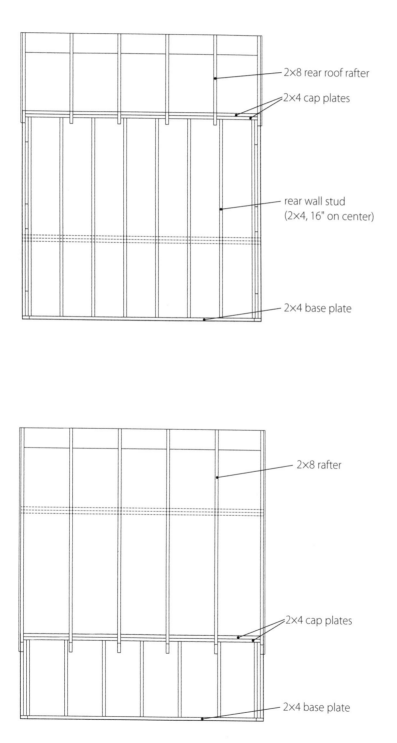

2×8 rear roof rafter

2×4 cap plates

rear wall stud (2×4, 16" on center)

2×4 base plate

2×8 rafter

2×4 cap plates

2×4 base plate

STEP 4: Build the Front Wall

The construction details of the front wall are shown in the bottom illustration. As you did for the rear wall, clamp together top and base plates and mark out placement of studs 16 inches on center. Using 16p nails, fasten the studs to the top and base plates, then fasten the blocking for the vent openings. Finally, nail ⅜-inch CDX plywood on the outside of the wall.

STEP 5: Build the End Walls

The end walls are built as shown in the illustration on page 239. One end wall has a door, the other a window, but the two walls can be framed at the same time. First cut a stud to the height of the front wall but slope the top to correspond to the sloped top plate.

Next, assemble the door wall on a large flat surface: Lay out the base plate and mark out the locations of the studs 16 inches on center and the placement of the door. The rough opening for the door will be 37½ inches wide and 6 feet 8¾ inches high. Set the stud you cut for the front wall at one end of the wall and lay studs in their determined spots. Dry-fit the header, jacks, ridgepole support, and blocking, and then nail together all pieces.

Finally, sheathe the door wall with ⅜-inch CDX plywood. Remember that the sheathing will have to cover the rafter, so make sure to allow an extra 8 inches above the top of the wall.

To assemble the window wall, proceed as above, laying out all pieces and marking stud placement and window header and sill placement. Cut all lumber and dry-fit it, then nail or screw together all pieces. As with the opposite wall, when you sheathe the window wall, allow for the rafter width at the top.

STEP 6: Erect the Walls and Add the Ridgepole

You'll need an extra pair of hands for this job. Once the walls are in place, brace each so that it remains perfectly vertical. Check the diagonals to make sure that the building is square before you nail or screw together all four walls.

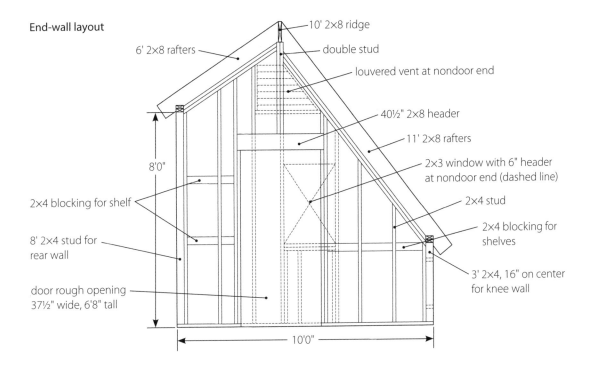

End-wall layout

10' 2×8 ridge
6' 2×8 rafters
double stud
louvered vent at nondoor end
40½" 2×8 header
11' 2×8 rafters
2×3 window with 6" header at nondoor end (dashed line)
2×4 blocking for shelf
8'0"
2×4 stud
2×4 blocking for shelves
8' 2×4 stud for rear wall
3' 2×4, 16" on center for knee wall
door rough opening 37½" wide, 6'8" tall
10'0"

Set the 10-foot 2×8 ridgepole in place on top of the double stud at the center of the greenhouse.

STEP 7: Install the Rafters

Rafters are cut as shown in the illustrations on page 238. Make one first and dry-fit it to be sure it's sized correctly. Note that the end rafter will overlap the vertical support stud under the ridgepole and may need trimming. You may also find that the header needs a little trimming at the end rafter.

After any necessary adjustments, cut the other rafters. For the rear of the roof, each rafter is set 16 inches on center and for the front half of the roof, where the glazing will be located, they are set 3 feet 4 inches on center.

STEP 8: Finish the Rear Half of the Roof

Sheathe the back half of the roof with ⅜-inch plywood cover the plywood with roofing felt and then with roofing shingles. Finish the shingles at the ridge. Later, they will be covered with a trim piece.

STEP 9: Install Glazing

For the front glazing, cut polycarbonate panels to 3 feet 4 inches wide and 7 feet 4 inches long. (For precise measurements, measure at the job site.) Because there are only three pieces of glazing in this greenhouse, you can also order glass to cover the windows. When ordering glass or polycarbonate glazing, be sure to allow a ¼-inch to ⅜-inch gap between panes so that you can screw cap pieces in place. The cap pieces should be 10 feet long and 2 inches by ½ inch. Refer to chapter 7 for information on installing polycarbonate or glass glazing.

For the roof glazing on the front half of the roof, rabbet a slot in the front trim so that it will cover the glazing, then run a bead of caulking along the top of the glass, set a trim piece in place, and nail or screw it down with finish nails. Run a bead of caulking along the back of this trim piece and nail another trim piece along the ridge of the structure, covering the top of the roof shingles and forming a watertight joint along the ridge.

STEP 10: Install the Door and Window

The greenhouse is now enclosed except for the window and door openings. To install the window, dry-fit it to ensure that it will sit in the opening. You may have to shim the window slightly on the inside to get it perfectly level. Once you are satisfied with the fit, nail or screw it in place.

To install the door, first measure the jambs and cut them to fit your rough opening. Slide the door into place and check that it is perfectly level. You may have to shim the sides slightly to ensure a perfect fit. Then, nail or screw it in place. Last, install the door handle.

STEP 11: Interior Sheathing

If you want, you can install waterproof sheetrock on the inside of the greenhouse (it's best installed over fiberglass insulation). As with all sheetrock applications, the corners will require taping and joint compound before the walls can be primed and painted.

STEP 12: Finishing Details

You can use measured and cut remainders from job lumber for shelving cleats. If you sheetrock the interior, be sure to screw cleats to the studs in the walls. Add shelves for a place to store tools and display flowers in pots. Empty pots, potting soil, and heavy items can be stored under the workbench.

The exterior of the shed can be finished with shingles or clapboards.

VARIATIONS AND UPGRADES

Besides using glass for some or all of your glazing, you can enclose an area under a shelf to serve as a lockable cupboard for storing pesticides and other hazardous materials.

You can also install louvers at the top of the end walls to allow more heat to clear the structure, but you'll need to measure them at the job site after the framing is completed. Building them is a job for an experienced craftsman: They can be made from thin ¼-inch by 3-inch or ¼-inch by 4-inch slats.

10. Multiuse Cold Frame

Materials

- Two 12' 2×8s or 2×10s
- Two 4' 2×8s or 2×10s
- Four 2' 4×4s
- 7' lengths of ½" PVC pipe placed 2' or 3' apart (for 2' spacing, use seven lengths; for 3' spacing, use five lengths)
- One piece of spun fleece, 8' by 16'
- Glass panes, no larger than 18" by 30" (with edges rounded so they aren't sharp)

I developed this frame to suit the changing seasons in the garden. Instead of moving plants from one frame to another, I simply move the frame. It consists of a basic raised growing bed that can be fitted with various covers, depending on the temperature and weather outside.

BUILDING THE FRAME

The first job is to set up the base. Because the frame will be used to grow food, it's preferable not to use pressure-treated wood. You can protect the wood with epoxy and paint instead.

Marking out the frame

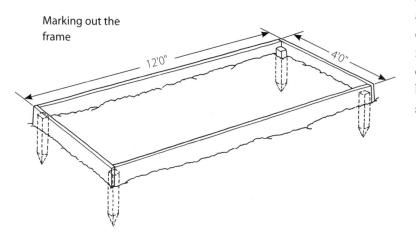

STEP 1: Construct the Frame

Mark out the frame and hammer the 4×4 posts into the ground at the corners. You can use 2×4s to construct the frame, but 2×8s or 2×10s are heavier, won't rot as easily, and will support the weight of the various frame covers. Nail the 2×8s to the corner posts with 16p nails. You may need another support in the middle of the frame to keep it from bowing.

STEP 2: Add Brackets for Pipes That Will Form Hoops

At 2-foot intervals along the outside of the wood frame, attach pipe brackets. You can insert ½-inch PVC pipes into these brackets to form arches that will support a polyethylene or fleece cover. To keep the weight of the snow from pushing the PVC pipes inward and causing them to collapse, the brackets at the ends of the bed can be fastened so that pipes inserted in them will slope outward slightly.

STEP 3: Cut Pipes for a Fleece/ Polyethylene Cover

For a 4-foot-wide bed, cut the pipes into 7-foot lengths. The hoops are covered with either spun fleece in summer to keep insects from getting to plants or with polyethylene in the fall to help extend the season. This hoop arrangement works best for low-growing plants such as lettuce, spinach, and root crops.

Screw pipe brackets or clamps to frame.

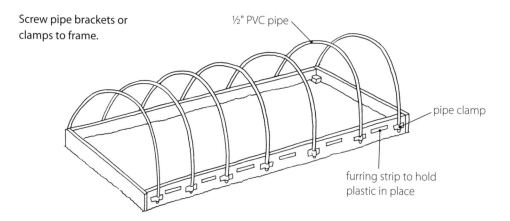

½" PVC pipe

pipe clamp

furring strip to hold plastic in place

STEP 4: Modify the Frame with Glass Panes and Clips

On some beds I use panes of glass tipped toward each other to form a cloche. Although we might think of cloches as being small, round glass "lids" for plants — much like overturned jars — in English market gardens a cloche is a glass pane about 2 feet tall with a metal clip at the top. These cloches may run for several hundred yards and can be moved to less mature crops as they are needed. They can protect plants from deer that are raiding the garden and from wind and can keep plants a bit warmer. In the cloche shown here, the glass panes sit in the dirt just inside the edge of the cold frame. To support the glass, I use glass cloche clips made of aluminum that I purchased in England several years ago. You can make similar clips by running a 2×4 through a table saw to cut two grooves ⅛ inch wide (or the width of the glass you're using). Make sure the grooves don't meet in the middle. Doing so prevents the wood from splitting and allows an air gap at the top of the glass panes. After the grooves have been cut, saw the 2×4 into 4- or 6-inch lengths to create a number of clips that can you can place at the peak of the glass panes. If each pane of glass is 18 by 24 inches, you'll use two clips for each section of the cloche. To close off the ends of the structure, simply lean two panes of glass against the frame and leaning panes and hold these in place with a stake in the ground. For air circulation when the weather is warm and dry, these end panes can be removed.

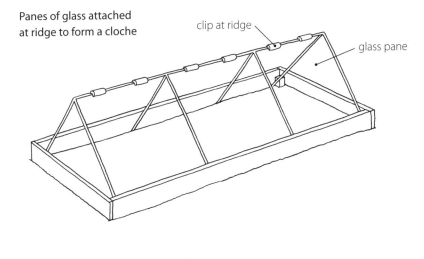

Panes of glass attached at ridge to form a cloche

clip at ridge

glass pane

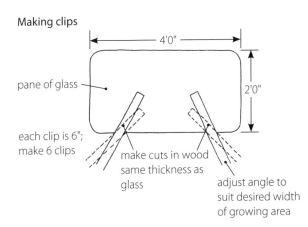

Making clips

4'0"

2'0"

pane of glass

each clip is 6"; make 6 clips

make cuts in wood same thickness as glass

adjust angle to suit desired width of growing area

11. Potting Bench

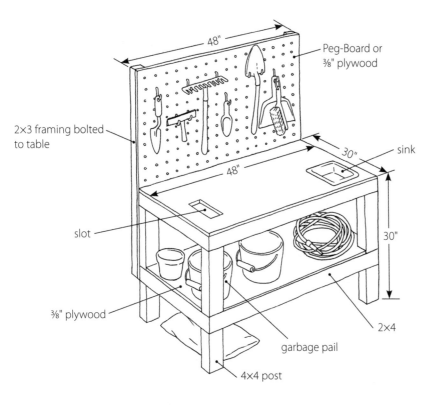

48"

Peg-Board or ⅜" plywood

2×3 framing bolted to table

30"

sink

48"

slot

30"

⅜" plywood

2×4

garbage pail

4×4 post

Schematic of bench

When you have the space to make use of them, potting benches are very handy in the greenhouse. This one is designed to be 48 inches wide and 30 inches deep. It is made with a waterproof plywood or laminate top with a slot in it so that garbage can be swept off the surface. A shelf underneath provides room for pots, tools, and compost; and the back, made of Peg-Board, enables you to hang small tools.

BUILDING THE BENCH

Materials

- Four 3' 3×3s for corner posts
- Four 4' 2×3s for shelf supports
- Four 30" 2×3s for shelf supports
- One 48" by 30" piece of ⅜" plywood or a similar-size piece of laminate for the bench top
- One 48" by 30" piece of ⅜" plywood for the lower shelf
- ¼" plywood to enclose the bench (optional)
- One 42" by 48" piece of Peg-Board or ⅜" plywood for the back of the bench
- Four 48" 2×3s to support the back
- Hinges, sink (optional), hose connections (optional), drain connections (optional), garbage pail, hooks (if installing a Peg-Board as the bench back)

Next, make the shelf supports: Each 2×3 has a lap joint at both ends. Dry-fit the legs and supports, then glue all pieces together and clamp them until they are dry. Finally, measure the diagonals to ensure that the bench is square.

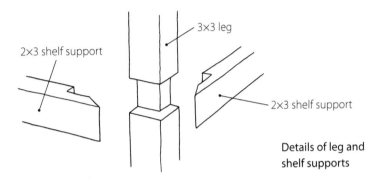

Details of leg and shelf supports

STEP 1: Build the Bench Frame

First, make the legs: Cut each 3×3 to the height of the bench (30 to 36 inches). On each, mark the height of the lower shelf 26 inches from the ground. Then, on each allow 2 inches for the width of the shelf support and mark this location. Cut a 1½-inch-deep slot at the top of each leg to hold the end of the shelf support.

STEP 2: Add the Top and Back

Use two 2×3s to support the plywood or Peg-Board back: one as a cross brace just below the level of the top of the bench and one as a cross brace at the height of the bench.

VARIATIONS AND UPGRADES

You can modify the dimensions of the bench to any length or width to suit the space you have available. You can plumb the space and add a small, inexpensive stainless-steel sink to the bench; a sink and hose connection would allow you to wash vegetables before taking them into the house or to clean pots when repotting plants. You can even arrange the drain line from this sink so that water moves through it directly into the greenhouse growing beds instead of the greenhouse drain. By enclosing the underside of the bench, you can create a lockable space for storing not only potting soil and small tools, but some hazardous materials as well.

Resources

GREENHOUSE & GARDENING ASSOCIATIONS

In addition to the following organizations, many state and local extension services have information on greenhouse design and construction. Check with your local extension service for recommendations and answers to your questions.

Hobby Greenhouse Association

www.hobbygreenhouse.org
A nationwide nonprofit association of hobby greenhouse growers who share knowledge and experience through HGA publications and programs. Encourages the formation of local chapters.

Royal Botanic Gardens, Kew

+44-20-8332-5655
www.kew.org
A scientific institution with the world's largest and most comprehensive living plant collection. Sponsors many publications, scientific conferences, and educational programs. A UNESCO World Heritage Site.

HOBBY & KIT GREENHOUSE MANUFACTURERS & SUPPLIERS

The following list of manufacturers and suppliers is only partial. Many manufacturers have dealers in all areas of the country. You can determine which manufacturers have a dealer near you and also view greenhouses and specifications by consulting their individual Web sites.

ACF Greenhouses

888-888-9050
www.littlegreenhouse.com
Features a wide variety of greenhouses and a full line of greenhouse supplies. Web site has a greenhouse resource center with information, guides, and heating and ventilation calculators.

Advance Greenhouses

877-228-0444
www.advancegreenhouses.com
Purveyor of greenhouses and greenhouse supplies. Web site offers information and links to sites for related products.

Atlas Greenhouse Systems, Inc.

800-346-9902
www.atlasgreenhouse.com
Member of the National Greenhouse Manufacturers Association. Serves both hobby and commercial growers.

B.C. Greenhouse Builders Ltd.

888-391-4433
www.bcgreenhouses.com
Hobby greenhouse kits to suit every budget, climate, and crop.

Cedar-Built Greenhouses (Cedar-Built Holdings Ltd.)

888-852-9302
www.cedarbuilt.homestead.com
Specializes in tax- and duty-free cedar greenhouse kits.

Charley's Greenhouse and Garden

800-322-4707
www.charleysgreenhouse.com
Supplier of greenhouse kits, custom structures, and many supplies and tools. Web site provides plenty of gardening and greenhouse tips.

Conley's Greenhouse Manufacturing and Sales

800-377-8441
www.conleys.com
Member of the National Greenhouse Manufacturers Association. Sells both commercial and hobby greenhouses.

CSI Hobby Greenhouses

303-273-9085
www.myhobbygreenhouse.com
Offers greenhouses built for extreme Colorado weather.

Curry's Greenhouses

800-861-1130
www.currygreenhouses.com
Offers hobby greenhouse kits and blueprints for galvanized-steel arched greenhouses and Quonset-style structures.

Envirocept Greenhouses, Etc.

888-326-8634
www.greenhouses-etc.net
Offers a variety of entry-level and more expensive kits as well as accessories.

Evergreen Greenhouse Mfg.

501-679-7118
www.evergreen-greenhouses.com
Sells greenhouse kits with polycarbonate glazing designed to withstand heavy snows and high winds.

FarmTek

800-457-8887
www.farmtek.com
Sells greenhouse kits and many supplies.

Farm Wholesale Greenhouses

800-825-1925
www.farmwholesale.com
Sells greenhouse kits that include Solexx high-density extruded polyethylene glazing.

Gardener's Supply Company

800-876-5520
www.gardeners.com
Offers a variety of greenhouse kits, including Northern Light greenhouses, as well as advice, accessories, and supplies.

Garden Styles

800-356-8890
www.gardenstyles.com
Offers many Danish-designed greenhouse kits. Includes kits with aluminum and redwood frames.

Garden Under Glass

631-424-5997
www.gardenunderglass.com
Sells prefabricated, ready-to-assemble kits, both freestanding and lean-to style. Regal Gardener greenhouses are aluminum with glass glazing.

Gothic Arch Greenhouses, Inc.

800-531-4769
www.gothicarchgreenhouses.com
Sells both hobby and commercial greenhouses of all styles and the supplies to go with them.

Growers Supply (A Division of FarmTek)

800-476-9715
www.growerssupply.com
Offers many kit greenhouses and a host of greenhouse and gardening supplies for hobbyists and professional growers.

Growing Spaces

800-753-9333
www.growingspaces.com
Sells energy-efficient geodesic dome greenhouses.

HobbyGardens

603-927-4283
www.hobbygardens.com
Specializes in kits to withstand heavy winter snows and winds. Offers a replacement guarantee on its PE film glazing.

Hoop House Greenhouse Kits
800-760-5192
www.hoophouse.com
Sells inexpensive, expandable kits for hobby gardeners.

International Greenhouse Company
888-281-9337
www.igcusa.com
Web site offers a handy comparison chart of all the company's kit greenhouses based on criteria such as cost, required base, frame material, glazing, and ease of assembly.

Keeler-Glasgow Co., Inc.
800-526-7327
www.keeler-glasgow.com
The company's galvanized-steel frames are constructed for strong gales, heavy rains, and blizzards. Installation services offered.

Poly-Tex
800-852-3443
www.poly-tex.com
Manufactures both hobby and commercial greenhouses and benches.

Santa Barbara Greenhouses
800-544-5276
www.sbgreenhouse.com
Sells standard and deluxe easy-to-assemble greenhouse kits, all with California redwood frames.

Spectrum Hobby Greenhouse Company
800-724-2659
www.spectrumgreenhouses.com
Sells English garden greenhouses with double-wall polycarbonate glazing.

Spirit Elements, Inc.
800-511-1440
www.spiritelements.com
Most structures of western red cedar with polycarbonate roof glazing. Wooden end walls and partial wooden side walls allow structures to serve as sheds or workshops as well.

Sturdi-built Greenhouse Mfg. Co.
800-334-4115
www.sturdi-built.com
Offers many sizes and styles of redwood and glass greenhouses.

Sunglo Greenhouses
800-647-0606
www.sunglogreenhouses.com
Greenhouses have aluminum frames and double-wall acrylic glazing.

Sunshine Garden House
888-272-9333
www.gardenhouse.com
Kits include automatic vent openers, redwood frames, and double-wall polycarbonate glazing.

Texas Greenhouse Company
800-227-5447
www.texasgreenhouse.com
Offers residential and commercial systems, starter kits, and more ornate steel- or aluminum-frame structures.

The Sun Country Greenhouse Company
204-757-4041
www.hobby-greenhouse.com
Manufactures one greenhouse style: an A-frame design with continuous roof vents and frame constructed of Canadian western red cedar.

Turner Greenhouses
800-672-4770
www.turnergreenhouses.com
Sells metal greenhouses with PE, fiberglass, or polycarbonate glazing along with many accessories.

Worldflower Garden Domes
512-431-9752
www.gardendome.com
Offers many geodesic dome greenhouse kits.

CUSTOM GREENHOUSE SUPPLIERS

British Conservatories
800-566-6360
www.britishrose.com
Offers architect-designed conservatories.

Buena Vista Sunrooms
800-747-3324
www.sunroom.com
Specializing in the design, sales, construction, and maintenance of all types of glazed structures, including sunrooms and solariums, greenhouses, and patio and garden rooms.

Clayton Hill Greenhouse Company
817-467-9370
www.claytonhill.com
Offers custom design and building as well as prefabricated structures.

Florian Greenhouses
800-356-7426
www.floriangreenhouse.com
Offers energy-efficient custom sunrooms, greenhouses, conservatories, and passive solar collectors.

Janco Greenhouses
410-381-5600
www.jancoinc.com
Designs custom greenhouses, conservatories, and solar rooms.

Under Glass Mfg. Corp.
845-687-4700
www.underglassusa.com
Exclusive manufacturer of Lord and Burnham custom greenhouses and solariums. Also sells less expensive kits.

LUMBER & WOOD INFORMATION

American Lumber Standard Committee
301-972-1700
www.alsc.org
A nonprofit organization of manufacturers, distributors, users, and consumers of lumber that administers an accreditation program for the grading of lumber which serves as the basis for the sale and purchase of all softwood lumber traded in North America.

American Wood Council
202-463-2766
www.awc.org
Wood products division of the American Forest and Paper Association. Develops design tools and guidelines for wood construction and provides technical information, standards, and education.

APA : The Engineered Wood Association
253-565-6600
www.apawood.org
A nonprofit trade association that works with member manufacturers to focus on the creation of new, strong engineered wood products through research and development.

California Redwood Association
888-225-7339
www.calredwood.org
A trade association promoting the use of California redwood as a construction material through information and education.

National Hardwood Lumber Association
901-377-1818
www.natlhardwood.org
A trade association founded to establish a uniform system of grading rules for the measurement and inspection of hardwood lumber.

Northeastern Lumber Manufacturers Association
207-829-6901
www.nelma.org
The rules-writing agency for eastern white pine lumber and the grading authority for eastern spruce, balsam fir, spruce pine fir (SPF) species grouping, and other eastern softwood lumber species.

Southern Pine Council
504-443-4464
www.southernpine.com
An organization of manufacturers of southern pine lumber providing information and education on the uses of southern pine. The organization's Web site offers useful tables on load-carrying capacity and spans for various sizes of pine lumber.

The Structural Board Association OSB Guide
905-475-1100
www.osbguide.com.
Provides information on oriented strand board and its uses.

TimberSIL
866-318-9432
www.timbersil.com
Promotes a new wood treatment process said to eliminate the problems of traditional treatment products. TimberSIL wood is promoted as non-toxic, noncorrosive, fire-retardant, arsenic-free, and effective against rot and decay.

Western Wood Products Association
503-224-3930
www.wwpa.org
A trade association of softwood lumber manufacturers that provides lumber grading, quality control, and product support services for those who use softwoods in construction.

OTHER BUILDING & FINISHING INFORMATION

Conproco, Inc.
800-258-3500
www.conproco.com
Manufacturer of repair mortars, mortar finishes, and base coats.

Dig Safe Inc.
www.digsafe.com
Web site provides a national call directory with Dig Safe numbers for every state for those who will be digging for foundations or power and water installation.

Eagle Panel Systems, Inc.
800-643-3786
www.eaglepanelsystems.com
Manufacturer of structural insulated stress skin panels.

Interlux
908-686-1300
www.yachtpaints.com
Manufacturer of many marine paints, finishes, and epoxies that perform well in greenhouse construction and maintenance.

The Last Straw
402-483-5135
www.strawhomes.com
An international journal of straw bale construction and other natural building methods.

Winter Panel Corp.
802-254-3435
www.winterpanel.com
Manufacturer of Structurewall and Curtainwall stress skin panels.

GLAZING SUPPLIERS

Many of the companies listed under Hobby & Kit Greenhouse Manufacturers & Suppliers also supply glazing.

CO-EX Corporation
800-888-5364
www.co-excorp.com
Manufacturer of premium polycarbonate sheeting, including Macrolux.

Solar Components Corporation
603-668-8186
www.solar-components.com
Manufacturer of solar glazing and panels.

Suntuf, Inc. (A Division of Palram Americas)
800-999-9459
www.suntuf.com
Manufacturer of corrugated polycarbonate panels.

HEATING SYSTEM SUPPLIERS

Charmaster Products
218-326-6786
www.charmaster.com
Manufacturer of indoor and outdoor wood furnaces.

Heatmor
800-834-7552
www.heatmor.com
Manufacturer of stainless-steel outdoor furnaces.

Southern Burner Co.
800-375-5001
www.southernburner.com
Manufacturer of heating units that require no electricity and run on natural gas or propane.

The Northland Outdoor Wood Furnace
218-778-6314
www.northlandoutdoorwoodfurnace.com
Manufacturer of outdoor wood furnaces.

GREENHOUSE ACCESSORIES SUPPLIERS

A number of the companies listed under Hobby & Kit Greenhouse Manufacturers & Suppliers also sell greenhouse accessories and supplies.

Burgon and Ball, Ltd.
+44-1202-684-141
www.burgonandball.com
British manufacturer of fine cutting and hand tools.

Greenfire
530-895-8301
www.greenfire.net
Organic and hydroponic gardeners emporium. Offers Shade Rite polyethylene sheeting.

Lee Valley Tools
800-871-8158
www.leevalley.com
Retail and mail-order supplier of gardening and woodworking tools.

Window Quilt
800-257-4501
www.windowquilt.com
Manufacturer of movable window insulation for attached greenhouses.

USDA Hardiness Zone Map

An unheated greenhouse will enable you to grow plants indoors that are hardy outdoors in one zone warmer. For instance, if you live in Zone 5, you can usually grow in a greenhouse those plants that are hardy in Zone 6.

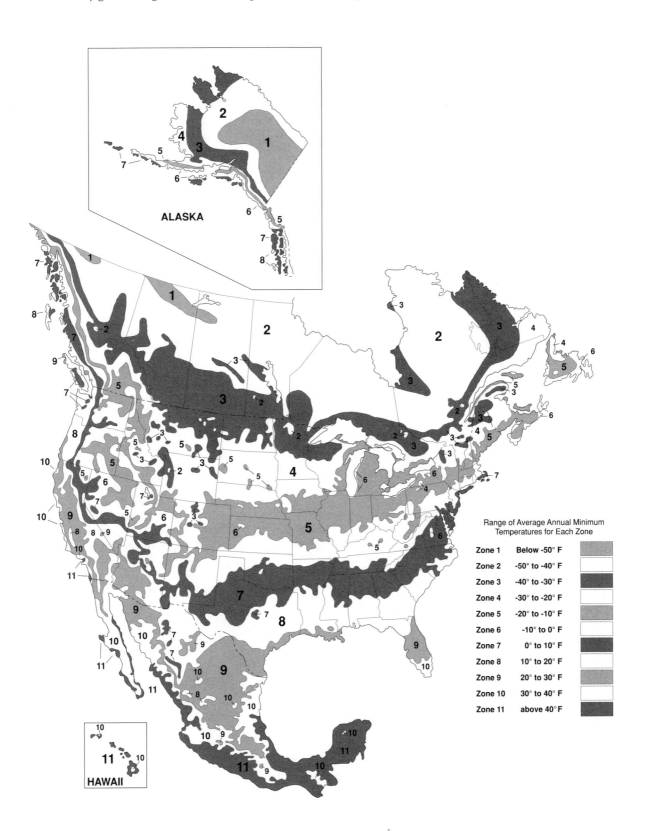

Range of Average Annual Minimum
Temperatures for Each Zone

Zone 1	Below -50° F	
Zone 2	-50° to -40° F	
Zone 3	-40° to -30° F	
Zone 4	-30° to -20° F	
Zone 5	-20° to -10° F	
Zone 6	-10° to 0° F	
Zone 7	0° to 10° F	
Zone 8	10° to 20° F	
Zone 9	20° to 30° F	
Zone 10	30° to 40° F	
Zone 11	above 40° F	

Index

Other Storey Titles You Will Enjoy

Be Your Own House Contractor, by Carl Heldmann.
The book to help you save 25 percent on building your
own home — without lifting a hammer!
176 pages. Paper. ISBN 978-1-58017-840-2.

Cold-Climate Gardening, by Lewis Hill.
Invaluable advice on landscaping, growing food, and warming up the soil for the
gardener plagued by early and late frosts, arctic winds, and inhospitable conditions.
320 pages. Paper. ISBN 978-0-88266-441-5.

Home Plan Doctor, by Larry W. Garnett
The essential companion to buying home plans, from understanding
basic design principles to requesting needed modifications.
224 pages. Paper. ISBN 978-1-58017-698-9.

Incredible Vegetables from Self-Watering Containers,
by Edward C. Smith.
A foolproof method to produce a bountiful harvest without
the trouble of a traditional earth garden.
256 pages. Paper. ISBN 978-1-58017-556-2.
Hardcover. ISBN 978-1-58017-557-9.

The Vegetable Gardener's Bible, by Edward C. Smith.
A reinvention of vegetable gardening that shows how to
have your most successful garden ever.
320 pages. Paper. ISBN 978-1-58017-212-7.

The Veggie Gardener's Answer Book, by Barbara W. Ellis.
Insider's tips and tricks, practical advice, and organic wisdom
for vegetable growers everywhere.
432 pages. Paper. ISBN 978-1-60342-024-2.

The Weather-Resilient Garden, by Charles W. G. Smith.
A defensive approach to landscaping, plus emergency and
long-term solutions for reviving weather-damaged landscapes.
416 pages. Paper. ISBN 978-1-58017-516-6.

These and other books from Storey Publishing are available
wherever quality books are sold or by calling 1-800-441-5700.
Visit us at _www.storey.com_.